The Word Made Flesh

The Word Made Flesh

A Theology of the Incarnation

Ian A. McFarland

WESTMINSTER
JOHN KNOX PRESS
LOUISVILLE • KENTUCKY

First edition
Published by Westminster John Knox Press
Louisville, Kentucky

19 20 21 22 23 24 25 26 27 28—10 9 8 7 6 5 4 3 2 1

Book design by Sharon Adams
Cover design by Mark Abrams
Cover art by Felix Spiske / felixspiske.com

Library of Congress Cataloging-in-Publication Data

Names: McFarland, Ian A. (Ian Alexander), 1963– author.
Title: The word made flesh : a theology of the incarnation / Ian A. McFarland.
Description: First edition. | Louisville, Kentucky : Westminster John Knox Press, [2019] | Includes bibliographical references and index. |
Identifiers: LCCN 2019002010 (print) | LCCN 2019009629 (ebook) | ISBN 9781611649574 (ebk.) | ISBN 9780664262976 (pbk. : alk. paper)
Subjects: LCSH: Jesus Christ—Person and offices. | Jesus Christ—History of doctrines. | Incarnation—History of doctrines.
Classification: LCC BT220 (ebook) | LCC BT220 .M39 2019 (print) | DDC 232/.8—dc23
LC record available at https://lccn.loc.gov/2019002010

♾ The paper used in this publication meets the minimum requirements of the American National Standard for Information Sciences—Permanence of Paper for Printed Library Materials, ANSI Z39.48-1992.

Contents

Preface

Although many of the ideas in these pages have been gestating for some time, I only began to set them to paper when I moved back to the United Kingdom to take up a position in Cambridge University. This book was thus written from a position of immense privilege, even beyond that which I already enjoyed as a man who is also white and who has held full-time university appointments throughout the past twenty years.

This privilege marks the book in various ways, many of which will have eluded me but will be embarrassingly evident to those who read it from social locations different from my own. But even as it stands, I cannot help but be aware that the sorts of problems that take center stage in this exploration of what it means to confess Jesus as the Word made flesh—the form of his existence before his birth and after his resurrection, the character of his relation to the Father and the Holy Spirit, the conceptual distinction between nature and hypostasis—may to many readers seem hopelessly abstract, far removed from the concrete realities of life for those who seek to live as faithful disciples in situations of deprivation and danger that I can scarcely imagine.

I have no defense against this charge other than to note that to write is unavoidably to be bound by the limits of one's own perspective. That rather obvious fact is certainly no excuse for ignoring, let alone discounting, other perspectives of which the writer is aware, and I have therefore tried to acknowledge and engage the views of other writers whose approach to the topic is different from my own, but whose concerns, both dogmatic and pastoral, I deeply respect. Moreover, it is my hope that the center of my argument—that all talk of divinity in Jesus must be controlled at every point by attention to the concrete particularity of his humanity—bears witness to a shared conviction that the measure of Christian God-talk is the life of this marginal Jew, who, whatever the privileges that may have fallen to him by virtue of his ontology, ancestry, gender, or class, claimed none for himself.

Yet as much as drawing attention to the privilege that has provided both the wider and more immediate contexts for my writing this book highlights its shortcomings, it is also provides a stimulus for giving thanks. For the advantages I have enjoyed in working at Cambridge have been an immeasurable gift, for which I am profoundly grateful. My gratitude extends, first of all, to my colleagues in the Faculty of Divinity, who have given me both a gracious welcome and countless models of excellence in theological scholarship to emulate. I am equally thankful to the Master, Fellows, and staff of Selwyn College, who provided me not only a place of tranquil seclusion where I was able to write much of this volume, but also a community of scholars and of friends that has enriched my life beyond all expectation.

Special thanks also are due to Professor Mona Siddiqi and the members of the School of Divinity at the University of Edinburgh, whose invitation to deliver the 2018 Croall Lectures gave me the opportunity to present a large part of this book before an audience whose friendly yet critical engagement with my ideas helped enormously in my revision of the manuscript. I am similarly grateful to Professor Dr. Hans-Peter Großhans and the Evangelical Theological Faculty of the University of Münster for their kind reception and robust discussion of a lecture version of chapter 7, which likewise proved very useful in helping me to clarify my ideas. And, of course, the final form of the text would not be before you at all without the support and careful work of Bob Ratcliff, Daniel Braden, and the rest of the production staff at Westminster John Knox, with whom it has been a pleasure to be able to work once again.

But my deepest thanks are reserved for my wife, Ann, and our two daughters, Maggie and Olive, who allowed their lives to be turned upside down by a move back across the Atlantic that was as little anticipated as it was desired. I will never forget it, and it is my hope that it may prove to be true that, when all is said and done, in this, too, all things will have worked together for the good.

Selwyn College
June 2018
The Feast of John the Baptist

Abbreviations

ANF   *Ante-Nicene Fathers.* Edited by Alexander Roberts and James Donaldson. American Edition. Grand Rapids: Wm. B. Eerdmans Publishing Co., 1975 [1867].

b.   Babylonian Talmud

CD   Barth, Karl. *Church Dogmatics.* 13 vols. Edited by G. W. Bromiley and T. F. Torrance. Edinburgh: T&T Clark, 1956–74.

DH   *Compendium of Creeds, Definitions, and Declarations on Matters of Faith and Morals.* Edited by Heinrich Denzinger, Peter Hünermann, et al. 43rd ed. San Francisco: Ignatius Press, 2012.

LW   Luther, Martin. *Luther's Works.* Edited by Harold J. Grimm et al. American Edition. 55 vols. Philadelphia: Fortress Press/ St. Louis: Concordia Publishing House, 1957–86. Continued as New Series.

LXX   Septuagint (the Greek OT)

m.   Mishnah

MT   Masoretic Text (of the Hebrew Bible)

NPNF²   *Nicene and Post-Nicene Fathers.* Edited by Philip Schaff and Henry Wace. 2nd series. Boston: Hendrickson Publishers, 1995 [1892].

NRSV   New Revised Standard Version

OTP   Maximus the Confessor. *Opuscula theologica et polemica.*

PG   Patrologia Graeca = Patrologiae Cursus Completus: Series Graeca. Edited by Jacques-Paul Migne. 162 vols. Paris, 1857–86.

RSV   Revised Standard Version

ST   Thomas Aquinas. *Summa Theologiae*. Blackfriars Edition. 60 vols. London: Eyre & Spottiswood, 1964–81.

WA   Weimarer Ausgabe = D. Martin Luthers Werke: Kritische Gesammtausgabe. 121 vols. Weimar: Hermann Böhlau, 1883–2009.

WA Br.   Weimarer Ausgabe, Part 4, Briefe/Briefwechsel (Correspondence). *See* WA

Introduction

A Chalcedonianism without Reserve

The name "Jesus" means "God saves" (see Matt. 1:21), and the conviction that God is the one and only Savior has always been central to those who look to Jesus as the "pioneer and perfecter" of their faith (Heb. 12:2). Its importance can be gauged from the fact that one of the favorite biblical texts of the earliest Christian writers was Isaiah 63:9 (LXX): "Neither an elder, nor an angel, but the Lord will save them because he loves them, and will spare them: he will set them free."[1] Yet those writers used this text in support of what to Jews and Gentiles alike seemed to be a claim much more contentious, if not downright outrageous. For since it was the defining belief of these same early Christians that *Jesus himself* is the agent of our salvation, the truth that God—and God alone—saves seemed to demand the conclusion that Jesus was none other than God. It was presumably following this chain of reasoning that already at the turn of the second century an anonymous Christian preacher declared, "Brothers and sisters, we ought to think of Jesus Christ as of God, as the judge of the living and the dead; and we ought not to belittle our salvation. For when we belittle him, we hope to get but little."[2] If Christians expect salvation from Jesus, then they cannot regard him as any less than God.

But how could they so regard him? For these same Christians were no less convinced that this Jesus was a human being, "born of a woman, born under the law" (Gal. 4:4), who was crucified under the Roman governor Pilate, died, and

---

1. See, e.g., Irenaeus, *Against Heresies* 3.20; and *Demonstration of the Apostolic Preaching* 88; Tertullian, *Five Books against Marcion* 4.22; Cyprian of Carthage, *Three Books of Testimonies against the Jews* 2.7; Methodius, *Oration concerning Simeon and Anna*. While in the LXX the finite verbs of Isa. 63:9 are all in the past tense, these writers always quote them as future.

2. See 2 Clement 1.1–2, in *Early Christian Fathers*, trans. and ed. Cyril C. Richardson (New York: Macmillan, 1970), 193; translations slightly modified.

1

was buried. To be sure, they also confessed that he was risen from the dead, but that further claim, albeit far more contestable as a biographical datum, did not in any sense qualify belief in his humanity. On the contrary, only one who had truly died could rise again, so precisely as the risen One, Jesus was confessed as one who had died—a defining feature of human existence, but emphatically not of divinity (Rom. 1:23, 1 Tim. 6:16; cf. Ps. 68:20).[3] And while there were early Christians (usually described as "docetists") whose belief in Jesus' divinity led them to deny his humanity, the majority tradition consistently affirmed it. The most obvious ground for this affirmation was the Gospel narratives themselves, which describe Jesus in explicitly human terms as someone who walked, talked, hungered, slept, wept, and so forth. Interestingly, these very ordinary human characteristics came to be seen as having soteriological implications of their own, as evident in Paul's judgment that "since death came through a human being, the resurrection of the dead has also come through a human being" (1 Cor. 15:21). So if at one level the confession of Jesus as Savior implied that he could be no less than God, at another level the fact that this Savior took human form seemed to be equally significant. For if God had determined that human salvation was to come through a human being, then no aspect of our humanity could be excluded from Jesus' life; rather, he had to become like us "in every respect" (Heb. 2:17) in order that every dimension of human life might be transformed by him. As Gregory of Nazianzus would put it in the fourth century, "that which he has not assumed he has not healed; but that which is united to his Godhead is also saved."[4]

And so Christians came to develop a Christology (that is, a formal account of the person of Jesus) characterized by the confession that he is both God and a human being. This dual confession was given classic form at the fifth-century Council of Chalcedon, which decreed that Christ is neither only God nor only a human being nor some sort of divine-human hybrid, but rather

> one and the same Son, our Lord Jesus Christ, the same perfect in divinity and also perfect in humanity, the same truly God and truly a human being composed of rational soul and body, the same one in being with the Father as to the divinity and one in being with us as to the humanity, like unto us in all things but sin. The same begotten from the Father before all ages according to the divinity and . . . born as to his humanity from Mary, the virgin mother of God, . . . one and the same Lord Jesus Christ, the only begotten Son, [who] must be acknowledged in two natures, without confusion or change, without division or separa-

---

3. Here and throughout this volume, I use "divinity" and "humanity" as alternative expressions for (and thus as synonymous with) "divine nature" and "human nature," respectively.

4. Gregory of Nazianzus, *Letter 101* (*To Cledonius against Apollinaris*), in *Christology of the Later Fathers*, ed. Edward R. Hardy (Philadelphia: Westminster Press, 1954), 218.

tion. The distinction between the natures was never abolished by their union but rather the character proper to each of the two natures was preserved as they came together in one person and hypostasis. He is not split or divided into two persons, but he is one and the same only begotten Son, God the Word, the Lord Jesus Christ.[5]

It is my contention in this book that a thoroughgoing commitment to Christology developed in these terms—a Chalcedonianism without reserve—continues to provide the most adequate account of Christian convictions regarding Jesus. I speak of a "Chalcedonianism without reserve" because in practice the Christology that has been typical of the Catholic, Orthodox, and Reformation traditions that all share allegiance to the council frequently fails to follow through fully on the implications of its teaching, especially with respect to the question of Jesus' humanity. The problem is not that his humanity is explicitly denied or even qualified, since that would be flatly inconsistent with the conciliar definition, but rather that it tends to be marginalized as a point of dogmatic interest.[6] In other words, although in the majority tradition Jesus' full humanity is formally affirmed, it is not viewed as integral to his identity, since it is only where his humanity is overshadowed by the power of his divinity that God is revealed.

This tendency is already visible in the document that perhaps more than any other is associated with the formulation of the Chalcedonian definition, Pope Leo the Great's *Tome to Flavian*, in which it is written that "each nature does what is proper to each in communion with the other. . . . One shines forth with miracles; the other succumbs to injuries."[7] While one might argue that Leo's intention here was simply to affirm the integrity of both Jesus' divine and human natures throughout the course of his ministry, his language is infelicitous. Most obviously, the idea that miracles display Jesus' divinity is clearly wrong: since miracles were performed by the Old Testament prophets, who were not divine, and since Jesus himself taught that his equally nondivine followers would perform miracles greater than his (John 14:12), the ability to do miracles clearly cannot count as evidence of divinity.[8] Furthermore, to argue

5. DH §301–302, trans. slightly alt.

6. It is striking, e.g., that for all the considerable theological sophistication Dante displays in the *Divine Comedy*, "the Word" nowhere appears in the poem as a human being, but only in the allegorical form of a griffin (*Purgatorio* 29–32), as a light of unbearable brightness (*Paradiso* 23), and as a circle (albeit one that assumes a vaguely human shape) of colored light (*Paradiso* 33).

7. DH §294.

8. This is not to deny that Jesus' miracles both were and continue to be a factor in his disciples' confession of him as divine (see, e.g., John 20:30–31), but only that they are but one such factor among many others that include much less spectacular acts of teaching, table fellowship, and even more ordinary features of his daily life. As will be discussed at various points in the pages that follow, because it is the *entirety* of Jesus' earthly existence, as vindicated in his resurrection from the dead, that displays his identity as the Word made flesh, no one aspect of that existence can be singled out as revelatory of his divinity apart from the rest.

that the divine nature "shines forth" anywhere in Jesus' life seems to contradict the fundamental Christian conviction that the divine nature is inherently invisible and thus not subject to perception in space and time (1 Tim. 6:16). But from the perspective of a Chalcedonianism without reserve, the chief problem with Leo's language is that it turns our attention away from Jesus' humanity by linking the revelation of the divine to special powers that are added to it, thereby implying that the quotidian realities of Jesus' flesh and blood are not in themselves a suitable vehicle for God's self-revelation.[9]

In order to avoid this kind of Christology, in which attention to Jesus' divinity had led in practice to the marginalization of his identity as a first-century Palestinian Jew, theologians in the modern era have sought to formulate alternatives that do a better job of honoring Jesus' humanity in all its historical, cultural, and physiological specificity. Two approaches have proved particularly influential. One, kenotic Christology, first arose among nineteenth-century German Lutherans, but subsequently spread beyond that confessional context and has been especially influential in the English-speaking world. The term "kenotic" comes from Philippians 2:6–7, which states that Jesus, "though he was in the form of God, . . . emptied [ekenōsen] himself, taking the form of a slave, being born in human likeness." Over against traditional Christologies, in which Jesus' divinity overshadows his humanity, kenoticists see in Paul's letter evidence for just the opposite: in order for God to fulfill the aim of becoming like us "in every respect" and become truly human (Heb. 2:17), Jesus must empty himself of divinity. Kenoticists share with Chalcedonians commitment to a Christology "from above," that is, an understanding of the incarnation as the unique enfleshment of the eternal Word of God, who comes down from heaven to dwell with us on earth below. But they argue that in order to lead a genuinely human life, with all its natural limitations, God must surrender certain divine properties (e.g., omniscience and omnipotence). So kenoticists confess that God is truly present in Jesus, but only in a changed (that is, ontologically compressed or diminished) fashion. In this way, for all their worries about the perils of Chalcedonianism, kenoticists share with Leo the assumption that Christ's humanity and divinity stand in an essentially competitive relationship with one another, such that where one nature is more visible, the other is less so. To be sure, kenoticists typically insist that in taking flesh the Word retains what they hold to be God's essential attributes of love, holiness, goodness, and truth; but if Leo depicted a Jesus whose humanity is eclipsed by his divinity, kenotic theologies

---

9. "Clearly . . . Jesus does not act as the 'one teacher' (Matt. 23:10) solely in virtue of his divine nature. . . . Both his sovereign lordship and his lowliness are human, just as they represent in human form . . . God's sovereignty and lowliness." Hans Urs von Balthasar, *Truth of God*, vol. 2 of *Theo-Logic*, trans. Adrian J. Walker (San Francisco: Ignatius Press, 2004 [1985]), 70.

suffer from the opposite problem, in that their emphasis on the integrity of the incarnate Word's humanity is purchased at the price of qualifying the confession of his perfect divinity.

Also dating from the nineteenth century, the major modern alternative to kenoticism seeks to avoid this competitive understanding of the relationship between divinity and humanity in Christ by defining Jesus' divinity in human terms. Although the range of variations on this strategy is too broad for its representatives to be considered a single theological "school," they can all be characterized as advocating a Christology "from below."[10] That is, they share the common worry that the language of the Word's descent "from above," common to kenotic and Chalcedonian Christologies, sets Jesus' humanity and divinity in opposition to each other, so that the one can be affirmed only at the expense of the other. To avoid this problem, they offer instead a Christology in which Jesus' divinity is defined by his humanity. In some cases, Jesus' divinity is equated with the perfect realization of some human characteristic (e.g., his God-consciousness, his openness to divine grace, or his dedication to the kingdom of God); in others his life as a whole is understood as constitutive of the divine being, such that God's very existence is conceived in historical terms.[11] Either way, Jesus' full humanity is not in tension with confession of his divinity since the latter is now defined in human, historical terms. But this coordination of divinity and humanity in the life of Jesus succeeds only by collapsing the two together, such that while humanity can now indeed serve as a vehicle for disclosing divinity, this is only because divinity is no longer clearly differentiated from humanity, but rather identified with some set of observable, creaturely characteristics.[12]

In short, whether ancient or modern, loyal to Chalcedon or critical of it, all these approaches end up so construing the relationship between divinity and

---

10. Though sometimes used to contrast the ancient Christologies of, e.g., Cyril and Nestorius, the terminology of "above" and "below" seems to have originated with F. H. R. Frank, who proposed that "our knowledge of Christ, as of God, moves from below to above [*von unten nach oben*]." F. H. R. Frank, *Zur Theologie A. Ritschl's*, 3rd ed. (Erlangen: Andreas Deichert'sche Verlagsbuchhandlung, 1891), 27; cited in Wolfhart Pannenberg, *Systematic Theology*, trans. Geoffrey W. Bromiley (Grand Rapids: Wm. B. Eerdmans Publishing Co., 1991), 2:279–80, n. 12. For criticism of the distinction, see, e.g., Nicholas Lash, "Up and Down in Christology," in *New Studies in Theology 1*, ed. Stephen Sykes and Derek Holmes (London: Duckworth, 1980), 31–46; and Wesley Wildman, "Basic Christological Distinctions," *Theology Today* 64 (2007): 285–304.

11. In rough terms, the former group (including thinkers as diverse as Albrecht Ritschl, Donald Baillie, and Catherine Keller) takes after Schleiermacher, while the latter (including Jürgen Moltmann, Wolfhart Pannenberg, and Robert Jenson) follow the lead of Hegel, for whom history is the theater of God's self-realization. I would also include contemporary advocates of non-Trinitarian Spirit Christologies (e.g., Roger Haight, SJ; Geoffrey Lampe; James Mackey) in the first group, inasmuch as they all correlate Jesus' divinity with his unique and exemplary receptivity to the Spirit.

12. Cf. the assessment in Kathryn Tanner, *Jesus, Humanity and the Trinity* (Edinburgh: T&T Clark, 2001), 10–11.

humanity that emphasis on one invariably obscures the distinctive significance of the other. Leo certainly had no interest in denying Jesus' humanity, but by stressing the miracles as the place where his divinity shines forth, the human fades into the background as a focus of theological interest. Modern Christologies, by contrast, seek to correct this traditional bias by highlighting Jesus' humanity, yet the result is simply the converse: the human qualities of Jesus come into relief, but at the price of Jesus' divinity being either heavily qualified (in kenoticism) or reduced to a particular set of distinctively human attributes (in Christologies from below). By contrast, a Chalcedonianism without reserve, holding firmly to the council's teaching that in Christ the divine and human natures are united "without confusion or change," refuses both Leo's linking the revelation of Jesus' divinity with the eclipsing of his humanity and the modern tendency for attention to Jesus' humanity to obscure either the fullness or the ontological distinctiveness of his divinity.

Fundamental to a Chalcedonianism without reserve is the principle that because the divine nature is inherently invisible and so not capable of perception (1 Tim. 1:17; cf. Col. 1:15; 1 John 4:12), when we look at Jesus, what we see is his humanity only. It follows that no aspect of that which we perceive in Jesus—his miracles, his faith, his obedience, or anything else—can be equated with his divinity; all are fully and exclusively human, and thus created, realities. Yet this claim need not entail any qualification of the confession that Jesus is God. On the contrary, in proposing a Chalcedonianism without reserve, I seek to uphold Martin Luther's claim that "whoever wishes to deliberate or speculate soundly about God should disregard absolutely everything except the humanity of Christ."[13] In other words, to know God *rightly*, one must look at Christ's humanity *only*—without claiming that what we see, hear, touch, or otherwise perceive of Jesus is anything other or more than human substance. Following that advice would seem to bring us crashing onto the shoals of blasphemy, inasmuch as Christ's humanity is created, and it is a fundamental conviction of Christians (and not only of Christians) that the created should never be identified with the Creator, because to do so is to commit idolatry—to honor as God that which is not God. To claim that Christ's humanity is the sole ground and source for right knowledge of God seems not simply to risk idolatry but actively to endorse it by identifying a creature directly with the Creator (cf. Rom. 1:25).

---

13. "Ideo repeto iterumque monebo: quicunque velit salubriter de Deo cogitare aut speculari, prorsus omnia postponat praeter humanitatem Christi." Martin Luther, Letter to Spalatin (February 12, 1519) in WA Br. 1:226. Cf. Kathryn Tanner's equation of "what the Trinity is doing for us" with "what is happening in the life of Christ," in *Christ the Key* (Cambridge: Cambridge University Press, 2010), 234.

Chalcedonian Christology seeks to avoid this pitfall by maintaining that Jesus' humanity, while inseparable from his divinity, is at no point to be identified with it. In order to avoid any such confusion of the divine and human, a conceptual distinction is drawn between *nature* and *hypostasis*. The definition of Chalcedon makes use of this distinction in its claim that in Jesus Christ "two natures," divine and human, "came together in one . . . hypostasis." But the precise character of the difference between nature and hypostasis only came to be clarified gradually in the decades following the conclusion of the council in 451.[14] The upshot of these postconciliar developments can be summarized as follows: nature refers to the *whatness* of an entity, as defined by its constitutive qualities or attributes (e.g., "immaterial intellect" as the definition of angelic nature).[15] By contrast, hypostasis (or person) applies to entities that have rational or spiritual natures, and which therefore take individualized form as *whos*.[16] In other words, to be a hypostasis is to have a personal identity: to be some*one* in addition to being some*thing*.

The conciliar language of the two natures constituting "one person and hypostasis" puts the claim that Jesus is a single someone at the heart of Chalcedonian Christology. Who is this someone? The Chalcedonian answer is, "God the Son, the second person of the Trinity." That is, Jesus is hypostatically (or personally) divine. His hypostasis is therefore not human, meaning that he is not, like the prophets of old, a *human* person who has received special divine powers but is rather from the beginning of his life a *divine* person: God the Son. Crucially, however, the Chalcedonian equation of hypostasis

14. The inchoate character of the distinction in the mid-fifth century is clear in the text of the definition itself, since the language of the two natures "coming together" (*syntrechein*) could easily be understood to suggest that the one hypostasis was the product of the union rather than its agent and ground. See chap. 3 below for more detailed discussion of the conceptual development that led to the mature (or "neo-Chalcedonian") doctrine of the hypostatic union.

15. Insofar as an entity's whatness is described in terms of particular qualities or attributes, a nature can be considered in abstraction from its instantiation in any particular being. Nevertheless (and as I hope my subsequent usage will make clear), I hold to the position that the human nature Christ assumes is concrete rather than abstract, in the sense that the "nature" assumed by the Word is an individual instance of humanity rather than a property or set of properties. For a fulsome discussion of the distinction, see Timothy Pawl, *In Defense of Conciliar Christology: A Philosophical Essay* (Oxford: Oxford University Press, 2016), 34–39.

16. *Hypostasis* continued to be used even in Chalcedonian circles in a more generic sense to refer to the concrete instantiation of any nature (e.g., Lassie as a particular hypostasis of canine nature); it is therefore useful to distinguish the hypostases of humans and angels as inherently personal, in distinction from the hypostases of other creatures (e.g., apple trees, *E. coli* bacteria, etc.). Importantly, the modification introduced by the adjective "personal" entails a shift in ontological categories; indeed, that is the upshot of the difference between nature and hypostasis as developed within a Chalcedonian theology: to qualify a hypostasis as a *person* is to affirm that it is not to be identified with a concrete instance of a nature as such, but rather with the subject whose concrete instance it is. See, e.g., Leontius of Byzantium, *Contra Nestorianos et Eutychianos* (PG 86.1:1277C–1280B).

with personal identity means that the claim "Jesus does not have a human hypostasis" does not entail any diminishment or qualification of the claim that he has a fully human *nature*.[17] For although the character of humanity as a rational nature is such that there cannot be a concrete instance of human being that is without any hypostasis at all (that is, it is impossible to have a human nature and to lack a personal identity), the distinction between nature and hypostasis—between *what* and *who*—means that there is no inconsistency in affirming that the hypostasis of the particular instance of human nature known as Jesus of Nazareth is divine. Indeed, that is just the point of the doctrine of the incarnation: the claim that in Jesus a person who is and has always been divine (viz., the eternal Son or Word) "became flesh" so as to live a fully human life. On this basis later Chalcedonians took up Cyril of Alexandria's description of the incarnation as a "hypostatic union," in which the hypostasis of the Son unites in his person both divine and human natures.

The upshot of applying the distinction between nature and hypostasis to the person of Jesus may be summarized in the following two theses:

1. When we perceive Jesus of Nazareth, we perceive *no one* other than God the Son, the second person of the Trinity.
2. When we perceive Jesus of Nazareth, we perceive *nothing* other than created substance, and thus nothing that is divine.

Together, these theses affirm that although the one *whom* we see in Jesus is none other than the Son of God, *what* we see in Jesus is simply and exhaustively human flesh and blood. Much of what follows in this book will take the form of the exposition of this double claim as foundational for an account of the incarnation capable of affirming the full and unsurpassable revelation of God in Christ without either diminishing his humanity or conflating it with his divinity. Furthermore, insofar as Jesus' status as Savior is understood to mean that he is the one in and through whose life all humanity and, with it, the whole creation are brought into eternal and unbreakable fellowship with God, this book also seeks to show that a Chalcedonianism without reserve can meet the challenge of providing a conceptual framework capable of affirming that finite creatures can dwell with God in their finitude, and thus that creation can be affirmed as unqualifiedly good in its difference from God. For the burden of the Christian claim that the Word became flesh is that God can draw infinitely near to the creature, even to the extent of rendering the creature's life inseparable from God's own, and yet the life

---

17. Although here I use the traditional language of Jesus not "having" a human hypostasis, this phrasing is infelicitous because, strictly speaking, a hypostasis is not something one *has*, but rather who one *is*.

of the creature is not thereby overwhelmed, but rather affirmed precisely in its createdness.

Therefore (and as paradoxical as it may seem), it is a central thesis of this book that an orthodox account of Jesus' divinity necessarily includes the affirmation that nothing divine can be perceived in him. All that can be perceived in him is his humanity, and because his humanity is purely and exhaustively human, no empirically identifiable feature of Jesus—his height, strength, speed, knowledge, gender, piety, or anything else—may be identified with the divine. A Chalcedonian understanding of the incarnation thus denies that Jesus' status as the "one mediator between God and humankind" (1 Tim. 2:5) depends on his possessing certain empirically observable characteristics that constitute a link or bridge between the human and the divine. This does not mean that God is to be sought behind or beneath Jesus' humanity. On the contrary, God is very much on its surface, so to speak, since God (or more specifically, the second person of the Trinity) is simply who Jesus is, and thus the one *who* is seen when he is seen—even though *what* is seen in any such encounter is purely human. In this way, Jesus mediates between Creator and creature not by standing in some imagined ontological space between God and the world (as Arius and other advocates of subordinationist Christologies believed), or by collapsing the distinction between them (as in modern Christologies from below), but by uniting in his person the being of God and humanity "without confusion or change, without division or separation."

The vision of the incarnation unfolded in this book is correspondingly broad, since it proposes that the Word's taking flesh initiates a comprehensive transformation of creation, reaching through humankind to bring the whole world to a glory—a renewed existence before God that is no longer subject to the futility of decay and alienation (Rom. 8:19–21; cf. 2 Pet. 3:13; Rev. 21:1). The incarnation has not always been conceived in this way. In line with Paul's correlation of Christ and Adam, as well as Jesus' interpretation of his mission in terms of repentance and forgiveness (Matt. 26:28; Mark 1:14; cf. Luke 24:47; Acts 5:31; 10:43; 13:38; 26:18), it has been common in the Christian tradition to conceive of the incarnation chiefly in terms of the doctrine of reconciliation, that is, as God's means of rescuing humanity from the effects of sin (viz., guilt, death, and damnation). By contrast, conceiving the incarnation in terms of glorification, as the means by which God bridges the divide between Creator and creature so as to draw creatures into God's own eternal life, suggests a "supralapsarian" interpretation of the Word's enfleshment. That is, because the "problem" that the incarnation addresses is overcoming the divide between Creator and creature, and because this divide is intrinsic to the very ontology of creation and is not a consequence of human sin, the Word's taking flesh is not dependent on and is thus logically prior to (*supra*) humanity's fall (*lapsus*). The ontological divide between transcendent Creator and finite creatures means that human beings simply cannot exist in communion with God (that is, "become participants of the divine nature," in the words of 2 Pet. 1:4) by the exercise even of their unfallen natural capacities; they can do so only as they become recipients of a gift of grace that supervenes on their nature. In short, God becomes incarnate because God wishes to share the divine life with us, so that the incarnation is part of God's plan for creation independently of human sin.

This sort of supralapsarian interpretation of the incarnation is not without precedent. It is found already in the late second century in the work of Irenaeus of Lyon, who maintained that in taking flesh the Word "did, through his transcendent love, become what we are, that He might bring us to be even what He is Himself."[18] A century and a half later, Athanasius of Alexandria—while anything but inattentive to the specifically redemptive dimensions of the incarnation—gave classic expression to the idea that God's purposes in taking flesh are not limited to redressing the effects of the fall when he wrote that the Word "was made a human being that we might be made God."[19] And to allude to a text that is the touchstone for a later chapter of this book, Maximus the Confessor's affirmation that "the Word of God, who is God, wishes always and everywhere to effect the mystery of his embodiment" likewise implies a commitment to divine enfleshment that is not contingent on the accidents of earthly history.[20] Much more explicitly, in the medieval period Robert Grosseteste and John Duns Scotus both affirmed that God's commitment to communion with human beings is such that the Word would have become incarnate even if humankind had not sinned.[21] Though very much a minority report at the time, variations on this perspective have gained considerable currency in modern theology. In the nineteenth century Friedrich Schleiermacher regarded the coming of Jesus not primarily as a remedy for sin, but as "*the completion, only now accomplished, of the creation of human nature.*"[22] And still more recently Karl Barth insisted that the logic of the claim that Jesus of Nazareth is none other than God demands that the

---

18. Irenaeus of Lyon, *Against Heresies* 5 (Preface), in *ANF* 1.

19. Athanasius of Alexandria, *On the Incarnation of the Word* 54; in Hardy, *Christology of the Later Fathers*, 107.

20. Maximus the Confessor, *Ambigua* 7 (PG 91:1084C–D).

21. Grosseteste develops his arguments in several texts, but most extensively in the second part of his *De cessatione legalium*. Scotus addresses the question in his *Ordinatio* 3, 7.3 (but cf. his *Reportatio Parisiensia* 3, 7.4). See the discussion in Daniel C. Horan, OFM, "How Original Was Scotus on the Incarnation? Reconsidering the History of the Absolute Predestination of Christ in Light of Robert Grosseteste," *Heythrop Journal* 52 (2011): 374–91.

22. Friedrich Schleiermacher, *The Christian Faith*, 2nd ed., §89, ed. H. R. Mackintosh and J. S. Stewart (Edinburgh: T&T Clark, 1928 [1830]), 366.

incarnation be understood as the first of God's decrees, prior even to the willing of creation. Barth reasoned that to confess that Jesus is God, and thus rightly affirmed as the ultimate object of faith, entails the belief that God has no identity more fundamental than Jesus. In other words, here stands the most complete account of who God is: God is just the One who became flesh in Jesus of Nazareth. Everything else that Christians claim to know about God, including God's identity as Creator, is therefore logically subsequent to God's determination to take flesh.[23]

Indeed, Barth's analysis suggests that traditional forms of incarnational supralapsarianism are not quite right precisely because they continue to explain the incarnation as a solution to a problem, albeit that of human finitude (i.e., overcoming the ontological distance between Creator and creature) rather than human sin. Against attempts to construe the incarnation in these terms, one might object that Christian convictions regarding God's omnipotence render problematic the idea that God is constrained to use certain means to achieve God's ends for creatures.[24] But Barth shows that the real difficulty with such approaches is that they conceive of the incarnation—and thus the person of Jesus—as a means to an end, and thus as theologically secondary: occasioned by and thus logically subsequent to more fundamental truths regarding the being and relationship between God and the creature (whether fallen or not). It is more in keeping with the centrality of Jesus to Christian faith to put it precisely the reverse. For if Jesus of Nazareth is truly God, such that Jesus discloses the fullness both of God's being and of God's will for creation without reservation or qualification (Col. 2:9), then (as Barth reasoned) God's determination to be Jesus must enjoy logical precedence over even the creation, let alone the fall (Col. 1:15). From this perspective, the work of creation follows from the primordial election of Jesus: because God elects to be Jesus, and because Jesus is a particular human being—one who breathes, eats, drinks, and bleeds, a Jew, the son of Mary, announced by Gabriel, and so forth—God's willing to be Jesus entails willing the whole created order, from angels to mud puddles and from the big bang to eschaton, within which Jesus lives, moves, and has his being. In other words, the existence of the world and the human beings within it depends on the incarnation rather than the other way around: the truth is not that God had to become flesh to save the world, but that the world's creation and consummation alike are rooted in God's will to be made flesh.

---

23. See Karl Barth, *CD* II/2 (1957), §33.

24. Calvin, e.g., affirmed that God could have effected communion with unfallen human beings apart from the incarnation, even as God enjoys communion with angels without having assumed angelic nature. See John Calvin, *Institutes of the Christian Religion* 1.12.6–7, ed. John T. McNeill, trans. Ford Lewis Battles (Philadelphia: Westminster Press, 1960), 471–73.

Now, all of this is not to deny that by taking flesh in Jesus, God does in fact bridge the divide between the infinite being of the Creator and the finite existence of creatures, or that in and through the incarnation of the Word God actually does break the power of sin. On the contrary, both the form and content of this book is predicated on the conviction that God does both these things in and as Jesus of Nazareth. Yet it remains the case that the incarnation is not best conceived as the solution to a problem, whether the problem is the incommensurability of finite and infinite or the destructive power of sin. The incarnation is instead more appropriately understood as the ground of our being, such that these "problems' are secondary, known and knowable by us as the obstacles to life in communion with God that they most certainly are only as they have been overcome and canceled in the person of Jesus. The bridging of Creator and creature in Jesus is therefore not a response to a logically prior divide, but rather the ground of that very distinction. It is just because God has determined first of all to share the divine life fully with the creature that God brings creatures into being, or, to put it still more sharply, creation happens because God wills to take flesh, and God cannot do that without bringing into being the world that flesh inhabits.

Thus, while affirming the priority of Christ does nothing to compromise his character as the "one mediator between God and humankind," it does require that this work of mediation be described carefully. For Christ is mediator not as a tertium quid positioned between two predefined realities, but rather the one in whom God and humankind acquire their identities as Creator and creature in the first place, that is, the one in and through whom the distinction between Creator and creature is itself established. After all, God is Creator only in relation to the creature, and so while God is eternally God apart from creation, because it is only through the Word who became flesh that all created things came into being (John 1:3; cf. Heb. 1:2), so it is only through the Word that God is Creator.

Conceiving the Word in this way, as the one who both grounds and defines the character of the relationship between God and creation, underlies the structure of this book, which falls into three main parts. The first uses the Johannine account of the Word as God on the one hand and nevertheless enfleshed on the other hand to introduce the distinction between Creator (chap. 1) and creation (chap. 2). This distinction cannot be described without stressing the radical discontinuity between the transcendent being of God and the radically contingent and finite existence of creatures—to the extent that I have titled part 1 as "The Great Divide." Moreover, the affirmation that creation is genuinely other than God, and that this otherness is the reason for creatures' vulnerability to the power of sin and death, is crucial to affirming not only Christ's status as mediator but also the utterly free and gracious character of his mediating work. Yet against the charge that in proceeding in this way I have compromised the christocentric focus of my argument at the outset, I seek in these two chapters to ground the distinction between Creator and creatures in the life of the Trinity. My point in so doing is to underline the claim that this distinction is inseparable from the being and act of the triune God and thus not a state of affairs that may be conceived apart from the One through whom it is bridged.[25] Thus, although in their focus on the Creator-creature distinction these chapters cover much of the same material found in my book *From Nothing*, it is my hope that their orientation to Christology keeps them from being dully repetitive of the arguments I developed there.[26]

The book's second part explores the meaning and defends the coherence of the claim that the bridging of the divide between Creator and creature happens through the Word taking on a creaturely life through a study of the doctrine of the hypostatic union. The analysis attends first to the claim that in taking flesh the Word remained just one *person*, the very Word or Son of God (chap. 3); it then moves to an exploration of the confession that the Word who became flesh was fully *divine* (chap. 4), and yet in taking flesh became no less fully *human* (chap. 5). These three chapters thus move from a discussion of the metaphysics of the incarnation through an exploration of the peculiar identity of the incarnate one as the God of the Jews, who in the fullness of time took on Jewish flesh so as to be born, suffer, and die. The third part of the book then shows how Jesus' victory over death in the resurrection gives rise to a new, redeemed mode of created existence that is rooted in God's own life and is thereby secured from the natural vulnerability of created being (chap. 6), culminating in a discussion of how the effects of God's taking human flesh spread through creation to catch up the whole world in glory (chap. 7). Finally, the book concludes with a brief discussion of the implications of this Chalcedonian framework for the traditional distinction between Christ's person and work.

In all this the point that I hope stands at the forefront is that the confession of the incarnation, that the Father's only begotten Son has come among us as one of us, is good news. It is *news* because it is incomprehensible. That God, who is not a creature, should nevertheless become a creature and, indeed,

---

25. "It is, then, proper for us to begin the treatment of this subject [of the incarnation] by speaking of the creation of the universe, and of God its Artificer, that it may be duly perceived that the renewal of creation has been the work of the selfsame Word that made it at the beginning." Athanasius, *On the Incarnation of the Word* 56.

26. Ian A. McFarland, *From Nothing: A Theology of Creation* (Louisville, KY: Westminster John Knox, 2014).

share creatures' radical estrangement from God, taking the form of a slave and humbling himself "to the point of death—even death on a cross" (Phil. 2:8)—is quite beyond our grasp. How can God be human without at any point ceasing to be God and Lord of all? The coherence of this claim can be defended (such defense is the aim of this book), but how it comes about can never be explained.

And the incarnation is more specifically *good* news. It is a mystery, but (in contrast to the original meaning of that word) not therefore something before which we are to fall silent. On the contrary, it is mystery that we have "been given to know" (Matt. 13:11; Luke 8:10) and that we are charged to proclaim (Matt. 28:19–20; Mark 16:15; cf. 1 Cor. 4:1; 9:16), because God has become a creature "for us and for our salvation," to wrench us from captivity to sin, death, and the devil (Rom. 7:23; 8:2; 2 Tim. 2:26) so that we might enjoy the glorious liberty of the children of God (Rom. 8:21). In this way, the point of a Chalcedonianism without reserve is finally to defend a still more fundamental theological claim: that while God is good, it is not necessary to be God in order to be good, since both now and in eternity the goodness of God the Creator is fulfilled in establishing the goodness of the creature too. For to proclaim the incarnation is to affirm the truth contained in Jesus' very name: that God saves. And because this salvation is effected in God's coming among us as Jesus, it does not depend on isolating some spark of divinity within us, and thus does not consist in the setting aside of our contingent and finite creatureliness in order to achieve some terminal apotheosis. Quite the contrary, it is precisely as creatures who are other than God that we are saved because God, in a love beyond all telling, has willed not to be other than us.

There is one more point that needs to be made before proceeding to the substance of the argument. It might seem odd that in a book that claims to take its lead from Luther's maxim that "whoever wishes to meditate or speculate soundly about God should disregard absolutely everything except the humanity of Christ," just one chapter has the humanity of Christ as its explicit subject. This fact might seem evidence that Chalcedonianism is guilty of just the shortcomings that its modern critics allege: a Christology in which (to use the vivid metaphor of Catherine Keller) the dogmatic frame covers over the picture of the human being who is ostensibly its subject.[27] Against this charge, I would simply say that the point of this book is not to say everything that can or even should be said about Jesus (see John 21:25!). It is rather to give an account of how and why his humanity is rightly understood as the center of Christology in spite (and indeed, just because) of the confession of Jesus

---

27. Catherine Keller, *On the Mystery: Discerning Divinity in Process* (Minneapolis: Fortress Press, 2008), 133.

as divine. That is, it seeks to show how things that Christians say about the hypostatic union, two natures, preexistence, ascension, and promised return do not divert us from Jesus' humanity, but rather—if rightly understood and explicated—serve precisely to turn our attention back to the life that extended from Mary's womb to Pilate's cross, on the grounds that this life, in all its seemingly provincial particularity, opens for us the mystery of the love that moves the sun and the other stars.

PART 1

The Great Divide

For my thoughts are not your thoughts,
    nor are your ways my ways, says the Lord.
For as the heavens are higher than the earth,
    so are my ways higher than your ways
    and my thoughts than your thoughts.
                                    —*Isaiah 55:8–9*

1

The Life of the Creator

Christians confess that all we see has been brought into being by God and that God is not brought into being by anything. For this reason they call God "Creator." But how does one begin to talk about this Creator God? In general, we talk about things because we encounter them in our experience: we bang our toes on rocks, we spy a shell on the beach, the rain drenches us. But the New Testament is very clear that we don't encounter God in that way: "No one has ever seen God" (John 1:18; 1 John 4:12).[1] At one level, this claim accords well with the traditional Christian conviction that God is utterly transcendent with respect to the created order. For if, as the claim of transcendence entails, God is not one thing among other things, then the fact that no one has ever seen God is not a matter of happenstance, but intrinsic to God's very nature. Put simply, a god we could see would not be God. As Augustine famously put it, "So what are we to say, brothers, about God? For if you have fully grasped what you want to say, it isn't God. If you have been able to comprehend it, you have comprehended something else instead of God. If you think you have been able to comprehend, your thoughts have deceived you. So he isn't this, if this is what you have understood; but if he is this, then you haven't understood it."[2] Considered further, however, such assertions seem to undermine the possibility of any talk about divinity at all, since if God can't be seen (with "seeing" standing in for every form of human perception), then God can't be known—and then even the claim that God is transcendent seems open to question. Indeed, if God is

---

1. All biblical translations are from the NRSV unless otherwise noted.
2. Augustine, "Sermon 52," in *Sermons III (51–94) on the New Testament*, ed. John E. Rotelle, OSA, trans. Edmund Hill, OP (Brooklyn, NY: New City Press, 1991), 57.

so radically inaccessible to us as to be beyond the very possibility of human perception, it's not clear how the word "God" could enter human language in the first place.

And yet it clearly has. It is a notable fact, upon which Christian missionaries from the earliest times to the present have capitalized, that every language seems to have a term that Christians have been able to appropriate to refer to the God they proclaim. And most Christians have interpreted this as evidence for the claim that God can be known in spite of the divine invisibility—not directly, to be sure, but by inference from what can be seen. For example, it seems that in light of the radical contingency of the entities that make up our world (whether with respect to their origin, development, or end), we are inevitably led to reflect on the overarching context that frames our experience of reality as a whole—and it is at that point that God-talk emerges.[3] From this perspective, "God" is an orienting point for reflection on the ontological horizon of human experience and can therefore be said to "appear" in the world at the limits of human thinking. Even here, however, "God" seems to function only as a verbal token that marks where our empirical resources for speaking about the world run dry, thus not signaling the kind of direct apprehension of an object that would allow specification of what (let alone who) God is.

THE PROBLEM WITH GOD-TALK

The inherently content-less character of the concept of "God" that emerges from reflection on its "natural" place in human speech seems to provide no ground for ascribing any positive predicates to God. Because "God" is not an object of immediate experience, but only a marker for where our experience comes up short, once the semantic space that "God" occupies has been identified, there is no experiential basis for going on from there to fill in its content. In short, if God is transcendent, then the claim that God is invisible follows quite naturally, as do various other forms of "negative" (or "apophatic") predication that speak of God in terms of what God is not. Thomas Aquinas, for example, argued that although reflection on the limits of human experience justified the inference *that* God exists, the "existence" thereby demonstrated is so peculiar that it allows no conclusions to be drawn about *how* God exists. Instead, he insisted, the most we can do is to show how the categories we

---

3. See Thomas Aquinas, *ST* 1.2.3. As Rowan Williams summarizes Thomas's "five ways," "the interpretive context that holds together the entire realm of causality and dependence is what is generally meant by 'God.'" Rowan Williams, *The Edge of Words: God and the Habits of Language* (London: Bloomsbury, 2014), 7.

normally use to describe existents do *not* apply to God.[4] In short, locating the semantic space occupied by "God" does not generate theological data; instead, it only returns us to the claim that God cannot be said to exist or to be known in the way that other entities exist and are known—as some *thing* that can be distinguished from other things. And this brings us back to the question of whether it is possible for God to be known at all, or whether, as thinkers from Xenophanes to Freud have supposed, all talk about God is finally just a projection of human wishes and prejudices into the void that we face when we confront the limits of experience.

In light of such considerations, how does the invisible God, the one "whom no one has ever seen or can see" (1 Tim. 6:16; cf. 1 John 4:20), come to be known as real and not just posited as a hypothesis or a piece of wish-fulfillment? Here, too, Scripture is clear: "It is God the only Son, who is in the bosom of the Father, who has made him known" (John 1:18 alt.). God can be known by us because God makes God's self known through the Son or (as named a few verses earlier in John's Gospel) the Word, who was not only *"with* God" from the beginning as the one who rests in the Father's bosom, but who *"was* God" (John 1:1). Exactly what it means to say that this happens—the coherence of the claim that this Word "became flesh and lived among us" (John 1:14) —will be the subject of part 2 of this book. The central point to be secured now is that the God whom we know through the Word is known only as God chooses to make God's self known to us in this way. This God is not an object we can identify and investigate on our own by any observation of or inference from the worldly processes, however carefully managed.

Importantly, adherence to this principle does not rule out the possibility of true knowledge of God apart from explicit reference to Jesus. After all, there is plenty of talk about God in the Bible before Jesus appears on the scene, and Christians (after some initial disagreement and with a few lingering exceptions along the way) have held firmly to the conviction that the Old Testament is no less God's word than the New. Moreover, it is clearly a central concern of the authors of the books of the New Testament to show that the God whose reign Jesus proclaims is not in every respect a heretofore "unknown God" (cf. Acts 17:23), but precisely the God of Abraham, Isaac, Jacob, Moses, David, and Israel's prophets (see, e.g., Matt. 2:5; 26:24, 31; Luke 22:37; 24:44; John 2:17; 12:14–15; Acts 13:33; 24:14; Rom. 9:33; 11:26; 1 Cor. 1:19, 31; Gal. 3:13; Heb. 10:5–7). Yet therefrom it does not follow that knowledge of this God is altogether independent of Jesus. Forasmuch as it is true that Jesus' divinity is

---

4. "Having recognized *that* something exists, we still have to investigate *the way in which* it exists, that we may come to understand *what it is* that exists. Now we cannot know what God is, but only what he is not; we must therefore consider the ways in which God does not exist, rather than the ways in which he does." Aquinas, *ST* 1, Preface to questions 3–11, trans. slightly alt.

inseparable from his witness to the God of Israel, so too is it the case that the knowledge of Israel's God is theologically indispensable for Christians because it is just *this* God whom Jesus reveals. In other words, because the God who is revealed in Jesus—the God who cannot be seen and so can only be made known definitively by the Son, who has seen him (John 3:11, 32)—is the God who elected Israel, truthful witness to Jesus' God cannot be given without using the language of Zion. Because Jesus is the revelation of this God, we need to know God's ways with Israel in order to understand fully who Jesus is, even as the knowledge of God that comes from Jesus, in turn, gives definitive form to our understanding of the God of Israel (see, e.g., Rom. 11:25–32; 1 Cor. 10:1–4).[5] These two points are inseparable: incarnation is misunderstood if it is not understood as the incarnation of the God of the Jews, and the identity of the God of the Jews is not fully understood apart from the incarnation.[6]

But what exactly can we say about the God who is known in this way? Clearly, if true knowledge of God comes through Jesus—whose life, in terms of both its immediate content and its broader Israelite context, is communicated in Scripture—then the words we use to talk about God must be grounded in the terms the biblical authors use to talk about God. And in this context it is significant that one of those things Scripture says about God is precisely that God cannot be seen. Of course, many things in the world—air, protons, physical forces like gravity and electromagnetism—also cannot be seen by the human eye, but they can be detected by other means: air can be felt, contained, and weighed; and even infinitesimal subatomic particles can be measured by their effects. But God, according to Scripture, is not subject to investigation in this way: if no one has ever seen God, this is not merely a matter of accident, nor a matter of our needing to use senses other than vision, but because God is only knowable as God is made known through the Son. So when Christians say that God is invisible, they mean that God is not detectible by us in any way whatsoever: cloud chambers and compass needles allow us to track the paths of protons and magnetic lines of force, but no apparatus we can construct allows us to track God.[7]

---

5. See chaps. 4 and 5 below for a more focused discussion of the implications of Jesus' Jewishness for Christian confession of his divinity and humanity alike.

6. It should go without saying (although the presence of this footnote shows that I fear it does need to be said) that this is a specifically *Christian* claim. Jews will not accept that knowledge of Jesus is decisive for full knowledge of the God of Israel—precisely because they do not view Jesus as the Word made flesh. And while Muslims do confess Jesus as the Word (Qur'an 3.45; cf. 4.171), they do not on this basis identify him with God, and so do not ascribe to him the definitive role for correct human knowledge of God that Christians do.

7. "How things are in the world is a matter of complete indifference for what is higher. God does not reveal himself *in* the world." Ludwig Wittgenstein, *Tractatus Logico-Philosophicus* 6.432, trans. D. F. Pears and B. F. McGuinness (London: Routledge, 1974 [1921]).

And yet Scripture proclaims not only that we can and do come to know God, but also that among the things we come to know is precisely that God is invisible. And, crucially, the biblical basis for this claim is not generalized reflection on the limits of human experience, but precisely God's own act of self-disclosure:

> Then the LORD spoke to you out of the fire. You heard the sound of words but saw no form; there was only a voice. . . . Since you saw no form when the LORD spoke to you at Horeb out of the fire, take care and watch yourselves closely, so that you do not act corruptly by making an idol for yourselves, in the form of any figure. (Deut. 4:12, 15–16)

In short, Christians claim that God is invisible because God has *shown* God's self to be invisible—self-contradictory though such a claim may seem. This showing culminates in Jesus: yet his being "the image of the invisible God" (Col. 1:15; cf. John 12:45; 14:9) does not cancel divine invisibility but confirms it, since it is precisely God's definitive self-disclosure in Jesus that gives rise to the claim that "no one has ever seen God." Thus, within a properly Christian theological perspective, divine invisibility is not to be understood as a conclusion derived from a lack of knowledge of God, but rather as the immediate content of God's own direct act of self-disclosure.[8] That is, God's invisibility is not inferred but *seen*, albeit indirectly, in the sense that when God makes God's self available to creaturely perception—whether in the call of Abraham, the burning bush, or the incarnation—God is never encountered as an object. Even in the case of Jesus, what is heard, seen, looked at, and touched (1 John 1:1) is never the divine nature itself, which always exceeds the creaturely medium through which it becomes known. In every encounter with the creature, God remains subject, so that although God thereby comes to be known objectively, the knower's absolute dependence on God's initiative in the process means that the God so known can never be objectified. To do so would be to identify the divine nature with a phenomenal reality in a

---

8. In this context, it is important to note that when in Rom. 1:20 Paul speaks of God's "eternal power and divine nature, invisible though they are," as having been "understood and seen through the things he has made," seemingly apart from any knowledge of Christ, his point is precisely that any putative human knowledge of God that is not the product of direct divine self-disclosure is bootless. Apart from revelation, human beings certainly talk about God; Paul concedes that they may even be said to know God (v. 21)—perhaps because they use language for God in a way that reflects some inkling of God's transcendence. But apart from God's own self-disclosure, such "knowledge" does not result in people honoring God as God; instead, in every case "they became futile in their thinking, and their senseless minds were darkened" (v. 21). In Jesus, by contrast, people see the invisible God in a way that enables them to give due honor to God. Apart from Jesus (even in the history of Israel), any such "seeing" only manifests what the Lukan Paul describes as "the times of human ignorance" that God has "overlooked"—and which in Christ are now brought to an end (Acts 17:30–32).

way that betrays the character of revelation as precisely the making known of the God "whom no one has ever seen or can see."

In this way, the biblical account of God reaffirms the fundamentally negative or apophatic observation with which our exploration of the word "God" began: our incapacity to say anything about *how* God exists. As such, it points to a much broader array of predicates that similarly highlight the impossibility of treating God as one object alongside others, and thus in any way at our disposal. Many of these (e.g., infinite, immense, immaterial, immortal, unchangeable, impassible, uncircumscribable) take the same morphologically negative form as "invisible." Others carry negative force, even if lacking a negative prefix, in denying that God is relative to any other entity (aseity), that God is in any sense composite (simplicity), or that God is contained in time (eternity). Whatever their verbal form, all such predicates point to the conviction that God cannot be treated as one item alongside others because God transcends the conceptual categories we use to distinguish one entity from another by ascribing to it certain qualities ("black," "round," "metallic") instead of others ("yellow," "oblong," "organic"). To say that God is transcendent, in other words, is to affirm that God does not fall under any category. As medieval theologians quipped, *Deus non est in genere*, "God is not a kind of anything."

Indeed, if God cannot be categorized, then it seems to follow that the only way to speak of God accurately is to speak of God negatively, using words like "invisible" to deny that the kinds of predicates (e.g., color, size) we generally use to differentiate items from one another can be applied to God. To be sure, the rhetorical effect of these terms can sometimes betray that intent, so that (e.g.) the attributes of unchangeability and impassibility have been understood to imply that God is static, inert, and indifferent with respect to the world in a manner that hardly accords with the Bible's characterization of God as "a devouring fire, a jealous God" (Deut. 4:24; cf. Exod. 34:14; Josh. 24:19; Ezek. 39:25). Rightly understood, however, the point of such attributes is not to define God by contrast with worldly realities, for that effectively reintroduces a scheme in which God is treated as one object among others (viz., *x* as opposed to *y*). But divine transcendence means that God isn't rightly understood as either like or unlike other entities in the sense of being characterized by some attributes rather than others: as big rather than small, black rather than white, here rather than there, or, most generally, *this* rather than *that*. Instead, the point of using negative predicates of God is to signal that God's distinctiveness is not properly expressed in terms of contrast with other entities.[9] To make

9. For a contemporary development of this point, see Kathryn Tanner, *God and Creation in Christian Theology: Tyranny or Empowerment?* (Malden, MA: Blackwell, 1988), esp. 28: "Whatever you say about God and the world, do not simply identify and oppose their attributes."

this point clear, the fifteenth-century theologian Nicholas of Cusa referred to God as *Non aliud*, "Not Other," not meaning to promote a pantheism in which God is identified with the world of nondivine being (i.e., as if "Not Other" were equivalent to "The Same"), but rather to suggest that the "difference" between God and the world has no ready analogue in our everyday experience.[10] God is "Not Other," insofar as "other" is a term used to designate one item among others in a series. In this sense, "Not Other"—itself, of course, a form of negative predication—highlights the role that all apophatic predicates play in keeping Christian talk about God faithful to Scripture's witness to divine transcendence.

And yet as important as these negative predicates are, their theological role is inherently formal. They discipline Christian speech about God so that at every point it respects God's reality as *totaliter aliter*: not (as often mistranslated) "wholly Other," as though God were defined by contrast with the world, but rather "wholly otherwise" with respect to the modes of existence that shape our experience and structure our ways of thinking. Although they derive from God's self-disclosure, in which God addresses human beings and so reveals God's self as God, they do not so much communicate positive information about God as to call into question our efforts to engage in such communication. They remind us of the unique character of the One with whom we have to do.

But Christian Scripture also includes no shortage of positive (or "cataphatic") claims about God, statements that do not deny but rather affirm definite attributes of God. Indeed, because these attributes are predicated of God, in whom, as the source of all reality, every created good is fully and unsurpassably realized, they are sometimes referred to as divine perfections. And yet it is not immediately clear how the ascription of any such qualities to God can be squared with God's status as "Not Other." For if God's being transcends and exceeds all our categories and concepts, what meaning can be ascribed to the divine perfections? Scripture may provide the words, but if God is transcendent, then their meaning cannot be such as to subsume God under the same categories that govern their everyday use; the result is that their theological application seems to be hopelessly equivocal. We may say that God is good, for example, but such affirmations can provide no more knowledge of God's goodness than knowledge of a dog's bark gives about the bark on a tree.

10. Nicholas of Cusa, *Nicholas of Cusa on God as Not-Other: A Translation and Appraisal of "De li non aliud,"* trans. Jasper Hopkins, 2nd ed. (Minneapolis: Arthur J. Banning Press, 1983). Cf. Robert Sokolowski's pithy summary of the significance of Thomas's characterization of the divine essence as simply "to be" (*esse subsistens*): "The contrast to *esse subsistens* is not differentiation, but nothing other at all." See Robert Sokolowski, *Presence and Absence: A Philosophical Investigation of Language and Being* (Bloomington: Indiana University Press, 1978), 179.

At one level, Christians will concede this point. That is, based on the witness of Scripture (and thus, so to speak, on God's authorization), they will want to affirm *that* certain qualities (e.g., goodness, wisdom, righteousness) are genuinely true of God, while at the same time allowing that God's transcendence means that they do not know *how* they are true of God. In short, they will admit that when they say that God is good, wise, or righteous, they do not fully understand what they are saying. But neither will they conclude that those words carry no meaning at all, because Christians maintain that there is a middle ground between predicating qualities of God in the same way that we do of other entities and pure equivocation. This third way is that of analogy. Thomas Aquinas offers the word "healthy" as an example of analogical predication found in everyday speech. He notes that the word "healthy" may be used to describe a person, her diet, and her urine, but that "healthy" is clearly not being used in the same way across these three cases since it is not possible to derive what it means to say that either a diet or urine is healthy from knowledge of what it means for a person to be healthy. At the same time, someone who understands all three uses of "healthy" can articulate the relationship between them (viz., that a healthy diet promotes health in a person, and that healthy urine reflects it) and so explain how these uses, while genuinely distinct, nevertheless stand in a meaningful relationship with one another and so are not simply equivocal.[11] In the same way, terms like "goodness" and "wisdom" apply to God in a way that cannot be understood on the basis of their application in everyday contexts (e.g., it is not simply a matter of a quantitative increase, as though God were wise like Socrates, only more so), but that somehow both encompasses and completes our everyday understanding of their meaning.

Given that in this life we remain incapable of perceiving how the terms we apply to God encompass and complete their everyday application, it follows that their deployment in theological contexts must hew closely to the biblical witness in order to ensure that they are interpreted in a manner consistent with God's own self-disclosure rather than simply following the conventions of everyday use. And because it is a Christian conviction that the divine life includes all perfections, a full accounting of them is not possible. Any enumeration of the divine perfections will therefore be selective, and efforts at classification will be unable to avoid a degree of arbitrariness. The categorization that I use is no exception and reflects the chapter's limited aims: not to provide a comprehensive doctrine of God, but only to offer enough of a characterization of what Christians mean by divinity to give a sense of the conceptual difficulties posed by the confession that God has become flesh. To this end, the divine perfections will be examined in terms of two main categories:

---

11. See Aquinas, *ST* 1.13.10.

the perfections of divine *love* (among which particular attention will be given to God's goodness, patience, and holiness) and the perfections of divine *presence* (among which God's unity, omnipotence, and glory will be highlighted).

This classification echoes Karl Barth's distinction between the perfections of divine loving and the perfections of divine freedom.[12] As Barth himself notes, the idea of a basic, twofold categorization of the divine perfections is well established in Christian tradition, although typically described using other terminological pairings (e.g., communicable and incommunicable, relative and absolute, moral and metaphysical) than that of love and freedom. Where Barth diverges from the tradition is neither in the character of his primary categories nor in the particular perfections associated with each of them, but rather in their ordering. For whereas traditional orthodoxies gave pride of place to the "incommunicable" or "absolute" perfections—those, like omnipotence and omnipresence, that pertain to God alone—Barth prioritizes the "communicable" or "relative" perfections of love in which creatures, too, may participate. He does so to indicate that the concrete and personal trump the abstract and metaphysical in matters of divine ontology, and it is in agreement with this principle that I begin with the perfections of divine love.

THE PERFECTIONS OF DIVINE LOVE

That love should be singled out as a foundational divine perfection may seem entirely natural in light of the biblical affirmation that "God is love" (1 John 4:8, 16), but given that Scripture (and indeed, the Johannine tradition in particular) also claims that God is "spirit" (John 4:24) and "light" (1 John 1:5), the priority of love cannot be secured on the basis of a single proof text. Additional support might seem to be provided by the repeated affirmation that God abounds in "steadfast love" (Exod. 20:5–6; 34:6; Num. 14:18; Deut. 5:9–10; 1 Kgs. 8:23; Ezra 3:11; Pss. 33:5, 18, 22; 62:12; 86:5, 13, 15; 100:5; and passim), but the focus in all these passages is God's covenant faithfulness to Israel, and thus God's "economic" activity in creation, rather than any immanent characteristic of the divine life. In any case, a theology that honors divine transcendence must be careful to ensure that the biblical witness to God is used to interpret the predicate "love" rather than the other way around; hence, noticing the frequency of scriptural references to divine love will not in itself be sufficient to establish its relative priority among the divine perfections. It is necessary instead to explain how love is characteristic of God independently of God's relationship to creatures.

12. Karl Barth, *CD* II/1: §§28–31.

The best way to meet this demand is once again to begin with the principle that we know God only as God chooses to make God's self known, and that God makes God's self known through the Word, who "became flesh and lived among us" (John 1:14). But what does it mean to make this kind of claim about the Word? How can this Word be in a position to reveal God? The answer is that "in the beginning" this Word was "*with* God" (John 1:1). In other words, the God whom Jesus reveals can be known because this God, though transcendent, is not closed in on God's self. There is nothing before the eternal God, who encompasses all beginnings and so is uniquely "in the beginning"; and the doctrines of divine aseity and simplicity mean that there is no nondivine reality in relation to or as a consequence of which God is God; and yet in this eternal and unconditioned form of existence, the Word is with God. Significantly, the Greek preposition used by the fourth evangelist is not *meta* or *syn*, the prepositions most typically rendered "with" in English, both of which connote a static collocation or coordination of distinct entities. It is rather *pros*, which is suggestive of a more dynamic relationship: the Word as "for," "up against," or (most crudely but also most evocatively) "toward" God. In short, God and the Word are not to be conceived as two things alongside one another. They are mutually implicated in another way.

It is in specifying the nature of this mutual implication that the perfection of love may be invoked: as Jesus testifies, it is as the Word made flesh and by love that he was joined to the God he calls Father before the foundation of the world (John 17:24). In other words, for the Word to be with God in the beginning is for the Word to have been joined to God in such a way as to be the Son of the Father. And it is only in consequence of this love—because the "Father loves the Son and shows him all that he himself is doing" (John 5:20)—that Jesus is able to reveal God, for "the Son can do nothing on his own, but only what he sees the Father doing; for whatever the Father does, the Son does likewise" (John 5:19).

But what exactly is the character of this love? It is importantly distinct from the human experience of love, which is not native to our being, but rather shapes our lives by coming upon us and changing both who we are and how we relate to others (cf. Rom. 5:5). We are before we love. But if God *is* love, there is no divine being prior to and apart from the divine loving, and thus no God who is Father apart from the love whereby the Father loves the Son. Love, therefore, is not an extrinsic quality that supervenes on and modifies God's existence. Instead, Father is the Father precisely in loving the Son, even as the Son is the Son precisely in receiving (and returning) the love of the Father. It follows that the Father's showing all things to the Son is not adventitious, as though the Father and the Son had some sort of existence independent of each other that would require a logically subsequent transfer of information in order for the Son to be able to reveal the Father; rather, the Father's showing is rooted in a still more fundamental giving to the Son of divine being itself: "For just as the Father has life in himself, so he has granted the Son also to have life in himself" (John 5:26). The love of the Father for the Son thus takes the form of a comprehensive self-bestowal, in which all that is the Father's—indeed, all that the Father is—is given to the Son, since the "Father loves the Son and has placed all things in his hands" (John 3:35; cf. 17:10). In short, the Father is the Father just as he gives life to the Son, even as the Son is the Son as he receives life from the Father: each thereby lives in the other (John 10:38; 14:10–11).

Yet as unfathomable as the gift by which the Father bestows all that the Father has and is on the Son may be, it does not exhaust the love of God, which also includes the Holy Spirit. The Spirit's character is notoriously enigmatic, for although associated with Jesus' life from his conception (Matt. 1:20, Luke 1:35) and through his baptism (Matt. 3:16 and pars.; John 1:32) and ministry (Matt. 4:1 and pars.; 12:28; Luke 4:18; John 3:34) to his resurrection from the dead (Rom. 1:4), the Spirit seems to be active behind, in, and through Jesus rather than to stand over against him as the Father does, so that, for example, Jesus never speaks *to* the Spirit (though he does address the Father *in* the Spirit; Luke 10:21).[13] But this feature of the Gospel narratives actually points to the Spirit's specific place within the divine life; for the Spirit is designated in Scripture equally as the Spirit of the Father (Matt. 10:20; cf. Rom. 8:11) and the Spirit of the Son (Gal. 4:6; cf. Acts 16:7; Phil. 1:19), and it is precisely as such—the one who, in searching "the depths of God," bears witness to the love of the Father and Son—that the Spirit is "the Spirit of God" (1 Cor. 2:10–11) and thus a third alongside these two. More specifically, the Spirit's role is to bear witness to Jesus (1 Cor. 12:3; 1 John 4:1)—the Son apart from whom there is no knowledge of the Father (Matt. 11:27 and par.; 1 John 2:23). In this way the Spirit confirms the love of God as not an abstract or impersonal property of divinity, but just that by which God is the Father who gives all that the Father is to the Son and, simultaneously, the Son who receives all this from the Father. So while the Spirit is no less integral to God's life than the Son, the Spirit subsists precisely as the Spirit of Jesus, the

---

13. This is not to say that the Spirit is not depicted as a distinct "character" in Scripture. Alongside the Gospel accounts of the Spirit alighting on Jesus at his baptism, in Acts especially the Spirit is depicted as one to whom it is possible to lie (5:3; cf. v. 9) and who speaks (10:19; 13:2; cf. 21:11). And yet even here, the Spirit's presence is identified so completely with Jesus' mission (John 14:26) that if the Son is identified as the object of the Father's love, the Spirit, though proceeding from the Father (John 15:26) in a manner distinct from the Son, is nevertheless so inseparable from the Son as at times to be identified with him (2 Cor. 3:14–18).

beloved of the Father (Matt. 3:17; 17:5 and pars.), and on that basis is known and confessed as the Spirit of God the Father, too.

In summary, to say that God is love is to confess God as Trinity: the Father, the Son, and the Holy Spirit. God is love in that the Father loves the Son in giving all that he is to the Son and confirming this in the Spirit, even as the Son loves the Father by glorifying the Father in the same Spirit, with the Spirit bearing witness to—and thereby sharing in—the mutual love of the Father and the Son. In other words, "love" characterizes God's concrete existence as these three, traditionally designated as hypostases or "persons." As realized in the communion of the three persons, the love of God is free, in that it is not involuntary or compelled, as though grounded in a reality either logically or ontologically prior to the act of the divine persons' loving one another. Rather, God loves freely, and thus willingly, since it is integral even to the human love of which God's is both the ground and goal that love can never be unintended, as though a lover could refrain from acknowledging her love as her own act. At the same time, the freedom of divine love does not make it a matter of choice or decision, as though God's freedom were to be understood as its cause. If love were in this way the product of some more fundamental divine activity (viz., the divine will), then it would not be strictly true that God simply *is* love.[14] For us, love is adventitious, in that we are before we love. It is not so for God, since the mutual love of the Father and the Son in the Holy Spirit is just what it means for God to be God: neither relative to or dependent on any nondivine reality, but simply the One who lives in and as three persons.[15]

The Divine Goodness

As a summary characterization of the divine being, love is the foundational divine perfection, and it encompasses many more. First and foremost, to affirm that God is love is to confess God's measureless *goodness*. The Bible proclaims that God is good (Mark 10:18 and par.; cf. Ezra 8:18; Neh. 2:8; Titus 3:4) no less than that God is love; indeed, insofar as the good is traditionally defined as

14. This problem is not solved by arguing (as does Bruce McCormack in *Orthodox and Modern: Studies in the Theology of Karl Barth* [Grand Rapids: Baker Academic, 2008], 271; cf. 192) that God's love is the product of an eternal decision; for though that position does affirm that God has "never" been other than loving, it still leaves love—and thus God's being as Trinity—logically subsequent to God's will and thus leaves open the possibility that God might have been other than loving.

15. In this way, the confession of God as Trinity provides the framework for interpreting the biblical claim that "God is love" as the primary and most concrete meaning of the traditional theological affirmation that God's being is in act: that is, God subsists as rather than being in any sense prior to the mutual love of the persons.

that which is desirable (and thus a fitting object of love), it might at first glance seem that goodness would have precedence over love in God's life, since it is precisely as something is good that it is worthy of love. Here again, however, it is crucial to mark the distinction between the divine and human, for whereas humans exist prior to their loving, so that it is precisely the perception of the good that elicits their love, in God there is nothing prior to love. The persons do not love one another as objects of desire, for because the mutual love of the persons is primordial (i.e., just what it means for God to be God), it is not prompted by any lack; indeed, it is not prompted by anything at all. Thus, while humans' love is a response to the good, God is good precisely in loving.

As already noted, the form that God's loving takes is precisely the eternal and infinite act of self-donation whereby the Father begets the Son in the power of the Spirit. So although it is the case that with respect to creatures, God is the supreme good (and thus preeminently desirable) precisely as the source of all perfections (and thus of every possible object of desire), the form that this goodness takes is just God's self-giving. And while this goodness is manifest in creation in the giving of being to that which is not God, it is active already and quite apart from creation in the love whereby the Father eternally gives the fullness of divinity to the Son in the Spirit, while the Son in the same Spirit returns this gift by eternally glorifying the Father. So the goodness of God is just this eternal process of self-bestowal in which the persons neither hold anything back nor claim any "reserve" of divinity for themselves in isolation, but rather subsist—whether in the mode of bestowal (the Father), reception (the Son), or witness (the Spirit)—by sharing divinity freely, unstintingly, and inexhaustibly.

The Divine Patience

Importantly, however, this sharing of being does not involve the overwhelming of the recipient by the gift. Even as in creation God gives rise to that which is other than God by allotting each creature its own integrity in space and time, so in the Godhead the mutual sharing of divinity among the three persons does not result in their confusion. On the contrary, the complete giving of divine being by the Father to the Son is accompanied by a letting-be that constitutes the Son not as a second Father but precisely as the Son, even as the Son's glorification of the Father does not entail any sort of diminishment but rather the Son's own acknowledgment of the Father's being as Father. And the Spirit's own unique mode of participation in this life is precisely to witness to the distinctiveness of the Father and the Son—and thereby to establish his own distinctiveness as Spirit. This eternal letting-be points to a second perfection of divine love: the divine patience.

In human terms patience carries the connotation of letting-be in the rather negative sense of putting up with someone: maintaining one's commitment to another in spite of that other's behavior. Scripture tends to characterize God's patience in similar terms (Rom. 2:4; 9:22; 1 Tim. 1:16; 2 Pet. 3:15; cf. Jer. 15:15; Rom. 3:25). But if God is (and therefore charges us to be) patient in this sense with the waywardness of other creatures, this is because patience in an expanded sense already characterizes the divine life. For if patience is a virtue at those times of strain or tension in relating, that is precisely because the one to whom patience is to be shown has her own integrity (even if, as in the case of the creature before God, that integrity is itself entirely a matter of God's own free bestowal). At bottom, patience is simply the acknowledgment of that integrity in life and action, and if it is proved in occasions of strain, it is presupposed quite independently of any such occasions arising. Insofar as God, as love, is Trinity, God is supremely and eternally patient precisely in not holding divinity as something to be hoarded (cf. Phil. 2:6), but in subsisting as three, each of whom subsists in a peculiar glory that, while inseparable from the other two, is distinctive and incommunicable.

The Divine Holiness

God's holiness is affirmed throughout Scripture (Josh. 24:19; Ps. 99:1–2; Isa. 5:16; 6:3; Rev. 4:8; 6:10) and, indeed, stands out from the other perfections thus far examined in that it is a matter of God's own self-identification: "I the LORD your God am holy" (Lev. 19:2; cf. 21:8). But what does it mean that God is holy? Most basically, that which is holy is set apart. So in Scripture whatever is declared holy, whether the priests, the inner precincts of the sanctuary, or the sacrifices offered there, is not to be combined or confused with the everyday. These created realities are, of course, holy only derivatively, by virtue of their having been set apart by the God who is holy by nature—and whose holiness is dangerous and, correspondingly, fearful (Exod. 19:16–23; cf. Heb. 12:18).[16] And yet God's people are not supposed to be repelled by the divine holiness. Quite the contrary, they are set apart so that they might share in God's holiness by adopting practices that are appropriate for life with God (1 Pet. 1:14–16; cf. Josh. 24:2–14; Gal. 4:8–9; Eph. 4:22–24).

Insofar as holiness is a matter of God's supreme distinctiveness as the one so set apart as to be incapable of comparison with any other (Exod. 8:10; 9:14; 1 Sam. 10:24; 2 Sam. 7:22; 1 Chr. 17:20; Isa. 46:9; Jer. 10:7), it might seem to

---

16. For the classic account of the holy as that which is at once terrifying and fascinating, see Rudolf Otto, *The Idea of the Holy*, 2nd ed., trans. John W. Harvey (New York: Oxford University Press, 1958).

be only another term for divine transcendence, but it is not. Transcendence is fundamentally an apophatic attribute: it does not ascribe any perfection to God, but simply notes the inability of human words, concepts, and categories to capture God. By contrast, holiness is a positive feature of divine being. God reveals God's self as holy, and this revelation takes the form of an appeal for human beings to live with God in holiness. Thus, while God's holiness, like all God's perfections, invariably exceeds our grasp, holiness does not simply refer to God's ontological distance from the creature, but is rather an intrinsic feature of God's own being. Quite apart from God's relationship to the world, God is holy in God's self, and this holiness is quite specifically a perfection—indeed, the culminating perfection—of the divine love.

God is love as Trinity, and this love is realized in the eternal sharing of divinity among the persons that is the divine goodness and the eternal letting-be of the persons that is the divine patience. To affirm the divine holiness is to signal that in this eternal giving-over and letting-be, God does not lack stability or integrity, as though God's goodness were heedless or God's patience a matter of indifference. Rather, because the eternal sharing and affirmation of divinity within the Trinity that constitute God's goodness and patience is just how God is love: they are rightly completed by the affirmation of the divine holiness, which is just God's constancy and steadfastness in being. To confess God as holy is, in other words, to affirm that God's incomparability is rooted in God's own eternal integrity as *this* God, in whom, precisely as Father, Son, and Holy Spirit, "there is no variation or shadow due to change" (Jas. 1:17).[17] God is thus holy precisely in God's identity as "I am" (Exod. 3:14–15; cf. John 8:58). And as a perfection of divine love, this holiness does not function to drive away or annihilate all that is not God. Rather, God calls us to be holy, too, which means that God's holiness is manifest precisely in inviting us to share in God's own constancy of being by adopting forms of life that reflect the inexhaustibly good and patient love that is the very life of God.[18]

17. The Protestant Scholastic equation of holiness with purity (e.g., J. A. Quenstedt, *Theologia didactico-polemica* 1.292; cited in Heinrich Schmid, *The Doctrinal Theology of the Evangelical Lutheran Church*, 3rd ed., trans. Charles A. Hay and Henry E. Jacobs (Minneapolis: Augsburg, 1961), 120; *Synopsis Purioris Theologiae* 6.40, ed. Dolf te Velde (Leiden: Brill, 2015 [1625]), 178) is justified just to the extent that purity is understood not as freedom from contamination (as though the divine holiness depended on God's being insulated from contact with the nondivine), but rather as God's free, eternal, unwavering, and effortless being as Trinity: as John Webster writes, "the sovereign act . . . in which he maintains his own triune being in its integrity and distinctiveness." John Webster, "The Holiness and Love of God," *Scottish Journal of Theology* 57, no. 3 (2004): 259.

18. "The 'You shall be holy' which corresponds to the 'I am holy' is not simply the indication of a state; it is a life-giving imperative that bids the creature to inhabit and act out the role to which the creature has been appointed by the Father's purpose." Webster, "Holiness and Love of God," 262.

THE PERFECTIONS OF DIVINE PRESENCE

The claim that God is love is foundational to the Christian understanding of God, for God is love insofar as God is Father, Son, and Spirit, and this three-fold designation is, in turn, rooted in the foundational confession that Jesus is Lord and Savior. For who is Jesus? He is many things: the Christ (John 20:31), Mary's child (Matt. 1:16), a Jew (John 4:9), a carpenter (Mark 6:3), a teacher (John 13:13), a healer (Matt. 12:15), a friend of tax collectors and sinners (Matt. 11:19 and par.), all of which will be discussed in greater detail later in this book. And yet he is Lord and Savior insofar as he is the only Son of the Father (John 1:18; 3:16, 18)—a status confirmed by the power of the Spirit through his resurrection from the dead (Rom. 1:4; 1 Tim. 3:16). And because only God can save, it follows that as Savior, Jesus, the Word made flesh, was "in the beginning" not only "with God," but also "*was* God" (John 1:1).

Yet there seems to be a problem here, for if the Word's status as the one who was *with* God the Father "in the beginning" is the ground of Christian explication of the claim that God is love, the affirmation that the Word *was* God risks undercutting it. For to say the Word *was* God connotes identity—a lack of ultimate distinction between the Word and God that seems to rob the "with" of its force and thereby evacuate love of its content. After all, in the human sphere love presupposes a clear distinction between lovers, because to speak of love is to speak of the power that draws distinct individuals together into a relationship of mutual trust and vulnerability. From this perspective, the claim that God is love only seems coherent if the divine ontology includes sufficient "distance" between the persons to allow the movement of one toward another as lover toward beloved, subject toward object. And herein lies a problem, for just as a divine love interpreted as "object-related" in this sense would be flatly inconsistent with the Christian conviction that God is one (Deut. 6:4), so a strong affirmation of God's oneness would seem to make it difficult to speak meaningfully of God as love.[19]

It is in this context that divine presence proves its worth as an appropriate complement to divine love and thus a foundational divine perfection. In order to make this case, however, it is important to eschew the term's spatial connotations. The mutual presence of the divine persons is not a matter of their

---

19. In this context, Katherine Sonderegger has rightly identified tritheism as a genuine risk for the kind of strongly Trinitarian interpretation of divine love championed by Barth and others. Yet her alternative proposal of speaking of the divine love as a disposition (born of her own prioritization of the divine unity and concomitant efforts to speak of divine love apart from the Trinity) is unpersuasive, because God's love is not characterized in 1 John or elsewhere in Scripture as a passive potential only actualized under certain conditions (as suggested by the example of fragility, which Sonderegger offers as a parallel), but just as God's own being and act. See Katherine Sonderegger, *The Doctrine of God*, vol. 1 of *Systematic Theology* (Minneapolis: Fortress Press, 2015), 477–90.

being open or available to one another by virtue of local proximity. God's transcendence of space and time renders any interpretation of the divine presence that draws on imagery of juxtaposition untenable. Instead, presence refers to the divine persons' inseparable mutual indwelling. This relationship, traditionally designated by the Greek term perichoresis, has no creaturely analogue precisely because it prescinds from any thought of separable entities relating to one another.[20] On a properly Trinitarian understanding of the persons, the Father is present to the Son as the one *in* whom the Son lives, even as the Father is *in* the Son as the one by whom the Son lives (John 10:38; 14:10–11; 17:21), and the two are one (John 17:11) precisely *in* the Spirit, who simultaneously confirms both the Son's identity as the beloved of the Father and his love for the Father.[21] In this way, the mutual presence of the divine persons refers not to the confrontation of three subjects, but to the undivided and indivisible subsistence of the one God in threefold repetition.

The love in and through which the divine persons are God is therefore not distributed among the persons as among three distinct centers of consciousness. To put it in the sharpest possible terms, the mutual presence of the divine persons is a perfect simultaneity of consciousness in and as the one divine life, such that (e.g.) for the Father not to be present to the Son would mean the end of the Father and the Son no less than the Trinity. Once again, divine love is not a modification of a prior personal existence, but just the mode of the persons' Trinitarian coinherence, their being one God in and through one another. And to affirm that God is eternally *present* in love specifies the perichoretic character of that love and thus is a vital qualification of it, precisely insofar as creaturely love does not take this form.

Despite this crucial disanalogy between the forms of divine and creaturely love, it remains the case that the intradivine pattern of presence in love has an external parallel in God's relationship to creatures. Translated to the sphere of space and time (where, in contrast to the transcendent life of God, different locations may be distinguished as up or down, right or left, and, most basically of all, here or there), the divine presence is rightly confessed as omnipresence. For no more than is the case for the relations among the divine persons is God's distinction from creatures a matter of location.[22] For the biblical authors there is no created place from which God is absent.

20. In order to avoid this interactive interpretation of perichoresis, Barth argues that the preferable Latin translation of the term is *circuminsessio* (mutual indwelling) rather than the more literal *circumincessio* (mutual interpenetration); see *CD* I/1:370.

21. In line with this position, Thomas avers that the best creaturely analogy for the Trinitarian relations is "in the intellect where the action of understanding remains in him who understands." Aquinas, *ST* 1.27.1.

22. "All [created] things are distant from God not by place, but by nature." John of Damascus, *On the Orthodox Faith* 1.13, in PG 94:853C.

Where can I go from your spirit?
  Or where can I flee from your presence?
If I ascend to heaven, you are there;
    if I make my bed in Sheol, you are there.
If I take the wings of the morning
    and settle at the farthest limits of the sea,
even there your hand shall lead me,
    and your right hand shall hold me fast.
                    (Ps. 139:7–10)[23]

This conviction receives further support from the Christian doctrine of creation from nothing. For if (as that doctrine teaches) God is the sole antecedent condition of the existence of every creature at every point of its existence, it follows that any creature exists only as God is present in it and giving it being.[24] And if this existence is a blessing (and if it were not, then its diminishment through suffering and death could not be judged an evil), then it follows that this presence is loving and, indeed, occasioned by love. So as within the Trinity the Son is never without the Father's presence as inexhaustibly self-bestowing love, so in God's works *ad extra*, the world does not exist except as the Father's self-bestowal in the Son is extended outward, with the Father's presence in the Son grounding the Son's presence in the world as the one in whom "all things hold together" (Col. 1:17).[25]

Since the advent of Derridean deconstruction, the concept of "presence" has acquired a bad reputation. Presence, it is argued—and especially the

---

23. It is worth noting the parallelism between "presence" and "spirit" at the beginning of this quotation, for the biblical claim that "God is spirit" (John 4:24) is fundamentally a claim about God's presence. Jesus makes this claim in response to the Samaritan's question about God's relationship to particular places: Where should God be worshiped—here or there, on Mount Gerizim or Mount Zion? "Jesus said to her, 'Woman, believe me, the hour is coming when you will worship the Father neither on this mountain nor in Jerusalem. . . . But the hour is coming, and is now here, when the true worshipers will worship the Father in spirit and truth, for the Father seeks such as these to worship him'" (John 4:21, 23). To say that God is spirit is thus, among other things, to deny that God is to be defined by location in any one place. Unlike finite beings, God is not exclusively here or there—as, of course, the Old Testament authors knew perfectly well (see, e.g., Jer. 23:24; 1 Kgs. 8:27; 2 Chr. 2:6; 6:18).

24. "Now since it is God's nature to exist [*Cum autem Deus sit ipsum esse*], he it must be who properly causes existence in creatures, just as it is fire itself [that] sets other things on fire. And God is causing this effect in things not just when they begin to exist, but all the time they are maintained in existence, just as the sun is lighting up the atmosphere all the time the atmosphere remains lit. During the whole period of a thing's existence, therefore, God must be present to it, and present in a way keeping with the way in which the thing possesses its existence." Aquinas, *ST* 1.8.1.

25. So Boethius writes that divine omnipresence should be understood to mean "not that he is in every place (for he is not able to be *in* any place at all), but that every place is present to him for him to hold [*ad capiendum*], although he himself is not held [*suscipiatur*] in any place." Boethius, *De Trinitate* 4, in *The Theological Tractates and the Consolation of Philosophy*, Loeb Classical Library 74 (Cambridge, MA: Harvard University Press, 1973), 20; translation mine.

omnipresence I have claimed for God—makes it impossible for difference to be taken seriously. It breeds a sterile and oppressive monism since the omnipresence of a God who is the source and key of all reality inevitably eclipses everything else and becomes the only reality worthy of attention. Against this perspective, the upshot of my argument is that divine presence, far from erasing difference, is the ground of difference, both within the Trinity and in creation. Within the Godhead one person does not subsume the others; neither do the three compete for a common space; rather, each sustains the others in and through their mutual presence in one another in love: the Father by begetting the Son in the Spirit, the Son by receiving the Father's gift of divinity in the same Spirit, and the Spirit, as the Spirit of the Father and the Son, as inseparable from either. In creation likewise, God's presence does not come at the expense of creatures' integrity but is its basis, since it is only as the Creator is present in creation at every point and every moment that creatures come to be and are sustained in their difference from God and one another.

The Divine Unity

As biblically well attested as God's omnipresence may be, it seems that God's oneness is even more fundamental: "Hear, O Israel: The Lord our God is one Lord" (Deut. 6:4 RSV; cf. Mark 12:29). This theme is sounded throughout Scripture (see Mal. 2:10; Rom. 3:30; Gal. 3:20; Eph. 4:6; 1 Tim. 2:5). It is clearly bound up with the God of Israel's claim to exclusive worship, and it also speaks to the unity of the divine being: *only* this God is to be worshiped, and this God is *one*.[26] Nevertheless, the divine unity is rightly viewed as a perfection of the divine presence rather than the other way round, for God is one precisely in the mutual indwelling of the Father, Son, and Spirit that constitutes the divine presence. And so, too, with respect to the creation, the divine unity is not any more than God's goodness best viewed as a "transcendental" property that is true of God insofar as it is true of every existent to be in some sense good (i.e., desirable) or one (i.e., this particular entity) merely by virtue of its existence. On the contrary, in a world where "there may be

---

26. The NRSV dissolves this tension by translating Deut. 6:4 as a demand for monolatry without any ontological connotations ("Hear, O Israel: The Lord is our God, the Lord alone"). Whether this is the best rendering of the Hebrew is questionable: for a compelling argument that it is not, see R. W. L. Moberly, "'Yahweh Is One': The Translation of the Shema," in *Studies in the Pentateuch*, ed. J. A. Emerton (Leiden: Brill, 1990), 209–16. In any case, for Christians Jesus' citation of the verse in Mark 12:29 (which follows the Greek of the LXX, where the "one Lord" language is unambiguous) should be theologically decisive—all the more so in that it would have actually suited the context better for Jesus to have described God as *monos* (alone) rather than *heis* (one), given that he is responding to a question about faithful practice ("Which commandment is first of all?") rather than divine ontology.

so-called gods in heaven or on earth—as in fact there are many gods and many lords," God's oneness—precisely as the unity of the Father and the Son in the Spirit—is known only through revelation: "For us there is one God, the Father, from whom are all things and for whom we exist, and one Lord, Jesus Christ, through whom are all things and through whom we exist" (1 Cor. 8:5–6; cf. 2:10–12).

In giving formal definition of the doctrine of the Trinity in the fourth century, Christians specified that God's oneness was a matter of God's nature or essence (Greek *ousia*), in relation to which the Father, Son, and Spirit were (as already noted) described as persons (Greek *hypostaseis*) or "modes of being" (*tropoi hyparxeōs*). By itself this sort of terminological distinction is of limited help in characterizing the divine unity, since the acknowledgment that Mary, Peter, and Paul share the same (human) essence is perfectly consistent with the claim that they are three separate individuals—which is just what Christians do *not* want to say about the divine persons. The difference, of course, is that while humanity is a general category that can take particular form in any number of discrete individuals (e.g., Thomas, Phoebe, Tokunboh, Sacajawea, and so forth in addition to Mary, Peter, and Paul), divinity is not a general category that can be considered independently of the divine persons (and which, therefore, might just as easily include four or six hypostases rather than three); rather, the one God simply *is* Father, Son, and Spirit.

At this point appeal to God's transcendence is helpful in order to guard against a false assimilation of the divine nature with created natures. Unlike creatures, God does not "have" or "instantiate" a nature, because there is no distinction between what God is and how or who God is. It is perfectly possible to talk about the characteristics of *E. coli* bacteria, sugar maple trees, or human beings apart from reference to any individual example of those species: even if our knowledge of the species is derived from the examination of many such individuals, the very idea of a species is predicated on the capacity of abstracting from the particular to the general. By contrast, to affirm that God is one is to insist that there is no such possibility when talking about God. God is not one as Napoleon (or *that* sugar maple tree or *this* bacterium) is one; that is, as *one rather than another* of the same type. Again, God's nature or essence is not a type: as "Not Other," God is not a type of anything and so is not "one" as an object we might contemplate alongside other objects—even if we were to conceive of God as the greatest object of all. God's oneness is not (any more than any of God's other perfections) a passive attribute; rather (and as with all God's perfections), God's being is act: God *is* one and is known by us *as* one in confronting us in Jesus as the God who is from all eternity Father, Son, and Holy Spirit.

The Divine Omnipotence

Because God's presence is not passive but is precisely God's way of being, both immanently as Trinity and *ad extra* toward creatures, God is always present in power that is unlimited by any nondivine reality. So it is that Christians confess God to be omnipotent or almighty. Although both these terms are standard elements of Christian theological vocabulary, they have the disadvantage of being all too easily understood as affirming divine power in the abstract—and so as entailing God's ability to do anything that does not entail a logical contradiction, which (insofar as it would include the possibility of God telling a lie, e.g.) is not something Christians have typically wanted to affirm.[27] A better translation of *pantokratōr* (the Greek term that stands behind "Almighty" in the English versions of the New Testament and Nicene Creed) is "all-ruler," which more accurately portrays divine "might" as God's active sovereignty over all things.[28] In the words of the mysterious sixth-century writer known to us as Dionysius the Areopagite, God is called almighty because "he preserves and embraces all the world. He founds it. He makes it secure. He holds it together."[29]

This sort of clarification regarding the character of the divine might help to answer the objection that divine omnipotence implies the selfish, oppressive, and arbitrary exercise of power over and against others. Here again, God's status as Creator is crucial: because every creature exists as the creature it is only as God holds it in being at every point of its existence, there is no way in which divine omnipotence can be understood as power that either resists or overwhelms the power of creatures. Quite the contrary, whatever power a creature has, it has only as a gift from God, and it makes use of that power only as God enables it to do so. Among creatures it is certainly the case that power is very often competitive: if another creature lives, moves, and has its being in my sphere of operation, my potential for action may be constrained; and in those

---

27. Here it is worth noting that denying God's power to do anything entailing a logical contradiction—decreeing that twice two equal five, e.g., or creating a stone so heavy that even God cannot lift it—is not to place restrictions on God's power, but simply to recognize the limits of human language. Since anything can be shown to follow from a contradiction, allowing talk about God's power to extend to logical contradictions would simply render theological discourse incoherent.

28. The situation is more complicated in cases where "Almighty" is used to translate the Hebrew *shaddai* in Old Testament texts like Gen. 17:1; 28:3; 35:11; Ruth 1:20–21; Job 5:17; 6:4, 14, and passim. Though the translators of the LXX consistently use *pantokratōr* (cf. 2 Cor. 6:18) for this term, the etymology of the Hebrew is uncertain at best, so that while the intent of the texts is clearly doxological, the precise quality the original authors intended to ascribe to God cannot now be determined.

29. Dionysius the Areopagite, *Divine Names* 10, in *Pseudo-Dionysius: The Complete Works*, trans. Colm Luibheid (New York: Paulist Press, 1987), 119.

cases my range of activity will correspondingly be enhanced if that competitor is removed.[30] By contrast, the withdrawal of God's power can never lead to an increase in creaturely capacities, but only to the creature's dissolution. With respect to the being of creatures, divine omnipotence is not a threat, as though it meant that only God has power; it means rather that all power comes from God, who, far from being jealous of creaturely power, is its ground.

And yet if God is omnipotent precisely as the "all-ruler," it might seem that God is "almighty" only relatively—with respect to that which is other than God—and not in God's self. For if Christians confess belief in "God, the Father Almighty," this is not because the Father rules over the Son and the Spirit, who, as fully divine themselves, are every bit as "almighty" as the Father.[31] Nevertheless, this creedal designation is important precisely for blocking any interpretation of the divine omnipotence as referring to sheer limitless, arbitrary power. For to say that it is precisely as *Father* that God is almighty is not to associate this term with the first person to the exclusion of the other two. Far from being the juxtaposition of two equiprimordial terms, the sequence of "Father" first and "almighty" second establishes a definite order of superordination and subordination, in which God is Father first of all, and only *as* Father is almighty as well. The meaning of the latter term must therefore be controlled by the former, such that we rightly confess God as "almighty" only as a specification of the more fundamental claim that God is Father.[32] For insofar as the might of the Father takes just the form of giving all power to the Son (Matt. 28:18; cf. John 5:21–23, 26–27; 1 Cor. 15:27), it is the case that in God, no less with God's life *ad intra* than with God's relationship to creatures *ad extra*, God is almighty as the one who gives power. Indeed, since within God this act of giving and receiving power is eternal and without limit, God is most perfectly almighty in God's self, quite apart from the work of creation. For as Trinity, God's power is no mere potential for activity, but just that activity by which God is God: the Father who in and

---

30. Importantly, such creaturely collocation does not necessarily entail competition, as the various forms of symbiosis in nature attest; moreover, even the reality of competition does not preclude mutually beneficial cooperation between individuals (though it does mean that my wife and I cannot both have the last cookie in the jar). For further discussion of this point, see pp. 56–59 below.

31. See, e.g., Aquinas, *ST* 1.33.1.2. Cf. Maximus the Confessor, *Disputatio cum Pyrrho*, PG 91:324A–B: "Obedience is not a property of God but of human beings, as the divine Gregory [of Nazianzus] says, . . . 'God is neither obedient nor disobedient, for such matters pertain to subordinates and those under authority.'"

32. Jean-Pierre Batut shows that this ordering emerged only gradually in the early church, as Christians struggled to integrate the "cosmological" and "Trinitarian" senses of Father in such a way that the Trinitarian sense of "Father" (viz., its status as a name) was understood to have precedence over the cosmological term *pantokratōr*. Jean-Pierre Batut, *Pantocrator: "Dieu le Père tout-puissant" dans la théologie prénicéenne* (Paris: Institut d'Études Augustiniennes, 2009), 61–63; cf. 57.

through the Spirit gives the fullness of divinity to the Son, who, in and by the same Spirit, ascribes all power to the Father.

The Divine Glory

In all that God is—as good, patient, holy, one, and almighty—God is glorious. To say this is certainly not to claim that glory is a higher perfection than any of the others, for if God is not composed of parts, then no perfection is higher or lower than any other: all are finally identical with God (i.e., they describe what God *is*, not simply features that God *has*), so that even the priority assigned to the perfections of love and presence in this chapter can only be relative and rhetorical. On just such relative and rhetorical grounds, nevertheless, glory is appropriately listed last among the divine perfections because it has a summative character. Specifically, it is the cataphatic complement to the apophatic confession of God's invisibility with which this chapter began. For at bottom it is the revelation of God's glory, which is just God's inexhaustible fullness of being, which is the root of a properly Christian apophaticism. In other words, it is because God is (cataphatically) revealed as the one who "dwells in unapproachable light" that God is (apophatically) confessed as the one "whom no one has ever seen or can see" (1 Tim. 6:16; cf. Isa. 6:1–5; Ezek. 1:26–28). So it is that on the Mount of Transfiguration, the revelation of the divine glory in Jesus takes the form of an ineffable brightness on which the disciples cannot bear to look (see Matt. 17:2–5 and pars.; cf. Acts 7:55; Rev. 15:8; 21:23).

Although the word for glory in biblical Greek (*doxa*) connotes brightness, the Hebrew word it translates (*kabod*) refers to weight (cf. 2 Cor. 4:17). The two terms are appropriately complementary, in that the Hebrew makes it clear that God's glory is not a mere surface phenomenon, a matter of appearance that may dazzle but lacks substance. Quite the contrary, it is "like a devouring fire" (Exod. 24:17; cf. Isa. 10:16). Insofar as glory is intrinsic to God's transcendent being, it is most properly located above the heavens (Pss. 113:4; 148:13), but its substantial character is indicated by the fact that it fills space when appearing on earth (Exod. 40:35; 1 Kgs. 8:11; 2 Chr. 5:14; 7:1–2; Ezek. 43:5; 44:4) and is, correspondingly, experienced as capable of moving from one place to another (Exod. 33:22; Ezek. 3:12; 9:3; 10:4, 18–19; 11:22–23; 43:2, 4). Most importantly, in contrast to the glory of creatures, which is ephemeral and naturally passes away (Prov. 14:28; Isa. 13:19; Jer. 13:11; 1 Pet. 1:24; cf. Isa. 40:6–7), God's glory is eternal (1 Pet. 5:10) and, as such, cannot be transferred to others but rather is exclusive to God alone (Isa. 42:8; 48:11).

It is thus the glory of God as Trinity to be from all eternity the one who is present in love. And yet as true as it may be that this glory depends on (and thus belongs to) no other, it is not for that reason something that God keeps to God's self. On the contrary, as a perfection of divine presence, the divine glory is just that which God discloses in making God's self known: that is, to see God is to see God's glory (Exod. 16:7; Deut. 5:24; cf. Exod. 33:18–23). If God's presence, as that which founds and sustains creation, is typically invisible, in the revelation of the divine glory God's presence is seen. And if in the Old Testament that disclosure is episodic and often a matter of ecstatic vision rather than public event (Isa. 6:1–5; Ezek. 1:26–28), these appearances carry the promise of a future in which the whole earth is to be filled with God's glory (Num. 14:21; Ps. 72:19; Isa. 4:5; Hab. 2:14), precisely so that the vision of divine glory that once was limited to Israel should include all nations (Isa. 40:5; 66:18–19). Moreover, this final revelation is not intended to overwhelm creatures, but rather to catch them up in God's glory, so that they might both live in and see by it (Rev. 21:10–11, 23–24). Yet while all this is in keeping with the principle that the divine presence supports rather than suppresses difference within the Godhead, it is not clear how a glory that is so bright as to be unapproachable can be understood to enhance rather than annihilate creaturely existence. The solution to this problem lies in the peculiar form in which divine glory is fully and definitively revealed in the life of Jesus; but before moving to that topic, it is necessary to explore in greater detail the character of created being in distinction from the divine. That is the subject of the next chapter.

2

The Being of Creatures

The previous chapter's outline of the Christian doctrine of God already contained a good deal about creatures. That should not come as a surprise, because even though God is not a creature, and thus not located on any "chain of being" or positioned within any of the other ontological frameworks we use to organize our thinking about creatures, we have no capacity to speak or think of God except by means of creaturely concepts and categories. If we know God, it is only because God has chosen to make God's self known to us as we exist in time and space, and this happens only as God makes use of created realities—voices, visions, bushes, fire, cloud, and so forth—to make visible God's essentially invisible presence. And so on the basis of these phenomena (which, precisely in their perceptibility, are not themselves divine), we talk about God, making use of the same words we use of creatures to speak of the one who cannot be seen—albeit with the proviso that however confident we may be *that* such words are true of God, we do not really understand *how* they are true of God. Specifically, we confess that God is good, patient, holy, and so forth, and that these terms, as used of God, are somehow related to (and reflected in) created goodness, patience, and holiness, while at the same time acknowledging that we are unable to specify just what that relation is.

Quite apart from the inseparability of theological and everyday vocabulary, however, talk of God involves discussion of creatures because God is Creator and thus the source and ground of created being. Although it is true that God might not have created the world (so that God is not necessarily Creator), the fact that God has in fact created the world, and that we are part of it, means that we know God by virtue of God's relation to creatures. Consequently, it is impossible for creatures to talk about God without talking about creatures, too, even if only to draw distinctions between, say, God's goodness or

43

patience considered as attributes of God's eternal life as Trinity, and God's goodness or patience as manifest externally in God's dealings with creation.

Nevertheless, up to this point the talk about creatures has been incidental and indirect. Creatures have been mentioned as the objects of God's love, goodness, patience, presence, and power, or as called to participate in God's holiness and glory, but no attention has been given to the character of created being in its own right. At most the denial that God is composite, conditioned, circumscribed, or even properly conceived as a kind of thing might naturally be taken to imply that all these qualities are true of creatures, so that although God is "Not Other" with respect to creatures, every creature without exception is "other" in relation to both God and all creatures distinct from itself. That is, to be a creature is to be here *or* there, now *or* then, matter *or* spirit, and, most fundamentally, *this* rather than *that*. But it remains to explore in greater detail the characteristics of this kind of being. What, in short, does it mean to be created and thus to be other than God?

"FROM NOTHING": THE CONTINGENCY OF CREATURES

The starting point for any theologically satisfactory answer to this question is the affirmation that the most fundamental truth of creation as a whole, which is shared by every creature individually in equal measure, is just that it is created. To be created is not to be self-originating, but to exist by the will and action of another—a creator. When Christians say that creation is the product of the Creator's will, they intend to deny that it is a necessary manifestation of the Creator's nature and to affirm instead that the whole of the created order is contingent, meaning that it might not have been.[1] Considered in these terms, it is possible to draw analogies between God's work of creation and acts of creation that we ascribe to human beings. For when we speak of a composer creating a symphony, a baker creating a cake, a designer creating a dress, or a carpenter creating a desk, we thereby indicate that the thing created is dependent for its coming to be on the will of its

---

1. This relationship between divine willing and contingency is a bit more complicated than this, in that (as noted in the preceding chapter) the coincidence of being and act in God (i.e., the claim that God's nature is identical with God's concrete "act" of existing as Father, Son, and Spirit) means that it is perfectly appropriate to speak of God's own, noncontingent existence as a matter of divine willing, which takes the form of the mutual love of the divine persons for one another. But although God may in this way be said to subsist as Father, Son, and Spirit willingly, the divine willing is not logically prior to the persons as it is logically prior to creation. In other words, God is Trinity willingly, but not because of a preceding act of divine willing; by contrast, creation exists only because of an act of divine willing to which it is logically subsequent.

creator, such that it would not have been, save for the creator's willing it to be. Yet when creatures do the creating, the contingency of the thing created is not absolute, because such creation always amounts to the modification and rearrangement, however radical, of already existing components, the properties of which shape the character of the thing created independently of the creator's will. Such "creation" is at bottom merely transformation, in which, for example, the baker blends flour, sugar, eggs, leavening, and oil to make a cake; or the composer draws on an established range of tones and timbres in order to produce a piece of music.

By contrast, since the end of the second century the overwhelming majority of Christians have denied that God creates in this way. Rather than fashioning creatures *from some already existing substance*, they maintain, God creates *from nothing*. It is important to take care in interpreting this phrase, for its grammar can be misleading. In everyday speech, the role of the prepositional phrase in a statement of the form "Mary created *x* from *y*" is precisely to specify the already existing material *y* out of which the created thing *x* was made: a chair made from wood, a bust made from marble, beer made from barley and hops, and so forth. In his reflections on the doctrine of creation, Anselm of Canterbury argued that to say that God created the world out of nothing in this sense, as though nothing were a kind of substance, would be to posit a contradiction by affirming that nothing is something—and thus not truly nothing. Likewise, he argued that the word "nothing" in the claim "God creates from nothing" could not be understood as having the same force as in the sentence "She meant nothing by that gesture," since that would be to claim that creation is an illusion, that it is truly nothing, which is evidently not what Christians mean when they say that the world is created. The only remaining alternative, Anselm argued, was to interpret "created from nothing" to mean "created, but not out of anything" (*factum sed non esse aliquid unde sit factum*).[2] Thus, in contrast to creatures' acts of "creating" various items out of already existing materials, in the divine work of creation God is the sole antecedent condition, the only factor contributing to the existence of the creature.

When seeking to give a quotidian parallel to this use of "from nothing," Anselm offers that of a person who is "saddened from nothing" (*contristatus de nihilo*)—that is, not on the basis of any external prompting or cause, but solely out of his own internal disposition.[3] This example illumines another aspect of the contingency of creatures' existence by pointing to its sheer gratuity. In

---

2. Anselm, *Monologion* 8; in *Complete Philosophical and Theological Treatises of Anselm of Canterbury*, trans. Jasper Hopkins and Herbert Richardson (Minneapolis: Arthur J. Banning Press, 2000), 18–19. Cf. Thomas, who notes that the *ex* of ex nihilo "signifies a sequence [and] not a material cause." Thomas Aquinas, *ST* 1.45.1.3.

3. Anselm, *Monologion* 8, 19.

other words, as a corollary of the claim that the world is not made "out of" some already existing substance, it also has no rationale, basis, or cause other than in the will of God. And it is at this point—and most especially in light of the analogy with spontaneous sadness that Anselm draws—that the doctrine of creation from nothing raises important questions about the character of God's creative work and of the world that is its product. After all, it would be natural enough to judge that a person who was "saddened from nothing" (that is, owing to no reason or cause external to themselves) was perhaps not altogether in his right mind—the victim of a melancholy disposition, perhaps, or more seriously, clinical depression. Similarly, the freedom or spontaneity of creation from nothing might appear as arbitrary: not, to be sure, a sign of divine lack or loneliness (impossible for a God who encompasses all possible perfections), but nevertheless something that in its utter and absolute non-necessity is not to be taken altogether seriously—a matter of whimsy that has no lasting significance in God's eyes.

This possibility of divine indifference is, however, foreclosed by reference to the identity of the Creator as the triune God. In fact, for Christians it is only in light of God's being as Trinity that the gracious character of God's creative work is fully and properly understood.[4] Seen in relation to the immanent form of the divine life, creation appears as an altogether natural extension of God's own Trinitarian being. For as Trinity, God's own life is from eternity a matter of donation, in which God subsists in the endless giving of divine being from the Father to the Son in the Spirit's power. And if God's life is in itself a sharing of being in this way, there is nothing arbitrary or odd in God's choosing to share being with that which is not God. To be sure, the description of this sharing as "natural" must not be taken to imply that it is in any sense necessary, as though God's creating were analogous to the sun's shining—an involuntary emanation or overflow of divinity that follows automatically from the fact of God's being God. Rather, it is "natural" in the way that it is natural for parents to give good gifts to their children (cf. Matt. 7:9–11; Luke 11:11–13): not as an impersonal or mechanical process, but as a fitting expression of identity that is not for that reason any less gracious. After all, one does not estimate a gift as any less worthy of gratitude because it is from a close friend or family member; quite the contrary, it is

---

4. See Aquinas, who maintains in *ST* 1.32.1.3 that one reason why knowledge of the Trinity was revealed was "in order to have a right view of the creation of things. For by maintaining that God made everything through the Word we avoid the error of those who held that God created by virtue of some necessity of nature [*ex necessitate naturae*]. By affirming that there is in him the procession of love, we show that God made creatures, not because he needed them nor because of any reason outside himself, but from love of his own goodness" (trans. slightly alt.); cf. *ST* 1.45.6: "the processions [*processiones*] of the divine Persons can be seen as types for the production [*productionis*] of creatures" (trans. alt.).

the gift that has no discernible ground in the identity or character of the giver that, precisely in its inherent and utterly unmotivated arbitrariness, is more likely to be regarded as an occasion for puzzlement or even distress rather than an act of generosity.[5]

In short, from a Trinitarian perspective the claim that creation is from nothing and so has no cause outside of God's self does not lead to the worry that God's creative work is without any rationale or motive. Because God, as Trinity, is love, eternally subsisting as the sharing of infinite being, it is thoroughly consistent—though for all that no less unfathomably gracious—that God should choose to share being in a finite mode by bringing into being entities that are other than God. And yet there arguably remains another sort of worry about the status of creatures that have been made from nothing. The charge of arbitrariness, which raises the question of creation's integrity from the side of the Creator (viz., Does God really take it seriously?), can be addressed by appeal to the consistency of creation with the inner form of God's own triune life; but a similar question can also be raised from the side of the creature. For even if we can be persuaded that God takes created being seriously, can creatures themselves do so if they are truly from nothing? The worry here is that to be *from* nothing is, for all practical purposes, to *be* nothing, so that "to be a creature is to be humiliated, devoid of integrity or power of self-movement or self-subsistence, and so lacking intrinsic worth."[6]

The force of this worry derives from the radically contingent character of created being according to the doctrine of creation from nothing. As already noted, the doctrine posits a strong disanalogy between God's work of creation and all creaturely processes of bringing to be. The latter are never acts of absolute origination but rather always entail the modification of some already existing substance. Thus, however much processes of creation within the world may alter the appearance and activity of whatever material is involved, the fact that this material is prior to and continues to subsist through the work of creation means that its being is fundamentally independent of its creator: a house's component materials subsist apart from the activity of the builder, and the fate of the completed structure is equally free of ongoing ontological entanglements with its creator. By contrast, the world and its creatures possess no such ontological inertia. Because God is the *only* antecedent condition of their existence, they have no being whatsoever independently of God's

---

5. It is in light of such reflections that I find myself unable to make much sense of Jacques Derrida's account of the gift in *Given Time*, vol. 1, *Counterfeit Money* (Chicago: University of Chicago Press, 1992).

6. John Webster, "*Non ex Aequo*: God's Relation to Creatures," in *God and the Works of God*, vol. 1 of *God without Measure: Working Papers in Christian Theology* (London: Bloomsbury T&T Clark, 2016), 108.

willing them to be.[7] The witness to the act of creation of John 1 is particularly striking in this regard: in contrast to the more ambiguous language of Genesis, the only entities present in this account of "the beginning" are God and the Word. And inasmuch as the Word *is* God, the conclusion follows that in the work of creation God is the only factor in play, giving rise to creatures' existence solely through (though, importantly, not out of) God's own divine being.[8] In short, to teach creation from nothing is to insist that in the work of creation there is *nothing but God*—which, again, seems to lead to the troubling conclusion that creatures are quite literally nothing in themselves.

The most obvious response to this worry is simply to note that for creatures to be nothing in or by themselves is not for them to be nothing at all, but just what it means to be created: that is, to exist solely (but really!) by God's gracious donation of being. This sort of derived or dependent mode of existence is only problematic if true or proper existence is defined as one that is independent of all external factors, causes, or conditions—that is, if true existence is equated with aseity and thus restricted to God alone. While it is certainly possible to stipulate such a definition, Christians (along with Jews and Muslims) have consistently demurred from the view that in order for something to be considered real, and thus worthy of regard, it needs to be divine. After all, such a claim is flatly inconsistent with the witness of Genesis, where the repeated refrain "And God saw that it was good" (Gen. 1:10, 12, 18, 21, 25; cf. 1:4, 31), implies that creatures have their own being, which is other than God's, and that this created form of being, for all that it is utterly dependent on God and therefore unable to subsist in, of, or by itself, has value in God's sight. In short, if the fact that the goodness of creatures derives from God does not vitiate the claim that they are good, neither should the fact that their being derives from God be taken to imply that their existence is in any sense deficient or illusory. Instead, created being both is and is good precisely as created—and thus in its dependence on the Creator.

This point is fully consistent with Athanasius of Alexandria's teaching that "the nature of created things, inasmuch as it is brought into being out of nothing, is of a fleeting sort, and weak and mortal, if considered in itself."[9] But arguably the whole point of the doctrine of creation is just to insist that

---

7. See Aquinas, *ST* 1.46.1: "The world exists just so long as God wills it [*quatenus Deus vult illum esse*], since its existence depends on his will as its cause." Cf. 1.104.1.2: "There is no more possibility of God's conferring on any creature that it be sustained in being [*esse*] on the cessation of his action than of his conferring on it that its being [*esse*] be uncaused by him" (trans. slightly alt.).

8. The point that creation ex nihilo is not creation *ex Deo* (that is, out of God's own substance) is another way of distinguishing God's willing of creation from an impersonal process of emanation, thereby securing both creation's utter gratuity and the radical difference between Creator and creature: creation is from God, but is in no sense part of God.

9. Athanasius, *Against the Heathen* 41 (PG 25:81C–D); in *NPNF*[2] 4:26, trans. alt.

a creature's existence is not rightly "considered in itself," as though having to rely on its own resources to continue in being. If the subsistence of creatures were dependent on their inherent capacities in this way, then creation would indeed be a nullity: unworthy of regard for the simple reason that when considered without reference to God, creatures are nothing, and nothing, as nonexistent, is just not a possible object of regard. In opposition to this scenario, however, Athanasius himself reminds his readers that every creature has its being in God, who

> seeing that all created nature, as far as its own inner principles were concerned, to be fleeting and subject to dissolution, . . . did not leave it to be tossed in a tempest in the course of its own nature, lest it should run the risk of once more dropping out of existence; but, because He is good He guides and settles the whole Creation by His own Word, Who is Himself also God, that by the governance and providence and ordering action of the Word, Creation may have light, and be enabled to abide always securely.[10]

In short, the fact that creation from nothing means that *behind* created being there stands nothing but God does not imply any defect or lack *in* created being, for the power of divinity is such that creatures need nothing but God in order to be. Precisely because in creation from nothing there is nothing but God that needs to be taken into account as the cause of created existence, the only possible threat to creatures' being is God—whose will is precisely that creatures should exist. The one possible threat thus turns out to be no threat at all, because, as Paul once put it, "If God is for us, who is against us?" (Rom. 8:31).

To be sure, if the radical contingency of creation does not mean that creaturely being should be regarded as defective, it certainly does render creatures' mode of being different from God's. As already noted, even if God, as the utterly transcendent source of the world, is "Not Other" than creatures, yet creatures most certainly are other than God. Indeed, this otherness is central to understanding the contingent character of created being. Within God the persons are distinct from one another—the Father is not the Son or the Spirit, and so forth—but each is nonetheless fully God. Because the giving of being that is the life of the Trinity is at once infinite and inexhaustible, that is, because what is given is nothing less than divinity itself, the recipients of this gift (viz., the Son and the Spirit) are themselves fully divine. Since the Father gives everything that he is to the Son in begetting and to the Spirit in spirating, then neither the Son nor the Spirit can be ontologically any less or other than the Father. For God to be God is just for God to give and receive

10. Athanasius, *Against the Heathen* 41 (PG 25:84A), 26, trans. alt.

being in this way, so that the diversity of hypostases does not open up any distinction of nature.

By contrast, the gift of being to creatures is not infinite. It therefore gives rise to an ontological gap between the God who gives and the creatures that receive being. In giving being according to limit and measure, God does not reproduce God, but opens up an ontological space (indeed, because the difference between finite and infinite is infinite, an infinite ontological space) between God and the creature. Crucially (and to counter yet another form of the worry that the doctrine of creation from nothing impugns the integrity of the creature), this is not because God's donation of being in creating is any less free and unstinting than in the divine life itself. The contrast between the giving of being within the Trinity and the giving of being by the Trinity to creatures is not that between a full and a qualified generosity. God's giving in creation is no less unrestrained than within the divine life itself, but it is a different sort of giving—one that has as its aim precisely that there should be alongside the inexhaustible and infinite fullness of divine being, which neither requires nor can receive any augmentation or supplement, another sort of being as well. Since there is no need whatsoever for any such multiplication of entities from God's side, the act of creation, whether considered as a whole or with respect to even the most ephemeral creature, can only be conceived as unstintingly generous: God gives being where no giving is called for, simply so that being may be enjoyed not only by God, but also by entities that are not God.

Still, the fact that creatures are not God means that in their difference from God, they are distant from God. To be sure (and as John of Damascus once noted), this distance is not a place but of nature.[11] As ontological, the space between God and creatures is not a matter of linear distance, since creatures' continued existence is secured entirely by God's presence, as the one in which they live, move, and have their being (Acts 17:28). Nevertheless, this distance is such that although God does not stand over against creatures (since God does not subsist—and thus cannot be defined—by reference to them), creatures do stand over against God. It is not the case that to be God is not to be a creature, because God is not properly defined over against or with respect to any nondivine reality; rather, as Aquinas argued, to be God is simply *to be*, without qualification.[12] But it is the case that to be a creature is to be other than God—to exist dependently, and thus not *a se*. This distinction is the substance of the scholastic teaching that creatures have a real relation to God (viz., the relation of creation, by which they exist), but that God does not

---

11. John of Damascus, *On the Orthodox Faith* 1.13, in PG 94:853C. For an English translation, see vol. 9 of *NPNF*².

12. See Aquinas, *ST* 1.3.4; cf. David B. Burrell, CSC, *Aquinas: God and Action* (Chicago: University of Chicago Press, 2008 [1979]), chap. 3.

have real relations with creatures. The point is not that God is indifferent to creatures; quite the contrary, the lack of real relations is a direct corollary of God's pure generosity as Creator, since it simply means that God, as God, is independent of creatures, neither augmented nor capable of being diminished by them.[13] It is just so that God is utterly generous in creating them. But, as other than God, creatures have no access to God: God sustains them, but this sustaining, the all-sufficient presence of the Not Other, is for that very reason one in which creatures, as other, have no intrinsic possibility of a life in communion with God, in which God is present to them in love in the same way that the divine persons are present to one another. God's transcendence does not rule out divine immanence in the sense of God's constant care for the creature as the very condition of its existence, but that same transcendence (which, again, is the very condition of the creature's existence) does seem to rule out the creature's direct encounter with God in the way that Christians claim takes place in Jesus. For it would seem that in order for such an encounter to take place, either God would need to confront the creature as a finite other, and thereby cease to be God, or the creature would need to receive the fullness of divine being, and thereby cease to be a creature.

"EACH ACCORDING TO ITS KIND": THE DIVERSITY OF CREATURES

As noted at the beginning of this chapter, creatures are not only different from God; they are also different from each other. God is three persons, but only one and the same God. Although there is (hypostatic) distinction in God, there is no ontological difference, for the Father, Son, and Spirit are so radically present to one another that even in their distinction from one another they remain utterly inseparable. Far from any one person excluding the other two, each person subsists only in and with the other two, as one life with a single and undivided will. If, as traditionally taught, the external acts of the Trinity are undivided (*opera Trinitatis ad extra indivisa sunt*), that is because the Trinity is just one actor.

By contrast, creatures are ontologically different from each another: separate actors with separate lives.[14] While God transcends categories (*Deus non*

---

13. See, e.g., Aquinas, *ST* 1.13.7. To give an earthbound example, my being an uncle is not a "real relation" for me, not because it is imaginary (as though I weren't really an uncle), but simply because my being is completely independent of the event that establishes the relation (viz., the birth of my nephew).

14. Although application of terms like "actor" and "life" to creatures in general may seem exaggerated, it is not without biblical support: "You are the LORD, you alone; you have made

est in genere), creatures can be categorized in any number of ways: by location, size, physical state, composition, form, biotic character, sentience, rationality. Equal in all respects, Father, Son, and Spirit are one God (Deut. 6:4; Gal. 3:20; 1 Tim. 2:5); creatures are many and manifold.

It is, of course, possible to consider the ensemble of creatures—creation as a whole—as a unity precisely in its difference from God. Indeed, for certain purposes there is good reason to do so. For in the face of every system for categorizing created being, and with the understanding that any number of such systems may have real value in illuminating the various sorts of relationships that obtain between creatures, there can be no ranking of creatures with respect to proximity to God. All creatures are equally—and infinitely—far from God by virtue of their having been created (none, even the highest of the seraphim, is in any sense divine); and all are equally—and absolutely— near to God as the one who sustains their existence (none, not even the most ephemeral of virtual particles, exists save by God deliberately and irresistibly holding it in being). Even if some version of the many-worlds version of quantum mechanics or multiverse accounts of cosmology were to prove correct, it would remain the case that all such "worlds" would be equally dependent on God for their existence.[15] To put the same point in other words, insofar as the universe (or multiverse)—however internally differentiated, and with its constituent components emerging and evolving over time—is sustained in its entirety by God and thus willed by God as a whole, it may be conceived as just one "thing."

Nor is this unity simply a matter of arbitrary conglomeration, analogous to referring to the different items in a time capsule as "one" solely by virtue of their having been collected in a single place. The unity of creation is certainly a matter of origination, in that the whole comes from and is sustained by the one God, but it also relates to the structure of created reality itself. Here the witness of Genesis 1 is significant, for it affirms not only that each creature is good considered in itself, but also that goodness pertains to

---

heaven, the heaven of heavens, with all their host, the earth and all that is on it, the seas and all that is in them. *To all of them you give life*, and the host of heaven worships you" (Neh. 9:6).

15. In this context it is worth noting that the traditional distinction between "heaven and earth" bears certain conceptual similarities to the multiverse theory, so long as "heaven" is taken to refer not to the visible array of stars and planets (and, by extension, to galaxies, nebulae, dark matter, and so forth), but, following the Nicene Creed, to the realm of the "unseen." For one point of this traditional division is to affirm that there exists a sphere (indeed, a very large and diverse sphere) of creation that is intrinsically imperceptible to and independent of those "earthly" creatures that inhabit the universe we can perceive. The parallel breaks down only insofar as Christians have tended to understand this imperceptibility as unidirectional, such that events on earth are known and can be affected by heavenly beings (viz., angels), while multiverse theories typically do not envision any sort of causal interaction between different universes.

creation as a whole: "God saw *everything* that he had made, and indeed, it was very good" (Gen. 1:31). The entirety of the created order, whatever its extent or the particular character of its differentiated complexity (e.g., whether or not it includes a plurality of "worlds"), is good—indeed, *very* good—and one in that goodness.[16]

And yet however much creation may be regarded a unity on the grounds that it is in its entirety uniformly and unilaterally dependent on God, other than God, and good in that otherness, it remains an internally differentiated unity made up of creatures that are distinct from one another.[17] They exist as very diverse types, each marked by its own set of constitutive attributes or properties (e.g., stars and flowering plants), and even within those types they may be further distinguished as separate individuals (e.g., Arcturus and Sirius, the rose bush to the right and the one to the left of the front door). In short, creation is a composite and, as such, subsists quite differently than God, who is not composed of parts. Nor is this diversity simply accidental; it is, rather, intrinsic to what it means for the world to be created. Within God the donation of being is total and, as such, gives rise to the Son, who is the perfect image of the Father, and to the Spirit, who at once bears witness to and participates in this complete intradivine repetition of divinity. Once again, as God gives being in this unlimited way, the result can only be the repetition of God's own life that is the Trinity: an eternal affirmation of the uniqueness, integrity, and self-sufficiency of divine being, in which the oneness of the Father is matched by the oneness of the Son, who in the Spirit are all together just one (John 10:30; 17:11). But creation is not the product of this infinite mode of giving. Because the gift of being to creatures is resolutely finite, no individual creature is able to reflect the infinite fullness of divine being. It follows that insofar as God nevertheless wishes to communicate that fullness to creation, creation necessarily takes differentiated form. As Thomas argued, God

---

16. "Seven times I have counted Scripture saying you saw that what you made is good. But on the eighth occasion when you saw all that you had made, it says they were not merely good but 'very good'—as if taking everything at once into account. For individual items were only 'good,' but everything taken together was both 'good' and 'very good.' This truth is also declared by the beauty of bodies. A body composed of its constituent parts, all of which are beautiful, is far more beautiful as a whole than those parts taken separately; the whole is made of their well-ordered harmony; though individual, the constituent parts are also beautiful." Augustine, *Confessions* 13.43, trans. Henry Chadwick (Oxford: Oxford University Press, 1991). Augustine's count of seven instances of "good" in the creation story reflects the Old Latin version of Genesis, which has an occurrence of "God saw that it was good" in v. 8 that is lacking in the Hebrew text on which most English Bible translations are based.

17. In the words of Austin Farrer, "The world is not a system, it is an interaction of systems innumerable." Austin Farrer, *Love Almighty and Ills Unlimited: An Essay on Providence and Evil* (London: Collins, 1962), 51.

brought things into existence so that his goodness might be communicated to creatures and re-enacted through them. And because one
single creature was not enough, he produced many and diverse, so
that what was wanting in one expression of the divine goodness might
be supplied by another, for goodness, which in God exists singly and
without variance [*simpliciter et uniformiter*], in creation is multiple and
separated [*multipliciter et divisim*]. Hence the whole universe shares
and represents the divine goodness less incompletely than any one
creature alone.[18]

Insofar as God transcends the totality of creation no less completely than
God transcends any single creature, even the sum of all finite creatures falls
short of God's infinite being. But that creation displays God's goodness
through a plurality of creatures more adequately than it could through a single one nevertheless reflects the logic of divine transcendence. If God were to
communicate God's goodness through just a single creature, the effect would
be to suggest that God might be located on the same scale with creatures, in
that God would be like this one creature, only incomparably greater. By contrast, the multiplicity of creatures is a more adequate representation of divine
goodness because this plurality serves as a reminder that the unity of perfections in God is utterly incommensurable with any form of creaturely unity.
From this perspective, creation is best conceived less as a reflection of divinity
(as in Plato's "moving image of eternity") than as its refraction into the finite
realm of time and space, a projection of the inexhaustible richness of God's
being into myriad nondivine forms.[19]

This diversity of created forms is every bit as good and glorious as the analogy of refraction—white light split into the colors of the rainbow—would suggest. For it is one of the wonders of creation that it is profoundly capacious:
a weaving of space and time able to sustain the rich diversity of beings, from
the simple to the complex, the material to the spiritual, and so forth, in and
through all of which God wills to share the gift of being. And yet though this
plurality of creaturely forms, considered both individually and as a whole, is
good, the fact of its being other than God entails further aspects of divergence
from the character of divine life beyond the sheer fact of multiplicity, including chiefly the relationships that obtain among the diversity of created beings.

God, as Trinity, is love: an inexhaustible donation and reception of divinity
in which each of the three divine persons subsists always and only in and by

---

18. Aquinas, *ST* 1.47.1, trans. alt.
19. Thus "we are not invited to consider creation a specimen or *imitation* or *reflection*. . . .
Creatures do not mirror or instantiate their Creator in this direct and commensurate way." Katherine Sonderegger, *The Doctrine of God*, vol. 1 of *Systematic Theology* (Minneapolis: Fortress Press,
2015), 366–67.

its relations with the other two. So, for example, if the Father were to cease to beget the Son, the being of the Father would be compromised no less than that of the Son, for the Father *is* Father precisely in the act of begetting the Son. That God is love thus means that divine being is marked by a radical and absolute mutuality in which the three persons are so bound up with one another that each exists only in and through the others. Not only does the being of one person never come at the expense of another, but each lives only by referring (whether through unstinting donation, thankful reception, or joyous glorification) their being to the other two in a ceaseless round of perfect and joyous communion that, in its inseparable unity, constitutes the one life of God.

By contrast, the unity of creation is not that of a single life, and the relationships of interdependence that obtain among creatures are correspondingly various. Indeed, if one follows Thomas and views angels as immaterial, then this one class of creatures (which Christians have generally viewed as being very large, as per Rev. 5:11) does not exist in any such state of interdependence; rather, each is its own species, sustained in being solely and directly by God, so that even though all share in worship of and service to God, each is ontologically independent of every other.[20] And even if attention is limited to the material (and leaving aside the possibility of parallel universes), the enormous distances between stars and galaxies severely restrict the range of interaction possible between us on earth and creatures elsewhere in the universe: all subsist as part of the same fabric of space-time and are subject to the same physical laws, but the distances are such that even the most cataclysmic events in other galaxies are unlikely to affect the conditions of our existence.[21]

---

20. See Aquinas, *ST* 1.50.4. Like all forms of created being, angels' ontological independence from one another is good in itself, insofar as it is a constitutive feature of their being as created by God. At the same time, it brings home again the fact that all forms of created being diverge from the radical mutuality of the Trinity—and thus with their existence grounded in grace rather than their (created) natures—do creatures come to share (by grace) the radical mutuality of existence that is proper to God by nature. In this context, it is important to note that while angels' natural immortality means that they are not threatened by death and thus have no need of resurrection, they stand in no less need than humans of being glorified.

21. While most galaxies are moving away from our own at high velocities, our nearest neighbor, the Andromeda galaxy, is projected to collide with the Milky Way in around four billion years' time. Leaving aside the fact that the increased luminosity of the sun will have long since wiped out all terrestrial life by that time, the enormous distances between stars means that the effect of such a collision on the solar system would likely be negligible, even if the resulting tidal forces were to sweep it outside of the Milky Way altogether. Cataclysmic events within our galaxy—massive gamma ray bursts, e.g.—could have serious consequences for life on earth, but they are also extremely rare. The hypothesis of a cosmic expansion culminating in a "Big Rip" that would tear apart the fabric of space-time itself certainly does speak to the ultimate interdependence of all matter, but, precisely as such, relates to the structure of the universe as a whole rather than to the interaction between particular entities within it.

On a more local scale, however, interdependence is much more in evidence. Most obviously, life on earth is utterly dependent on the energy received from the sun, as well as on the physical conditions (orbital eccentricity, axial tilt, the presence of a magnetic field, and so forth) ensuring that this energy is sufficient to sustain life without overwhelming it.[22] And within the earth's biosphere, life requires liquid water and other chemicals to metabolize the sun's energy, whether through processes of photosynthesis (plants), ingestion (animals), or decomposition (fungi).[23] In these exchanges of energy within the biosphere, there is much that can be seen as exemplifying a beautiful reciprocity between the needs of various classes of organism (e.g., the carbon cycle), and within particular ecosystems the contributions of different biota to a stable and balanced system is well established.[24] Still more profound examples of interdependence can be found in the symbiotic relationships between individual species: humans benefit from colonies of bacteria in their bowels, and mature ruminants cannot digest food at all apart from a highly diverse gut ecosystem. In still other cases the mutual dependence of symbiotic species is so intimate as to generate what in effect are compound organisms (e.g., algae and fungi in lichens, or corals and dinoflagellates).[25] Finally, interdependence among members of the same species can be so profound as to lead some to speak of the resulting collectives (e.g., social insects like termites, ants, and bees, but also the naked mole rat among mammals) as superorganisms.[26]

And yet while the interdependence of thousands of species within a single ecosystem may be striking in its combination of intricacy and comprehensiveness, the achievement of balance in the aggregate is inseparable from relationships of competition and conflict in detail. Quite simply (and again, in sharp

22. Even the giant tubeworms that live near deep sea thermal vents depend indirectly on sunlight, since their metabolism depends on the presence of free oxygen that is released by photosynthesis elsewhere in the biosphere.

23. In associating the main types of biotic metabolism with the three great multicellular kingdoms, I do not mean to exclude the myriad forms of terrestrial microorganisms, among which all three of these modes of metabolizing energy, along with chemosynthesis as a fourth, may be found.

24. More controversial is the Gaia hypothesis, formulated by James Lovelock and Lynn Margulis, according to which the biosphere as a whole is understood as a self-regulating system in which organisms interact both with each other and abiotic systems to maintain conditions of life on the planet. See, e.g., James Lovelock, *Gaia: A New Look at Life on Earth* (Oxford: Oxford University Press, 2000).

25. Insofar as it is now widely accepted that the eukaryotic (nucleated) cells that are constitutive of all protists, plants, fungi, and animals are evolutionarily the product of the symbiosis of prokaryotic ancestors (as evidenced by, e.g., the fact that eukaryotic mitochondria carry their own DNA), it can be argued that all terrestrial multicellular life has a basically symbiotic character.

26. See, e.g., Bert Holldoble and E. O. Wilson, *The Superorganism: The Beauty, Elegance, and Strangeness of Insect Societies* (New York: W. W. Norton, 2009).

contrast to the relationship of persons and nature in the Godhead), the flourishing of a whole ecosystem not only does not entail but is flatly inconsistent with the equal flourishing of all constituent parts.[27] Animals (along with some protists) subsist by consuming other organisms, and while it is clear that, for example, predation by wolves helps to maintain the overall fitness of the caribou herd by removing older, weak, and sick individuals, it remains the case that the well-being of the wolf pack and the herd alike comes at the expense of the individuals that are culled in this way. Moreover, for all the many ways in which ecosystems achieve a kind of stability in which populations of creatures (if not all particular individuals) flourish in common, the introduction of new species, climate change, and other environmental factors can also lead to situations in which the success of one species comes at the expense of another.[28] And the most direct competition occurs between members of the same species, who vie for the same resources (whether space, nutriments, or, for organisms that reproduce sexually, reproductive partners), with the result that success for one can only come at the expense of some other. No one has described this situation with more vivid imagery of competition within and between species than Charles Darwin:

> Nature may be compared to a surface covered with ten thousand sharp wedges, many of the same shape and many of different shapes representing differing species, all packed closely together and all driven by incessant blows: the blows being far severer at one time than another; sometimes a wedge of one form and sometimes another being struck; and one driven deeply in forcing out others; with the jar and shock often transmitted very far to other wedges in many lines of direction.[29]

This is not so much nature "red in tooth and claw" (an image that describes the relationship between a relatively quite small number of species), as nature constrained by the sheer physicality of organisms bumping up against each other, so that the "self-regulation" of ecosystems, as well as the evolution of

---

27. Again, angels constitute a special case, since their immateriality means that God does not sustain their existence through any system of created causes. Because angelic existence, unlike that of living creatures composed of matter, is not dependent upon the acquisition and use of material resources, there can be no competition among angels.

28. Although the question continues to be debated, there is some evidence that human migration to the Americas contributed to the population collapse of indigenous megafauna. And there seems to be little doubt that human migration led to the extinction of the giant moa in New Zealand, as well as (albeit probably more indirectly) to the disappearance of the dodo on Mauritius.

29. Charles Darwin, *Natural Selection: Being the Second Part of His Big Species Book Written from 1856 to 1858*, ed. R. C. Stauffer (Cambridge: Cambridge University Press, 1975), 208; cf. the parallel, shorter passage in his *On the Origin of Species* (London: Murray, 1859), 67.

new species, are processes in which the flourishing of some individuals (and even whole species) comes at the expense of others.

Importantly, these features of creaturely existence need not (and, given Christian convictions about the character of creation, should not) be taken to impugn the essential goodness of creation. It is certainly true that both protologically (Gen. 1:29–30) and eschatologically (Isa. 11:6–9; 65:25) the Bible suggests that God wills creation to be a peaceable kingdom, without competition among creatures. Yet with respect to the latter, it must be emphasized that this is precisely an eschatological vision and thus is linked to a fundamental transformation of the conditions of created existence sufficiently radical to be characterized as the creation of a new heaven and earth (Isa. 65:17; 66:22; cf. 2 Pet. 3:13; Rev. 21:1). The situation in Genesis is different since it is precisely the vegetarian ecology in which God has given to "everything that has the breath of life . . . every green plant for food" (1:30) that is described as "very good" (1:31). Still, the point of transition from universal vegetarianism to carnivorous existence is not specified for any creature except human beings, and in that case it is described not as an act of human presumption but as a divine gift associated with the renewal of creaturely existence after the flood (Gen. 9:1–3); this fact cautions us against taking it as a declension from an ideal state. Although current patterns of competition among creatures are destined to come to an end, that does not render them illegitimate or evil in the present. If we are assured that someday "the lion shall eat straw like the ox" (Isa 11:7; 65:25), in the present time God seems quite happy with the order in which the young lion catches its prey (Job 38:39; Ps. 104:21; Isa. 31:4; Amos 3:4).

At the same time, such reflections should not be taken to justify human indifference to the natural order. The Bible's recognition of the rhythms—and indeed, the terrors—of the natural world (stated with particular power in Job 40:15–41:34) does not imply that whatever is in nature is necessarily right, and the primordial charge given to human beings to till and keep the earth (Gen. 2:15; cf. 1:28) suggests that our species has an obligation to make practical judgments about the management of terrestrial life.[30] Given the conditions of material existence, however, all such judgments, in addition to being debatable in content, will invariably entail checks on the flourishing of some creatures (possibly including some human beings) in the present time. Because living creatures are individually finite and inhabit a finite world, creaturely interdependence entails mutual limitation

---

30. So, notwithstanding the fact that God in Gen. 9:3 explicitly gives human beings permission to use "every moving thing that lives" for food, there is every reason for human beings to reflect on whether or not in the twenty-first century the ecological effects of animal husbandry on the terrestrial environment are so severe as to demand a return to vegetarianism.

alongside mutual sustenance and support.[31] The three divine persons are not in any respect threatened by one another: each one lives entirely in and by the other two, such that at no point does the flourishing of one come at another's expense; quite the contrary, it is the nature of divinity that the "expense" of giving whereby the divine life is sustained does not diminish any person but rather constitutes the persons as the one God. The relationships between material creatures tend to operate much more on a zero-sum basis, with the gain of one entailing loss by another via processes that are generally involuntary and competitive, if not always violent. There is also donation among creatures, but even the most generous giving comes at a cost, diminishing the being of the one who gives, and correspondingly is only capable of being shared among a limited number of others. The diversity of God's being both reflects and promises inexhaustible abundance fully, if distinctly, shared among the divine persons; the diversity of created being is more ambiguous: it is the source of flourishing, delight, and abundance, but also of lack, threat, and destruction.

And all this has serious consequences for the character of God's presence in creation. Because God is "Not Other," sustaining creation as the origin and ground of created being and, precisely as such, subsists wholly otherwise than created being, God is invisible. As noted in the previous chapter, this invisibility is intrinsic to God. It is certainly not a barrier to God's presence in creation; on the contrary, it is just in God's unique and incomparable mode of subsistence that God is also able to found and sustain the world. But God's presence in creation is not the same sort of presence that is found in the Trinity, and this fact accentuates the problem of God's unknowability by creatures, and thus of the possibility of mutual communion between God and

---

31. Absent the (questionable) feasibility of mining operations on the moon or elsewhere in the solar system, as well as the (relatively) small quantities of additional matter that accrue to the earth from meteorite impacts, the amount of material available for living beings is fixed and confined to the area bounded by the outer limits of the earth's atmosphere. The question of whether creation as a whole is finite does not admit of an altogether straightforward answer. If the universe is, as seems the case, "flat" (i.e., has zero curvature), then it is infinite in extent; that is, if one were to proceed in a given direction forever, one would never return to one's starting point. But our knowledge of the contents of the universe is limited to the "observable universe" (i.e., that which is causally connected to us and of which it is therefore possible to have knowledge); it therefore does not include what may exist beyond the limits of observation (a distance of around 46.5 billion light years in every direction), let alone the contents of possible parallel universes. And since we cannot be affected by what is outside the observable universe, the universe may be taken to be functionally finite, and it is on this basis that cosmologists offer estimates of the universe's total baryonic (viz., ordinary) mass (ca. 10^{53} kg) and the total number of baryons it contains (ca. 10^{80})—unimaginably large, but nevertheless finite quantities. It follows that even if we had access to more of the stuff of the universe than we do, there would still be limits on the amount of resources available for the flourishing of material creatures.

creatures. In the Trinity, God is fully known because each divine person is fully present to the others precisely in the infinite donation and reception of divine being. But where God gives rise to that which is not God, God's giving, though no less utterly gracious and unselfish than within the Trinity, is not complete. It follows that God is not present in creation in the same way that God is present within the Godhead. Instead, God's presence is hidden—and this as a very condition of bringing what is not divine into being. Thus a logical condition of God's creating a world seems to be that God should be invincibly invisible to and unknown by it.

This invisibility is not absence, as though God had to withdraw to make space for creatures.[32] As already noted, the doctrine of creation from nothing means that God's uninterrupted presence is a necessary condition of the creature's existence at every moment of its existence. But it is a condition of finite existence, which is existence as another (and thus *in genere*), to be distinct precisely from the God who is "Not Other." For God to be present to a creature as that which the creature might encounter, it would be necessary for God also to be other, one item in the world rather than the one who sustains the world, and thus to cease to be God. Such a finite God would indeed need to withdraw to make space for creatures, even as every creature, by virtue of taking its particular place in creation, prevents that space from being occupied by any other creature.[33] In this way, the diversity of creatures suggests that God's radical, sustaining presence *in* the world as Creator precludes God's objective presence *to* creatures as one who can be known and loved.

---

32. This is the position of Jürgen Moltmann, who invokes the kabbalistic concept of *zimsum*, or contraction, as the precondition of God's creative work. See Jürgen Moltmann, *God in Creation: A New Theology of Creation and the Spirit of God* (New York: Harper & Row, 1985), 86–93.

33. This point is not disproved by instances of creaturely symbiosis: my gut bacteria live inside me, but only because my insides contain physical space in which they can live. Indeed, even though Thomas Aquinas denies that angels are material—which seems to preclude their taking up space—he nevertheless maintains that they do have place, since to argue otherwise would be to ascribe to them the divine attribute of omnipresence (see Aquinas, *ST* 1.52.1–3). A more serious objection to the idea that any place can be occupied exclusively by one creature comes from the world of quantum mechanics, within which the phenomenon of superposition teaches that a single particle (e.g., an electron orbiting an atomic nucleus) occupies multiple positions simultaneously; but even here the particle will "collapse" to a single position when measured. Although it is a matter of consensus among physicists that the particle has no single position until measured, the fact remains that we only *experience* entities, even at the quantum level, as having a single position (indeed, if the Copenhagen interpretation of quantum mechanics is correct, we *cannot* experience them otherwise, because they do not exist as distinct entities unless and until they are measured). See Noson S. Yanofsky, *The Outer Limits of Reason: What Science, Mathematics, and Logic Cannot Tell Us* (Boston: MIT Press, 2013), 176–94.

"FOR EVERYTHING A SEASON":
THE TRANSIENCE OF CREATURES

When considering creation's diversity, it is precisely creatures' presence to one another that emerges as a significant threat to their flourishing since that presence—what Austin Farrer called their "mutual externality"—marks each as a different entity from and irreducibly other than all the rest.[34] That distinctness and otherness is in itself good, a consequence of each creature enjoying its own existence as God intends it should; but it is also ineluctably sets every creature in some respect over against its fellow creatures: occupying its own space and requiring its own material resources, which cannot be shared fully with any other creature. (I may certainly share my bread with my neighbors, but whatever portion they eat, I cannot, and vice versa.) At a basic level, in short, my enduring as a creature in whatever place I occupy and by whatever means I employ precludes any other creature subsisting just there and by those means. Creaturely presence is thus relative and ambiguous, in that the presence of other creatures is at once a condition of my existence (since I cannot live without a place to stand, air to breathe, water to drink, food to eat, others of my kind to give me birth and promote my nurture) and a limit to it (since other creatures' use of space, air, water, and so forth compete with my own). In this it contrasts with the mutual presence of the divine persons, which is absolute (the radical copresence of circuminsession) and utterly self-constituting, since far from competing for resources, it is by an infinite and endless life of mutual donation, reception, and glorification that the Father, Son, and Spirit subsist as God. Divine diversity, rooted in love, is both inseparable from and an eternal celebration of presence; creaturely diversity is just not correlated with love in this way.

Yet if one aspect of creatures' distinction from God is the combination of competition and collaboration that structures their presence to one another, an even more pronounced way in which creatures differ from God relates to their lack of mutual presence. For however much my presence to other creatures and their presence to me may be a matter of ambiguity (both a condition of and a limit to my existence), the fact is that most creatures are not—and indeed cannot be—present to me at all. As noted above, the vast expanse of the universe and the absolute speed limit established by the velocity of light means that the overwhelming majority of these distances that separate me from other creatures cannot be crossed: absent some all but unimaginable

---

34. Austin Farrer, *Finite and Infinite: A Philosophical Essay* (New York: Seabury Press, 1979 [1943]), 246; cf. 283, where he refers to this "mutual and incoherent externality" as "the real scandal of finitude."

technological developments, I will never be present to living creatures (if there should be any) on even the nearest stars, let alone in the most distant galaxies or possible parallel universes. And, of course, the finite character of created existence means that even where I am able to cross an intervening distance, whether across the street or over an ocean, any experience of creaturely presence gained in my new circumstances is matched by a loss of presence to those I leave behind. My experience of presence is a shifting between different, highly localized environments, in the movements between which I exchange the presence of one very small subset of creatures for another.

Nor is space the only barrier to creatures' mutual presence. An even more insurmountable barrier is posed by time. Even though my spatial mobility is limited, I can nevertheless go some way to determine my physical location, but I have no such power with respect to time: I come to be at a particular point in time and am thereafter carried along by time.[35] If I was absent when an event took place, I can never become present to it (I might, of course, hear tell of or view visual records of a past event, but I cannot affect it in any way). And while I can anticipate and prepare to be present to creatures in the future (e.g., at a concert next week, a reunion in five years' time), this reduces to a matter of waiting, in the knowledge that the anticipated event may never take place—or that I may no longer exist when it does. Indeed, this last possibility points to the fact that the barriers to presence posed by time are not merely the irretrievability of the past and the uncertainty of the future, but, most fundamentally, creatures' inherent transience. The finitude of creatures is not simply a matter of physical extent, but also of temporal duration. Here, too, the contrast with God is stark: "Of old thou didst lay the foundation of the earth, and the heavens are the work of thy hands. They will perish, but thou dost endure; they will all wear out like a garment. Thou changest them like raiment, and they pass away; but thou art the same, and thy years have no end" (Ps. 102:25–27 RSV). Creatures are present as they come to be, and they cease to be present when they pass out of being.[36]

---

35. The physics of special relativity mean that this is not quite true: I can affect my relative location in time by changing my velocity: if I move relatively faster than other creatures in my immediate environment, I will find myself to have moved forward in time at a faster rate than those who have remained at (relative) rest. But except at speeds that are unlikely ever to be technologically feasible, these effects will be vanishingly small; and in any case, however large and precisely calculated such efforts may be, all movement in time remains strictly unidirectional: I might jump ahead days, years, or decades, but time's arrow only moves forward, so that whatever times I have overleaped will be irretrievably in my past and thus not present to me. Still, the possibility of relativistic "time travel" may be taken as a theoretical proviso to be set alongside all statements made in this section about the experience of time's passing.

36. Again, immaterial angels would stand in a different category: while they, too, are created (so that it is not the case that they always existed), they do not pass out of existence but are held to subsist eternally once brought into being.

To be sure, creatures' temporal finitude should no more be taken as a blight on their goodness than should their occupying only a finite region of space. The Preacher is clear on this point:

> For everything there is a season,
>   and a time for every matter under heaven:
> a time to be born, and a time to die;
> a time to plant, and a time to pluck up what is planted;
> a time to kill, and a time to heal;
> a time to break down, and a time to build up;
> a time to weep, and a time to laugh;
> a time to mourn, and a time to dance;
> a time to throw away stones, and a time to gather stones together;
> a time to embrace, and a time to refrain from embracing;
> a time to seek, and a time to lose;
> a time to keep, and a time to throw away;
> a time to tear, and a time to sew;
> a time to keep silence, and a time to speak;
> a time to love, and a time to hate;
> a time for war, and a time for peace.
>
> (Eccl. 3:1–8)

That everything has its time is part of its created goodness—its distinct form of being as the creature it is, which includes its being *now* rather than *then* as much as to be *here* rather than *there*. Indeed, the Preacher's words here go further still, for they affirm not simply the time given individual creatures in their particularity, but also the various types of relations that obtain among them during that time: planting and plucking, killing and healing, love and hate, war and peace. In line with the conclusions of the previous section of this chapter, both work of cooperation and competition, two basic forms in which creatures live out their mutual presence to one another, are affirmed as intrinsic to God's will for created being. For insofar as finite creatures can subsist only by way of varying rhythms of cooperation and competition, one could hardly affirm the inherent goodness of creation otherwise.[37]

The point remains, however, that the transience of creatures means that all such relationships are necessarily temporary. Indeed, although certain forms of creaturely interaction (e.g., gravitational attraction between massive bodies, or the continued "noise" of the big bang in the form of cosmic background radiation) can operate across enormous stretches of space and time, for the

---

37. "As we love our own distinct being, we must endure the conditions of its possibility," and these conditions include, e.g., that the activity of any creature "has a passive aspect insofar as its form is limited and determined—often broken and spoiled—by the conditions set to it by . . . its neighbours." Farrer, *Finite and Infinite*, 258, 279.

most part spatial and temporal distance mean that creatures neither are nor ever can be present to one another. Again, this fact does not impugn creation's goodness. That creaturely existence, whether considered at the level of the individual or the species, should be temporally limited is not in itself an evil but, arguably, entirely consistent with creatures' intrinsically finite mode of being. This is true even when the "time" of a specific creature is short. We simply have no basis for defining what a proper length of existence is for any creature, such that its failing to attain it should be judged an evil. If it is true, as the Preacher also says, that God "has made everything beautiful in its time" (Eccl. 3:11 RSV), on what basis are we able to judge what that "time" is in any particular case? Is it any more reasonable to say that a human being should be expected to live to a certain minimum age than that one should grow to a certain minimum height? Although the idea that all creatures should live to the full age attainable by their species has a certain appeal, it arguably buys into a prejudicial sort of teleology, according to which life as lived now, in the present moment, is less than fully good. Here Ruth Page's insistence on "Teleology now!" provides a valuable corrective to the urge to equate creaturely flourishing with a given creature's achievement of any particular outcome (e.g., a ripe old age), since such an equation subverts a fundamental principle of a properly Christian theology of creation, namely, God's joy in the sheer existence of creatures at every point of their existence, such that every moment of a creature's existence is "an end in itself."[38]

These observations do not imply that human beings should adopt an attitude of indifference to every instance of creaturely transience; to do so would mean disregarding the biblical understanding of human responsibility for the tending of creation. My point is simply that such judgments are properly made within the context of appreciating that the goodness instantiated by every creature is particular to that creature and so cannot simply be subsumed under a general law, however helpful certain sorts of generalizations may be as guiding principles for acts of judgment. For example, the fact that life is in general better than death does not preclude the judgment that under a given set of circumstances it may be licit not only not to prevent a creature's death, but even to pursue it (e.g., the case of HIV viruses infecting human beings). In short, human judgments about which actions constitute faithful witness to the goodness of all creation and God's concern for all

38. Ruth Page, *God and the Web of Creation* (London: SCM Press, 1996), 63. At the same time, this emphasis has to be balanced with Oliver O'Donovan's insight that the very idea of creaturely flourishing cannot escape some reference to a temporally extended, natural teleology justifying the claim that an acorn flourishes in becoming an oak, a colt in becoming a stallion, and so forth. See Oliver O'Donovan, *Resurrection and the Moral Order: An Outline for Evangelical Ethics* (Grand Rapids: Wm. B. Eerdmans Publishing Co., 1986), 35.

creation are appropriately contingent, based on analysis of particular circumstances obtaining in any given case.

One way of conceiving the goodness of created existence in its transience both in its relation to and radical distinction from the being of the Creator is by way of the patristic distinction between the one divine Word, or (in Greek) Logos, through whom all things came into being (John 1:3), and the diverse *logoi* of individual creatures. Developed in great detail by the seventh-century theologian Maximus the Confessor, the language of Logos and *logoi* has certain parallels with Thomas's vision of the relationship between God and creatures cited above: God, the Logos, seeks to share the divine goodness with that which is not God, and so doing refracts the richness of divine life through myriad nondivine forms, the *logoi* of individual creatures, each of which displays some aspect of the undivided fullness of divinity.[39] Yet the use of the Greek term *logos* brings out the temporal dimension of created existence in the way that Thomas's image does not. *Logos* has a broad array of meanings. It can be translated "word," "speech," and "reason"; in the context of patristic references to the diverse *logoi* of creatures, it is often rendered "nature" or "principle." For present purposes, however, I suggest that "story" is a particularly appropriate rendering. The Creator Logos is the fullness of God's being, who personally instantiates the never-ending story of the love of the Father and the Son in the Spirit, which is the life of the Trinity. By contrast, the *logoi* of creatures are smaller stories that individually display and together illustrate particular aspects of the inexhaustible fullness of the divine life. Insofar as creatures endure for widely varying time spans, ranging from days to years to centuries in the case of organisms and anything up to billions of years for nonliving beings, their particular *logoi* may be compared to sentences, paragraphs, chapters, or even volumes within a larger story. The key point, however, is that each is finite in duration: it has a beginning and an ending, and as such, in its coming to be and passing away, displays both its own particular goodness and its relationship to other *logoi*. Moreover, the full and final significance of each created *logos* is properly understood not only in relationship to the other *logoi* that lie in more or less close proximity to it, but also in light of the one Logos who is its origin and goal, and in relation to whom creation can be seen as a temporal analogue to the eternal story of God's love.

This picture of the place of individual creatures in the larger story of creation is quite different from Macbeth's despairing soliloquy in Shakespeare's play. It is true that from the universe's origins straight through to "the last

---

39. See Maximus the Confessor, *Ambigua* 7 (PG 91:1077C–1080B), in *On Difficulties in the Church Fathers: The Ambigua*, ed. and trans. Nicholas Constas, 2 vols. (Cambridge, MA: Harvard University Press, 2014), 1:95–96.

syllable of recorded time," any living being has only "his hour upon the stage / And then is heard no more"; but that does not render its existence a mere "shadow" without significance.[40] It simply means that its significance is not self-contained and thus is not self-evident. As with any sentence (or paragraph or chapter), its meaning emerges only when read in the context of the larger story of which it is a part. Again, temporal finitude is no more a fault or a defect than finitude in space: the two rather define the basic character of created being as precisely created and thus not divine—but no less good for all that.

And yet here, too, the defining characteristics of created goodness seem to pose an impermeable barrier to genuine, mutual communion between Creator and creature. For although the Creator sustains the creature in its spatial and temporal particularity—as just *this* being, existing uniquely and unsubstitutably in a given time and place—this creative work seems unavoidably hidden: inherently invisible and thus incognito. For the only way for God to be known by the creature would be for God to become a *logos* alongside the other *logoi*, and thereby to cease to be the one Logos who transcends the many *logoi* as their infinite source. Moreover, if the comprehensibility of the *logoi*—their very status as refractions of divine goodness, witnesses to the divine story and not simply meaningless "sound and fury"—depends on their being "read" within the context of the eternal Logos, then the latter's unavailability is fatal to the very aim of creation: that God should share the blessings of existence with creatures in such a way that existence might be received as a blessing and not a curse. So it is that creatures' transience, their lack of presence to one another, combined with a transcendence that renders God phenomenally absent to creaturely perception, threatens to give support to Macbeth's despair: the limits of created existence—its contingency, diversity, and temporality—lacking any larger context of order or meaning, seem doomed to dissolve into hopeless, pointless fragmentation.

Once more, the obvious solution to this problem would be for the Logos to appear and provide the frame for understanding the ground and goal of created existence, but to do so would mean for the Logos to assume a place within space and time, and thus, seemingly, to cease to be the Logos who, as Creator, transcends them both. On the one hand, then, nothing and no one other than God can disclose God's self to creatures in such a way as to invite them to share the love of the triune life; on the other hand, God can only do so by assuming a finite, material form that would put God in the same position of all other finite beings: able to affirm self only at the expense of others. Whatever fulfillment such a god might promise, and however much support,

---

40. William Shakespeare, *Macbeth* 5.5.21, 25–26, 24.

encouragement, and power it may offer, the fact that the space it occupies necessarily excludes others seems to force the conclusion that any such being will be no more than one *logos* among many and, to the extent that it seeks to be more, will in the final analysis only eclipse rather than fulfill the meaning of other *logoi*. A God who sustains creatures must remain invisible to them, since only so can God be God. By becoming visible, God would cease to be God, with the result that—once again—it appears to follow that the unavoidable consequence of God seeking to effect genuine communion with creatures would be the dissolution of creaturely existence. The claim that it need not be so is the burden of the doctrine of the incarnation, to which we now turn.

PART 2

The Bridge

Very truly, I tell you,
    you will see heaven opened
and the angels of God
    ascending and descending upon the Son of Man.
                                    —John 1:51

3

"One and the Same"

"And the Word became flesh and lived among us, and we have seen his glory" (John 1:14). So the Gospel of John declares, but if the analysis of Creator and creature presented in part 1 is correct, it does not seem credible. To be sure, the problem here is not that the divine needs to keep its distance from the world—the eternal from the temporal, being from becoming, the changeless from the changeable—in order to avoid contamination by (and subjection to) worldly processes of degradation and decay. God and the world are not opposed in this sense. On the contrary, creatures subsist only by virtue of God holding them in being, so that it is precisely the most intimate presence of God at every point in space and at every moment of time that is the one necessary and sufficient condition of there being a world at all. In this way, God's integrity is not threatened by proximity to the world, and the creature's integrity demands it.

But if divine and created being are compatible, they are not commensurable, and in this respect the distinct ontologies of Creator and creature seem to pose an insuperable limit to the possibility of their genuine communion. For their incommensurability means that while creatures are always present to the God who is their sole source and ground, a transcendent God cannot be present to the creature in the same way. The Creator-creature relation is marked by a fundamental asymmetry, deriving from the fact that while creatures are absolutely other than God, God is "Not Other" with respect to creatures. Precisely as Creator, God is the infinite source of all that exists and, as such, not one existent among others (i.e., one more item in a universal inventory) who can be identified by way of contrast with creatures, in the way that creatures may be distinguished from one another through comparison and contrast. Even the *via negativa* of theological apophaticism is not properly

71

a means of drawing a contrast between God and the world but rather as a strategy for highlighting the impossibility of locating God on any of the ontological scales (e.g., physical, temporal, modal) used to categorize creatures.[1]

In this way, the very comprehensiveness of divine presence in the world renders it essentially hidden. For although it is emphatically not the case that God needs to absent God's self in order to make space for creatures, the fact that God is not one entity among others entails that the divine nature is intrinsically and unchangeably invisible. For God to become flesh (or any other created and thus finite reality) would be for God to be present at a particular place and time, and thus not to be the omnipresent Creator and Sustainer of the world.[2] Only within the Godhead is divine presence directly experienced, as in the life of the Trinity each of the persons is fully present to the others in the eternal donation and reception of the fullness of divine being. But creatures do not receive this fullness. As I have emphasized, to receive the gift of finite rather than infinite being is simply what it means to be created and so is not a defect; yet it does seem to preclude the mutual presence of Creator and creature to one another. The incommensurability of divine and created natures means that for God to be present to the creature would be either for God to cease to be God, or for the creature to cease to be a creature.[3] The idea that the Word might become flesh, that divine and human natures might somehow be united, therefore seems to be a conceptual nonstarter.

NATURE AND HYPOSTASIS

To answer this question, as indicated in the introduction to this volume, it is necessary to shift theological focus from Jesus' two natures considered in themselves to the distinction between nature and hypostasis. This language antedates the christological debates that rocked the churches from the fifth

1. It is in this context that the importance of understanding the phrase *totaliter aliter* as referring adverbially to God's "wholly otherwise" *mode* of existence and not to some "Wholly Other" *content* of the divine being is especially clear. A "Wholly Other" God could only stand over against the world and would thus be commensurable with creatures (as one entity among others), but precisely not compatible with them—exactly the converse of the Creator God's relationship to the world. See p. 25 above.

2. One might imagine that God could be omnipresently "visible" as, say, a mist surrounding and pervading the whole of creation, along the lines of Augustine's famous image (in *Confessions* 7.5) of the sea containing and permeating a sponge; but that would not really solve the problem since it would entail that God could be quantified, with different creatures containing different "parts" of God, and larger objects containing more of God than smaller ones.

3. For an arresting account of how the presence of God can only mean the annihilation of the creature, see Katherine Sonderegger, *The Doctrine of God*, vol. 1 of *Systematic Theology* (Minneapolis: Fortress Press, 2015), 225.

through the eighth centuries, having been forged as a specifically Christian terminological distinction in the formulation of the doctrine of the Trinity. Although the term *hypostasis* had been functionally synonymous with substance or essence (*ousia*) in Hellenistic Greek and was treated as such even at the Council of Nicaea (325), later in the fourth century the two terms began to be distinguished.[4] Crucial here was the work of the so-called Cappadocian theologians (Basil of Caesarea, Gregory of Nazianzus, and Gregory of Nyssa), who in their formulation of Trinitarian doctrine taught that God, though one and undivided in substance, nevertheless subsisted as three co-eternal, equally divine hypostases: the Father, the Son, and the Holy Spirit. The basis of this distinction was anchored in a revised definition of hypostasis as "mode of subsistence" (*tropos hyparxeōs*), thanks to which the Cappadocians could distinguish hypostasis from substance or nature as answering the question of *how* rather than *what* an entity is. So the doctrine of the Trinity teaches that God *is* one, but is so *as* the eternal communion of Father, Son, and Spirit.

The relationship between the one *ousia* and the three hypostases outlined by the Cappadocians precludes any relative priority: unity is not an achievement of the three (tritheism), nor is the threefold hypostatization a subsequent modification of the unity (modalism). No compromise or qualification of monotheism was intended: the so-called Nicene Creed that emerged in the wake of the Cappadocians' work as the consensus statement of the new Trinitarian orthodoxy began with the ringing affirmation of belief in "one God," and the classical Trinitarian principle that the works of God in the world are undivided shored up the claim that God is a single subject, and that Christians have, correspondingly, only a single object of worship.[5] And it is precisely as the one God whose nature is incommensurable with any finite reality and transcends all categories that the divine presence in creation is hidden and God rightly confessed as invisible: the One "whom no one has ever seen or can see" (1 Tim. 6:16).

As noted above, however, the divine presence is not hidden within the Godhead; rather, the life of the Trinity is just the mutual presence of the Father, Son, and Spirit to one another, as constituted through the relationships of

---

4. In defending the consubstantiality of the Father and the Son, Nicaea anathematized anyone who declared that the Son is "of a different hypostasis or *ousia*" from the Father. DH §126.

5. The doctrine of the Trinitarian appropriations, according to which particular economic actions are associated specifically with one of the divine persons, does not compromise this principle, since its aim is not to weaken the confession that all three persons are equally and indivisibly active in all God's works, but only to affirm that each is active in a distinctive way that reflects its eternal mode of subsisting within the divine life. So in the creeds, for example, creation is "appropriated" to the Father, not as the unique action of the first person (a claim that would contradict John 1:3; Col. 1:16; and Heb. 1:2), but as reflecting the Father's status as the font or source (*aitia*) of divinity within the Godhead.

giving and receiving named by the technical terms "begetting" and "spirating."[6]
At one level this point may seem trivial—it would make no sense to say that
God is hidden from God—but the structure of divine presence is significant.
Presence is, after all, a relational term. It would make no sense to affirm that
presence is an intrinsic or eternal attribute of a God who is not hypostatically
differentiated.[7] Presence is intrinsic to divinity insofar as the divine life is that
of the three hypostases, which may (to use the language of Thomas Aquinas)
be characterized as "subsistent relations," that is, relations that are not accidental but intrinsic to the divine *ousia*.[8] In this way (and as argued in chap. 1
above), divine presence within the Trinity is hypostatic: God is eternally present quite apart from the creation of the world because as the Father, Son, and
Holy Spirit are present to one another.

Moreover, as the Creator who brings all things into being from nothing
and sustains them in being, God is present *in* the world quite apart from the
incarnation, but God becomes fully and definitively present *to* the world as
one with whom creatures can engage so as to be perceived, known, and loved
by them only as the Word becomes flesh. And yet according to a Chalcedonian Christology the incarnation does not entail any change in the divine
nature; because God does not become other than God in taking flesh, divinity
remains as invisible and unknowable as ever. The Word may have been "from
the beginning," but the flesh taken by the Word may be "heard, . . . looked at
and touched" (1 John 1:1) only because it is created stuff and so not divine at
all. And because the divine nature remains invisible and inaccessible even in
the incarnation, the divine may only be experienced as present to the world
hypostatically, in the person of the Son, sent into the world by the Father in
the power of the Spirit to live a human life. In taking flesh and thereby join-
ing the life of the Creator to that of the creature, the Son both demonstrates
and effects God's will that the infinitely generous love by which God lives in
God's self should be opened also to creatures.

The incarnation, no less than creation, is a work of grace. Nothing com-
pels God to take flesh. Yet in the same way that the divine sharing of being

6. Western theology has traditionally recognized four relations within the Trinity: paternity
(of the Father to the Son), filiation (of the Son to the Father), active spiration (of the Father and
the Son to the Spirit), and passive spiration (of the Spirit to the Father and the Son). These designations are less valuable for the specific terminology employed (which is, truthfully, not very
illuminating) than for securing the principle that the relations among the persons are mutual
and reciprocal, so that no person is "passive" in the sense of being the inactive or inert "object"
of another person; rather, all are in their relations "active," whether in the mode of donation or
reception.

7. This is not to say that non-Trinitarian (e.g., Jewish or Muslim) monotheism is ontologically incoherent, but only that the category of presence could not play the same role in such
accounts of God as it does where God is confessed as Trinity.

8. Thomas Aquinas, *ST* 1.29.4 (cf. 1.28.2).

in creation reflects the eternal and infinite sharing of being within the Trinity, it is a mark of the essential consistency between God's works *ad extra* and God's being *ad intra* that the hypostatic mode of God's presence to the world in Jesus also reflects the hypostatic structure of God's presence to God's self in eternity. In creation, God through the Word determines that the gift of being should not be reserved to God alone, and in taking flesh God, again through the Word, determines that this gift should be enhanced so as to allow creatures to share in God's very own life by participating in the loving presence of the divine persons to one another. In short, the incarnation shows that God intends not simply that other entities should exist, but that they should exist *in God*. This does not make incarnation the continuation or completion of creation: there is nothing incomplete or defective in created being as such that demands for it to be supplemented by the incarnation.[9] That God should not only bring creatures into being but also be present to and for them is grace upon grace; but what sense does it make to say that God, though remaining utterly invisible with respect to the divine nature, has become present in this way?

This question is all the more pressing in light of the fact that the Christian God is not unknown prior to the incarnation. The New Testament affirms clearly that God spoke "in many and various ways" (Heb. 1:1) to people long before Jesus came on the scene, and the fact that the canonical evangelists themselves so frequently justify their claims about Jesus by reference to these previous acts of divine speech means that God's presence to creatures cannot be dated only from the first Christmas.[10] After all, it is hard to conceive of a God who "used to speak to Moses face to face, as one speaks to a friend" (Exod. 33:11), in other than personal terms. And, as Thomas points out, because in God essence and existence are one and the same, it is coherent to speak of "God" as a personal agent even apart from reference to Father, Son, or Spirit.[11] But this God is still not an entity in the world: when "the

9. Given the fall, of course, it is very much the case that the incarnation also reverses the declension of created being back to the nothingness from which it came by reestablishing it on a renewed basis: no longer secured merely extrinsically by God's gift of finite being, the existence of creatures is now sustained by God from within, anchored in God's own life, rendered through the flesh of Christ inseparable from the creature's life (see the discussion in Kathryn Tanner, *Jesus, Humanity and the Trinity* [Edinburgh: T&T Clark, 2001]). But this mission of repair is necessitated only by the perversity of creatures themselves and is not consequent upon any defect in created existence as such.

10. Matthew is particularly fond of noting that events in the life of Jesus "fulfill" the words of the prophets (1:22; 2:15, 17, 23; 4:14; 8:17; 12:17; 13:14, 35; 21:4; 26:54, 56; 27:9), but similar language is used by the other evangelists as well (see Mark 14:49; Luke 4:21; John 12:38; 19:28, 36; cf. Acts 1:16; 3:18).

11. Thomas argues that affirming a real distinction between nature and hypostasis in the case of the Trinity is problematic, for since by definition "everything that is not the divine nature is a creature," and since Christians do not view the divine hypostases as creatures, it follows that the relations that constitute hypostases are the same thing (*idem*) as the divine nature (*ST*

Lᴏʀᴅ spoke to you out of the fire," the Israelites are reminded, "you heard the sound of words but saw no form; there was only a voice" (Deut. 4:12), and even Moses was not able to see God's face (Exod. 33:19–20).[12] Apart from the incarnation, God may appear, but precisely not as a concrete object that can be seen and handled, in line with the contrast drawn in Hebrews between revelation as "a blazing fire, and darkness, and gloom, and a tempest, and the sound of a trumpet, and a voice whose words made the hearers beg that not another word be spoken to them," and as "Jesus, the mediator of a new covenant" (Heb. 12:18–19, 24). The same God is involved in both cases, but the mode of revelation is quite different. God's appearances in the pyrotechnics on Sinai or, earlier, in the burning bush are not incarnational, because although in these and other Old Testament theophanies God makes God's self known through created forms, God is not to be identified with those forms: the burning bush is not God. By contrast, Christians confess that Jesus *is* God: not just a medium through which God communicates, but one whose every phenomenal feature may be predicated directly of God (e.g., God's hands, God's hair, God's hunger, etc.). In the language of mature Chalcedonian theology, the confession that Jesus' *hypostasis* is that of the second person of the Trinity means that he is rightly named as God, even though the only *nature* that we can or do perceive is fully and exclusively human.

Yet it took some time for this way of distinguishing between nature and hypostasis to develop. For all the ingenuity displayed by the Cappadocians when they deployed these terms to formulate the doctrine of the Trinity, they tended to conceive nature and hypostasis as corresponding to "universal" and "particular," respectively.[13] In the early fifth century, however, hypostasis began to shift from the sense of concrete particular to personal

---

1.28.2; cf. *ST* 3.3.3.1). His point is not that the distinction of persons in the Godhead is in any way illusory (see *ST* 1.28.3), but only to remind us that the word "person," like all words, "is not used in exactly the same sense of God as of creatures" (*ST* 1.29.3). And so it is coherent to speak of "God" as personal apart from explicit reference to the three hypostases, whereas it makes no sense to speak of "humanity" as personal apart from reference to a particular human being or set of human beings.

12. Cf. the stunning periphrasis of Ezek. 1, where after an elaborate description of the human form that appears above the fiery chariot by the river Chebar, the prophet claims not to have seen God, but only "the appearance of the likeness of the glory of the Lᴏʀᴅ" (v. 28). This restraint notwithstanding, later rabbinic tradition forbade the reading of "the chapter about the Chariot" in the synagogue (Megilloth 4.10; cited in Francis Watson, *Text and Truth: Redefining Biblical Theology* [Edinburgh: T&T Clark, 1997], 289).

13. See, e.g., Basil of Caesarea, Epistle 214, in *NPNF*[2] 8:254. At the same time, Gregory of Nazianzus gestures toward the idea if not the terminology of the later christological distinction between nature and hypostasis in his letter *To Cledonius against Apollinaris*, where he contrasts the ontology of the Trinity as three "he's" and one "it" with that of Christ, where there are two "it's" (which Gregory identifies as "natures") but only one "he" (in *Christology of the Later Fathers*, ed. Edward R. Hardy [Philadelphia: Westminster Press, 1954], 217).

identity, following the lead of Cyril of Alexandria, who used the language of "union according to hypostasis" to affirm Jesus' status as a single subject.[14] But although this Cyrilline usage is arguably reflected in Chalcedon's claim that in Christ "each of the two natures . . . came together in . . . one hypostasis," the meaning of those words remained far from clear at the time they were penned.[15] Only in subsequent decades did a consensus emerge among Chalcedonian theologians that speaking of the incarnation in this way means that "hypostasis" is not to be interpreted substantially as referring to some-*thing* (whether universal or particular) in Jesus, but rather as identifying the some*one* Jesus is—namely, the second person of the Trinity.[16] In other words, according to what came to be known as the doctrine of the hypostatic union, the "one hypostasis" was not to be understood as a product of the two natures coming together, but rather as the agent and locus of that union.[17] This agent is identical with the eternal Word, who, having from all eternity lived a divine life with the Father and the Holy Spirit, in these last days has assumed a human nature, too, and so now lives a human life as well.[18] It is on this basis that (as argued in the introduction) Chalcedonian Christology entails the confession that *what* is seen in Jesus is simply and exhaustively created human flesh and blood, even though the one *whom* is seen is no less than the eternal Word, the second person of the Trinity.

This understanding of the incarnation suggests a parallel between our experience of Jesus and our experience of any other human being: *what* we perceive

---

14. Of course, Cyril also could use the term "nature" in this way, as seen in his appropriation of the slogan "one incarnate nature of the Word" (see, e.g., Cyril, *Epistle* 45.6). But his talk of one hypostasis was both more frequent and more momentous, if Aloys Grillmeier is right to interpret Nestorius's insistence that Christ possessed two hypostases as reflecting his fidelity to the Cappadocian understanding of hypostasis as the instantiation of a nature. From this "Cappadocian" perspective, denying that Christ had a human hypostasis would mean denying the concrete particularity—and thus the reality—of his humanity. See Aloys Grillmeier, SJ, *Christ in Christian Tradition*, trans. John Bowden (Louisville, KY: Westminster John Knox Press, 1995), 1:457–63.

15. DH §302.

16. See p. 7 above. The ontological ambiguity of the "one hypostasis" in the Chalcedonian definition is also perceptible in the Council's rehabilitation of Theodoret of Cyrrhus and Ibas of Edessa, both of whom had objected to Cyril's attribution of suffering to the divine Word. It is thus no accident that in 553, when the Second Council of Constantinople sought to close the question by anathematizing anyone denying that the Word "has only one hypostasis who is our Lord Jesus Christ, one of the Holy Trinity" (DH §424), it also condemned the anti-Cyrilline writings of Theodoret and Ibas.

17. In other words, "the one Hypostasis of Christ does not originate from a union of natures taken by themselves, but from the will of the Word's preexistent Hypostasis." Dumitru Staniloae, *The Person of Jesus Christ as God and Savior*, vol. 3 of *The Experience of God: Orthodox Dogmatic Theology*, ed. and trans. Ioan Ionita (Brookline, MA: Holy Cross Orthodox Press, 2011), 34.

18. *"The person is a unique 'who'* that exists and knows himself as the subject of a nature or of a complex set of qualities out of which he can bring forth acts that are always new, and in which he supports and receives the acts of other personal and impersonal factors." Staniloae, *Person of Jesus Christ*, 27.

is physical substance—some*thing*—that can be subjected to the same forms of measurement and analysis as any other chunk of matter; and yet in perceiving this particular configuration of substance, we see a person—some*one*.[19] This quotidian experience of knowing human persons helps to make sense of the claim that when we look at or listen to Jesus, the one *whom* we see and hear is no one other than God, although at no point can *what* we see or hear be identified with the divine nature, which remains utterly transcendent and thus incapable of creaturely perception. Thus, although God has, as Creator, always been fully present in creation, only in the incarnation is this *seen* to be so: not because the divine *nature* becomes visible in Jesus, but because the *hypostasis* of the Word assumes (and so can be known in) a nature that *can* be seen.

"BECAME TRULY HUMAN"

The Nicene Creed declares that through the incarnation the one, eternal Son of God "became truly human." In order to rule out the interpretation of this creedal claim as meaning that divinity is changed or transformed into humanity, Chalcedonian Christology understands "became truly human" to mean that the divine hypostasis of the Son or Word, without ceasing to be divine, assumed a human nature as Jesus of Nazareth, such that it is true to say that whatever Jesus does, God does. In other words, the confession that Jesus' hypostasis is that of the Word means that the designations "Jesus," "Christ," "son of Mary," "God," "Son of God," "Word," and so forth are fully convertible: any one of these designations can always be substituted for any other without changing the referent or the truth value of the statement in which it is found. For example, if it is true that Jesus is born of Mary, it is also true that the Son of God is born of Mary (so that, following the decision of the fourth-century Council of Ephesus, Mary is rightly confessed as Mother of God, or *Theotokos*). Likewise, if it is true that Christ died on the cross, it is true that God died on the cross. If it is true that the Word is eternal, infinite, and immense, so is Jesus; and if Jesus hungers (Matt. 21:18), weeps (John 11:35), or is in anguish (Luke 22:44), then it follows that those same actions both may and must be predicated of the Word as well.

---

19. Thomas Aquinas (citing Augustine) draws an analogy between this kind of seeing to explain how we will be able to *see* God's *invisible* essence in heaven: "Our glorified eyes will see God as now they see the life of another. For life is not seen by bodily eyesight as though it were visible in itself as a proper object of sight; it is an indirect sense-object, not itself perceived by sense, yet straightaway [*statim*] known in sensation by some other cognitive power" (*ST* 1.12.3.2). Importantly, this "other cognitive power" is not deduction or inference: in the text on which Thomas draws for this analogy, Augustine specifically differentiates this future knowledge of God from that we now derive deductively from our experience of the physical world.

This semantic rule is a crucial implication of the hypostatic union: because in Jesus both divine and human natures are united in one hypostasis, any of the properties (*idiomata* in Greek) of either nature are rightly predicated of the single hypostatic "someone" that Jesus is. So, because it is "proper" to a human nature to hunger, thirst, grow tired, and so forth, those properties are rightly ascribed to the enfleshed Word, even as that same Word, as one of the Trinity, also continues to possess those perfections of eternity, infinity, immensity, and the like that are proper to the divine nature. Known as the *communicatio idiomatum*, or communication of attributes, this rule does not mean that in Jesus the divine *nature* wept or died, or that Christ's *humanity* were eternal or invisible, as that would violate the Chalcedonian principle that "the distinction between the natures was never abolished by their union but rather the character proper to each of the two natures was preserved as they came together."[20] In order to avoid the implication that the properties of the two natures are changed or confused by the incarnation (as though, again, one were transformed into the other), the predications associated with the communication of attributes can be given more precise form, specifying (e.g.) that the Word died *according to* (or *in*) *his human nature*, or that the one born of Mary is eternal *according to* (or *in*) *his divine nature*.[21] In summary, to confess with Chalcedon that the Son of God, in becoming truly human, remained truly God, means to affirm that Jesus is a single someone, identical with the eternal Word, who lived simultaneously a fully divine and a fully human life, each with all of its inherent and inalienable attributes.

Presupposing this conceptual framework, the Second Council of Nicaea confessed "one and the same Christ as both invisible and visible Lord, incomprehensible and comprehensible, unlimited and limited, incapable and capable of suffering, inexpressible and expressible in writing."[22] The Chalcedonian distinction between nature and hypostasis serves to answer the charge that such language is incoherent by arguing that the ontology of Jesus provides a degree of latitude with respect to the question of whether these predicates are being applied to the "same thing." For while they *are* being applied to the same person (viz., Jesus of Nazareth), because this particular person has (or "hypostatizes") two distinct natures, each with its own characteristic properties, they are *not* being applied to the same nature. In short, seemingly

20. DH §302; cf. the seventh anathema of the Second Council of Constantinople, DH §428.

21. "For the sake of greater clarity, and in order to avoid insidious ambiguities and errors, we must commonly add to these propositions [expressing the communication of attributes] certain distinguishing expressions, for the Scripture itself does so also [e.g., Rom. 9:5; 1 Pet. 4:1]." Martin Chemnitz, *The Two Natures of Christ*, trans. J. A. O. Preus (St. Louis: Concordia Publishing House, 1971 [1578]), 197.

22. Norman P. Tanner, *Decrees of the Ecumenical Councils*, 2 vols. (Washington, DC: Georgetown University Press, 1990), 1:162.

incompatible predicates are not so when predicated of a subject who has more than one nature.[23] There is therefore no basis for the worry that the Word's assuming a human nature, with its characteristically nondivine properties of visibility, passibility, and so forth, might entail any loss or diminishment of the divine perfections that are intrinsic to the persons of the Trinity.

This way of understanding the distinction between Jesus' two natures is crucial for avoiding the idea that the incarnation entails the claim that the divine nature is more present in Jesus than anywhere else in the created realm. Because a God who creates from nothing sustains every creature in existence in every aspect of its existence at every moment of its existence, God is always already maximally present everywhere in creation, since in God's absence nothing created could exist at all.[24] Although God's transcendence means that the divine presence in creation is hidden, its all-pervasiveness means that it makes no sense to conceive of the incarnation in terms of its quantitative augmentation in Jesus. The difference between God's presence in Jesus and God's presence in every other creature must therefore be qualitative: God is not any more present in Jesus than anywhere else in the world, but God is present in him in a distinctly different way.

One way to conceive of this difference is by drawing an analogy between God's relationship to the world and an author's relationship to her novel. Even as God is the immediate ground of every created thing and event, so a writer determines every feature within the "world" of her novel, from the minutest details of the setting to the thoughts and actions of each and every character.[25] And just as God, as Creator, is already fully present in every creature and therefore cannot be any more present in Jesus than anywhere else, so too, the author of a novel cannot be any more the source of one character's features and actions than any other's. Instead, what distinguishes Jesus is that God claims his life and actions as God's own. Thus, while God as Creator is the immediate cause of all created events, only in the case of Jesus is it true

23. I understand this position to be consistent with the approach to the problem of christological predication offered by Timothy Pawl, although Pawl does not assign the nature-hypostasis distinction the same place in his analysis that I do. See Timothy Pawl, *In Defense of Conciliar Christology: A Philosophical Essay* (Oxford: Oxford University Press, 2016), especially chap. 7.

24. See the discussion of Thomas on p. 36 n. 24 above. John Duns Scotus did not see creation from nothing as entailing divine presence in this way, but his rationale (that a creature, once created, enjoys some ontic autonomy with respect to its origin in the divine will) seems to depend on eliding the distinction between primary and secondary causes. See the discussion in Michael Sylwanowicz, *Contingent Causality and the Foundations of Duns Scotus' "Metaphysics"* (Leiden: Brill, 1996), 177–86.

25. The novelist or playwright analogy is often associated with the philosophical theologian Austin Farrer, but it had already been introduced on a more popular level by Dorothy Sayers. Cf. Austin M. Farrer, *A Science of God?* (London: Geoffrey Bles, 1966); and Dorothy L. Sayers, *The Mind of the Maker* (London: Methuen, 1941). See also C. S. Lewis, *Mere Christianity* (New York: HarperCollins, 2000 [1952]), 4.3.

that whatever Jesus does, God does.[26] That is what it means to claim that in Jesus, God assumes (or "hypostatizes") a human nature.[27] And here too, an analogy can be drawn with the relationship between an author and her novel, such that God's taking flesh in Jesus (incarnation) may be understood as parallel to an author who makes herself a character in her novel (call this "inscription").[28]

This analogy is particularly helpful in making sense of the Chalcedonian insistence that the divine and human natures are united in Christ "without confusion or change." To see how this is the case, note that an author, considered in her own "nature" as the creator of the fictional "world" of the novel, possesses all the traditional "absolute" or "incommunicable" divine attributes with respect to that world, being omnipotent (the sole condition of all that happens in the novel) and therefore both omniscient (knowing all that happens within that world) and omnipresent (immediately and equally present to every event related in the narrative). And yet considered in her "nature" as a character "inscribed" within the novel, the author does not possess those attributes. As a character, she is not omnipresent, since as one character among others in the story, she is at any given point in the narrative at one place rather than another. Nor is she omnipotent, since her activity as a character within the novel is framed by the same circumstances that limit other characters' actions. Thus, even if she (as author) grants herself (as character) superhuman or miraculous powers, these necessarily fall short of omnipotence, insofar as within the world of the novel the "inscribed" character's exercise of even the most extraordinary abilities is necessarily relative both to the setting and to the actions of other characters, so that in her "nature" as character (again, in contrast to her "nature" as author), she will never be the sole antecedent condition for any event in the novel. Finally, while there are (as far as I can see) no logical problems posed by the idea of an "inscribed" character's being omniscient with respect to the world of the novel, neither does there seem to be any reason to conclude from the mere fact of inscription that such a character as an infant or adolescent had the same level of knowledge she enjoys as an adult—let alone

26. "All bodies are Christ's [viz., God's], including mine and yours, but they are not his body personally, but only bodies under his lordship and power." Martin Luther, WA 41.481.6–7.

27. It may be added here that because God alone is the cause of everything that is, only God can hypostatize a created nature: "Only because of the uniqueness of the form of causality that is proper to God as creator is he alone free to 'become' human, to adopt a created nature hypostatically without being in any way alienated from what he is eternally." Thomas Joseph White, OP, *The Incarnate Lord: A Thomistic Study in Christology* (Washington, DC: Catholic University of America Press, 2015), 197.

28. Probably the clearest instance of this situation in literature is the character of Dante in the *Divine Comedy*. Of course, not all first-person narratives suggest so close an identification between author and character (e.g., in *À la recherche du temps perdu* the relationship between the first-person narrator and the author is far more ambiguous).

that she possesses the same knowledge of other characters and circumstances as she does in her "nature" as author.[29] So too, there need be no difficulty in denying that Jesus is omnipresent, omnipotent, or omniscient according to his human nature, in spite of his being confessed as hypostatically identical to the second person of the Trinity.

In this way, the analogy between incarnation and "inscription" provides a framework for distributing the various things Christians predicate of Jesus between the divine and human natures while affirming that the Word nevertheless remains the one subject of all of them. For example, just as adherence to Chalcedonian doctrine of the hypostatic union makes it necessary to confess that the Son of God was buried and that the son of Mary is the Creator, so the identity of the author and the inscribed character means that it is equally true to say that Dante fainted after hearing the tale of Paolo and Francesca and that Dante is the one who determined that Paolo and Francesca are damned. And just as Jesus lies in the tomb in his human nature only and creates according to his divine nature only, so fainting pertains to Dante's "nature" as character (since it is inconsistent with his "nature" as author to be at any point unconscious with respect to the world of the poem), and the fate of particular characters is determined by Dante in his "nature" as author (since it does not pertain to his "nature" as character to decide the eternal destiny of any other human being). The Word is the sole, unique, and undivided subject of all Jesus' actions (since Jesus just is the Word), but he is born according to his human nature only (since the divine nature does not come to be), and he remains invisible according to the divine nature only (since it belongs to the human nature to be seen). Once again, because the natures of Creator and creature are incommensurable, they are not in competition, so that in taking flesh it is neither the case that the divine perfections are foregone by the Word, nor that those perfections displace or cancel the essential characteristics of humanity; for

---

29. As noted by Kasper Bro Larsen, the Gospel of John in particular seems to ascribe, if not omniscience, at the very least a supernatural level of knowledge to Jesus (see, e.g., 1:48; 2:24–25; 4:17–19; 13:3; cf. 16:30) that creates problems for his integration in the narrative (see Kasper Bro Larsen, "Narrative Docetism: Christology and Storytelling in the Gospel of John," in *The Gospel of John and Christian Theology*, ed. Richard Bauckham and Carl Mosser (Grand Rapids: Wm. B. Eerdmans Publishing Co., 2008), 354. Against this worry, Marianne Meye Thompson has argued that any treatment of Jesus as Savior presupposes some unlikeness to other human beings. See Marianne Meye Thompson, *The Incarnate Word: Perspectives on Jesus in the Fourth Gospel* (Peabody, MA: Hendrickson, 1988). In line with my own emphasis on the integrity and thus the ordinariness of Jesus' humanity (discussed further in chap. 5 below), I would not want to stress as much as Thompson does any extraordinary (human) qualities of Jesus as definitive of his identity as Lord. At the same time, it does not seem to me that Jesus' possession of supernatural knowledge (understood as a particular charism) in itself poses any threat to his humanity or to the narrative integrity of the fourth Gospel.

"Christ was a human being, and he willingly assumed and held all things human, sin excepted."[30]

As John of Damascus pointed out many centuries ago, all analogies between created and divine realities necessarily fall short, and that between God and a human author is no exception to that rule.[31] Most obviously, in the case of the incarnation, enfleshment pertains to just one of three divine hypostases, and there is no analogous plurality of hypostases in the case of a novelist.[32] Nevertheless, the parallels are sufficiently strong to counter the charge that incarnation necessarily entails a diminishment either of Jesus' divinity or of his humanity. They may be summarized in three points, as follows:

1. In both the case of the Word's incarnation and a novelist's inscription, there is a hypostatic identity between the Creator/author and creature/character; that is, by fiat of the Creator/author (who is the sole arbiter of what is real in the world brought into being), they identify and refer to the same someone.[33]

2. Incarnation/inscription entails a change with respect to the number of "natures" hypostatized by the Creator/author; specifically, all the while continuing to hypostatize a divine/authorial nature (since the Creator/author could not cease to do so without removing the very condition of the possibility of the existence of the world within which incarnation/inscription takes place), the assumption of a created/character nature brings with it all the ontological constraints (e.g., existence relative to the created world's temporal and spatial parameters) that obtain for every other entity within the world.

30. Martin Luther, WA 9:442.20–21; cf. 15–18: "Just as the eye of Christ did not see every-thing when it was closed, but truly slept, so, too, his soul did not see everything. For the Deity, joined equally and fully both to Christ's body and to his rational human soul, did not forego ignorance of the mind any more than bodily weakness."

31. "For one must not take examples too absolutely and strictly: indeed, in examples one must consider both what is like and what is unlike. For if they were like in all respects, they would be identities and not examples, and all the more so when dealing with divine matters. For one cannot find a [creaturely] example that is like [the divine] in all respects, whether with respect to theology or the economy." John of Damascus, *On the Orthodox Faith* 3.26, in *Hilary of Poitiers, John of Damascus*, vol. 9 of *NPNF²*, trans. slightly alt.

32. This point of dissimilarity is important as a means of checking the temptation to see in the analogy an argument for the so-called *extra Calvinisticum*, since in the case of God (in contrast to the author) there are divine hypostases who do not become incarnate, so that it is possible to acknowledge that there are divine persons (viz., the Father and the Spirit) who subsist apart from the flesh after the incarnation without concluding that the person of the Word does so.

33. For this reason the example of inscription is quite different from the analogy David Brown proposes between the incarnation and the practice of the method actor. See David Brown, *Divine Humanity: Kenosis and the Construction of a Christian Theology* (Waco, TX: Baylor University Press, 2011), 250–59. The problem with the latter from a Chalcedonian perspective is that Jesus is not a preexisting character *to whom God conforms* (the equivalent of the "Nestorian" doctrine of the *homo assumptus*, in which the human being Jesus has a subsistence and identity ontologically distinct from his relationship to the Word); rather, the Word simply *is* Jesus.

3. Nevertheless, the act of incarnation/inscription does not entail that the Creator/author undergoes any diminishment, either with respect to her hypostatic identity as Creator/author, or with respect to her attributes as one who, quite apart from the act of incarnation/inscription, hypostatizes a divine/authorial nature.[34] No more than an author experiences herself as in any way limited by virtue of becoming a character in her novel is there any reason to suppose that God would experience any sort of loss in taking flesh. In neither case does incarnation/inscription modify the basic point that the world develops entirely and in every respect under the Creator/author's direction.

In all these respects the analogy provides a serviceable illustration of what it means to confess that in the incarnation the divine and human natures are united "without confusion or change" in the one hypostasis of the Word.

The analogy also has the further benefit of helping to make clear that the incarnation—God's becoming a human being—is not an event or development in the life of the Word. To think of the incarnation as though it were such a development fails to pay due regard to divine transcendence by (again) suggesting that the incarnation entails something like a movement of God from heaven to earth, as though Creator and creature existed on the same ontological plane. But this is a mistake: nothing "happens" to God in becoming a human being, any more than anything happens to an author who inscribes herself as a character in her novel.

At first glance, this claim may seem inconsistent with the biblical descriptions of the Word as the one who has "come down" (John 6:38), who is "from heaven" (John 3:13, 31; 1 Cor. 15:47), who has "emptied himself" (Phil. 2:7), and of course, who "became flesh" (John 1:14). Yet once it is accepted (again, following the principles of Chalcedonianism) that in all these cases it is the hypostasis of the eternal Word who is the subject of the actions, then what is being described can be interpreted neither as a transformation (in which God changes from one thing into another) nor as a relocation (in which God is first in one place and then moves to another). To think of the incarnation in these terms, as something that happens to the Word, treats eternity and time

---

34. There is a similarity here to traditional Lutheran understanding of the incarnation, in which the "self-emptying" of Phil. 2:7 refers to Christ's deportment in his humanity (viz., *as* incarnate) and not to the act of incarnation as such (see WA 17/2:238–45). The difference is that Lutherans have often suggested that this deportment (what one might call "dispositional kenoticism") was a matter of restraint on Jesus' part rather than a function of his specifically human vocation (see, e.g., WA 45.239.32) and thereby pushes precisely toward the kind of "ontological kenoticism" of divine self-limitation introduced by the nineteenth-century Lutheran Gottfried Thomasius in his *Christi Person und Werk: Darstellung der evangelisch-lutherischen Dogmatik vom Mittelpunkte der Christologie aus*, 5 vols. (Erlangen, 1852–1861).

as though they could be plotted along a single narrative sequence, as though the Word's taking flesh were analogous to my becoming a father or moving to Cambridge. For the Word to become incarnate is just for the Word to assume a particular human life as the Word's very own. In so doing, the Word neither ceases to be God (since the Word could not cease being God without also ceasing to be the Word) nor migrates from one place to another (since One who is omnipresent cannot move). To put the matter sharply, while it is certainly true that during the last ice age (or at any other time before Jesus' birth) the Word was not enfleshed, it would be a logical mistake to conclude that the Word then subsisted in heaven in an unenfleshed state. For no proposition that attributes temporal existence to the Word can be true prior to the Word's taking flesh.[35]

This same line of reasoning also calls into question the idea that the Word existed apart from the flesh (*Logos asarkos* in Greek) prior to the Word's having been made flesh (the *Logos ensarkos*). To the extent that the *Logos ensarkos* just *is* the eternal Word of God, there is no fully satisfactory way of talking about the state of the Word "before" the incarnation, since the very language of "before" locates heaven and earth on a single temporal sequence and thus casts the incarnation as a development in the life of the Word. But to conceive the incarnation in this way undermines the Chalcedonian claim that the Word and Jesus are fully convertible terms by reducing Jesus to the status of the Word's avatar: a temporal manifestation of a reality more fundamental, yet ultimately elusive.[36] But if it is true that the Word simply *is* Jesus, such that Jesus, and not some power in or behind him, is the object of Christian hope, then although Christians will find themselves compelled to confess that the Word, as God, is eternal, they will find themselves equally constrained to acknowledge that they cannot speak of the Word apart from the flesh, not even as the one who is to become enfleshed (*incarnandus*); rather, they will confess that adherence to the doctrine of the incarnation entails the affirmation that there is no Christianly adequate way of referring to the Word except

35. "Moses could certainly have said, 'It is true now that the Son of God exists' but he could not have said truly, 'The Son of God exists now.' That proposition, which attributes temporal existence ("now") to the Son of God, is the one that became true when Jesus was conceived in the womb of Mary." Herbert McCabe, OP, *God Matters* (New York: Continuum, 2010 [1987]), 50. Cf. Yves Congar, *The Word and the Spirit*, trans. David Smith (London: Geoffrey Chapman, 1986), 95: "It is possible to speak of the Word *without* Jesus' assumption of humanity, although it is not possible to speak of the Word *before* the incarnation."

36. The problem here is not that it is impossible for the Word to become incarnate more than once (against this claim, see Aquinas, *ST* 3.3.7), but rather a failure to grasp that in taking flesh God encounters us *as* a creature and not simply *through* a creature, so that Christian faith is not simply a matter of trusting what Jesus says (although, of course, it is certainly also that), but trusting *him* as Lord and Savior.

as the one who *has been made* flesh (*incarnatus*). For Jesus says, "Very truly, I tell you, before Abraham was, I am" (John 8:58)—and this "I" is just *the Word made flesh*.[37]

Interpretations of the incarnation in which taking flesh is understood as a development or episode in the life of the Word suffer from two difficulties. First, by locating the preexistent and the incarnate Word on a single narrative continuum, such interpretations invariably treat humanity and divinity as ontologically commensurate, as though God were capable of being conceived generically, as a particular instantiation of a nature, and thus as a kind of thing alongside other things.[38] When God is understood in these terms, then the divine and human natures cannot help but be seen as competing for space within the life of Jesus, who thereby comes to be conceived as some sort of divine-human hybrid in a manner incompatible with Chalcedon's insistence that in him the two natures are united "without confusion or change."[39] Second, interpreting the incarnation as an episode within the life of the Word implies that the Word changes in taking flesh (i.e., becomes different than it was before). But positing such a change is inconsistent with the claim that in Jesus "the whole fullness of deity dwells bodily" (Col. 2:9), since a Word who changed in becoming incarnate would not be identical with (and thus could not embody the fullness of) the Word's preexistent life. Thus, if Jesus is to be confessed as embodying "the whole fullness of deity," then the incarnation cannot be understood to involve any change in the Word. On the contrary, it can only count as revelation in the definitive and unsurpassable sense that

37. The "before" in this verse is thus best interpreted as affirming Jesus' divine identity as transcending time rather than as referring to a temporal "preexistence" apart from the flesh. For what Augustine wrote of God as such applies no less to the incarnate Word: "It is not in time that you precede times. Otherwise you would not precede all times." Augustine, *Confessions* 11.16, trans. Henry Chadwick (Oxford: Oxford University Press, 1991), 230.

38. In order to avoid this reification of divinity, Kathryn Tanner goes so far as to argue that proper attention to the implications of divine transcendence justifies the conclusion that "the only nature Christ has, strictly speaking, is a human one." Kathryn Tanner, "David Brown's *Divine Humanity*," *Scottish Journal of Theology* 68, no. 1 (2015): 112. Such language is a provocative reminder of the need to resist the ever-present temptation to view "nature" as an overarching class within which the types "human" and "divine" (along with "angelic," "bacterial," etc.) can be located; but insofar as the tradition speaks of two natures, and as a means of securing the point that divinity is not nothing, there is reason to continue to speak of a "divine nature"—so long as one remembers that "nature," like any other attribute, can only be predicated of God analogically.

39. This sort of problem can be seen, e.g., in David Brown's description of the incarnation as the "merging of two natures into a single consciousness" (*Divine Humanity*, 253), as well as in Brian Bantum's explicit characterization of the hypostatic union as a matter of "mixture" or "hybridity." See Brian Bantum, *Redeeming Mulatto: A Theology of Race and Christian Hybridity* (Waco, TX: Baylor University Press, 2010), 98. In this context, it is worth recalling that the immediate occasion for the drafting of the Chalcedonian definition was to condemn the Christology of Eutyches, who maintained that there were two natures before the incarnation, but only one afterward, thereby implying that Jesus was neither divine nor human.

Christians wish to claim for it if in taking flesh the Word remains *un*changed: subsisting in a human nature without undergoing any alteration whatsoever with respect to its divinity.[40]

In summary, the incarnation does not mean that the Word ceases to live in the Father's bosom or beyond time. It is therefore not rightly conceived as any sort of movement from above to below, in which the Word leaves heaven (however partially or temporarily) for life on earth. Incarnation is better conceived as a kind of projection of the eternal, heavenly life of the Word (who remains eternal and heavenly) in and as the temporal lifespan of Jesus of Nazareth.[41] On this understanding, the distinction between *Logos asarkos* and *Logos ensarkos* cannot be understood as referring to successive states in the life of the Word, since it is a category error to construe the relationship between God (who transcends time) and any aspect of (temporal) creation in terms of "before" and "after." Instead, incarnation is simply the life of the Word in its entirety ("the whole fullness of deity") translated into finite, "bodily" form: that is just what it means to say that the Word is revealed fully and without qualification in Jesus.[42]

Nevertheless, talk of the *Logos asarkos* should not be dismissed altogether. It is appropriate in two very specific contexts. First, it is justified as a means of identifying an ontological presupposition of the incarnation, rather than asserting that the Word subsists in an unenfleshed state before the incarnation. While the latter claim is to be avoided, the former serves as a legitimate

---

40. By virtue of taking flesh, the Word becomes open to new forms of predication (e.g., "born of the Virgin Mary," "crucified under Pontius Pilate," "buried," and so forth) that would not be applicable apart from the incarnation. But viewed from the perspective of divine ontology, these are not properly understood as changes in the Word's life, in the sense of episodes in a narrative that begins before Jesus' conception and continues after his resurrection (as would be the case if the incarnation were analogous to, e.g., a king temporarily assuming the life of a beggar and then having various adventures in that role); rather, they should be viewed as parts of a comprehensive identity description that serves to pick out the Word as *this* particular human being, defined by the full temporal span of his earthly life from birth to death.

41. The image of projection ("as on a cinema screen") comes from Herbert McCabe, "Aquinas on the Trinity," in *Silence and the Word: Negative Theology and Incarnation*, ed. Oliver Davies and Denys Turner (Cambridge: Cambridge University Press, 2004), 92.

42. Adopting this perspective provides a means of addressing the worry expressed by Bruce McCormack (among others) that affirming the Trinity as logically prior to the incarnation opens a gap between God's immanent being and God's external acts that renders the latter arbitrary and thereby introduces the specter of a *Deus absconditus* "behind" the *Deus revelatus*. Drawing a distinction between God's *being* triune eternally and God's *willing* to be God-for-us in time is necessary if we are to affirm (as McCormack grants we must) that God would be God even without us. And against the charge that positing such a distinction introduces a *Deus absconditus*, it should be sufficient to note that to claim that Jesus *is* the Word made flesh is precisely to deny any God behind (and thus potentially different from) the God revealed in Jesus, since the point of confessing that "the Word became flesh" in Jesus is to affirm that *this* is just who God is. See Bruce McCormack, *Orthodox and Modern: Studies in the Theology of Karl Barth* (Grand Rapids: Baker Academic, 2008), esp. chaps. 7–8.

shorthand means of affirming the incarnation's free and gracious character over against the idea that the Word is inherently or necessarily enfleshed.[43] It is in this sense that the biblical passages speaking of the Son or Word coming down from heaven are most profitably understood: the spatial imagery of condescension serves as a metaphorical way of communicating the contingency of the incarnation as a matter of divine grace.[44] Second, affirmation of the *Logos asarkos* has a legitimate role in preserving the Chalcedonian principle that in the hypostatic union the divine and human natures are united "without confusion or change," so that the Word is rightly confessed as *asarkos* with respect to the divine nature (which is and remains essentially incorporeal even after the incarnation) and *ensarkos* with respect to the human nature (which is and remains essentially embodied). In short, while the phrase *Logos asarkos* should not be deployed *descriptively* (i.e., as an account of the life of the Word over some particular narratable period), it may be used *regulatively* (i.e., as a means of securing certain specific dogmatic points with respect to the meaning of the incarnation).

"A NEW THEANDRIC ENERGY"

The central challenge of this chapter has been to explain how a truly transcendent God can become perceptible—and thus genuinely present—to finite creatures without thereby ceasing to be God. I have argued that the Chalcedonian distinction between nature and hypostasis provides a means of addressing this problem: in taking flesh the hypostasis of the Word can be perceived by virtue of assuming a created and visible *human* nature (Col. 1:15; Heb. 1:3; cf. 1 John 1:1), even though *God's* nature remains as transcendent (and thus as intrinsically imperceptible) as ever. Thus, although grasping *what* God is remains beyond our ken as creatures, we encounter and thereby come to know *who* God is in and through the psychosomatic particularity of Jesus in just the same way that we perceive and know anyone as the person she is in and through her concrete human nature. By teaching that the Creator is disclosed to creatures not by any sort of appearance of the divine substance, but personally, by living the life of a creature, the doctrine of the hypostatic union seemingly allows us to have our cake and eat it, too, by affirming that God remains unknowably transcendent according to the divine nature but genuinely known according to the human nature of Jesus of Nazareth.

43. See Karl Barth, *Learning Jesus Christ through the Heidelberg Catechism*, trans. Shirley C. Guthrie (Grand Rapids: Wm. B. Eerdmans Publishing Co., 1981 [1961]), 77; cited in Darren O. Sumner, "The Twofold Life of the Word: Karl Barth's Critical Reception of the *Extra Calvinisticum*," *International Journal of Systematic Theology* 15, no. 1 (January 2013): 53.
44. "Filius enim Dei est sua deitas, sed non est sua humanitas." Aquinas, *ST* 3.3.7.3.

And yet, on a little further consideration, this putative solution seems only to reinscribe the problem on a different level by so emphasizing the distinction between the categories of hypostasis and nature as to render vacuous the claim that we genuinely come to know the divine in Jesus. For on Chalcedonian terms it seems that the price of securing the principle that we truly experience and thereby come to know a divine *hypostasis* in Jesus is giving up any claim to experience the divine *nature*, which remains utterly transcendent and thus stubbornly unknowable even in the incarnation. And if that is true, then the claim that God is revealed in Jesus seems problematic, for what can it mean to speak of the revelation of God without the revelation of the divine nature? It is certainly possible to stipulate that Jesus' hypostasis is divine; but when combined with an insistence that all that actually is or can be seen in Jesus is a particular instantiation of human nature ontologically indistinguishable from that of any other human being, then it becomes difficult to see what difference the incarnation makes for our understanding of God. We may well say that by virtue of the hypostatic union, everything that Jesus does, God does; but the terms of that very same doctrine suggest equally that everything we perceive Jesus doing is done by him in his human nature, since that is the condition of our being able to perceive it at all.[45] And it thereby becomes hard to see how our knowledge of Jesus enables us to say anything substantively about the nature of *God*. In short, hewing to a "Chalcedonianism without reserve" seems to create a situation where maintaining a proper distinction between the two natures (in line with the principle that they are combined "without confusion or change") effectively decouples them from each other (thereby violating the parallel claim that they are combined "without division or separation").

In short, although the confession that Jesus is God (i.e., that his hypostasis is divine) remains in force, insofar as the strictly Chalcedonian terms on which the confession is made mean that the nature of this God is no less invisible after the incarnation than before, then we seem to be in the odd situation of having to conclude that Jesus, though none other than God, contributes nothing to our knowledge of God's attributes, properties, or characteristics, since these all pertain precisely to the divine nature that "no one has ever seen or can see." Of course, it has never been the contention of Christians that

---

45. It remains true, of course, that it is possible to affirm of Jesus, as of any other creature, that God, as Creator, is the primary cause of all his actions, but we do not perceive God so acting in Jesus any more than we do in any other creature, for (following the creeds) the work of creation is a matter of faith, not sight. Alternatively, that Jesus performs miracles is, as noted in the introduction (above), not to be understood as a manifestation of his personal divinity, but rather of the divine power of the Holy Spirit operative in his human nature in the same way as in any other human being who performs miracles; cf. note 53 below.

Jesus is the sole source of knowledge of divinity, since the revelation of God in Jesus is inseparable from the preceding history of God's dealings with Israel as recorded in the Old Testament, which gives clear testimony to God's being faithful, merciful, present, powerful, righteous, and so on long before the first Christmas. But if, in Jesus, God is revealed not simply through created means (burning bushes, night visions, heavenly voices, and the like) but *as* a creature, then Jesus has a unique status, such that all descriptions of the divine nature, from wherever they may have been derived, must be assessed and interpreted by reference to his life and work. But how can this be done if the human form of that life, precisely because it is created, renders it as opaque to divinity as that of any other creature?

As a first step to addressing this dilemma, it is useful to note once again that the hypostasis is not some sort of third thing that links the natures by standing above, behind, or between them. Indeed, the hypostasis is not any kind of "thing" at all apart from the natures, but just the particular one who subsists in and as the natures, so that, in the words of John of Damascus, "the two natures are one Christ, and the one Christ is two natures."[46] Thus, if the Word assumes a human nature as one who from eternity subsists in the divine nature, whatever communion exists between the divine person and the human nature must include the divine nature as well. In other words, because a hypostasis may be named divine only as it shares in the one divine essence, it is impossible to confess that Jesus is *hypostatically* divine without also confessing that he—the human son of Mary—is also divine *essentially*.[47] This is not to say that the assumed human *nature* is or becomes divine, but it is to insist that if it is indeed true that in Jesus "the whole fullness of deity dwells bodily," then there is no human *activity* of Jesus that is not also divine.[48]

---

46. John of Damascus, *On the Orthodox Faith* 3.19. The Damascene is here drawing on Maximus the Confessor's characterization of the two natures "from which, in which, *and which* Christ is." See, e.g., his *OTP* 1 (PG 91:36C), 6 (PG 91:68A), and 19 (PG 91:224A); *Ambigua* 5 (PG 91:1052D) and 27 (PG 981:1269C); and *Epistles* 12 (PG 91:488C) and 15 (PG 91:573A). For a discussion of the derivation and significance of the three clauses, see Dmitri Bathrellos, *The Byzantine Christ: Person, Nature, and Will in the Christology of Saint Maximus the Confessor* (Oxford: Oxford University Press, 2005), 108–11.

47. "If the hypostasis of the λόγος has been truly and really imparted to the assumed flesh, undoubtedly there is a true and real presence between the divine and human nature, since the hypostasis of the λόγος and the divine nature of the λόγος do not really differ." J. A. Quenstedt, *Theologia didactico-polemica* (Wittenberg: Apud Johannem Ludolphum Quenstedt & Elerdi Schumacheri, 1685), 3.87; cited in Heinrich Schmid, *The Doctrinal Theology of the Evangelical Lutheran Church*, 3rd ed. (Minneapolis: Augsburg, 1961), 316; cf. 314: "For, by the personal union, not only the person, but, since person and nature cannot be separated, the divine nature also has entered into communion with the human nature."

48. Is the converse also the case, so that there is no divine activity of the Word that is not also human? This is the central point at issue in the *extra Calvinisticum* debate. The question permits of no easy resolution, since in addressing it we arguably run up against the limits of language's ability to apply predicates across the Creator-creature divide. But if, argued earlier, the idea of

In order to make proper sense of this claim, it is necessary to be clear about the meaning of the term "activity." My use of the term in a christological context derives from Eastern Orthodox theology, where the category of "activity" or "energy" (from *energeia*, the Greek word for activity) is closely related to nature and yet distinct from it. Specifically, energy refers to a given nature's characteristic modes of operation, such that while an entity's energy is not the same as its nature, energy corresponds to nature, such that a being's energies are, so to speak, symptoms of its nature.[49] Since any entity operates in particular ways that are characteristic of its nature (from photosynthesizing in the case of green plants, to singing in the case of whales, to moving at a velocity that is identical for all observers in the case of a photon), it is a feature of any nature to have its own distinct energy. Thus (and to bring us back to Christology), insofar as Christ has two natures, it follows that Christ also has two distinct energies, or modes of activity—a principle of mature Chalcedonian Christology enshrined in the acts of the Third Council of Constantinople in 680–681.[50]

At this point it may seem that the concept of energy is not likely to be very productive in explaining how Christ's human activity can disclose the divine, for if energies correspond to natures, then it would seem to follow that here, too, what Christ does according to one nature will have no bearing on our knowledge or experience of the other. Yet in the Orthodox understanding of energies, there is a further qualification to be made that blocks this inference, for while creatures cannot share in the divine *nature* (since if they were to do so, they would, by definition, become divine), they can participate in the divine *energies* without ceasing to be creatures.[51] Here the metaphor of energies as

---

an unenfleshed *Logos* "before" the incarnation is to be rejected, it is hard to see the grounds on which it could be defended afterward. For while it remains appropriate to speak of a *Logos asarkos* as a means of affirming that the incarnation does not alter the essential properties of the divine nature, the claim that Jesus, the Word made flesh, remains immaterial and incorporeal according to his divine nature cannot be allowed to entail the claim that the presence and activity of the eternal Word are at any point distinct from the presence and activity of Mary's son. To do so would mean to have failed to honor the principle that Jesus just *is* the Word, as opposed to a form or manifestation of the Word.

49. Maximus the Confessor defines *energeia* as a nature's "constitutive power" (*systatikē dynamis*) in *Ambigua* 5; see his *On Difficulties in the Church Fathers: The Ambigua*, 2 vols., ed. and trans. Nicholas Constas (Cambridge, MA: Harvard University Press, 2014), 1:33.

50. See DH §556: "We likewise proclaim in [Christ], according to the teaching of the holy Fathers, two natural volitions or wills and two natural actions [*physikas energeias*], without division, without change, without separation, without confusion."

51. "The doctrine of grace for Gregory Palamas (as for all of Orthodox theology) . . . is founded on the distinction of nature and energies in God: 'Illumination or divine and deifying grace is not essence, but the energy of God,' he says. . . acting in man, changing his nature, entering into a more and more intimate union with him, the divine energies become increasingly perceptible, revealing to man the face of the living God." Vladimir Lossky, *In the Image and Likeness of God*, ed. John H. Erickson and Thomas E. Bird (Crestwood, NY: St. Vladimir's Seminary Press, 1985), 59, citing Gregory Palamas, *Capitula physica, theologica, moralia, et practica* 69 (PG 150:1169).

symptoms of a nature comes into its own, for just as one may exhibit the symptoms of a disease without having it, so it is possible that a creature might by grace be enabled to act in a divine manner without becoming divine. In other words, participation in the divine energies does not entail any confusion of human and divine: human beings remain human, acting according to their own proper natures (viz., as embodied souls moved by a fallible will); but by grace humans may participate in the divine energies, with the result that their activity may take forms that are symptomatic of divine nature.[52] The most arresting example of such participation is miracles—acts performed by, in, and through human bodies that exceed normal human abilities—but other examples include living unselfishly, bearing witness to the gospel in the face of persecution, or forgiving others' offenses.[53] In such cases, human beings may be said to perform human acts (that is, acts performed by a human body with a human soul set into motion by the operation of human will and intellect) divinely, thereby participating in the divine energies.[54]

Human beings are able to act in this way through the gift of the Holy Spirit. This is especially clear in the case of Jesus, for whom the entirety of

52. Maximus the Confessor makes much of this in *Ambigua* 42 (PG 91:1316A–1348D); see especially 1341D, where he distinguishes the principle (*logos*) by which human nature operates as body and soul from its mode (*tropos*) of operation, understood as "the order [*taxis*] whereby it naturally acts and is acted upon, frequently alternating and changing, without however in any way changing nature along with it." Maximus, *On Difficulties in the Church Fathers* 2.173; cf. *Ambigua* 5 (PG 91:1049D), where Maximus clarifies that whatever the incarnate Word does, however miraculous, he does as a soul properly and naturally moving the body (*autourgikōs psychēs dikēn physikōs to symphyes sōma kinousēs*).

53. It may seem that this line of argument is equivalent to Leo I's vision of divinity shining forth via miracles in his *Tome to Flavian* criticized in the introduction (above). But while Leo argues that miracles reveal Christ's divinity, the present point is that miracles provide a basis for characterizing God, on the prior assumption that Jesus is (hypostatically) divine. That is, my reference to miracles here, unlike that in Leo's *Tome*, has no apologetic force in establishing Jesus' divinity, but is limited to helping shape Christian characterizations of God once Jesus' divinity has been accepted on other grounds. In this context, it may be helpful to contrast two analogies (both used in classical Lutheran theology) to illustrate God's actions in Christ. The first is that of the heated iron: just as the sword placed in flames assumes the properties of the fire—e.g., glowing, burning—without ceasing to be iron, so Christ's human nature takes on the properties of the divine nature without ceasing to be human. This analogy arguably does succumb to the problematic implications of Leo's *Tome* because it suggests that the divine nature (viz., the glowing fire) is not simply visible, but is so visible as to mask the human nature (viz., the blackness of the iron). By contrast, the second analogy, that of the soul in the body, has the advantage of maintaining the hiddenness of the divine, for though the soul's activities (seeing, speaking, etc.) are clearly perceived through the body, the soul itself remains invisible: all that is seen are the bodily members in motion. Cf. Chemnitz, *Two Natures of Christ*, 289–91 and 296–97.

54. "The mind of Christ which the saints receive . . . [1 Cor. 2:16] comes along not by any loss of our mental power, nor as a supplementary mind to ours, nor as essentially and personally passing over into our mind, but rather as illuminating the power of our mind with its own quality [*poiotēti*] and bringing the same energy [*energeian*] to it." Maximus the Confessor, *Chapters on Knowledge* 2.83 (PG 90:1163B), in *Selected Writings*, trans. G. C. Berthold (New York: Paulist Press, 1985).

his earthly career from his conception (Matt. 1:18; Luke 1:35) to his baptism (Matt. 3:16 and pars.), to his sojourn in the wilderness (Matt. 4:1 and pars.), to his teaching (Luke 4:14–18; 10:21) and miracles (Matt. 12:28; cf. Acts 10:38), to his death (Heb. 9:14) and resurrection (Rom. 1:4; 1 Tim. 3:16; 1 Pet. 3:18) is ascribed to the work of the Spirit. He promises the disciples this same Spirit (John 14:26; 16:13; cf. Luke 24:49; John 7:39; Acts 1:8), which he ultimately bestows upon them (John 20:22; cf. Acts 2:4); and it is to this Spirit that the gifts that manifest God's presence and power in the church are attributed (1 Cor. 12:4–13; Gal. 5:22; cf. Rom. 15:19; 1 Cor. 2:4). Thus, although the divine nature remains invisible in the incarnation, its characteristics nevertheless become visible in Jesus' humanity through the Spirit's power: "The Son shows his person and hides his nature. The Spirit hides his person and shows the divine nature by pointing to the Son."[55]

In Orthodox theology this process of Spirit-enabled activity is understood to culminate in the state of deification (*theoōsis* in Greek), where human life is so uninterruptedly receptive to the Spirit's grace as to participate in the divine energies continually.[56] Although in Orthodox thought the divine light that is the visible expression of these energies is perceptible even now (as it was to the disciples on the Mount of Transfiguration), prior to the eschaton human beings do not participate in the divine energies continually, raising the question of how one knows which of their acts should actually be counted as the product of such participation—especially given deep-seated Christian convictions regarding the pervasive character of sin in human life (see 1 John 1:8). Even miracles (i.e., manifestations of supernatural power) cannot by themselves be taken as a trustworthy criterion of God's presence, for the Bible is quite clear that "signs and wonders" can be performed under demonic no less than divine influence (see, e.g., 2 Thess. 2:9; Rev. 13:13–14; 16:14). Only if some concrete individual were understood to enjoy full and uninterrupted participation in the divine energies characteristic of deified existence would there be a reliable criterion of assessment, since every act performed by such a person would conform to—and thus be a reliable guide to the content of—the

---

55. Vladimir Lossky, *Dogmatic Theology: Creation, God's Image in Man, and the Redeeming Work of the Trinity*, ed. Olivier Clément and Michel Stavrou, trans. Anthony P. Gythiel (Yonkers, NY: St. Vladimir's Seminary Press, 2017), 62; cf. Lossky, *In the Image and Likeness of God*, 65: "If the visible has become invisible (by the Ascension), this has happened in order that the invisible—the fire of uncreated grace—might become visible in us."

56. It should be noted that although this characterization of the Orthodox theology of deification reflects the highly influential neo-Palamite synthesis promoted by theologians like Vladimir Lossky, John Meyendorff, and Dumitru Staniloae, it is not shared by all modern Orthodox thinkers. For a discussion of the differences between Lossky and John Zizioulas in particular, see Aristotle Papanikolaou, *Being with God: Trinity, Apophaticism, and Divine-Human Communion* (Notre Dame, IN: University of Notre Dame Press, 2006).

modes of activity characteristic of the divine life. And because it is a matter of Christian conviction that Jesus has the unimpeded openness to grace characteristic of deification from birth, all his human activities, including his healing of the sick and forgiving of sins, but also his practices of table fellowship and laying down his life, serve as a touchstone for Christian talk about the divine nature: they are all human acts, since they are performed by a human body activated by a human soul, but they are performed in a divine mode.[57] On this basis, the problem of Jesus' capacity to reveal the divine nature can be addressed by following Dionysius the Areopagite and affirming the presence in Christ of a "new theandric [i.e., divine-human] energy," such that while in Jesus the divine and human energies (like all the properties of his two natures) remain distinct, the hypostatic union dictates that in the case of Jesus—and Jesus alone—the human mirrors the divine, so that in each of his acts Jesus does human things divinely and divine things humanly.[58]

Of course, Christians do not claim that Jesus is completely deified during the course of his earthly ministry. Insofar as Jesus hungers, thirsts, tires, bleeds, and exhibits other typical features of human life in this world, it is clear that his body does not enjoy the properties of glorified existence prior to his resurrection from the dead.[59] For Jesus no less than anyone else, "this perishable body must put on imperishability, and this mortal body must put on immortality" (1 Cor. 15:53). For his earthly actions to be a reliable index of divinity, however, it not necessary that he be deified in every respect, but only in his will, as the source of those actions.

In order to see why this is the case, it is necessary to briefly examine the place of the will in Christian accounts of human being. From the earliest

---

57. "For the corporal nature has not become God but, just as the Word did not change and remained what he was though becoming flesh, so also the flesh became the Word without having lost what it had. . . . The humanity of Christ is a deified nature that is permeated by the divine energies from the moment of the Incarnation." Vladimir Lossky, *The Mystical Theology of the Eastern Church* (Cambridge: James Clarke & Co., 1957), 146. Cf. Maximus the Confessor, *OTP* 9 (PG 91:120A).

58. "One could say, then, that he experienced suffering in a divine way . . . and that he worked miracles in a human way, since they were accomplished through his flesh (for he was not naked God). . . . Knowing this, the teacher [Dionysius the Areopagite] said, 'As for the rest, He did not do divine things after the manner of God,' for they were not done only divinely, as if separated from the flesh . . . , 'neither did He do human things in a human way,' for they were not done solely by the flesh . . . for He was not merely a Human being. Instead, as God having become man, he lived His life among us according to a certain new theandric energy." Maximus, *Ambigua* 5, in *On Difficulties in the Church Fathers*, 1:49 (PG 91:1056A–B). The citations from Dionysius comes from his *Letter 4*.

59. While Jesus is reported as eating after his resurrection (Luke 24:42–43; cf. John 21:15), given the wider context it seems reasonable to assert that this has ceased to be a matter of physical necessity for him. Cf. the speculation on the role of food in glorified existence in Augustine, *The City of God against the Pagans* 13.22, ed. and trans. R. W. Dyson (Cambridge: Cambridge University Press, 1998).

period of the church, Christians have associated the will with humans' status as free and responsible beings—a status that gives them a distinctive (though not necessarily unique) relationship to God.[60] As noted in the previous chapter, all creatures are products of God's will and, as such, are made to exist in conformity with that will. All terrestrial creatures other than human beings do this automatically and necessarily because they lack wills of their own. In other words, their behavior is instinctive: determined by their genetic programming to follow particular, characteristic patterns that define them as the creatures they are, they invariably act according to their natures, which, since they have been created by God to act in just that way, cannot deviate from God's will for them. By contrast, it is a peculiarity of human beings that their natures include a will, which means that humans' actions do not supervene upon them as the inevitable products of their natures (i.e., as matters of instinct), but rather are experienced by each individual as her own, and thus as matters of personal agency.[61] That human beings have wills, in short, means that they own their deeds, but creatures without wills cannot: humans' actions do not simply come upon them but are enacted by them in a way that can never be reduced to the impersonal outworkings of nature.[62] The fact that human beings have wills, by virtue of which their actions are not the immediate products of their God-given natures, allows for the logical possibility that they may sin, or deviate from God's will in their actions. Indeed, it is a foundational conviction of Christianity that they invariably do so.

Because of this proclivity to sin, the actions of human beings cannot reliably be taken to participate in the divine energies. If Jesus' will is deified, however, it follows that none of his humanly willed actions involve any deviation from God's will for him. And that his will is deified follows from the terms of

60. Not unique because traditionally angels were also understood to possess wills, and in light of contemporary understanding of the vastness of the universe, there seems no reason to rule out the possibility of other material creatures on other planets also endowed with wills.

61. This is not to say that human beings do not have instincts, but only to note that they experience their instinctual drives (e.g., procreation) as occasions for the exercise of personal decision and responsibility.

62. Given that there are any number of human actions, from sweating to laughing to being perplexed, that are not "willed" in the sense of being "consciously intended," it is important that human willing be identified with *agency* rather than *control*; that is, to have a will is to experience oneself as an "I" who owns one's actions (viz., "*I* did them") rather than as some power by which an essentially disembodied "I" exercises control over the body. That such "ownership" extends beyond the realm of intentional acts is reflected in the fact that we quite naturally use the first-person pronoun for "involuntary" actions (e.g., "I was confused," "I'm sweating") no less than for acts that are more clearly the product of deliberation and decision (e.g., "I promised to stay," "I unlocked the door"). So although the degree to which human actions are matters of conscious choice varies widely, all remain ineluctably part of the actor's identity as a personal agent—and thus are bound up with the will. It is in light of this understanding of the will that it is possible to understand what Cyril of Alexandria may have meant when he wrote, "In a rational nature nothing natural is involuntary" (cited in Maximus the Confessor, *Disputatio cum Pyrrho*, PG 91:296A).

the hypostatic union. For because Jesus' human will is (like every other aspect of his human nature) hypostatized by the eternal Word, it is necessarily free of sin (Heb. 4:15), since the Word, as God, is inherently incapable of sinning by virtue of its participation in the divine nature.[63] Consequently, because Jesus is the particular person he is (viz., the second person of the Trinity), all Jesus' human actions participate in the divine energies, making them reliable indices of the divine that allow us to affirm, on the basis of the attributes revealed in those actions, that the divine nature is merciful, compassionate, righteous, and so forth.

Because this knowledge comes by way of the participation of Jesus' human nature in the divine energies, it does not entail the claim that the divine nature becomes visible, still less comprehensible, through the incarnation. Once again, the divine nature is in no way changed when the hypostasis of the Word takes flesh, but, having been united with humanity "without confusion or change," remains in every respect utterly transcendent. Therefore, when Christians affirm, on the basis of Jesus' actions, that God is loving and merciful, wise and powerful, or anything else, they must also recognize that because these terms are being predicated of the divine nature, which transcends all creaturely categories, they can only apply to God analogically. So when we use them, we are not saying that God is, say, loving as Jesus was only much more so. We are saying something more like when we come to know God's love in glory, we will see that it exemplifies and perfects what we have come to know humanly as love in Jesus (and indeed, that Jesus exhibits the love we will see in God in its most perfect creaturely form), though in a manner that will be evident only a posteriori and not definable on the basis of any sort of extrapolation from worldly experience—even our experience of Jesus. In short, what we are doing when we say that God is loving, just, merciful, and so forth, is claiming that insofar as we can humanly apply these predicates to Jesus, and insofar as we understand Jesus to be none other than God's Son in the flesh, these predicates also apply (albeit in a way we cannot truly fathom) to divinity as well. We ascribe such predicates to God in profound ignorance of their full meaning for God; but because we derive them from the activities of the human being who is the Word made flesh, we can nevertheless

---

63. Christ's will "is wholly and thoroughly deified by its agreement and concord with the Father's will, and can properly be said to have truly become divine in virtue of the [hypostatic] union." Christ's humanity is not for that reason any less human, since for Maximus "nothing at all changes its nature by being deified," and indeed, all human beings raised to glory will in that state share the same perfect attunement of their wills with God's that Christ enjoyed from birth. See Maximus the Confessor, *OTP* 7, in Andrew Louth, *Maximus the Confessor* (New York: Routledge, 1996), 187. Cf. Maximus's *OTP* 20 (PG 91:236D): "But as for the Savior's willing according to his human nature, even though it was natural, it was not open to fault [*psilon*] like ours . . . since it has been perfectly deified above us in the [hypostatic] union, because of which it is actually sinless."

be confident that we apply them truly and that their character corresponds (albeit in a way we cannot fully know or describe) to their divine archetype.

The upshot of this claim is that if the analysis of the hypostatic union presented in this chapter is sound, then the distinction between nature and hypostasis at the heart of Chalcedonian Christology has among its benefits the ability to honor both the negative (or apophatic) and positive (or cataphatic) dimensions of Christian theology. The good news of the incarnation is precisely that in Christ, God has come among us so as to make it possible to speak about God cataphatically. Our knowledge of God is no longer (as was the case in the various Old Testament theophanies) limited to instances where God has made God's self known through created realities that are themselves not God and so cannot finally be means by which God is fully present to us. Because Jesus is God, we can say that in seeing Jesus, we see God. At the same time, because in Jesus we see not the nature but the person of the Son, the incarnation allows us to hold fast to the principle of the invisibility of the divine nature. So although the incarnation provides firm ground on the basis of which Christians can make claims about God's love, power, wisdom, mercy, and so forth, the fact that these and other qualities are manifested by God the Son in his incarnate form, and thus humanly, means that we remain ignorant about what these things are in God eternally. Because there is no common measure between the being of a creature and that of the Creator, only an analogous relationship can be posited: we know that love applies to God, and we trust that the content of that love will be clear to us in glory in a manner that will be fully coherent with our experience of Jesus; but in the present we cannot simply extrapolate from the love that God shows us in Jesus to what love means in God eternally. Honoring Chalcedon in this way means that Jesus, as God, is the chief source and touchstone, but also, as human, the limit to our ability to understand and talk about God truly.

In this way, a Chalcedonianism without reserve addresses the challenge with which this chapter opens: how the confession that "the Word became flesh and lived among us" (John 1:14) can be squared with the absolute and inherent transcendence of God. The distinction between hypostasis and nature in Chalcedonian Christology makes it possible to affirm that while the divine *nature* never becomes human or in any way subject to either physical or conceptual circumscription, the *person* of the Word can, without ceasing to be divine, also assume a human nature. That is why Chalcedonians answer the question "Who is Jesus?" by saying that he is the Word of God made flesh: one divine hypostasis who may and must be confessed as truly human as well as truly divine with respect to nature.

In providing a conceptual framework for a characterization of Jesus' ontology, the Chalcedonian distinction between nature and hypostasis is important as a means of defending the Christian claim that Jesus is Savior—a role that can be ascribed to God alone—in a manner that honors the integrity of his humanity. But for all its value, the picture Chalcedon gives of Jesus is radically incomplete, in much the same way that to identify me as fully (and only) human, while entirely true, gives only a very incomplete picture of who I am. When we ask who someone is, we want more than an ontological description, however helpful such a description may be in clarifying the kind of entity about which we are speaking. We want to know not simply the kind of being about whom we are talking, but also the way in which the entity in question goes about living as that particular kind of being—the distinctive histories, behaviors, attitudes, habits, character traits, and so forth that distinguish that individual from all others. In short, to understand fully *who* they are, we need to know something about *how* they are. The next two chapters will seek to answer the question of who Jesus is from that perspective. The terms of that answer will continue to be Chalcedonian, but developed in terms of identity description rather than simply a specification of ontological type. Following the order of the creed, we begin with an exposition of Jesus' divinity.

4

"Perfect in Divinity"

In the preceding chapter I argue that the confession that Jesus is the Word made flesh does not entail that the Word subsisted in an unenfleshed state prior to the incarnation. The latter assertion, I maintain, implies that the incarnation is a development in the life of the Word, and therefore that the portion of the Word's life predating the incarnation is not revealed through the incarnation. But if Jesus is the temporal projection of the life of the Word *in its entirety*, such that it is indeed the case that in him "the whole fullness of deity dwells bodily," then there can be no such remainder hidden behind the one who takes flesh from Mary.

Importantly, however, this does not mean that there was no knowledge of God prior to the incarnation of God. Any such claim would be flatly inconsistent with the New Testament's affirmation that long before Jesus' birth, "God spoke to our ancestors in many and various ways by the prophets" (Heb. 1:1). And insofar as the New Testament writers agree that Jesus is Israel's Messiah, and thus the one who inaugurates the kingdom of Israel's God, they are one in presupposing that God was (and is) known to Israel.[1] In the second century when Marcion challenged this conviction by teaching that the God of Israel was other than the Father of Jesus, he was promptly condemned. It follows that Christian teaching about Jesus needs both to insist on the one

---

1. "For classical Christianity, the New Testament interprets but does not cancel the Old. That is why a form of Judaism lives in the church and the church cannot understand itself without coming to terms with the Judaism within it." Michael Wyschogrod, *Abraham's Promise: Judaism and Jewish-Christian Relations*, ed. R. Kendall Soulen (Grand Rapids: Wm. B. Eerdmans Publishing Co., 2004), 167; cf. 180, where Wyschogrod adds that the God of Israel, precisely as the God of *Israel*, "remains inaccessible to all those who wish to reach him and, at the same time, to circumvent this people."

hand that there is no Word of God other than Jesus Christ, while maintaining on the other hand that Jesus does not exhaust either the reality of God or the content of human knowledge about God. After all, the very confession that Jesus is the Word of God incarnate seems to assume some prior knowledge of the God whose Word Jesus is.

As already suggested, this prior knowledge is most naturally understood as passing through Israel, since the Christian confession of Jesus as Israel's Messiah directly associates him with Israel's God. Nor does this reference to Israel undermine Luther's principle that our talk about God should be derived from attention to Jesus' humanity, since it is the human Jesus himself who teaches that the Hebrew Scriptures bear witness to him when he says, "If you believed Moses, you would believe me, for he wrote about me" (John 5:46). Indeed, claiming that Jesus' identity as the eternal Word is properly understood only by way of reference to the God of Israel is decisive for Christian understanding of divinity. For it means that to confess Jesus as perfect in divinity is not in the first instance to ascribe to him a set of attributes (whether communicable or incommunicable, absolute or relative), but rather to identify him with *this* God: the one who chose the people of Israel and thereby became the object of their worship (see Exod. 20:2–3). And so to understand what it means to confess that Jesus is divine, we need to know who this God is.

PRELIMINARY CONSIDERATIONS:
THE DIVINE NAME

Israel's God is neither a human being (Num. 23:19) nor an angel (Isa. 63:9), but the fact that this God is addressed as a "you" (see, e.g., Gen. 15:2; Exod. 5:22; Num. 11:11; Deut. 21:8; 2 Sam. 7:18–29) shows that the object of Israel's worship is nevertheless personal, in the sense of being someone rather than something. Now, because personal beings, whether human or divine, are identified by name, the most obvious way of saying who Israel's God is, is to give that God's name. According to the Bible, Israel learns God's name in connection with the very event whereby this God becomes identifiable as *Israel's* God in the first place: the exodus.[2] Because this event takes place in a cultural context characterized by a plurality of deities, when this God calls

---

2. The Bible is, to be sure, not completely consistent on this point. Although God says to Moses, "I appeared to Abraham, Isaac, and Jacob as God Almighty, but by my name YHWH I did not make myself known to them" (Exod. 6:3 alt.; cf. Gen. 17:1; 35:11), we also read that both Abraham (Gen. 13:4; 21:33) and Isaac (Gen. 26:25) did in fact call on the name of YHWH (see also Gen. 4:26).

Moses to lead the people of Israel out of bondage in Egypt, Moses quite reasonably asks just who this would-be liberator God is:

> Moses said to God, "If I come to the Israelites and say to them, 'The God of your ancestors has sent me to you,' and they ask me, 'What is his name?' what shall I say to them?" God said to Moses, "I AM WHO I AM." He said further, "Thus you shall say to the Israelites, 'I AM has sent me to you.'" God also said to Moses, "Thus you shall say to the Israelites, 'YHWH, the God of your ancestors, the God of Abraham, the God of Isaac, and the God of Jacob, has sent me to you': This is my name forever, and this my title for all generations. Go and assemble the elders of Israel, and say to them, 'YHWH, the God of your ancestors, the God of Abraham, of Isaac, and of Jacob, has appeared to me, saying: I have given heed to you and to what has been done to you in Egypt.'" (Exod. 3:13–16 alt.)

This is a complicated passage. Moses asks for God's name, and God gives three responses in quick succession: first, "I AM WHO I AM"; second, "I AM," and third, "YHWH" (normally rendered in English, following ancient Jewish convention, as "the LORD"). Biblical scholars have long recognized that there is wordplay in the relationship between the "I AM" ('ehyeh in Hebrew) of Exodus 3:14 and the (traditionally unvocalized) four consonants known as the Tetragrammaton (YHWH) in the following verse, although it is unclear what, if any, etymological relationship actually holds between them. Christian theologians have tended to focus on the "I AM" statements (not least because of the way they are echoed by Jesus in passages like John 6:20; 8:24, 58; 18:6) as providing a description of the divine essence, and thus as communicating an ontology (e.g., God as ho ōn, ipsum esse subsistens, or the "Ground of Being") as much as an identity.[3] Yet arguably it is only with the third response that God actually satisfies Moses' request. For since Moses is not told to communicate "I AM WHO I AM" to the Israelites, it does not seem that God intends this formula as the answer to Moses' question "What shall I say to them?" And although Moses is instructed, "Say to the Israelites, 'I AM has sent me to you,'" it is only with the giving of the Tetragrammaton that God provides a response that corresponds to the terms in which Moses made his request by placing this designation in apposition to "the God of your ancestors." Still

---

3. Kendall Soulen points out that the Cappadocian theologians Gregory of Nazianzus (in *Theological Orations* 30.17) and Gregory of Nyssa (in *Against Eunomius* 3.9) not only largely ignore Exod. 3:15, but even go so far as to interpret Exod. 3:14 as evidence that God is essentially unnameable (see R. Kendall Soulen, *Distinguishing the Voices*, vol. 1 of *The Divine Name(s) and the Holy Trinity* [Louisville, KY: Westminster John Knox, 2011], 51–52). By contrast, Thomas Aquinas explicitly states that the Tetragrammaton is the most proper name of God. Aquinas, *ST* 1.13.11.1.

more significantly, it is only at this point that God says, "This is my name forever" (cf. Exod. 6:3; 33:19). Moreover (and moving beyond the particular textual features of Exod. 3), it is YHWH that serves in practice as God's name in the Hebrew Scriptures, appearing "more than twice as often as all other divine names combined (some 6,000 times in all)."[4]

This God is clearly identified in the Bible as the Creator (Gen. 2:4; Pss. 33:6; 124:8; 134:3; Isa. 42:5; 44:24; 45:18) and thus as the God of all peoples (Ps. 36:7; Isa. 25:6; 56:7; cf. Dan. 7:13–14), but is most frequently character-ized (and more importantly, comes to be known) as God in and through his dealings with a particular people: Israel, or the Jews. Indeed, the point of the revelation of the divine name to Moses is precisely for God to make this people "my people," so that this people might, in turn, "know that I am the LORD your God" (Exod. 6:7). So when Christians confess that Jesus is God, what they mean is that Jesus is *this* God, YHWH, the God of Abraham, Isaac, and Jacob, the God of the Jews. The Chalcedonian claim that Jesus is perfect in divinity therefore means that he has rightful possession of this name (Heb. 1:4) and therefore is identical with just this God.

Yet as vital as the identity between the God of Israel and the Word made flesh is to Christian confession, specifying the relation between them is no easy task.[5] This is certainly not because there is any dearth of reference to the God of Israel in the New Testament, or any question that it is just this God in whose name Jesus has come, but because the modes of speech that Jesus and, fol-lowing him, the New Testament writers employ when speaking of God sug-gest both identity and difference between the rabbi from Nazareth and the one who called to Moses from the burning bush. Interestingly, most theologians of the church's early centuries were inclined to a straightforward identification between the God who spoke to Moses and the Word made flesh in Jesus. They argued for this identification on the grounds that the Word, as the one through whom all things were made (John 1:3; cf. Ps. 33:6), should be understood as the means of divine self-communication not only when enfleshed as Jesus, but also prior to the incarnation in the various Old Testament theophanies.[6] In short,

---

4. Soulen, *Distinguishing the Voices*, 10. On p. 12 he goes on to note that while the New Tes-tament does not employ the Tetragrammaton, it includes over 2,000 instances of perpiphrastic constructions reflecting the Jewish practice of avoiding the divine name; cf. Julius Boehmer, *Die neutestamentliche Gottesschen und die ersten drei Bitten des Vaterunsers* (Halle: Richard Mühlmann Verlagsbuchhandlung, 1917).

5. For a superlative account of this problem, on which I draw heavily in what follows, see Bruce Marshall, "Do Christians Worship the God of Israel?," in *Knowing the Triune God: The Work of the Spirit in the Practices of the Church*, ed. James J. Buckley and David S. Yeago (Grand Rapids: Wm. B. Eerdmans Publishing Co., 2001), 231–64.

6. See, e.g., Justin Martyr, *First Apology* 1.63; and Justin Martyr, *Dialogue with Trypho* 56; Irenaeus of Lyon, *The Demonstration of the Apostolic Preaching* 44–46; Tertullian, *Against Marcion* 3.9; 5.19.

since it is through the divine Word that God communicates with human beings so as to make God's self known, it seems to follow that the one who spoke to Abraham in Ur of the Chaldeans, to Moses on Mount Sinai, and to Ezekiel on the banks of the Chebar was the Word.

Yet while this position has a certain prima facie plausibility, it runs into serious problems in light of the fact that the evangelists consistently portray Jesus distinguishing himself from the God of Israel. Although John does depict Jesus appropriating the divine "I am" (6:20; 8:24, 58; 18:6; cf. the Synoptic invocation of Ps. 110 in Matt. 22:44 and pars.), much more common— even in John—are those cases where Jesus is described as sent by (and thus in some sense evidently other than) Israel's God. In arguing with the Sadducees over the resurrection, for example, Jesus refers to "the God of Abraham, and the God of Isaac, and the God of Jacob" as "he" rather than "I" (Matt. 22:32 and pars; cf. John 8:39–40). Similarly, if Paul occasionally uses language that seems to elide the distinction between Jesus and Israel's God (e.g., Rom. 9:5), in general he distinguishes very clearly between "God" (viz., the one who called Abraham, as in Rom. 4 and Gal. 3) and "Jesus Christ" (e.g., Rom. 1:7; 5:11; 7:25; 8:39; 15:6; 1 Cor. 1:3; 8:6; 15:15; 2 Cor. 1:2–3; 13:13; Gal. 1:3; Phil. 1:2; 1 Thess. 1:1, 3; 2 Thess. 1:1–2; 2:16). Moreover, the very designation of Jesus as the "Son" of (Israel's) God, especially as spoken by a heavenly voice at Jesus' baptism and transfiguration (Matt. 3:17; 17:5 and pars.; cf. 2 Pet. 1:17), implies that Jesus, for all that he is the Word made flesh, cannot straightforwardly be equated with that God.[7] And finally, the direct identification of the God who called Abraham and Moses with the not-yet-enfleshed Word brings back the problem of the *Logos asarkos* and thereby subverts the claim that "the whole fullness of deity dwells bodily" in Jesus.

All this might suggest that the God who appeared to the patriarchs and the prophets should instead be identified with the one Jesus called "Father."[8] There certainly can be no question but that in the New Testament this term is applied without any evident distinction both to the one who sent Jesus and to the God of the Old Testament—perhaps most strikingly in Jesus' reference to the temple in Jerusalem as "my Father's house" (Luke 2:49; John 2:16).[9]

7. "Jesus never invokes as God anyone but Israel's Lord, and never talks to himself. Taken together, these two elements in the narrative mean that the God of Israel cannot simply be the same as the person of the Word or Son." Marshall, "God of Israel?," 248.

8. This position, too, is not without patristic support, including Gregory of Nazianzus in *Theological Orations* 5.26, as well as (again!) Irenaeus in *Against Heresies* 1.22.1. It is also strongly bound up with the creedal appropriation of the work of creation to the Father (seen already in the late first-century text 1 Clement 19.2).

9. So it was that in the second century Marcion was only able to make a distinction between Israel's God and Jesus' Father by rejecting most of the books in what became the New Testament canon and heavily editing the rest.

Also, while the phrase "God the Father"—again, evidently none other than Israel's God—appears over a dozen times in the New Testament, there is no such reference to "God the Son" or "God the Holy Spirit." Moreover, insofar as the Old Testament writers freely employ the phrases "the word of God" (e.g., 1 Sam. 9:27; 1 Kgs. 12:22; cf. Isa. 38:4; Jer. 1:4; 16:1; Ezek. 7:1; 11:14) and the "spirit of God" (e.g., Num. 24:2; 1 Sam. 10:10; Ezek. 11:24; cf. Judg. 3:10; 6:34; Isa. 11:2; 61:1), it seems natural enough in light of later Trinitarian developments for Christians to identify the "God" whose word and spirit are so designated with the one that they, following Jesus' example, call "Father."

Yet despite the apparent exegetical merits of such a move, there are significant theological problems with identifying the God of Israel with any of the Trinitarian persons individually. Most obviously, the three divine persons do not subsist individually, but only in inseparable communion with one another. Because the Trinity is just one God, it is (as already noted) an ancient principle of Christian theology that the actions of the divine persons in the world are undivided. While it is indeed the case that only the Son takes flesh, this very act implicates and reveals the Father and the Spirit. That is, although only the Son is enfleshed, we know him as the Son only as we understand him to have been sent by the Father in the power of the Spirit, who together effect the work of redemption.[10] In short, because each of the persons is God only in relation to the others, it is inconsistent with the doctrine of the Trinity to imagine the revelation of one person in isolation from the rest without falling into tritheism. It is a matter of Christian confession that each of the divine persons is fully and truly God, but if the God of the Old Testament is identified with any one of the persons alone, such that in the Old Testament theophanies this one person, whether Father or Son, is—and thus can be—known apart from the others, then this God cannot be identified with the Trinity, since according to Trinitarian doctrine knowing any one of the persons is impossible apart from knowledge of the other two.

Considerations like these led Augustine to judge that while the mode of divine revelation in the Old Testament theophanies "remains obscure,"

---

10. In this context, it is important to note that the claim that only the Son (and not the Father or the Spirit) assumes flesh is no violation of the undivided character of the Trinity's acts *ad extra*, because the incarnation is not an act in this sense. As per the analysis of the incarnation in the previous chapter, the Son is not "doing" anything in taking flesh, since the work by which the human nature of Jesus is sustained and empowered is as much the work of the whole Trinity as is the case with any other human being. To be sure, it is true that by virtue of the incarnation the Son is born, eats, drinks, heals, suffers, dies, and is raised, and that none of these things can be predicated of the Father or the Spirit; but at the level of primary cause, the whole Trinity remains equally the cause of the Son's being born, eating, and so forth, and not the Son in isolation, while at the level of secondary cause it is the human will of the Son that causes his actions. In short, for the Son to take flesh and so to become a human being is not for the Son to *do* anything independently of the Father and the Holy Spirit.

nevertheless, at least in the case of God's speaking to Adam in the garden, "no reason can be given from the context against understanding this of the [whole] trinity."[11] Indeed, Augustine was inclined to go rather farther than this and argue that the point of the Old Testament theophanies was "to represent the invisible and intelligible God—not only the Father, but the Son too and the Holy Spirit."[12] That sort of claim must be judged to go beyond the evidence: whatever sort of anticipations of a tri-hypostatic God the Old Testament talk of God's "word" and "spirit" may be thought to provide, it falls short of a revelation of the Trinity, as should be evident from the fact that Trinitarianism has never commended itself to Jews, notwithstanding what to Christian ears may sound like "hypostatic" treatment of God's *memra* (word) and *shekinah* (presence) in rabbinic literature. Still, if Christians do well to refrain from claiming that God is revealed as Trinity in the Old Testament (since the explicit distinction of persons is known only by way of the incarnation), their confession of Jesus as the definitive revelation of Israel's God does give them reason to claim that the God of the Old Testament is properly identified with the Trinity. That is, although Israel's God can only be known *as Trinity* with the Word's taking flesh as Jesus, the claim that it is just *Israel's God* who became known in this way demands that the one who called Abraham, spoke to Moses out of the burning bush, and appeared in a vision to Isaiah was not the Father or the Son or the Spirit in isolation, but the one God of Israel—who is the Trinity.

To be sure, this conclusion, too, is not without its problems. Most obviously, it produces a kind of narrative incoherence since it carries the rather awkward implication that Jesus, in addressing the God of Israel, is talking at least partly to himself.[13] Likewise, the Nicene Creed's affirmation that it is the Holy Spirit in particular who "has spoken through the prophets" sits uneasily with a refusal to identify any Old Testament talk of God with one divine person in distinction from the others. Nevertheless, the identification of the God of the Old Testament with the Trinity rather than any one of the Trinitarian persons arguably does the best justice to the claim that in the life of Jesus, Israel's God is fully revealed. For this reason, the story of Israel's God is rightly called Jesus' story, because in his flesh Jesus is "the image of the invisible God" (Col. 1:15; cf. John 1:18)—that is, the God of Israel (Deut.

---

11. Augustine, *The Trinity* 2.18, ed. John E. Rotelle, OSA, trans. Edmund Hill, OP (Hyde Park, NY: New City Press, 1991).

12. Augustine, *Trinity* 2.25.

13. See Marshall, "God of Israel?," 254. As discussed below, however, Jesus is only relatively infrequently depicted in the Gospels as addressing "God" as such, in distinction from the Father. Though some of these instances are quite striking (e.g., the cry of derelictcion in Matt. 27:46 and par.), Jesus' recorded speech patterns tend to report him as distinguishing him from the Father more than from God as such (see Luke 23:34, 46).

4:12, 15) who, through the incarnation, is known to be triune.[14] Insofar as Jesus *is* the Word, he does not *reveal* the Word; rather, he reveals the Triune God whose Word he is. And so if we want to know what it means to say that Jesus is fully divine—what it means to confess that he is the incarnation of the God whose name was revealed to Israel—it is necessary to examine what Israel came to learn about this God in the centuries between that fateful encounter with Moses on Sinai and Jesus' birth. Three titles in particular emerge from such an examination as decisive for characterizing Jesus' divinity: Lord, Savior, and Son. We will review each of them in turn.

LORD

By the first century, Jewish respect for the holiness of the divine name meant that it was no longer spoken casually, or even in the course of worship in the synagogue.[15] As already noted, the New Testament suggests that Jesus himself followed this practice, using surrogate terms or periphrasis to designate Israel's God without vocalizing the divine name, not least in the opening petition of the Lord's Prayer: "Hallowed be your name" (Matt. 6:9 and par.; cf. John 12:28).[16] The evidence of the Septuagint in particular suggests that the title "lord" (Greek *kyrios*) had long since been appropriated as a surrogate term to be read or spoken in place of the Tetragrammaton, as does the Masoretic convention of pointing the four Hebrew consonants of the Tetragrammaton with the vowels for *'adonai*, the Hebrew word for "lord" (hence the English practice of marking the Tetragrammaton by the orthographic convention of printing "the Lord").[17]

14. In this way, Herbert McCabe is undoubtedly right to claim that "The entire Bible, spanning all history, is, all of it, the story of Jesus of Nazareth" is the most appropriate way to speak of Jesus' "preexistence." Herbert McCabe, OP, *God Matters* (New York: Continuum, 2010 [1987]), 51.

15. While it is sometimes affirmed (following the rabbinic tradition recorded in m. Yoma 3:8; 4:2) that the divine name was only spoken by the high priest on the Day of Atonement, the evidence is a bit more complicated (see the discussion by David B. Capes, "YHWH Texts and Monotheism in Paul's Christology," in *Early Jewish and Christian Monotheism*, ed. Loren T. Stuckenbruck and Wendy E. S. North [London: T&T Clark International, 2004], 124). Still, there seems little doubt that by the first century pious Jews vocalized the Tetragrammaton only in a very limited set of circumstances.

16. For a more fulsome account of the evidence, see Soulen, *Distinguishing the Voices*, 194–98.

17. Textual evidence shows a range of orthographic conventions for writing the divine name in the Second Temple period, including the use of paleo-Hebrew script, four dots, and Hebrew letters in Greek manuscripts, alongside the substitution of *'adonai/kyrios* for the Tetragrammaton (see Capes, "YHWH Texts," 122; cf. Soulen, *Distinguishing the Voices*, 52). It is, of course, impossible to know for certain how any of the former were read out loud, although the change of script seems to suggest that something other than the putative original vocalization of the divine name ("Yahweh") was to be spoken.

Such evidence suggests that by the time of Jesus, in Jewish practice the words "God" and "LORD" had an identical referent: both were used to identify the one God of Israel, who was "the LORD" (i.e., YHWH). With this convention in mind, it should come as no surprise to discover that in the New Testament the Greek *kyrios* is used as a surrogate for the divine name (as indicated by the absence of a definite article in the text, as in, e.g., Matt. 1:22; 4:7 and par.; 21:9 and pars.; 22:37 and pars.; Luke 1:16, 76; Acts 3:22; Rom. 10:13), in addition to being used as a title for Israel's God (e.g., Matt. 11:25; Luke 1:32; Rev. 4:8, 11; 21:22). More striking, however, is the frequency with which it is also applied to Jesus (e.g., Mark 16:19; Luke 1:43; 10:41; 11:39; John 6:23; 11:32; Acts 1:21; 4:33; 7:59; Rom. 5:1, 11; 13:14; 14:14; 1 Cor. 5:4; 11:23; Eph. 6:24; 1 Tim. 6:3, 14; Heb. 13:20; Jas. 2:1; 2 Pet. 1:16; Jude 4, 17, 21; Rev. 17:14; 22:20–21). These instances are clearly distinct from the evangelists' report of the merely honorific use of *kyrios* by Jesus' contemporaries as a title roughly equivalent to "sir" (see Mark 7:28; John 4:11, 15, 19, 49; 5:7; 6:34; 8:11; 9:36). For his followers, Jesus is not simply one alongside others, but the one and only "Lord of all" (Acts 10:36). The term's specifically theological significance is evident in the early Christian hymn quoted by Paul in his Letter to the Philippians:

> Let the same mind be in you that was in Christ Jesus,
>
> who, though he was in the form of God,
> > did not regard equality with God
> > as something to be exploited,
> but emptied himself,
> > taking the form of a slave,
> > being born in human likeness.
> And being found in human form,
> > he humbled himself
> > and became obedient to the point of death—
> > even death on a cross.
> Therefore God also highly exalted him
> > and gave him the name
> > that is above every name,
> so that at the name of Jesus
> > every knee should bend,
> > in heaven and on earth and under the earth,
> and every tongue should confess
> > that Jesus Christ is Lord,
> > to the glory of God the Father.
>
> (Phil. 2:5–11)

Here Jesus' status as one worthy of worship is directly connected with his having received "the name that is above every name" (cf. Heb. 1:4; John 17:11–12), which cannot be other than the Tetragrammaton. It is as the recipient of the divine name that Jesus is to be confessed by all creation as "Lord" (*kyrios*, without a definite article).[18] In short, he is to be honored as "Lord" because he bears the name of the Lord.

And yet it is important to note that even as he is so honored, he is explicitly distinguished from God the Father. For while (as noted above) the New Testament writers do refer to God (i.e., the Father) as Lord, yet such usage is not frequent—even as, conversely, Jesus is only very rarely identified directly and without qualification as "God" (e.g., John 20:28). Instead, and as suggested by the many variations on the phrase "God the Father and our Lord Jesus Christ" found in the Pauline corpus in particular (Rom. 1:7; 15:6; 1 Cor. 1:3; 2 Cor. 1:2–3; 11:31; 13:13; Gal. 1:3; Eph. 1:2–3, 17; 5:20; 6:23; Phil. 1:2; Col. 1:3; 3:17; 1 Thess. 1:1, 3; 3:11, 13; 2 Thess. 1:1–2; 2:16; Phlm. 3; cf. 1 Pet. 1:3), rather early there emerged among Christians a bifurcation of terminology, in which the word "God" was applied to the one Jesus called "Father," while the title "Lord" was associated with Jesus. Importantly, this division of terms is not understood by Paul as implying any qualification of the oneness of God, on which Paul continues to insist (see Gal. 3:20), following the ancient biblical confession of the Shema (Deut. 6:4). Indeed, in a formulation that seems to be influenced by the Shema (as indicated by the use of italics in the quotation below) and precisely as a means of distinguishing the identity of the God worshiped by Christians from other divinities, Paul writes: "Even though there may be so-called gods in heaven or on earth, . . . yet *for us there is one God*, the Father, from whom are all things and for whom we exist, *and one Lord*, Jesus Christ, through whom are all things and through whom we exist" (1 Cor. 8:5–6).[19]

Clearly, "God the Father" and "the Lord Jesus Christ" are not the *same* (i.e., Jesus is not the Father), yet they are named together precisely in order to stress that the God of Israel (and thus of Christians) is nevertheless *one*, in contrast to the plurality of deities among the nations.[20] And while it would

18. Soulen argues that in appropriating this passage from what scholars now view as a preexisting early Christian hymn, Paul "identifies the first person as the one who gives the divine name, the second person as the one who receives it, and the third person as the one who awakens its acknowledgment, in the second person to the glory of the first." Soulen, *Distinguishing the Voices*, 12.

19. Soulen gives careful attention to the parallels between this text and Deut. 6:4 in *Distinguishing the Voices*, 34–36; for another indicative text, if not quite so obviously parallel, see Eph. 4:4–6: "There is . . . *one Lord*, one faith, one baptism, *one God* and Father of all, who is above all and through all and in all."

20. In this context, one might cite Gal. 3:20, where Paul contrasts the confession of God as "one," as revealed in the promise made to Abraham and fulfilled in Christ, with the giving of the law, which, insofar as it, in Paul's reading, entails an (angelic?) mediator, "is not one." Here, too, the confession of Jesus and God the Father in their distinction seems for Paul somehow to reflect rather than compromise the oneness of God.

certainly be anachronistic to read into Paul's words the later doctrine of the Trinity, they may quite naturally be taken to reflect the basic conviction underlying that later teaching: the one who encounters us in Jesus is none other than the God who brought all things into being and sustains them in being.

What does it mean to say that Jesus is the Lord, and thus the one who rightly lays claim to "the name that is above every name"? What does this tell us about Jesus' divinity? Surely the first point to be made in answer to such questions is that the one who takes flesh in Jesus is unique: just *this* one, and so not to be confused with any other (that is, any nondivine, created) being. Here it is significant that an alternative name of God given in Exodus is "jealous" (Hebrew *qannā'*): "You shall worship no other god, because the LORD, whose name is Jealous, is a jealous God" (Exod. 34:14; cf. Deut. 4:24; 5:9; 6:15; Nah. 1:2). Indeed, when the people of Israel declare their intention to serve the Lord, Joshua goes so far as to cite God's jealousy as a reason why that commitment is beyond their abilities: "You cannot serve the LORD, for he is a holy God. He is a jealous God; he will not forgive your transgressions or your sins" (Josh. 24:19). The God who comes in Jesus is not one in a series or among many, but instead demands exclusive loyalty. For the people to offer anything less—seeking to serve this God *and* someone or something else—shows that they have failed to understand who this God is by treating the Lord as one value among many rather than the one source and ground of all that is.

In this respect, to identify Jesus as the Lord is to highlight the transcendence of the God who takes flesh, though with transcendence now understood not simply as a formal property of divine being, but as a defining feature of God's revealed identity: to be transcendent is to be known as just this one, not an instance of a particular kind (one god among a variety of deities, whether real or imagined), but one who is known only as named; that is, as incomparable and unique. In line with this point, God's name can only be received (rather than constructed or deduced) and, even once given, is never at the disposal of the recipient ("You shall not take the name of the LORD your God in vain"; Exod. 20:7 RSV). In short, to know God as the Lord is to know God as the sole determinant of God's identity. In this context, although (as argued above) the "I AM WHO I AM" of Exodus 3:14 may not be the answer to Moses' request for the divine name, it does make clear the significance of that name (viz., YHWH) when it is given in the next verse: who God is, is entirely a matter of God's own designation.[21]

---

21. In this context, the Gospel of John's combining the designation of Jesus as "Lord" with Jesus' own self-designation as "I am" clearly echoes the juxtaposition of those two designations in Exod. 3.

And yet it would be misleading to suggest that the identification of Jesus as Lord points simply to God's inaccessible and ultimately forbidding character. Even within Exodus, the interpretation of the divine name as "Jealous" is preceded by a rather different exegesis:

> The LORD descended in the cloud and stood with [Moses] there, and proclaimed the name, "The LORD." The LORD passed before him, and proclaimed,
>
> > "The LORD, the LORD,
> > a God merciful and gracious,
> > slow to anger,
> > and abounding in steadfast love and faithfulness."
> >
> > (Exod. 34:5–6)

This scene is the response to Moses' request to see God's glory (Exod. 33:18). God famously demurs, noting (in a manner consistent with the divine transcendence) that it is impossible for a creature to behold the divine "face" (Exod. 33:20). Nevertheless, the point of the revelation of the divine name is not that God should be hidden, but for God to be known. To be sure, God is known precisely *as the Lord*—as the true God rather than an idol—only insofar as human beings recognize that God's fullness exceeds their capacity as knowers. Such knowledge is indirect, partial, "in a mirror, dimly" (1 Cor. 13:12), a knowledge marked by awareness of the utter incommensurability between the knower and the one known. But it is nevertheless knowledge, not ignorance. And in condescending to be known by creatures as the Lord, this God is known as one who is "merciful and gracious, slow to anger, and abounding in steadfast love and faithfulness." For this God might well have determined not to have been known, since (unlike the gods of Babylon, who require the service of humankind in order to secure divine well-being), God has nothing to gain from creatures; indeed, it is just for this reason that God can be unqualifiedly gracious and merciful to them. So, once again, God's transcendence, far from being an impediment to the intimacy with creation implied by the proclamation of divine mercy and love, is its enabling condition.

In this respect, the fact that this God should take flesh in Jesus, the Lord of Israel definitively manifesting that lordship by living as an Israelite among Israelites, while certainly not an eventuality that could have been predicted, nevertheless may be seen as a profoundly appropriate exemplification of God's identity as the Lord. To say that Jesus is truly divine is thus in the first instance to say that Jesus is this transcendent Lord, known only as he gives himself so to be known. He is the one whose essence cannot be grasped, whose glory cannot be comprehended, and yet whose life is manifest as one of grace, mercy, and steadfast love lived among and for the people God has chosen, so that through them all peoples might be blessed.

SAVIOR

As these last observations make especially clear, "Lord" should not be understood as a neutral designation, affirming that the God of Israel holds immense power and authority (lordship), but without any indication of whether this power is exercised for good or ill. Such neutrality is ruled out by the recognition that "the Lord" is God's name, which was given to the people of Israel precisely to identify the agent of their liberation: "I am the Lord your God who brought you out of the land of Egypt, to be their slaves no more; I have broken the bars of your yoke and made you walk erect" (Lev. 26:13; cf. Exod. 20:2; Deut. 5:6). The being and power of the Lord are thus known as they are active in securing the well-being of creatures, whether in calling them into existence in creation or protecting their existence from the threat of annihilation in the course of the history that follows from creation: "The God of Israel is a redeeming God; this is the only message we are authorized to proclaim, however much it may not seem so to the eyes of unbelief."[22] It should thus come as no surprise that the term "Savior," like "Lord," is used in the New Testament to refer to the God of Israel (Luke 1:47; 1 Tim. 1:1; Jude 25). But Jesus, too, is confessed as Savior (Luke 1:69; 2:11; John 4:42; Acts 5:31; 13:23; Eph. 5:23; Phil. 3:20; 2 Tim. 1:10; Titus 1:4; 3:6; 2 Pet. 1:1; 1 John 4:14); and his status as Savior is evidently bound up with his being Lord (2 Pet. 1:11; 2:20; 3:2, 18).

Still, however closely connected the terms "Lord" and "Savior" are in Scripture, they differ as designation and description, respectively. That is, "Lord" identifies who this God is (viz., YHWH, who took flesh as Jesus of Nazareth), while "Savior" specifies what this God does. In this respect, if to call Jesus "Lord" is to stress the transcendence of the one who becomes incarnate, to call him "Savior" is to stress that this transcendent one becomes known in deeds of mercy and love. In other words, it is by reference to a commitment to the people of Israel manifest in saving work that "the Lord God" is to be picked out from the "many gods and many lords" (1 Cor. 8:5)

---

22. Wyschogrod, *Abraham's Promise*, 119. This is true of God's power even when exercised in judgment (see Heb. 12:6; Rev. 3:19; cf. 1 Cor. 3:13–15), so that destruction is not the effect of God's power, but what happens when God's power is withdrawn: see Ps. 104:29; cf. Jer. 4:23–26, where the effect of divine anger is the reversion of the world to its primordial state of "waste and void," suggesting the withdrawal of God's inherently saving power; so too, the flood in Gen. 7:11 comes about through God's removal of the barriers that hold back the waters of chaos.

who over the long history of human religious practice have been promoted as appropriate objects of worship. This God is the one *who brought Israel out of the land of Egypt*, and it is because of this specificity that Paul has no choice but to tell the Athenians on the Areopagus, who have not experienced this act of salvation, that the God he announces to them is not a God they already know, perhaps under a different name ("Zeus") or dimly, as sort of conceptual abstraction ("the Good," "the Unmoved Mover"), but precisely "the unknown God" (Acts 17:22–34).

From this perspective, the claim with which I began this book—that the name "Jesus" means "God saves"—is true, but in light of the specific identity of Israel's God, insufficiently precise. The name "Jesus" (a Greek transliteration of the Hebrew *Yeshuaʿ*, an alternative form of *Yehoshuaʿ*, or Joshua) is theophoric and so is more accurately rendered, "YHWH saves" or "YHWH is salvation" (cf. Matt. 1:21). Again, that YHWH, the Lord, is appropriately described as Savior is bound up with the events of the exodus: the divine name is revealed to identify the one who saves Israel from bondage. To be sure, the Lord was also the God of Israel's ancestors; but as much as God spoke with the patriarchs, establishing his covenant with them and promising to their descendants the land of Canaan, this relationship entailed only the promise rather than the fact of salvation—and so did not include the revelation of the divine name: "I appeared to Abraham, Isaac, and Jacob as God Almighty, but by my name 'The LORD' I did not make myself known to them" (Exod. 6:3).[23]

Yet this experience of the exodus, though definitive for Israel's experience of God as Savior, cannot be taken to exhaust that title's significance. For even as one swallow does not make a summer, neither can a single act of salvation be taken to establish deity. Even though it be granted that the Lord worked salvation for Israel at one particular point in the history of the Egyptian New Kingdom, that fact by no means guarantees God's power to effect salvation at other times and places, against more substantial opponents than Pharaoh. For this God to go on to insist, "You shall have no other gods before me" (Exod. 20:3; Deut. 5:7), is justifiable only if there is no situation in which God is unable to save. It is on the basis of this conviction that Israel's identification of the God of the exodus with the Creator of heaven and earth should be understood. For only an agent who is the sole source of all creaturely being can coherently be confessed as "Savior" in a truly comprehensive and unsurpassable sense: as able to guarantee the existence of the creature against every conceivable threat to its integrity.

---

23. The same sort of increase in the specificity of human knowledge of the divine identity that Christians claim comes with the incarnation is thus already found in the Hebrew Scriptures: Abraham knows the same God as Moses—but not (at least according to later tradition) as the one whose name is YHWH.

And yet interpreting salvation in this sense, as rescue from peril, is finally insufficient. After all, even a cursory glance at the histories of people having no connection with Israel makes clear that human beings, whether considered individually or in groups, may experience deliverance in various ways quite apart from any direct encounter with the Lord. And the Bible itself teaches that the same God who brought "Israel up from the land of Egypt" also brought "the Philistines from Caphtor and the Arameans from Kir" (Amos 9:7) without the latter knowing God as Savior. Nor does the Old Testament suggest that rescue from Egypt renders members of Israel immune from subsequent vulnerability to any of the various sorts of peril that threaten human existence. It thus seems that salvation does not cancel creation or change the basic contours of creaturely existence, with its characteristic alteration of birth and death, destruction and upbuilding, killing and healing (Eccl. 3:1–8; cf. Gen. 8:22; Matt. 5:45). Indeed, while Israel certainly experiences concrete acts of deliverance, ranging from the founding event of the exodus to the more small-scale and temporary victories described in the book of Judges, the point of all of them is finally for the people simply to be able to live a very everyday sort of life in their own land (Deut. 8:7–10; 1 Kgs. 4:25; cf. Eccl. 2:24; 3:13). Thus, as much as God evidently intends that Israel prosper, when considered simply in terms of its physical characteristics, the content of that prosperity does not seem any different in kind from that either hoped for or actually experienced by other nations.[24]

In this way, accounts of salvation framed in terms of God's power to rescue from danger, or to overcome the many sources of resistance to God's will for creatures' flourishing, require augmentation because they are sufficiently abstracted from the details of the process and ultimate purpose of God's saving work as to obscure the content of Israel's blessing. To make good this deficit, it is important to recognize that, in biblical perspective, salvation is not just understood negatively, as freedom *from* various dangers, but also positively, as a freedom *for* a relationship of intimate communion with God that exceeds anything creatures are able to achieve by their own powers. It is this second form of freedom that distinguishes Israel from its neighbors, for only of this people is it true that they no longer exist simply as creatures under God's power, but rather are called by God's power to covenant relationship with God. In this context, the claim that "salvation is from the Jews" (John 4:22) is for Christians not simply an observation regarding Jesus' biological ancestry, but also decisive for understanding what it means to be saved.

24. To be sure, there emerges within Israel the conviction that at some future date God will intervene to change the basic conditions of created existence for the better; yet here, too, the anticipated benefits are not limited to Israel but are conceived as universal in scope (see, e.g., Isa. 2:2–4; 11:1–9; 65:17–25).

As Creator, God sustains everything that exists with an equal intensity, since no part of creation can exist in any respect except by God's willing that it does so. God's care thus extends to every creature in particular, paramecia no less than humans, Egyptians no less than Israelites; but in its very universality, this creative work is *general*: extending in like manner to all creatures always and everywhere, regardless of their spatiotemporal location. As that which sustains the world as a whole, God's creative work stands (so to speak) "behind" the realm of space and time. By contrast, the work of salvation whereby material creatures are brought into a life of covenant with God takes place within time and space and so is necessarily *particular*: defined by specific moments and places—identifiable theres and thens that stand in relationships of varying proximity to other theres and thens.[25] In this way, salvation entails a qualitative shift in God's relationship to the creature, no longer merely sustaining the creature in existence, but also calling it to live out that existence in conscious relationship with its Creator.

Thus, the revelation of God as Savior marks a qualitative shift in the character of existence for the people of Israel. By virtue of having been chosen by a God who is Savior, the Israelites do not necessarily live longer, healthier, or wealthier lives than gentiles; but, unlike gentiles, they live in the understanding that their lives have been claimed by God, defining them as God's people and the Lord as their God: "I am the LORD your God, who brought you out of the land of Egypt, to be *your* God" (Num. 15:41; cf. Deut. 4:34; 14:2; 1 Sam. 12:22; Ps. 135:4). The work whereby God holds all creatures—human and nonhuman, Jew and gentile—in their being remains unchanged (as it must do, if creation is to continue in existence), but it is now supplemented by God's acting within the world to make God's self known directly to a particular set of creatures—the people of Israel—as a Thou who, while not one object alongside other objects, is nevertheless experienced in genuine objectivity as one who is not a creature, but the Lord.

Yet the point of God's self-manifestation to Israel is not simply to communicate the fact that the Lord—rather than Baal, Molech, or some other entity—is God (see 1 Kgs. 18:39). Again, the reason the knowledge of God's

---

25. Could not salvation, too, be conceived in general terms, with God having determined to call each and every person independently of anyone else, as Abraham was called? One might argue that God's relation to the angels takes this form (at least under a Thomist angelology, in which angels are immaterial, such that each is its own species and thus ontologically independent of the rest), but it seems not well suited to human beings, whose existence is one of radical interdependence. In this context, it is crucial to notice that the call of Abraham includes not simply blessing for Abraham and his direct descendants, but also through him for all people: "In you all the families of the earth shall be blessed" (Gen. 12:3; cf. 18:18). It seems consistent with this structure of salvation for the church to confess that God calls each person individually only in and through that individual's relationships with other human beings.

name is important is that it is bound up with a particular understanding of what it means to be saved. What distinguishes the case of Israel is that for them—and for them alone—rescue is the occasion for God's calling the people into a relationship of covenant, characterized by mutual recognition and obligation both of God to Israel and of Israel to God. Thus, integral to Israel's experience of salvation is the assumption of a whole range of responsibilities—commandments, statutes, and ordinances (Deut. 8:11 and passim)—that are not binding on other peoples and yet shape even the most seemingly trivial matters of this people's day-to-day existence.[26] And yet because these obligations form this people's existence as one of profound intimacy with God (the Old Testament writers' repeated recourse to marital imagery for the relationship between Israel and the Lord is no accident), they are received as blessing rather than burden.[27]

In order to appreciate the degree to which the life of the covenant stands at the center of the Israelite understanding of salvation, it is only necessary to note that for the biblical writers the chief threat to Israel's well-being in its postexodus history comes not from without, but from within. For though Israel will never be other than a small state in relation to the great empires of Egypt, Assyria, Babylon, and the rest, and so will be tempted to channel its collective energies toward securing its borders against military conquest, in both the Law and the Prophets Israel's own unfaithfulness to God appears to be a much greater risk to its flourishing than does any external power. In short, once it has been constituted as a people by having been rescued from Egypt, Israel needs to be saved from itself every bit as much as from the great empires of the ancient world. Although Israel has been called to covenant with God, the disparity between divine transcendence and human fecklessness renders the people unable to fulfil its terms (Josh. 24:19). For this reason, a number of the commandments, statutes, and ordinances that give substance to the covenant have to do precisely with procedures for restoring the community's relationship with God in the aftermath of a rupture caused by some transgression—sin—on the part of the people (see, e.g., Lev. 5:1–6, 16; 23:23–32; Num. 15:22–34; cf. 1 Kgs. 8:47–48; Ezek. 18:30), so that the Lord's status as Savior includes not only the act of calling Israel into a covenant relationship, but also of providing the means to sustain that relationship when Israel fails to honor it. From this perspective, it is of a piece with the Christian confession of Jesus as truly divine that the "salvation" his name

---

26. The rabbis would later quantify the difference: while Israel was given 613 commandments (b. Makkot 23b), the gentiles are obliged to keep only the seven so-called Noachide laws (b. Sanhedrin 56a).

27. As evident in the Jewish celebration of *Simchat Torah*, "Rejoicing with the Torah," which marks the conclusion of the annual cycle of Torah readings in the synagogue.

describes is precisely that by which "he will save his people from their sins" (Matt. 1:21).[28]

In summary, salvation may be described an intensification of God's relationship to what is not God. Creation is already a product of divine love, as God chooses, graciously and not driven by any need, to give being to that which is not God. But in salvation God loves the creature in such a way as to invite the creature's love in return. No more than in creation is this work of salvation prompted by any lack on God's part: God does not gain from the creature's love any more than God gains from the creature's being: as the very term "salvation" suggests, the benefit here accrues entirely to the creature. But if that is already the case in creation, in which the creature's life is utterly bound to God, in salvation God takes the further step of binding the divine life to the creature. As a result, the creature's life is now sustained not only *by* God but *in* God, who is no longer simply "the LORD God" (Gen. 2:4, 5, 7), the Creator, but "the LORD *your* God" (Exod. 6:7; 16:12; 20:2 and passim), the Savior: the One who, in electing Israel, has publicly declared the divine life to be the guarantor of the creature's life and thus made the creature's story God's own.[29]

SON

From a Christian perspective the incarnation is the culmination of the saving work of Israel's God, as this God's commitment to the creature takes unsurpassable form in God's actually living a creaturely life. And yet at this very point the language used by Christians to characterize Jesus' divinity becomes especially challenging. For in the New Testament arguably no title is more central to the characterization of Jesus' divinity than "Son," which in large

---

28. Of course, this attention to saving Israel from the effects of its own transgressions does not exclude salvation from external threats. In Luke's infancy narrative, Zechariah explicitly ties the hope of a Savior to God's promise to rescue the people "from our enemies and from the hand of all who hate us" (Luke 1:71; cf. v. 73); and Revelation also portrays Jesus' work of salvation as including victory over external powers, both earthly and supernatural (see, e.g., Rev. 19:11–21).

29. Thus cf. Heb. 6:13, 15–19:

> When God made a promise to Abraham, because he had no one greater by whom to swear, he swore by himself. . . . And thus Abraham, having patiently endured, obtained the promise. Human beings, of course, swear by someone greater than themselves, and an oath given as confirmation puts an end to all dispute. In the same way, when God desired to show even more clearly to the heirs of the promise the unchangeable character of his purpose, he guaranteed it by an oath, so that through two unchangeable things [viz., God's own intrinsic unchangeableness as Creator and the oath he swore to Abraham], in which it is impossible that God would prove false, we who have taken refuge might be strongly encouraged to seize the hope set before us.

part is why it came to be his particular designation in the later formulation of the doctrine of the Trinity. And yet, unlike "Lord" and "Savior," "Son" is never used in the Old Testament as a title for Israel's God. On the contrary, when used in a specifically theological context, "son" refers either to Israel (Exod. 4:22; Hos. 11:1) or to Israel's king (2 Sam. 7:14; Ps. 2:7), who, unlike the rulers of so many of the other peoples of ancient Near East, was *not* regarded as divine.[30] In this respect, "Son" seems a much less promising focus for understanding Jesus' divinity than other biblically attested titles like "Wisdom" or "Word." For each of these terms is also applied to Jesus in the New Testament (the former in 1 Cor. 1:24, 30; the latter in John 1:1, 14; Rev. 19:13), and both are much more clearly associated with the divine being in the Old Testament (e.g., for wisdom: Ezra 7:25; Prov. 8:22–31; Jer. 51:15; and for word: Gen. 15:1; 1 Kgs. 12:24; Ezek. 21:1).[31] By contrast, even in the New Testament the designation "Son" evidently distinguishes Jesus from the one he calls "Father" and thus seems to imply that Jesus is other than Israel's God rather than a manifestation of divine presence.

And yet further examination of the biblical texts suggests that matters are more complex than these preliminary observations suggest. For although in the New Testament the title "Son" clearly distinguishes Jesus from the *Father*, it does not thereby necessarily distinguish him from *God*. This is certainly not to suggest that the one Jesus calls Father is any other than the God of Israel, but only that the way in which the Jesus of the Gospels identifies the two is such that the Son's distinction from the Father does not in any straightforward way imply his distinction from God.[32] In this respect, the title "Son," in addition to being deployed more widely and frequently in the New Testament than either "Wisdom" or "Word," also does much more than these

---

30. Mention may also be made here of the plural "sons of God" (*bene-ha-'elohim*) in Gen. 6:2, 4 (cf. Deut. 32:8; Job 38:7), which seems to refer to supernatural (viz., "angelic") beings who elsewhere are portrayed as inhabiting God's heavenly court (see also Job 1:6; 2:1; cf. 1 Kgs. 22:19). Additionally, in Deut. 14:1 RSV (cf. Hos. 1:10 RSV) the whole people of Israel are called "sons of the LORD your God" (*banim . . . leYHWH 'elohekem*).

31. In this context one might also think of the title "Christ," or "Messiah"; but although this title is applied to Jesus in the New Testament more often than any other, it does not seem to be taken by the biblical writers as implying divinity. The few verses seeming to suggest otherwise do so precisely by linking "Christ" with other titles (e.g., "Son" in Matt. 16:16; John 11:27; cf. Matt. 26:63 and pars.; "Lord" in Matt. 22:41–45 and pars.).

32. Cf. the discussion on pp. 102–6 above. It is a weakness of Wolfhart Pannenberg's analysis that he fails to note this difference and equates Jesus' self-differentiation from the Father with self-differentiation from God (see his *Systematic Theology*, 3 vols., trans. Geoffrey W. Bromiley [Grand Rapids: Wm. B. Eerdmans Publishing Co., 1988–93], 1:263–64; 2:372–79). As already noted, Paul's deployment of God-language is different from that typical of the Gospels, but here, too, the way in which Jesus is distinguished from the Father does not function to impugn his own divine status; for though Paul is very consistent in reserving the term "God" for the Father, he is equally consistent in giving the Son the equally divine designation "Lord."

other two designations to clarify the specific character of Jesus' divinity: it is constituted by his relation to another, the one he calls "Father."

Two examples may help to illustrate this point. The first comes in the immediate aftermath of John's account of the feeding of the five thousand. The episode begins with one of the few instances in the Gospels where Jesus explicitly speaks of "God the Father"; moreover, he does so in a context where his own self-designation as "Son" seemingly confirms his own subordinate (and thus nondivine) status: "Do not work for the food that perishes, but for the food that endures for eternal life, which the Son of Man [Jesus] will give you. For it is on him that God the Father has set his seal" (John 6:27). As the discourse progresses, however, things become more complicated; Jesus goes on to identify "the work of *God*" with belief "in *him whom [God] has sent* [Jesus]" (6:29), and then he draws a contrast between Moses and the Father ("Very truly, I tell you, it was not Moses who gave you the bread from heaven, but it is my Father who gives you the true bread from heaven," 6:32) that parallels language used earlier in the Gospel to distinguish between Moses and Jesus ("The law indeed was given through Moses; grace and truth came through Jesus Christ," 1:17). Finally, Jesus refers to the "Father" (no longer identified as "God") and "Son" (no longer qualified as "Son of Man") as joint agents in the work of human redemption: "This is indeed the will of my Father, that all who see the Son and believe in him may have eternal life; and I [the Son] will raise them up on the last day" (6:40). In summary, as the discourse progresses, it depicts a set of relations in which the Son is indeed other than the Father, but, as the agent of resurrection, not quite so clearly other than God.

The second example also comes from John and takes the form of a discourse characterized by movement from what at first appears to be a fairly clear distinction between Jesus and (Israel's) God onward to their seeming identification. The crucial sequence begins when Jesus says to "the Jews," "If God were your Father, you would love me, for I came from God and now I am here. I did not come on my own, but he sent me" (John 8:42). In denying that God is the "Father" of his opponents, Jesus implicitly claims that distinction for himself, though in the process he appears to distinguish himself from this God as the one from whom he came and by whom he was sent. A few verses further, however, the perspective shifts: now Jesus' relationship with the "Father" is explicit, while the term "God" is associated with his opponents' misunderstanding of divinity and so moves to the background: "If I glorify myself, my glory is nothing. It is my Father who glorifies me, he of whom you say, 'He is our God'" (John 8:54). And as Jesus proceeds to describe the intimacy of this relationship with his Father, he goes so far as to apply to himself the form of God's own self-designation to Moses: "Very truly, I tell you, before Abraham was, I am" (John 8:58; cf. Exod. 3:14).[33] Here in the space of a few verses Jesus' way of distinguishing himself from the Father quickly leads to one of the most explicit reports of his self-identification with Israel's God anywhere in the New Testament.

To be sure, the interpretation of "Son" is complicated by the fact that in the New Testament the title is applied to Jesus in several different forms: "Son of Man" (chiefly though not exclusively in the Gospels), "Son of David" (limited to the Synoptic Gospels, though cf. Rom. 1:3; Rev. 22:16), "Son of God" (more typical of the Epistles), and "Son" without any further modification.[34] It is a matter of broad scholarly consensus, based in the patterns of usage found in the New Testament, that "Son of Man" was used by Jesus himself as a means of self-reference. What Jesus intended to convey by this phrase is less clear, since the Hebrew/Aramaic idiom on which it is based can have the purely anodyne meaning of "human being" and, as such, serves precisely to stress the nondivine character of the one so named (see, e.g., RSV: Ezek. 2:1, 3, 6, 8 and passim; Dan. 8:17).[35] At the same time, it is also the title given to the eschatological ruler described in Daniel 7:13, and at various points in the New Testament it is clearly applied to Jesus, both by himself and others, with this figure in mind (e.g., Matt. 10:23; 13:41; 16:27–28 and pars.; 19:28; 26:64 and pars.; Luke 18:8; John 3:13; 5:27; 6:62; Acts 7:56; Rev. 1:13; 14:14).[36] Yet though this heavenly "Son of Man" clearly acts in God's name and exercises divine power, the Danielic context suggests that he is to be understood as an agent of God rather than as himself divine (though see Matt. 16:27; Mark 8:38). The same may be said with even greater confidence of the messianic title "Son of David."

33. Lest there should be any doubt as to Jesus' meaning here, the evangelist notes that in response to this declaration, the crowd tries to stone him, applying the punishment for blasphemy specified in Lev. 24:16.

34. It should also be noted that there is one instance of "son of Mary" (Mark 6:3) and another of "son of Joseph" (John 6:42; cf. Matt. 13:55; Luke 3:23), but in context these phrases clearly function as informal (and noncontroversial) means of identifying Jesus as a member of the local community rather than as formal titles for him.

35. In this context it is interesting that one of the places in the New Testament where "Son of Man" is most clearly used in a theologically neutral sense is Matt. 16:13, when Jesus asks the disciples, "Who do people say that the Son of Man is?" And yet this question elicits from Peter one of the most theologically charged confessions made by any character in the Gospels: "You are the Messiah, the Son of the living God" (Matt. 16:16).

36. Vermes took the view that all historical uses of "Son of Man" from Jesus' lifetime were of the theologically neutral variety, and that the association of Jesus with the figure from Daniel resulted from the efforts of "apocalyptically minded Galilean disciples." Géza Vermes, *Jesus the Jew: A Historian's Reading of the Gospels* (Philadelphia: Fortress Press, 1981 [1973]), 186. But it is hard to see how even the most apocalyptically minded would have interpreted a purely neutral Aramaic idiom in this way without some precedent in Jesus' own usage, especially given the failure of the title (which appears over eighty times in the Gospels but only three times in all other New Testament books combined) to become part of Christian confessional language outside of descriptive accounts of Jesus' earthly ministry.

The situation with "Son" and "Son of God" is more complicated. The latter is generally applied to Jesus by others rather than used by Jesus of himself (though see John 5:25; 10:36; 11:4); by contrast, "Son" without modification is more typically placed by the evangelists on Jesus' own lips (Matt. 11:27 and pars.; 24:36 and pars.; 28:19; John 5:19–23, 25–27; 6:40; 8:36; 14:13; 17:1), in addition to being used by the Father at Jesus' baptism and transfiguration (see Matt. 3:17; 17:5 and pars.). Moreover, although "Son of Man" appears far more commonly as Jesus' means of self-designation in the Gospels, "Son" is typically coupled with explicit reference to the Father, while "Son of Man" is not.[37] To be sure—and in sharp contrast to their evaluation of the title "Son of Man"— New Testament scholars tend to doubt that the historical Jesus ever referred to himself as "Son" or "Son of God." By contrast, it is a matter of broad scholarly consensus that Jesus addressed God as Father (*Abba*; see especially Mark 14:36; cf. Rom. 8:15; Gal. 4:6), and though such usage was not unprecedented, the Gospel writers clearly regarded it as having been distinctive, such that (1) Jesus' addressing God as "Father" implies his own identity as "Son," and (2) because the one Jesus addresses as "Father" is evidently Israel's God, Jesus' identity as this Father's Son means that he is the "Son of God."[38] This is certainly the logic that John portrays as driving negative reaction to Jesus' use of Father language during the course of his ministry: "For this reason the Jews were seeking all the more to kill him, because he was . . . calling God his own Father, thereby making himself equal to God" (John 5:18; cf. 10:33).

While John is the Gospel in which this sort of pairing of "Father" and "Son" is most extensive, it is by no means absent from the Synoptics. In addition to the divine confession of Jesus as Son at his baptism (Matt. 3:17 and pars.) and transfiguration (Matt. 17:5 and pars.), as well as the so-called "Johannine thunderbolt" (Matt. 11:27; Luke 10:22), we might point to the fact that in

---

37. In this context, compare John 13:31, which juxtaposes "Son of Man" and "God" ("Now the *Son of Man* has been glorified, and *God* has been glorified in him") and John 17:1, which juxtaposes "Father" and "Son" ("*Father*, the hour has come; glorify your *Son* so that the Son may glorify you"). Indeed, the general lack of association of "Son of Man" language with "Father" language (one exception is John 6:27, discussed above) is a good reason for doubting that the former carries strong connotations of divinity.

38. "It is not Jesus' designation of himself as Son but his *proclamation of God as Father* that forms the basis for the use of the image of Son to describe his relationship to God." Ingolf U. Dalferth, *Crucified and Resurrected: Restructuring the Grammar of Christology*, trans. Jo Bennett (Grand Rapids: Baker Academic, 2015 [1994]), 108 (though see also p. 128, where Dalferth notes that the association of the title "son" with Davidic kingship meant that the confession of Jesus as Messiah would have reinforced his status as "Son"). Although references to God as Father appear in postexilic Old Testament books (see Isa. 63:16; 64:8; Jer. 3:4, 19; Mal. 2:10) and continue into the Second Temple period (see, e.g., Tob. 13:4; Wis. 14:3; Sir. 51:10; 3 Macc. 5:7; 6:3), the vocative form that seems to have been favored by Jesus was relatively rare. For a comprehensive review of the textual evidence, see Angelika Strotmann, *"Mein Vater bist du!" (Sir. 51:10): Zur Bedeutung der Vaterschaft Gottes in kanonischen und nichtkanonischen frühjüdischen Schriften* (Frankfurt: Josef Knecht, 1991).

Mark—by consensus the earliest of the Gospels—the narrative both opens with the identification of Jesus as "Son of God" (1:1) and comes to a climax with the centurion's echoing this confession at the foot of the cross, thereby becoming the first human character in the Gospel to designate Jesus by this title (15:39). Slightly differently, but to no less climactic effect, Matthew depicts Peter supplementing his confession of Jesus as Messiah at Caesarea Philippi with the declaration that he is "Son of the living God" (16:16); and he closes his Gospel with the risen Jesus' command to baptize all the nations "in the name of the Father and of the Son and of the Holy Spirit" (28:19). Finally, Luke introduces the title "Son" in connection with the annunciation of Jesus' birth (1:32, 35), even as the boy Jesus pointedly identifies Israel's God—and not the worried Joseph—as his Father (2:48–49). Alongside the witness of the Gospels may be added the full breadth of the remaining books of the New Testament (see, e.g., Acts 9:20; 20:28; Rom. 1:3–4; 5:10; 8:3; 1 Cor. 15:28; 2 Cor. 1:19; Gal. 2:20; Eph. 4:13; 1 Thess. 1:10; Heb. 1:8; 1 John 1:3; 2:23; Rev. 2:18). It is therefore clear that although the title "Son" is not used for Israel's God in the Old Testament and serves in the New to distinguish Jesus from one he called "Father" (who is Israel's God), it is nevertheless as much a means of characterizing Jesus' divinity as "Lord" and "Savior." But what exactly does it tell us about what it means for Jesus to be divine?

Clearly, unlike "Lord" and "Savior" the meaning of "Son" as a summary description of Jesus' divinity cannot be determined simply by reference to the use of the term in the Old Testament. At the same time, neither can the Christian deployment of the title simply be divorced from Old Testament usage without calling into question the identification of Jesus with Israel's God. With these two points in mind, I argue that while "Son" is not used as a divine title in the Old Testament, its deployment in the New does pick up certain features of the Old Testament's characterization of Israel's God. Thus, without wanting to claim that there is any direct appearance of the Son in the Hebrew Scriptures, I maintain that there is good reason to affirm that the revelation of the Son in and as Jesus is not only consistent with but also a fitting development of the Old Testament depiction of God.

Briefly, if the title "Lord" points to God's transcendence of the world and "Savior" to God's love for the world, "Son" highlights God's presence in and to the world.[39] Having made this point, however, there are immediately two cautions to be issued. First, to say that the title "Son" highlights the biblical

---

39. Cf. Dalferth, *Crucified and Resurrected*, 128: "What this title highlights is not the aspect of sovereignty but *God's nearness to Jesus himself* and the *nearness of God to us in and through Jesus*." Note, too, that in this respect the theological force of "Son" corresponds with "Wisdom" and "Word," both of which are associated in the Old Testament with the work of creation (see Prov. 8:22–31; cf. Wis. 7:22 and Ps. 33:6; cf. Sir. 42:15, respectively).

theme of divine presence is, once again, not to equate the Old Testament theophanies with the appearance of the Word not yet made flesh. The Son is not the mode of divine presence to the world as such, as in the Logos theologies of the church's early centuries. That sort of approach casts Jesus as mediator in just the wrong sense: as an ontological intermediary between God and the world and thus as less than fully divine. Second, to relate the "Son" to divine presence is not to suggest that the Father or the Spirit are absent. Because God is one, none of the divine persons are any more present in creation than any other, since it is the undivided work of all three persons, the one Creator, that sustains creation at every point of its existence. Indeed (as will be discussed at greater length in chap. 7), the Son's current absence from the world is an important dimension of Christian belief (see, e.g., Mark 16:19; Acts 1:9–11; 1 Cor. 11:26) that may be contrasted with the ongoing presence of the Spirit (John 16:7; Rom. 5:5; cf. Ps. 104:30), whose role in prompting us to call directly on the Father (Rom. 8:15–16; Gal. 4:6; cf. Matt. 6:9 and par.) implies the latter's presence as well.

That having been said, the claim that during the time of Jesus' earthly ministry the Son is present in a way (viz., enfleshed) that the Father and the Spirit are not does reflect a tension in certain of the Old Testament theophanies, in which God is portrayed as one who is both intrinsically inaccessible (and in that sense distant) and yet somehow capable of drawing near. This tension is especially clear in the figure called "the angel of the LORD." In many contexts, this entity seems to be just what the designation suggests: an emissary of God who, as such, is both different from and presumably subordinate to the God who sends him (see, e.g., Num. 22:22–35; Judg. 6:21–22; 1 Kgs. 19:5–7; 1 Chr. 21:12–20; Zech. 1:11–12). In other cases, however, the situation is not so clear-cut. Consider the following passage:

> The angel of the LORD found [Hagar] by a spring of water in the wilderness, the spring on the way to Shur. And he said, "Hagar, slave-girl of Sarai, where have you come from and where are you going?" She said, "I am running away from my mistress Sarai." The angel of the LORD said to her, "Return to your mistress, and submit to her." The angel of the LORD also said to her, "I will so greatly multiply your offspring that they cannot be counted for multitude." And the angel of the LORD said to her,
>
> "Now you have conceived and shall bear a son;
>   you shall call him Ishmael,
>   for the LORD has given heed to your affliction.
> He shall be a wild ass of a man,
>   with his hand against everyone,
>   and everyone's hand against him;
> and he shall live at odds with all his kin."

So she named the LORD who spoke to her, "You are El-roi"; for she said, "Have I really seen God and remained alive after seeing him?" (Gen. 16:7–13)

Throughout the bulk of the story, the supernatural character who appears to Hagar is named "the angel of the LORD," but at the end the designation suddenly shifts to "the LORD"; and, as if to emphasize the point, Hagar (with the evident consent of the narrator) names the one whom she has seen "God." A similar situation obtains in the very theophany where the divine name is given:

> Moses was keeping the flock of his father-in-law Jethro, the priest of Midian; he led his flock beyond the wilderness, and came to Horeb, the mountain of God. There the angel of the LORD appeared to him in a flame of fire out of a bush; he looked, and the bush was blazing, yet it was not consumed. Then Moses said, "I must turn aside and look at this great sight, and see why the bush is not burned up." When the LORD saw that he had turned aside to see, God called to him out of the bush, "Moses, Moses!" And he said, "Here I am." Then he said, "Come no closer! Remove the sandals from your feet, for the place on which you are standing is holy ground." He said further, "I am the God of your father, the God of Abraham, the God of Isaac, and the God of Jacob." And Moses hid his face, for he was afraid to look at God. (Exod. 3:1–6)

Once again, the entity referred to as "the angel of the LORD" at the beginning of the passage is designated as "the LORD" or "God" two verses further on— and then goes on to declare, "I am the God of your father."

Given that it is in the story of Hagar that the phrase "the angel of the LORD" makes its first appearance in the Bible, and that its appearance in the account of Moses at the burning bush corresponds to arguably the most important Old Testament theophany, the fact that in both cases there is such evident slippage between "the angel of the LORD" and "the LORD" is surely noteworthy. Other examples can be given (e.g., Gen. 22:10–14; Judg. 13:2–22), alongside the encounter between Abraham and the three men by the oaks of Mamre (Gen. 18:1–33), where there is no mention of the angel, but there is a similar mix of identification and distinction between the "men" and "the LORD." In no case is there any suggestion that there is more than one LORD involved. The implication is rather that the one sent by—and thus in some sense distinct from—the LORD is nevertheless none other than the LORD. And it is just such a situation that we find with respect to the deployment of "Son" in the New Testament, who is sent by God and yet is somehow identified with God (Matt. 10:40 and pars.; Luke 10:16; John 5:24, 30, 36; 8:42; 12:44–45). All this is not to say (with the early Fathers) that the Son may simply be equated with the angel of the LORD, but rather that in the revelation of the Son in the

New Testament, the sorts of identity-in-distinction between the appearance of God ("the angel of the Lord") and God's own self ("the Lord") found in the Old Testament assume clearer contours. As "the image of the invisible God," Jesus the Son is in some sense other than the Father he images, and yet also truly God—the one in whom "all the fullness of God was pleased to dwell" (Col. 1:15, 19; cf. John 14:9).

There are, of course, other ways beside reference to the ambiguous figure of the angel of the Lord by which divine presence is affirmed in the Old Testament.[40] For example, as the people are about to leave Mount Sinai during the exodus, God responds to Moses' complaint, "You have not let me know whom you will send with me," with the assurance: "My presence will go with you, and I will give you rest" (Exod. 33:12, 14). In the narrative that follows, this presence takes physical form in the descent of a cloud that signals to the Israelites when to pitch or strike camp during their wilderness wanderings (see Exod. 40:34–37; cf. Num. 9:17–22). This presence is obviously a benefit: it guides them in their journeying (Exod. 13:21–22) and even functions as a protective shield between the people and their adversaries (14:19–20). At the same time, the symbol of the cloud retains the tension between inaccessibility and proximity characteristic of the "angel of the Lord." Forasmuch as the cloud signals God's presence, it is also a mark of divine hiddenness: God descends (Exod. 34:5) and speaks "out of the cloud" (24:16), which generates a "thick darkness" (Deut. 5:22) and functions thereby as a divine "covering" (Ps. 105:39).

In this context, it is important to note the connection between the imagery of God's presence in the cloud and the language of divine glory (Hebrew *kabod*, Greek *doxa*) in the Old Testament. On the one hand, the cloud is the medium through which God's glory appears to Israel (e.g., "the glory of the Lord appeared in the cloud," Exod. 16:10; cf. 24:16; Num. 16:42); on the other hand, the cloud functions as a means of concealing (and thus protecting the people from) the divine glory, the appearance of which is "like a devouring fire" (Exod. 24:17; cf. Ezek. 1:27). It is the evidently destructive power of the glory that renders the cloud an impediment to human approach

40. A fascinating passage with respect to early Jewish belief regarding the degree to which an angel could serve as a mode of divine presence is Isa. 63:9, which in the Hebrew of the MT (followed by the RSV and most English versions) reads, "The angel of his presence [*mal'ak pānāyw*] saved them," in contrast to the LXX, which renders the verse "It was no messenger or angel, but the Lord himself [*autos kyrios*; NRSV: "his presence"] that saved them." As already noted (see p. 1 above), the latter was frequently cited in the early church as a means of bearing witness to the qualitative difference between God's presence in Jesus and in the angels as claimed already in New Testament texts like Heb. 1:5–7, 13–14. See Basil Studer, *Trinity and Incarnation: The Faith of the Early Church*, ed. Andrew Louth, trans. Matthias Westerhof (London: T&T Clark, 1993), 47.

(Exod. 40:35; cf. 1 Kgs. 8:10–11; 2 Chr. 5:13–14). The divine glory is simply too dangerous be encountered directly; and because it must be mediated, the most one might hope to glimpse is "the appearance of the likeness of the glory of the LORD" (Ezek. 1:28).[41]

Nevertheless, all of this is predicated on the Lord's willingness to be present to Israel. Solomon expresses the paradox involved here: "The LORD has said that he would dwell in thick darkness. I have built you an exalted house, a place for you to dwell in forever" (1 Kgs. 8:12–13). The idea of the God whose glory is wrapped in darkness dwelling in a house of human construction is recognized as deeply paradoxical: "But will God indeed dwell on the earth? Even heaven and the highest heaven cannot contain you, much less this house that I have built!" (8:27). But, as Michael Wyschogrod has pointed out, "the question does not invite the response that God does not dwell in this house."[42] On the contrary, even before Solomon begins his prayer of consecration, God has already come to be present in the house (8:10)—but that very presence, ironically, keeps even the priests authorized to serve God in the temple at bay (8:11).

So in the Old Testament, God is very much present to Israel; indeed, the presence is coeval with the revelation of the divine name, and as such, is integral to God's identity as the God of Israel (Num. 35:34). This presence is not simply the hidden presence by which God holds all creatures in being, but a matter of personal revelation whereby God makes God's self known uniquely to the Israelites as "the LORD." At the same time, this presence is also fearsome and correspondingly ambiguous: "a blazing fire, and darkness, and gloom, and a tempest, and the sound of a trumpet, and a voice whose words made the hearers beg that not another word be spoken to them" (Heb. 12:18–19; cf. Deut. 4:11; 5:22–25; 6:15). By contrast, when God becomes present in the flesh, it is not the people but the incarnate Lord himself who is threatened with destruction, as Jesus lays down his life for his friends (John 15:13–15; cf. 10:15b).

To be sure, it is important not to overstate the difference here. The God who took flesh in Jesus remains "a consuming fire" (Heb. 12:29; cf. Deut. 9:3); and if Jesus calls his followers friends, it is equally true that long before Jesus' birth, "the LORD used to speak to Moses . . . as one speaks to a friend" (Exod. 33:11; cf. 2 Chr. 20:7; Ps. 25:14; Isa. 41:8; Wis. 7:14, 27). And this is just what we should expect, since in both Testaments it is the same God who

---

41. Isaiah boldly claims to have seen "the Lord sitting on a throne," but the remainder of the description suggests that his vision did not extend beyond the hem of the divine robe, which "filled the temple" (Isa. 6:1)—and soon enough even this vision was obscured as "the house filled with smoke" (6:4).

42. Wyschogrod, *Abraham's Promise*, 169.

wills to be present in such a way as to be known and addressed by human beings—a measure of intimacy that was already viewed by Israel as astounding long before the Word took flesh: "For what other great nation has a god so near to it as the LORD our God is whenever we call to him?" (Deut. 4:7). To confess Jesus as Son is thus not to contrast divine presence with a previous absence, but rather to affirm presence as a defining characteristic of Israel's God, which in Jesus takes the new and surprising, but (at least according to the first evangelist) not altogether unanticipated form of God's dwelling with God's people as one of God's people (Matt. 1:23).

So what does it mean to confess with the Nicene Creed that Jesus is "perfect in divinity"? It means to say that, as Son, he is both Lord and Savior; but crucially, it is no less to say that the Savior and Lord is this one, the Son. As such, it is to confess as well that the one who takes flesh in Jesus is the Creator, but not Creator in the abstract sense of First Cause or Unmoved Mover. The reality of the one who takes flesh in Jesus is not a matter of deduction from human experience. If this God is known as the Creator "of all that is, seen and unseen," it is by virtue of already being known as the Lord, the God of Israel. And so to confess Jesus as God is to affirm that he is indeed the Creator and, as such, transcendent, loving, and present—but always only by virtue of his being the Lord and Savior of Israel, who dwells among his people. For if Jesus is not *this* God, then as far as Christian confession is concerned, he is not God at all. And yet because this God is definitely revealed in and as Jesus of Nazareth, the precise character of his divinity is finally known only in the perfection of the humanity with which it has been inseparably united. That perfection is the subject of the next chapter.

5

"And Also Perfect in Humanity"

The aim of the previous chapter was to speak concretely about Jesus' divinity by clarifying that the God who Jesus is, and thus whom he reveals, is the God of Israel, so that it is by reference to this God that Jesus' divinity is to be interpreted, and that we understand what it means to confess Jesus as Lord, Savior, and Son. The chapter's focus was thus primarily on Jesus' divine identity, or *hypostasis*, rather than his divine *nature* and its perfections. To be sure (and in line with the treatment of the divine perfections in chap. 1), the upshot of the argument is that to confess Jesus as Lord, Savior, and Son is also to acknowledge him as the one who is present in love, since such ascriptions are inherent in the creedal confession of Jesus as *"one* Lord," "the only *Son*," who came "for us and for our *salvation*." Nevertheless, because Jesus' unity, presence, and love can be known by us only as they take perceptible form, we experience these attributes as they are manifest in a substance that is not divine but created: flesh. As I argued in the introduction, this does not mean that Jesus' possession of the divine nature is in any sense merely partial or deficient, but only that, in line with the Chalcedonian principle that in him the divine and human natures are united "without confusion or change," the incarnation does not render divinity any less transcendent, and thus any more a possible object of human perception than it was prior to the Word's becoming flesh. After Jesus' birth no less than before it, divinity "dwells in unapproachable light" that "no one has ever seen or can see" (1 Tim. 6:16).

Yet if the divine substance remains as inaccessible as ever, the fact that a divine person has assumed human nature means that it is possible to speak of hearing, seeing, and touching God (1 John 1:1). Because human nature, as created, is available to us in this way, it differs absolutely from the nature of the Creator, and it is just because God is transcendent in this radical sense,

127

existing wholly otherwise (*totaliter aliter*) than creatures, that God can become incarnate. For since the Creator's presence never crowds out the creature's, neither the divine nor the human nature needs to be diminished to make room for the other when the Word takes flesh. That is why Jesus may be confessed as both "perfect in divinity and also perfect in humanity."

And yet in what does this dual "perfection" consist? With respect to divinity, the question is fairly easily answered: since God is not an instance of a kind, but simply the one, unique, and transcendent Lord, utterly unconstrained in the divine ability to exercise God's loving presence, for Jesus to be "perfect in divinity" is for him to possess all the divine perfections in their fullness, since any variation from this fullness would render them other than *God's* perfections, thereby making Jesus other than divine. The situation with Jesus' humanity is more complex, because "human being," unlike "God," is not a singular entity but applies to an indefinite number of numerically distinct and separable beings, characterized by variation in gender, size, color, temperament, and innumerable other features.[1] It is evidently impossible for any one human being to manifest all these variations simultaneously: Jesus cannot be at once brown-, green-, and blue-eyed (and for him to have multicolored eyes would, of course, just be a further particular variation) or both Jew and Gentile. In light of this it has been common enough in the history of the church to suppose Jesus' perfect humanity as meaning that he possesses what are taken to be the most perfect of these variations (e.g., male rather than female sexual characteristics, light rather than dark skin), or that he perfectly realizes the defining features of human nature (e.g., reason, virtue, freedom, God-consciousness, and so forth).

However common this sort of thinking has been, it does not have any basis in Scripture, nor is it integral to Jesus' role as the Savior of all people, whatever their individual variations. To be sure, it is crucial to Jesus' salvific role that he be fully human, "like his brothers and sisters in every respect" (Heb. 2:17). But the very fact of variation in the human species indicates that no particular individual or *hypostatic* property (e.g., biological sex, eyes of a particular color, etc.) can be regarded definitive of human *nature* in such a way that would require its having been assumed concretely by Jesus in order to satisfy the classical soteriological principle, "That which he has not assumed he has not healed."[2] Considered purely from this perspective, Jesus' role as Savior requires neither that he exhibit any particular human trait (e.g., maleness rather than femaleness),

---

1. Although God subsists in three distinct hypostases, these three are inseparable: to be (the one) God is just to be Father, Son, and Spirit. By contrast, to be human is to be distinctive: Mary or Martha or Lazarus, but not Mary and Martha and Lazarus.

2. Gregory of Nazianzus, *Letter 101* (*To Cledonius the Priest against Apollinarius*), in *NPNF*[2] 7:440; see p. 2 above.

nor that he be superior to other human beings with respect to any particular human capacity (as, e.g., the strongest, swiftest, or smartest human being who ever lived). To confess that Jesus' humanity is "perfect" is therefore not to claim that it is better than anyone else's, but simply to affirm that it is complete: lacking nothing of what is necessary to his being truly human.[3] Indeed, within a Chalcedonian framework the *perfection* of Jesus' humanity connotes chiefly its *ordinariness*: for him to be "perfect in humanity" is for him to be a perfectly ordinary human being.[4] In this context, it is worth noting that the evangelists recognize full well that Jesus struck many of his contemporaries in just this way: as a human being like any other (see Mark 6:3 and par.).[5]

Of course, to insist that Jesus' humanity is, ontologically speaking, perfectly ordinary is not to deny that it is distinctive. The same citizens of Nazareth who saw Jesus as a member of an unremarkable local family fully well recognized his "wisdom" and "deeds of power" (Mark 6:2 and par.). Indeed, that was precisely the occasion for their taking offense at him: the fact that nothing about him, humanly speaking, suggested any basis for the vocation he began to pursue after his baptism. In one respect, this sort of apparent mismatch should come as no surprise in light of the picture of God's election given in the Old Testament, where it is explicitly stated that the election of Israel has no basis in any extraordinary qualities the people possess (Deut. 7:7; cf. 1 Sam. 9:21; 16:7).[6] From this perspective, the distinctiveness that counts

3. One can make this point without presuming to be able to provide an exhaustive list of the traits that are constitutive of humanity. Since the set of individuals comprising humankind is continually being augmented by new additions with their own distinctive characteristics, and given the scriptural claim that we do not know what our completed humanity will look like (only that it will be manifest as a likeness to Jesus; see 1 John 3:2; cf. 2 Cor. 3:18), there is no need to deny that there is an "essence" of humanity, but every reason to affirm that it will be known only eschatologically. See Ian A. McFarland, *Difference and Identity: A Theological Anthropology* (Cleveland: Pilgrim, 2001), 131–43.

4. Importantly, to be "perfect in humanity" does not mean that Jesus has only human genetic material, since by the best current estimates over half of the cells that make up an average human being are microorganisms (including eukaryotes, prokaryotes, and viruses) with distinct, nonhuman genomes. It follows that for Jesus to be fully (i.e., typically and ordinarily) human means for his body to incorporate lots of nonhuman biota. And, of course, like all human beings, his humanity is through its processes of respiration and digestion constantly taking in (and through exhalation, defecation, and excretion) letting out various substances. To be human is thus to be utterly tied to and permeated by the nonhuman environment. For an excellent analysis of this point, see Rebecca Copeland, "Remembering the Word: A Decentered Approach to Two-Natures Christology" (PhD diss., Emory University, 2018), 172–75.

5. "For, if 'man' is truly to become the language of God, this cannot occur by straining man's nature toward the super-human, or by his wishing to stand out by becoming greater, more splendid, more renowned and stupendous than all others. He will have to be a man like everyone because he will be a man for everyone, and he will exhibit his uniqueness precisely through his ordinariness." Hans Urs von Balthasar, *Seeing the Form*, vol. 1 of *The Glory of the Lord: A Theological Aesthetics*, trans. Ermo Leiva-Merikakis (San Francisco: Ignatius 1989 [1967]), 457.

6. Paul develops this point to argue that election is always based in God's will rather than in any qualities possessed antecedently by the elect (Rom. 9:6–16).

for the purposes of vocation is not in the first instance the particular attributes (that is, the specific variations on human nature) a person may possess, but the way in which she lives them in relation to her environment.

In short, if the Word's becoming flesh is the means by which God establishes communion with creatures, the way to understand the nature of the fellowship God seeks (and thereby to come fully to terms with the character of the God who seeks it) is to examine the kind of human life the incarnate Word led. Thus, as the previous chapter focused on the character of Israel's God in order to address the question of who became incarnate in Jesus, so the present chapter, working from the conviction that Jesus is indeed this God made flesh, follows the reverse course: seeking to understand this God's character more fully by looking at Jesus' human life. It remains vital to maintaining the spirit of Chalcedonian Christology, however, that even the most strikingly distinctive features of his life be viewed as variations on ordinary human nature rather than exceptions to it.

BORN

Perhaps no fact is more decisive for the affirmation of Jesus' humanity than the confession that he was "born of a woman" (Gal. 4:4). And yet having stressed that Jesus' humanity is perfectly ordinary, such that his status as Lord and Savior does not require that the hypostatic properties (i.e., variations on human nature like gender, height, hair color, intelligence, and so forth that mark him as the distinct individual he is) be in any sense extraordinary or exemplary, it is an awkward fact that precisely with respect to Jesus' birth Christians affirm features of his humanity that are seemingly anything but ordinary, beginning with the creedal claim that he was born "of the virgin Mary." If Jesus was born of a virgin, then his humanity was certainly not typical in terms of the mode of its origination, since his conception involved no human father but was rather (again following the creed) effected "by the Holy Spirit" (cf. Matt. 1:18–23; Luke 1:26–35).[7]

Of course, to affirm that Jesus' humanity was extraordinary in its mode of origination does not entail that it is for that reason other than ordinary in substance. Still more to the point, insofar as his distinctive mode of conception is

---

7. This does not mean that the Spirit (rather than Joseph) was Jesus' father; rather, to say that Jesus "was conceived by the Holy Spirit" is precisely to deny that he had a biological father. The point is that Mary becomes pregnant by the power of God's will rather than by the infusion of divine DNA. In this same context, the cavil that biological parthenogenesis (of the sort that occurs among, e.g., water fleas and hammerhead sharks) cannot issue in a male offspring is clearly beside the point of the story, which is precisely that Jesus' conception is miraculous.

not in any sense essential to his identity as the eternal Son, the second person of the Trinity, it is not required for him to fulfill his vocation. It is certainly true that Matthew understands Jesus' virginal conception as a sign of his messianic status, since it fulfills the prophecy of Isaiah 7:14; but the claim that Jesus is divine does not depend on his having been so conceived. Precisely because Jesus is not a hybrid in whom divinity replaces some component of his human nature, his status as the Son of God—the claim that his hypostasis is the second person of the Trinity—is ontologically independent of whether or not he had a human father.[8] To be sure, given the strongly patriarchal culture of the ancient Mediterranean, in which a man's physical ability to beget sons was a means of securing power and prestige (see Ps. 127:4), the mode of Jesus' conception suggests that from his very origin his life challenges established modes of securing and exercising power.[9] On these grounds, Jesus' virginal conception might be described (following medieval Scholastic terminology) as *conveniens*—appropriate or fitting—but not as something on which his status as the Word made flesh hinges. There are, however, two other aspects of Jesus' humanity, established at birth, that do seem to be integral to his identity as Lord and Savior: that he was *sinless* and that he was a *Jew* (and more specifically, a descendant of David). Because both claims seem inconsistent with the affirmation that Jesus' vocation does not require his possessing particular, extraordinary qualities, they demand further discussion.

The claim that Jesus was sinless has clear scriptural support (Heb. 4:15; 2 Cor. 5:21; 1 Pet. 2:22; 1 John 3:5). Since it is not mentioned in the Gospels and is not justified in other New Testament texts on the basis of any sort of assessment of Jesus' behavior, Jesus' sinlessness is not best understood as an empirical claim, but as a theological corollary of his status as Savior, on the grounds that only one who is himself without sin is able to "save his people from their sins" (Matt. 1:21; cf. 1 Tim. 1:15) by forgiving them (Matt. 9:2 and pars.; Luke 7:48; cf. Heb. 2:17). The problem is that forgiving sins is, in biblical perspective, an exclusively divine prerogative (see Mark 2:7), and while Christians certainly are happy to conclude that Jesus is divine, this confession implies that Jesus' sinlessness is not simply a contingent feature of his humanity (as though it were the case that while he did not in fact sin, he might have done so in principle), but intrinsic to his identity as the Son of

---

8. See the discussion in Joseph Ratzinger, *Introduction to Christianity*, trans. J. R. Foster (London: Burns & Oates, 1969), 208.

9. As the nineteenth-century American preacher Sojourner Truth is reported to have said, "Whar did your Christ come from? From God and a woman! Man had nothin' to do wid Him." Frances D. Gage, "Reminiscences by Frances D. Gage: Sojourner Truth," in *History of Woman Suffrage*, ed. Elizabeth Cady Stanton, Susan B. Anthony, Matilda Joslyn Gage, 3 vols. (Rochester: Charles Mann, 1887), 1:116.

God. In other words, if Jesus is divine, then he was not merely without sin, but impeccable—utterly incapable of sinning. Is this claim consistent with his being fully human?

One might answer this question by noting that insofar as Christians teach that human beings were created in a sinless state and thus deny that sin is inherent in human nature as such, Jesus' sinlessness is not in itself inconsistent with his being fully human. But insofar as Christians claim that the first human beings committed sin, and that all other human beings *except* Jesus have followed suit, to confess Jesus as sinless seems to place him outside the company of the rest of the human family.[10] From this perspective, one might concede that the particular form of Jesus' humanity—like that of any other human being—will have distinctive features that mark him off from every other member of the species, and still one might worry that the claim that Jesus is sinless goes too far, since it makes his humanity not merely unique, but also utterly exceptional.

A first step toward addressing this concern may be made by noting the common Christian teaching that all human beings in the state of glory will be incapable of sinning, however much they may sin in the present (and even if, following the Western theological tradition, their natures have been so damaged by the fall that on earth they sin necessarily). And since even in glory human beings remain fully and genuinely human, Christ's inability to sin cannot in itself be held to be inconsistent with the claim that he is fully human. So if the rest of us can hope for a state in which sinning is humanly impossible, then Christ's impeccability cannot be judged ontologically incompatible with his humanity.

And yet theological concerns about Jesus' impeccability arguably have less to do with abstract considerations about the ontological compatibility between that claim and his full humanity than with the concrete features of Jesus' earthly existence as described in the New Testament, as summed up in the biblical affirmation that he was "tested as we are" (Heb. 4:15; cf. 2:17–18). This claim is certainly consistent with the belief that Jesus *did* not sin when faced with temptation, but one may still wonder whether he can be said to have been "tested as we are"—that is, to have undergone the human

---

10. In Catholic teaching the virgin Mary constitutes a separate case, in that she is confessed both to have been born without sin (the doctrine of the Immaculate Conception) and to have remained sinless throughout her life (see *Munificentissimus Deus*, §5). Crucially, however, the congenital sinlessness whereby Mary overcame all sin was not a product of her own capacities, but rather was a privilege granted "in view of the merits of Jesus Christ" (*Ineffabilis Deus*, §1). In this respect, Mary's sinlessness is different from Jesus', such that while she is (in Catholic teaching, at least) an exception to the norm of post-Adamic human sinfulness, she is not an exception in the same way as Jesus is, since her sinlessness does not preclude a dependence on Jesus' merits shared with the rest of the human family. See DH §2803.

experience of temptation—if he *could* not sin. This concern may, however, be addressed by distinguishing between the reality of being tempted, which is constituted by the simple fact of being enticed or urged to sin (e.g., Jesus' experience in the wilderness, as described in Matt. 4:1–11 and par.; cf. Mark 1:12–13), and the psychological experience of indecision or struggle when faced with two or more possible courses of behavior. The worry that Christ's impeccability is incompatible with his genuine humanity results from confusing these two situations. There are many sins that I do not commit and that I am not in the least inclined to commit: murder, theft, the public berating of colleagues, the sexual abuse of children. If someone were to urge me to commit any of these (or any of an indefinite number of other) sinful acts, it would be true that I had been tempted, though (at least based on my experience to date) I would not be in the least inclined to succumb to that temptation. For Christians to claim that Jesus is impeccable is, from this perspective, simply to affirm that he experiences *all* temptation in this way (unlike myself, for whom there are other sins for which my being tempted *is* accompanied by psychological struggle). And this claim could only be taken to impugn the genuineness of his humanity if it were also true that one were somehow *less* human in those areas where one did not struggle to avoid sin than those where one did. But that is surely not the case. On the contrary, assuming that we have been created for lives of blessedness, then it is when we regard the prospect of sinning as utterly without attraction and, indeed, as genuinely repulsive that we are *most* genuinely human. If the lack of struggle with sin as experienced by human beings even now may be taken as a genuine, albeit episodic, anticipation of the grace to be experienced fully in the state of glory, then the fact that Jesus happened to enjoy that fullness of grace throughout his earthly ministry cannot be taken as inconsistent with his humanity.

And if we should ask how it is that Jesus happened to enjoy that fullness of grace, the answer is the same one would give when explaining how any human being happens to enjoy a peculiar manifestation of grace: through the gift of the Holy Spirit. It is, indeed, central to the confession of Jesus' full humanity that the Spirit is the source of all his human graces, from his faithful teaching to his acts of hospitality and to his miracles.[11] Given the specific character of

---

11. That the Son is the *subject* of all Jesus' human actions (in a manner unique to Jesus as the Word incarnate), while the Spirit is their effective *cause* (in a manner identical to all human beings) is a crucial point emphasized by the seventeenth-century Puritan John Owen, who wrote that the "only immediate *act* of the person of the Son on the human nature was the *assumption* of it into subsistence with himself," while "all other actings of God in the *person of the Son* towards the human nature were voluntary, and did not necessarily ensue on the union mentioned; for there was no transfusion of the properties of one nature into the other, nor real physical communication of divine essential excellencies unto the humanity." John Owen, *Pneumatologia*, vol. 3 of *The Works of John Owen*, ed. William H. Goold (Carlisle: Banner of Truth, 1972), 160–61.

the claim that Jesus was impeccable, however, it is not sufficient to claim that the Spirit merely happened to keep Jesus from sin at every point during his life, but necessary to say something about how the Spirit's activity makes Jesus humanly impeccable (i.e., that the Spirit graces the operation of his human nature in such a way that sin becomes objectively impossible for him). In other words, granted that Jesus, as the Word of God, could not sin, how can his sinlessness be understood as a feature of his concrete human existence?

Given that Jesus' impeccability anticipates the situation of all glorified human beings, answering this question requires further reflection on the character of the glorified state as it relates to human willing. Here I take it as a basic principle, first clearly articulated in the Christian tradition by Augustine, that human willing follows desire (i.e., that human beings *will* what they *want*).[12] If this is so, then it follows that people struggle to will the good when their desires are not oriented toward it. Since God, as the source of all goodness and thus the highest good for all creatures, cannot but be desired (since humans desire whatever it is they desire only insofar as they view it as a good), human sin—the will's turning away from God—can only be the result of an imperfect apprehension of God. Now, the reason why humans are incapable of sinning in glory is because in glory they have unimpeded perception of God: the beatific vision.[13] It follows that the necessary presupposition of Jesus' impeccability is that he enjoys the beatific vision from the moment of his conception.

Is this claim that Jesus experienced even this much of the state of glory while on earth consistent with the principle that he "had to become like his brothers and sisters in every respect" (Heb. 2:17)? Thomas Aquinas was sensitive to this concern and addressed it by arguing that although it is fitting for Jesus to grow through time into all those aspects of human blessedness that other human beings also acquire over time, an exception needs to be made for those qualities, the absence of which would be inconsistent with his identity as God's Son.[14] Thus, insofar as impeccability is intrinsic to the person of the

12. To deny this point by, say, holding to a radically libertarian notion of the will as undetermined by anything other than itself makes nonsense of any attempt to explain human actions, for one can no longer appeal to motives (i.e., what the agent wanted) to explain a particular behavior, but only to the "free" decision of the will. The result, as Charles Mathewes puts it, is that the "explanation of our actions then ends invariably in the raw existentialist claim 'so I willed it.' But that ends up rendering one's identity a riddle; for why should I, a reflective, deliberative agent, identify myself with this willing 'I'?" Charles T. Mathewes, *Evil and the Augustinian Tradition* (Cambridge: Cambridge University Press, 2001), 54. For further discussion of the point, see Ian A. McFarland, *In Adam's Fall: A Meditation on the Christian Doctrine of Original Sin* (Oxford: Wiley-Blackwell, 2010), 75–79.

13. So Thomas derives impeccability from the possession of the beatific vision, on the grounds that "the will of one who sees God's essence necessarily clings to God, just as now we necessarily will to be happy." Thomas Aquinas, *ST* 1.82.2, trans. alt.

14. Aquinas, *ST* 3.19.3.

Word (since God cannot sin), and insofar as a human being may be impeccable only by virtue of enjoying the beatific vision, it is necessary for Jesus to
have had from conception an unimpeded vision of the divine will. And in the
case of Jesus, as for all human beings, the beatific vision is properly understood as a gift of the Holy Spirit.[15]

Note that if we follow this line of reasoning, the claim that Jesus' *person* had
to be sinless in order to fulfill his ministry does not require any qualification
of the principle that Jesus' human *nature* did not need to have any exemplary
characteristics in order to fulfill his vocation as Messiah. For although Jesus'
sinlessness is realized *in* his human nature (viz., via the purity of his human willing as enabled by his possession of the beatific vision), it is not derived *from* it:
he is sinless because he is the Son of God, not because he is the son of Mary.[16]

Things are just the converse with respect to Jesus' Jewishness, for a human
being is a Jew if and only if one is a biological descendent of Abraham through
the line of Isaac and Jacob. So while it is certainly true that because Jesus is
a Jew, the second person of the Trinity is a Jew, he is a Jew because he is the
son of Mary, not because he is the Son of God.[17] In short, Jesus' Jewishness
is a matter of his ancestry: it is, after all, only because he was born of a *Jewish* woman in particular that it is possible to affirm that he was "born under
the law" (Gal. 4:4), and thus a member of God's covenant people (see Rom.
9:4–5).[18] Thus, while Jesus' sinlessness is not visible as such, but is rather
inferred from his identity as God's Son, his Jewishness is a very much an

15. It is important to note that according to Thomas the beatific vision is not natural to Jesus if
viewed from the perspective of Christ's humanity, since it is not caused in Christ (any more than in
any other human being) by the properties of human nature itself (as with all human beings, it is the
product of grace given by God over and above the created properties of human nature); but Thomas
says that Jesus' sinlessness *can* be called natural in the sense of his having had it from his conception,
by virtue of the causal efficacy of the divine nature, which was from the outset hypostatically united
to the human nature. See Aquinas, *ST* 3.2.12. For a comprehensive contemporary defense of the
idea that Jesus enjoyed the beatific vision during his earthly ministry, see Simon Francis Gaine, *Did
the Saviour See the Father? Christ, Salvation and the Vision of God* (London: Bloomsbury T&T Clark,
2015). See also Thomas Joseph White, OP, *The Incarnate Lord: A Thomistic Study in Christology*
(Washington, DC: Catholic University of America Press, 2015), chap. 5.

16. Jesus' sinlessness is a matter of his hypostasis, which means that it is not the result of
his lacking a human father (as, e.g., Aquinas argues in *ST* 3.31.1.3). As already noted, Jesus'
hypostatic identity as the second person of the Trinity is independent of the circumstances of
his conception. Since his sinlessness is a function of this identity, it follows that it, too, stands
irrespective of his paternity (or lack thereof).

17. In rabbinic Judaism a person's status as a Jew is determined by the mother's status (see
b. Qiddushin 68b; cf. m. Qiddushin 3:12 and m. Yevamot 7:5), which dovetails nicely with the
Christian belief that Jesus had no biological father, but this matrilineal principle seems to be a
postbiblical development not clearly attested until the second century. See Shaye D. Cohen,
"The Origins of the Matrilineal Principle in Rabbinic Law," *Association for Jewish Studies Review*
10, no. 1 (Spring 1985): 19–53.

18. As already noted (see p. 115 n. 26 above), Gentiles are not "born under the law," according to Jewish teaching.

empirical fact. As such (and quite in contrast with the idea of Jesus' being without sin), it does not appear ever to have been a matter of dispute. The accounts of Jesus' ministry provided by the evangelists give no indication that even Jesus' opponents thought him other than a Jew (if objection is made to his being named as "King of the Jews" in John 19:21, it is evidently on the grounds of the office thereby ascribed to him rather than to his ethnicity).[19] Likewise, although Talmudic references to Jesus are uniformly negative, in no case does his Jewishness appear to be called into question.[20]

Granted that Jesus' being a Jew is clear biblical teaching, what is its significance? Jesus had to be sinless in order to be able to overcome the power of sin. But what was the point of his being Jewish—born not simply human but also "under the law"? If Jesus' being without sin singles out a feature of his earthly humanity that marks him as different from all other human beings—the Savior in distinction from all those who stand in need of saving—then according to Paul, Jesus' Jewishness is just the opposite: a point of profound solidarity with other people. As he puts it, Jesus was "born under the law, in order to redeem those who were under the law" (Gal. 4:4–5). Insofar as God's promise of blessing was made to the Jews, it is imperative that it be fulfilled among the Jews, so that it is to them, God's chosen people, that Jesus is sent (see Matt. 15:24; cf. 10:6; 19:28).[21] Thus, if Jesus is God's Son eternally, in taking flesh as a Jewish human being he becomes a brother to all other Jews and thereby makes them with him sons and daughters of God. Such at least seems to be Paul's thinking, in light of his teaching that the aim of the redemption Jesus provides to those under the law is "that we might receive adoption as children" (Gal. 4:5). Indeed, it is through the receipt of the same Spirit bestowed on Jesus at his baptism (where, according to Matt. 3:17 and pars., God explicitly names him as Son) that Jesus' fellow Jews receive confirmation of their status as God's children: "because you are children, God has sent the Spirit of his Son into our hearts, crying, 'Abba! Father!'" (Gal. 4:6).

Of course, the adoption as God's children that is enjoyed by those under the law is through Jesus extended to the Gentiles as well; indeed, most of Paul's correspondents in Galatia are evidently Gentiles, for he reminds them

19. At one point in the Gospels, Jesus' Jewish opponents call him a "Samaritan" (John 8:48), but, given that this accusation is joined with the claim that he is possessed, it is evidently to be understood as an insult rather than a literal description—all the more so given the accounts of Jesus' interactions with Samaritans elsewhere in the Gospels (see Luke 9:51–53; 17:14–18; John 4:7–9).

20. The extent and proper assessment of references to Jesus in the Talmud are matters of considerable debate, but none of the texts with a claim to refer to Jesus denies that he was a Jew. For a fine recent study, see Peter Schäfer, *Jesus in the Talmud* (Princeton, NJ: Princeton University Press, 2007).

21. See also Luke's account of how, when newly arrived in a city, Paul would always first preach Jesus in the synagogue (Acts 9:20; 13:5; 14:1; 17:10; 18:1–4, 19; cf. 28:16–23).

(as he could not possibly have done if writing to Jews) that prior to the proclamation of the gospel they "did not know God," but "were enslaved to beings that by nature are not gods" (Gal. 4:8). So too, Jesus had taught that while he has been sent in the first instance to Israel, he also has "other sheep that do not belong to this fold" (John 10:16). It is on this basis that after his resurrection he sends his followers out to "proclaim the good news to the whole creation" (Mark 16:15) and to "make disciples of all nations" (Matt. 28:19). Nevertheless, the discipleship to which all are invited involves being made heirs of the promise given to Abraham and his children (Gal. 3:29; cf. Rom. 4:13) by being grafted into the covenant people (Rom. 11:24).

In this way, the God who created the world proves to be the God of the Jews by living in the world as a Jew, thereby making the life of this people to be God's own life and God's promises to his people utterly indefeasible. For if God is born a Jew, then there is no longer even the logical possibility that God might destroy the people of Israel and raise up in their stead a new nation "greater and mightier than they" (Num. 14:12; cf. Deut. 9:14), since for God to destroy Israel after assuming Jewish flesh would be a matter of self-destruction. At this point, however, it is important to note that, according to the New Testament, Jesus' vocation as Messiah requires that he be not only a Jew, but also (and still more specifically) a descendant of David. It should thus come as no surprise that Jesus' Davidic descent is affirmed at various points throughout the New Testament (e.g., Rom. 1:3; 2 Tim. 2:8; Rev. 22:16; cf. Matt. 15:22; Mark 10:47–48; Heb. 7:14), and that two of the Gospels take considerable care to document it.[22] Although Jesus himself is recorded as treating the point with a certain amount of irony (Matt. 22:41–45 and par.); nevertheless, it seems clear that the early church saw Jesus' Davidic ancestry as crucial to his claim to be the Messiah (see John 7:41–42).

Is the claim that Jesus' messianic status is contingent upon his having been born both a Jew and of David's line consistent with his perfectly ordinary humanity? Yes, in the sense that there is nothing in itself extraordinary about being Jewish, or even being of Davidic descent: neither quality marks Jesus as uniquely gifted with respect to other human beings. Still, to say that Jesus needed to be a descendant of David in order to fulfill his vocation doubtless

22. It might seem odd that the two evangelists who give the most attention to Jesus' Davidic descent through Joseph are also the two who stress that Joseph was not, in fact, Jesus' biological father (Matt. 1:20–23; Luke 1:26–35; cf. 3:23); but given the character of adoption in first-century Jewish culture, there would have been nothing inconsistent with the affirmation of Jesus' being conceived without Joseph's involvement and his being counted as Davidic by virtue of being claimed by Joseph as his son (as passages like Matt. 1:24; 2:13–21; 13:55; and Luke 2:48 indicate was the case). See the discussion in Raymond Brown, *The Birth of the Messiah: A Commentary on the Infancy Narratives in the Gospels of Matthew and Luke*, 2nd ed. (New York: Doubleday, 1993), 505–13.

does posit a particular (even if not unique) characteristic of his humanity as integral to his saving work. The point remains, however, that this quality is not significant because it marks any sort of intrinsic excellence. After all, the Old Testament is replete with examples of Davidic descendants who were both foolish and wicked. Its significance lies rather in its being testimony to God's faithfulness to the promise that it is through Israel that the nations are to be blessed (Gen. 22:18; 26:4), and that the destiny of Israel should, in turn, be bound to the throne of David, which God has established forever (2 Sam. 7:16).

So if Jesus is born *sinless* and indeed impeccable, because only one who is without sin can be the Savior, then he is born a *Jew*—and more specifically, a descendant of David—because only a Jew can be the particular kind of Savior promised by God, namely, one who is Israel's Messiah, "Christ the Lord" (Luke 2:11 RSV). In this context, it is worth remembering that the term "Messiah" means "anointed," and that in the Old Testament anointing is the way in which individuals are set apart for particular ministries to the people of Israel, especially for the roles (or "offices") of prophet (1 Kgs. 19:16), king (1 Sam. 16:1, 11–13), and priest (Exod. 30:30). Furthermore, the association of election to these tasks with the practice of anointing serves as a reminder that, as often as not, the heroes of Israel's history were not distinguished by any intrinsic qualities, but simply by the fact of having been set apart—and only thereupon enabled—by God to do great things (see, e.g., Exod. 3:11–12; Judg. 6:15–16; 1 Sam. 9:21–10:1; Isa. 6:5–7; Jer. 1:6–8; Amos 7:14–15). As the culmination of Israel's history, the one in whom all God's promises are fulfilled (2 Cor. 1:20), Jesus has long been understood by Christians as "anointed" in a comprehensive sense, such that God perfects in him all three Old Testament offices of prophet, king, and priest. We will explore these dimensions of Jesus' ministry (traditionally referred to as the doctrine of Christ's threefold office, or *munus triplex*) by way of the defining points in the creedal narrative of Jesus' ministry: that he suffered and died (in the balance of this chapter) and is risen and ascended (in chap. 6).

SUFFERED

That Jesus was considered a prophet during his ministry is well attested (see, e.g., Matt. 21:11, 46; Luke 7:16; John 6:14; cf. Mark 8:28 and pars.). And at one level it seems very natural to associate his status as a prophet with the confession that he "suffered under Pontius Pilate," for it is a commonplace of New Testament teaching that the prophets suffered (e.g., Matt. 5:12 and par.; 23:29–34; Luke 11:49–50; Acts 7:52; 1 Thess. 2:15; Jas. 5:10; Rev. 16:6). At the same time, it is often cited as a serious defect of the classical creeds that they reduce the whole of Jesus' earthly ministry to his suffering. In moving straight from his birth to the fact that he "suffered" (the Apostles' Creed) or, even more restrictively, "was crucified" (Nicene Creed), the creeds rush past what are arguably the most genuinely "prophetic" dimensions of his work, bypassing the evangelists' rich accounts of Jesus' healing, teaching, and practices of table fellowship in a narrow focus on his trial and execution. And while the creedal affirmation that Christ's suffering happened "under Pontius Pilate" rightly situates the incarnation in the midst of secular history, the creedal focus on Jesus' passivity before earthly political power has arguably served to eclipse attention to the concrete—and often politically subversive—features of his ministry. As womanist and feminist theologians in particular have pointed out, one result has been to encourage passivity among his followers, especially among those of his followers who subsist at the margins of church and society.[23] If the effective content of Jesus' prophetic ministry is reduced to his suffering, it seems to follow that the good disciple is one who endures suffering, with little attention to the rather obvious fact that the defining practices of Jesus' ministry, his healing the sick and associating with outcasts, reflect a commitment to alleviating suffering. To be sure, Jesus warns his followers that such commitment will itself entail suffering (see Matt. 10:24–25; cf. 5:10–12; Luke 21:12; John 15:20); but it is a suffering that comes from challenging the present order rather than passively acquiescing to its demands.

And yet, however infelicitous in practice the theological deployment of "suffered under Pontius Pilate" has been, the phrase is able to bear a more expansive interpretation. Insofar as Pilate was prefect of Judea through the whole course of Jesus' ministry,[24] it is not necessary to limit Jesus' "suffering" under him to his last days in Jerusalem, all the more so if "suffering" is not equated with experiencing physical or psychological pain, but is interpreted in its etymological sense (from the Latin *suffere*) as to bear, endure, or undergo. In this sense, saying that Jesus "suffered under Pontius Pilate" affirms his concrete, historical humanity, but now with a focus on the fact that the whole of his earthly ministry was defined by relationships with other human beings, in response to whom he undertakes the particular practices of healing, teaching, reproof, feasting, and so forth that define him precisely as "a prophet

23. For now-classic formulations, see esp. Dolores Williams, *Sisters in the Wilderness: The Challenge of Womanist God-Talk* (Maryknoll, NY: Orbis Books, 1995); and Daphne Hampson, *Theology and Feminism* (Oxford: Basil Blackwell, 1990). On the other hand there have been feminists in particular who have sought to defend the liberating potential of kenotic language, from Rosemary Radford Ruether's interpretation of the incarnation as a divine self-emptying, in her *Sexism and God-Talk: Toward Feminist Theology* (Boston: Beacon Press, 1983), 1–11, 134–39; to Sarah Coakley's advocacy of human kenosis in contemplative prayer, in her *Powers and Submissions: Spirituality, Philosophy, and Gender* (Malden, MA: Blackwell, 2002), 3–39.

24. The years of Pilate's prefecture were 26–36; Jesus' ministry is conventionally dated as extending from 30 to 33.

mighty in deed and word before God and all the people" (Luke 24:19). For in the Old Testament, too, the ministry of the prophet is one of "suffering" in that it is radically contingent, continually shaped by interaction with the context within which that ministry takes shape. If it is a defining feature of the divine nature to be unconditioned by any nondivine reality, it is an index of the humanity of the incarnate Word that he is known only as his life is conditioned, constrained, and otherwise defined by interaction with the characters and circumstances in relation to which he lives, moves, and has his being. In just this way, he fulfills the office of prophet.

Even as consideration of the prophetic character of Jesus' ministry allows for a broader understanding of his suffering, so it provides a basis for reclaiming the language of kenoticism, or the Word's self-emptying. As I have already argued, it is a mistake to suppose that the mere fact of taking flesh in itself entailed any sort of diminishment of Jesus' divinity. The self-emptying consists rather in what follows upon his "being found in human form," namely, the fact that, as a human being, "he humbled himself" (Phil. 2:7–8). To be sure, he took "the form of a slave, being born in human likeness" (2:7); but given that there is nothing inherently servile about human existence (quite the contrary, according to texts like Gen. 1:26–28 and Ps. 8:3–8), the "form of a slave" must be seen as a particular—and deliberate—modification of the human form. That is certainly how Jesus himself interprets the shape of his ministry:

> The kings of the Gentiles lord it over them; and those in authority over them are called benefactors. But not so with you; rather the greatest among you must become like the youngest, and the leader like one who serves. For who is greater, the one who is at the table or the one who serves? Is it not the one at the table? But I am among you as one who serves. (Luke 22:25–27; cf. John 13:1–16)

In short, the kenosis of the Word is not a matter of giving up divinity for humanity (as though to take human flesh were eo ipso to be a servant), but rather describes the mode by which the eternal Word lives out his human life as Jesus of Nazareth.[25] So while we most certainly do see an emptying of the Word in Jesus' ministry, it is not defined by the *fact* of the incarnation

---

25. So Luther's sermon "Two Kinds of Righteousness":

The term "form of God" . . . does not mean the "essence of God" because Christ never emptied himself of this. Neither can the phrase "form of a servant" be said to mean "human essence." But the "form of God" is wisdom, power, righteousness, goodness—and freedom too; for Christ was a free, powerful, wise man, subject to none of the vices or sins to which all other men are subject. He was pre-eminent in such attributes as are particularly proper to the form of God. . . . [But] for our sakes he became as one of us and took the form of a servant, that is, he subjected himself to all evils. ("Two Kinds of Righteousness," in *Career of the Reformer I, LW* 31:301) (that Jesus, according to Luke 2:52, "increased in wisdom and in years, and in divine and human favor," hardly accords with the notion that his enfleshment is a matter of his constant and progressive humiliation), but by its *form*, as he "became obedient to the point of death—even death on a cross" (Phil. 2:8). In other words, it is by emptying himself of any claim to earthly distinction that Jesus exemplifies the life of a prophet.

Considerations of space (as well as limits of competence) make it impossible to embark on anything close to an exhaustive account of Jesus' ministry as portrayed in the canonical Gospels, let alone to engage fully with the debates over the historical accuracy of those accounts. I do take it that these Gospels are the oldest accounts we have of Jesus' life.[26] I also think that there is good reason to view them as generally reliable records of his ministry.[27] But I have no interest in defending their inerrancy: the obvious discrepancies between the evangelists' accounts, from the genealogy of Joseph through the day of Jesus' crucifixion, render frankly incredible the claim that the contents of the

---

Cf. the Lutheran Scholastic Johann Gerhard, who maintained that the incarnation itself may be called an *exinantio*, or emptying, only *improprie*, but that in "sensu biblico sive secundum stylum apostoli Phil. 2 exinanitio proprie accipitur pro ipsa Jesu Christi sive Λόγου incarnati κενώσει." Ioanni Gerardi, *Loci theologici*, 9 vols., ed. E. Preuss (Berlin: Gust. Schlawitz, 1863–75 [1610–22]), locus 4, caput 14, §§293–94.

26. That the noncanonical gospel texts, including the Gospel of Thomas, are significantly later and, where they incorporate genuine historical information about Jesus, overwhelmingly (though not exclusively) dependent on the canonical Gospel texts, I take to have been established convincingly by Simon Gathercole, *The Composition of the Gospel of Thomas: Original Language and Influences*, Society for New Testament Studies Monograph Series 151 (Cambridge: Cambridge University Press, 2012); see also Francis Watson, *Gospel Writing: A Canonical Perspective* (Grand Rapids: Wm. B. Eerdmans Publishing Co., 2013).

27. Although Luke Timothy Johnson believes that the data are simply lacking to produce detailed reconstructions of Jesus' life and ministry, he thinks there is ample evidence to suggest that the Gospels accurately portray Jesus' characteristic activities, as well as certain basic facts surrounding his birth and death, in *The Real Jesus: The Misguided Quest for the Historical Jesus and the Truth of the Traditional Gospels* (San Francisco: HarperSanFrancisco, 1996). A different sort of argument is presented by Richard Bauckham, *Jesus and the Eyewitnesses: The Gospels as Eyewitness Testimony*, 2nd ed. (Grand Rapids: Wm. B. Eerdmans Publishing Co., 2017). While Bauckham's book is not an argument for the historical reliability of the Gospels as such, the case he makes for the close connection between the Gospel accounts and eyewitnesses to Jesus' ministry obviates the concern of classic form-critical analysis, to the effect that the Gospels are too far removed from the events they purport to narrate to be taken as reliable sources for knowledge of Jesus' ministry. I leave aside the attempts to improve upon the Gospel accounts that have emerged from the various "quests of the historical Jesus" pursued over the last 200 years. The sheer variety of the results of these efforts tends to undermine the claim that any of these biographies succeeds in providing a more reliable account of Jesus than that found in the New Testament. Moreover, although these various "quests" have typically been motivated by the desire to present a picture of Jesus freed from traditional religious conventions, the alternatives presented tend to replace these with the religious sensibilities of the author, casting Jesus as liberal Protestant, political revolutionary, Cynic sage, and so forth. It does not follow, of course, that the risks of such projection can be avoided by eschewing historical-critical investigation in favor of uncritical reading of the Bible, but it does suggest that our knowledge of Jesus is not significantly enhanced when the biblical sources are viewed as duplicitous or defective rather than basically trustworthy.

Gospels are in every detail historically accurate. That they include embellishment, invention, rearrangement, and plain old factual error seems to me indisputable—but also perfectly consistent with the claim that they give faithful witness to the basic character of Jesus' life and work.[28]

To give a sense of how that life is to be understood theologically, I will focus on three episodes recorded in the Gospels, dealing, respectively, with three especially significant features of Jesus' prophetic ministry: his role as teacher, as healer, and as friend of sinners.[29] I have not chosen these particular episodes either because they have a strong claim to historical accuracy (on the contrary, each of them seems to have been subject to careful editing in order to bring to the fore points of particular theological salience), or because I judge them to be typical examples of Jesus' practices of teaching, healing, and befriending (in fact, each has quite distinctive features), but because they are compelling accounts of how Jesus' ministry—his human exercise of the divine power and authority that he possesses as the eternal Son—was shaped by responsive attention to the circumstances of those he teaches, heals, and befriends.

Episode 1: The Samaritan Woman (John 4:1–42)

The evangelists generally depict Jesus' teaching in settings that alternate between the atmosphere of the large lecture hall and the small seminar room: on the one hand, he holds forth before large crowds, whether in the open air or the synagogue (Matt. 9:35; Luke 4:16–27; John 6:25–59); on the other hand, he gives more detailed, private instruction to his disciples (Mark 4:34; Matt. 10:5–42; John 13:31–16:33).[30] In contrast to either of these models, Jesus' conversation with the Samaritan woman is described as a one-on-one encounter

---

28. "Reading these stories, one learns who Jesus is. . . . Many of the individual episodes serve as biographical anecdotes, 'true' if they illustrate his character authentically even though the particular incident they narrate never happened, and the overall shape of the narrative portrays something of Jesus' identity." William C. Placher, *Narratives of a Vulnerable God* (Louisville, KY: Westminster John Knox, 1994), 92.

29. Cf. Friedrich Schleiermacher, *The Christian Faith*, ed. H. R. Mackintosh and J. S. Stewart (Edinburgh: T&T Clark, 1989 [1928]), 441 (§103): "The prophetic office of Christ consists in his teaching, prophesying, and working miracles." Schleiermacher picked out these three elements on the grounds of their correspondence to the work of the Old Testament prophets; my list seeks rather to identify those aspects of Jesus' ministry that appear as especially distinctive in the records of the evangelists, though still corresponding to traditional prophetic activity. While teaching and healing correspond rather well to the first and last of Schleiermacher's categories, it is more of a stretch to link prophesying with forgiving sinners; yet the latter may be seen as part of a broader pattern of interacting with marginalized persons, which has at least some echo in the Old Testament prophets—as Jesus himself suggests in Luke 4:25–28.

30. Sometimes these two categories are blended: in both the Matthean Sermon on the Mount and the Lukan Sermon on the Plain, the narrator begins by specifying that Jesus addressed his disciples in particular (Matt. 5:1–2; Luke 6:20), but concludes by noting that the crowds heard him (Matt. 7:28; Luke 7:1).

from which even his closest disciples are absent (a point specifically noted in John 4:8).[31] Nor is the setting especially suggestive of teaching: Jesus is evidently unknown to his interlocutor (so that, unlike other Gospel characters, she does not approach him as a well-known teacher), and they meet at a well—not a place where one would normally expect religious instruction. And finally, the fact that the principals are a Jewish man and a Samaritan woman renders the encounter profoundly irregular, as the woman herself notes (v. 9).[32]

And yet it is precisely the irregularity and sheer contingency of this encounter that allow it to bring out in striking fashion important features of Jesus' character. Clearly, Jesus is not here communicating already formulated teachings that could as easily be given from a mountaintop, on the plain, or in the temple precincts. The encounter is, rather, profoundly dialogical, with the content taking shape through the back-and-forth of conversation. The woman soon recognizes, of course, that Jesus is no ordinary traveler ("Sir, I see that you are a prophet," v. 19) and on that basis seeks to explore with him specifically theological matters ("Our ancestors worshiped on this mountain, but you say that the place where people must worship is in Jerusalem," v. 20), but what Jesus teaches is specific to her situation. Thus, when she returns to town to report what has happened, she does not refer to "living water" (the ostensible subject of Jesus' teaching in vv. 7–15) or to the nature of true worship (vv. 21–24), or even to the fact that Jesus claims to be the Messiah (v. 26); instead, she says simply, "Come and see a man who told me everything I have ever done! Is this not the Christ?" (v. 29 alt.).[33]

At first glance, the reader might be inclined associate the woman's words here to Jesus' comments about her marital relations (vv. 16–18), especially in light of the fact that Jesus' miraculous knowledge is a theme accentuated by John in particular among the evangelists (see 2:24–25; 6:64; 16:31–33; cf. Matt.

31. Leaving aside cases where Jesus instructs an individual in the context of engaging a larger group (e.g., Matt. 8:18–22; Luke 11:27–28), other one-on-one teaching episodes include Jesus' encounters with Nicodemus (John 3:1–20), Martha (John 11:17–27), and Mary (Luke 10:38–42), though in none of these cases is it explicitly stated that his disciples were absent (and in the case of Mary we are explicitly told that Martha was present, though engaged in various chores). The account of Jesus' encounter with the rich man in Mark 10:17–22 (cf. Matt. 19:16–22) might also fall in this category, though in the Lukan parallel (18:18–26) it is clear that others are present who overhear the conversation.

32. Modern translations tend to take the second half of John 4:9 ("For Jews have no dealings with Samaritans," as the RSV puts it) as a parenthetical comment by the narrator, presumably on the grounds that a first-century Palestinian Jew like Jesus would not have needed any explanation for the woman's surprise at his addressing a Samaritan. But given the way that reading interrupts the narrative flow, and in light of the fact that later in the dialogue the woman returns to the theme of the incompatibility between Jews and Samaritans (v. 20), it seems to me entirely reasonable to agree with the Authorized Version in ascribing the comment to the woman herself.

33. The NRSV rendering of John 4:29b, "He cannot be the Messiah, can he?" is both cumbersome and inexact, since the Greek text reads *ho Christos*, not (as in v. 25a) *Messias*.

26:33–34 and pars.). But given that in this case Jesus' display of such knowledge comes in the middle of his discourse rather than as a climactic revelation at the end (contrast John 1:48–50), and remembering that in the balance of the conversation the woman engages Jesus in a manner that demonstrates considerable theological literacy, culminating with a discussion of the role of the Messiah, it seems odd to suppose that the one matter that stuck in her mind would be Jesus' reference to her marital status.[34] Nevertheless, there is something to be said for the idea that the aspect of Jesus' ministry highlighted by this story is his knowledge of the situations of those he encounters. In the face of more abstract debates over the extent of Jesus' human knowledge (of the "Could he speak Mandarin?" variety), attention to its specifically personal dimensions serves as a helpful reminder of the way in which the evangelists depict him as knowing others in such a way that they become known to themselves. In addition to the Samaritan woman, one might cite as examples of this phenomenon Jesus' encounters with Peter at the lakeside (Luke 5:1–10), Zacchaeus (Luke 19:1–10), the woman with the hemorrhage (Matt. 9:20–22 and pars.), and the man born blind (John 9:1–38), all of which suggest that as Jesus comes to know people, their "inner thoughts"—and thus their situation before God—are "revealed" (Luke 2:35).[35] It is presumably this experience, rather than Jesus' factual knowledge of her biography, that has impressed the woman of Samaria.[36] And it is also in this way that Jesus' human knowledge is properly equated with the knowledge of God: not by virtue of its extent (as though it entails Jesus' knowledge of the binomial theorem or the biology

---

34. It also seems odd to interpret Jesus' single sentence, "You are right in saying, 'I have no husband'; for you have had five husbands, and the one you have now is not your husband" (vv. 17b–18) as equivalent to his telling the woman "everything I have ever done" (v. 29).

35. For a nice discussion of the character of Jesus' human knowledge with particular focus on answering the charge that his congenital possession of the beatific vision is incompatible with his acquiring knowledge experientially, see Gaine, *Did the Saviour See the Father?*, chap. 6.

36. The near-consensus view among commentators that Jesus' comments on the Samaritan woman's husband are intended as a condemnation of her behavior must be challenged. Given the cultural context of first-century Palestine, her multiple marriages can hardly be taken as indicative of moral fault on her part, for marriage was a contractual arrangement controlled by males, who arranged the match and, when convenient, also had the power to nullify it (see Matt. 5:31–32 and pars.), so that Jesus himself elsewhere interprets the practice of divorce as a manifestation of specifically male hard-heartedness (Matt. 19:3–8). Seen from this perspective, Jesus' words to the Samaritan woman are best read not as an indictment of her, but rather of those who have tossed her from husband to husband. More specifically, his assertion that "the one you have now is not your husband" confirms her own assessment of her situation ("I have no husband," v. 17a) in a way that effectively amounts to a declaration of annulment: "What you have said is true!" (v. 18b), notwithstanding the fact that her marriage may be recognized as legal and binding in her community. If Jesus' words are interpreted in this way—as a declaration of liberation from a relationship that she has long since understood to have no claim on her—one can make much better sense of the enthusiasm with which she touts Jesus' knowledge of her life story to the citizens of Sychar.

of trilobites), but with respect to its quality as a knowledge that corresponds perfectly to the situation of the one who is known.

Episode 2: The Canaanite Woman (Matthew 15:21–28)

Of course, being known fully is not necessarily a pleasant experience. The examples of the rich young man (Matt. 19:16–22) and, more catastrophically, Judas (John 13:21–30) show that Jesus' teaching, with its ability to bring people's inner thoughts to light, can work to the detriment as well as to the benefit of his auditors. If the knowledge that people receive from their encounters with Jesus is to function as good news—the work of a Lord who is also Savior—then it has to be accompanied by the conviction that the Jesus who knows who we are is also a source of blessing to us in our vulnerability and weakness.[37] That Jesus' ministry has just this character is illustrated by the story of his encounter with the Canaanite woman in Matthew 15.

To first-century Jewish ears, the designation "Canaanite" would have had uniformly negative connotations.[38] The Canaanites were those whom Israel had dispossessed in taking up residence in the promised land (see Gen. 12:6; Exod. 13:11; Neh. 9:24). They are hated by God (Exod. 23:23–24; cf. Ezek. 16:3), and Israel is charged with their destruction (Deut. 20:17; cf. Num. 21:1–3; Josh. 17:18; Judg. 1:1–4). All intercourse with them is forbidden, lest close association with them tempt Israel to abandon their covenant with the Lord (Exod. 23:32–33; 34:11–16; Deut. 7:2b–4; Ezra 9:1; cf. Judg. 2:1–3). From this perspective, the fact that Jesus, when followed by a Canaanite woman shouting for him to heal her daughter, "did not answer her at all" (Matt. 15:23) is exactly the sort of behavior one would expect from a pious Jew. That the disciples, by contrast, urge him to speak to her, if only to send her away, shows them up as willing to sacrifice principle for practicality. But Jesus does not yield to their entreaties, insisting, "I was sent only to the lost sheep of the house of Israel" (v. 24).

Yet because Jesus, though ignoring her, evidently does not send her away, the woman persists; and since following after Jesus has done no good, she falls prostrate before him to renew her plea for aid. At this point Jesus at last speaks to her directly: "It is not fair to take the children's food and throw it

37. In this context, it is important to note that in Mark's telling of the story of the rich young man, the evangelist specifically notes that "Jesus, *looking at him*, *loved him* and said, 'You lack one thing; go, sell what you own, and give the money to the poor, and you will have treasure in heaven; then come, follow me'" (10:21). The problem is thus not that Jesus was in any sense ill-disposed, but that the man was unwilling to accept the very advice that he sought from Jesus.

38. By contrast, the Markan version of the story uses less prejudicial language. The woman is there described in more ethnographically neutral terms as "a Gentile, of Syrophoenician origin" (7:26).

to the dogs" (v. 26).[39] In so speaking, Jesus has exposed the situation of this woman in the most cutting way possible: she is not merely a Gentile (and therefore not part of the covenant), but a Gentile of the lowest order—one of those whose wickedness was the occasion for God driving them from the land (Deut. 9:4). Seen from this perspective, to criticize Jesus' language as evidence of ethnic prejudice unworthy of the Messiah is to fail to take seriously the meaning of Israel's election. It is not merely a matter of historical accident, as though God might have chosen another people, since in truth God loves all peoples equally. That is just not biblical teaching, however much it may accord with modern, liberal sensibilities. To be sure, God rules and, by God's providence, provides for all nations (see Amos 9:7). But although the people of Israel are not distinguished from other nations by any intrinsic qualities, Israel alone—in spite of its own objective unworthiness and legacy of faithlessness—is and remains the unique object of God's love (Deut. 7:7–8; cf. Num. 23:8–9; Amos 3:2). Those of us who are Gentiles may wish it were otherwise, that God's commitment to Israel were finally not something to be taken all that seriously. But even if the witness of the Old Testament were not sufficient, Jesus' words here render any such supposition utterly untenable. Gentiles are not part of the covenant people and, as such, have no claim whatever on the grace and mercy of Israel's God.

It is to the credit of the woman (who here shows a level of theological acumen missing from many subsequent Christian commentators) that she does not contest Jesus' judgment: "Yes, Lord, yet even the dogs eat the crumbs that fall from their masters' table" (Matt. 15:27). She accepts that Gentiles can have no expectation of—let alone any right to—the blessings that God has promised to Israel. She does not even suggest that she, as a Gentile, should by some particular or extraordinary act of divine condescension receive a special blessing (on the side, as it were) directly from the hand of the Lord. Instead, she concedes that God's blessings are given exclusively to Israel, but she argues that these blessings are so abundant that they naturally spread over and beyond the limits of the chosen people in such a way as to benefit the Gentiles as well. So it is that all nations—even the hated Canaanites—will be blessed through Abraham's progeny: not because Jesus brings blessing to Gentiles alongside (let alone instead of) Jews, but because although God's blessings come to Israel alone ("I was sent only to the lost sheep of the house of Israel"), their infinite richness causes them naturally to spill over to benefit all nations.

---

39. As various commentators have pointed out, there is doubtless some irony intended by the evangelist here, since the Greek word used to describe the woman's act of prostration (*proskynein*, Matt. 15:25) literally means to assume the posture of a dog (*kyōn/kynos*).

At this point in the story, the Canaanite gains her blessing: "Woman, great is your faith! Let it be done for you as you wish" (v. 28). It would be a mistake, however, to suppose that she gains it by way of exchange, as though her daughter's health were restored as a reward for her great faith. Rather, her faith is precisely that God's blessing is already there, bestowed so fully that its benefits have overflowed Israel's table and are there for the taking. Jesus' words to her are simply an affirmation of what she has already claimed: the ability as an outsider to recognize and draw on the abundance of what has been granted to Israel in the person of Jesus.[40]

Episode 3: The Sinful Woman (Luke 7:36–50)

Although the story of the woman with the alabaster jar of ointment is found in all four Gospels, the version found in Luke differs significantly from the other three, which all tie the story to the passion narrative. According to Matthew and Mark it is when Jesus is dining "at Bethany in the house of Simon the leper" that an unnamed woman enters and pours a jar of costly ointment on his head. The disciples grumble about the waste, but Jesus defends the woman, arguing that she has performed a prophetic act by proleptically anointing his body for burial (Matt. 26:6–13; Mark 14:3–9). John (12:1–8) introduces some minor variations: the setting is now the house of recently raised Lazarus; the woman is identified as Lazarus's sister, Mary; and the ointment is applied to Jesus' feet rather than his head. But he agrees with the first two evangelists on the other features of the story, including its location in Bethany, the complaint of the disciples (though John identifies Judas alone as the complainant), and the association of the anointing with Jesus' forthcoming burial.

It is a matter of scholarly consensus that Luke made use of Mark in writing his Gospel, and he follows Mark in naming the host of the meal where the anointing takes place as Simon (Luke 7:40, 43–44). The relation between Luke and John is obscure, but this story is one piece of evidence suggestive of some connection, since only these two evangelists share the detail that the woman anointed Jesus' feet rather than his head (cf. Luke 7:38 and John 12:3).[41] Yet the similarities between Luke's version of the story and that of

---

40. One might draw a parallel here between the Canaanite woman and another biblical Gentile, Ruth, who walks behind the reapers in Boaz's field, gleaning the excess of the harvest (Ruth 2:3–10; cf. Lev. 19:9–10; 23:22; Deut. 24:21, all of which specifically instruct that the gleanings be left for "the alien").

41. Both Luke and John also note that the woman used her hair when caring for Jesus' feet, but in Luke her hair is used to dry the tears she has used to wash his feet *before* she pours out the perfume, while John writes that she applied her hair *afterward* to wipe off the ointment itself. For a summary discussion of the relationship between Luke and John, see Joseph A. Fitzmyer, *The*

the other evangelists end here. First of all, at fifteen verses, Luke's account is twice the length of any of the other three. With respect to content, Luke completely decouples the story from Jesus' passion (it appears just a little less than a third of the way into his Gospel); moreover, he shifts the setting from the environs of Jerusalem to Galilee and describes the host as a Pharisee rather than a leper. The most significant feature of Luke's account, however, is that the woman (who, as in the other Synoptics, is unnamed) is explicitly introduced as "a sinner" (v. 37), and it is on this point that his telling of the story turns. Thus, while Luke, like the other evangelists, records that the anointing gives rise to complaint (in this case by the host himself), in Luke alone the complaining is not directed at the woman for wasting the ointment, but at *Jesus* for allowing himself to be touched by a known sinner. Indeed, if in the story of the Samaritan woman, Jesus' knowledge of other people establishes his identity as a prophet, in Luke's story of the sinful woman, Jesus' apparent lack of knowledge is used to call that identity into question: "If this man were a prophet, *he would have known* who and what kind of woman this is who is touching him—that she is a sinner" (Luke 7:39).

To be sure, the subsequent narrative makes it quite clear that Jesus knows the woman's character (v. 47), but the issue of his knowledge remains important for what Luke communicates here about Jesus' ministry. As suggested above, the Samaritan woman seems to have received Jesus' knowledge of her past as good news—a likely sign of his messianic status (John 4:29). For the Canaanite woman this status (for, according to Matt. 15:22, she addressees Jesus using a messianic title) serves as the basis for her trust that his blessing will come even to someone who is not a member of the chosen people. But the case of the anonymous woman in the Pharisee's house is different. Unlike the Samaritan and the Canaanite, she is evidently a Jew, but one who, as a sinner, has proved faithless to God's covenant and thus dismissive of God's blessing; and yet she is forgiven. In this context, that we are not told the content of the woman's sins (only that they were, in Jesus' words, "many") is just as well, for it allows us to imagine the worst—and thereby to understand that no sin is beyond the reach of divine forgiveness.

It is important also to note the way in which the forgiveness of the woman is described by Luke. As was the case with the Canaanite woman, a cursory reading might seem to suggest a logic of exchange, according to which forgiveness is granted as recompense for the woman's love, as demonstrated by

---

Gospel according to Luke I–IX: A New Translation with Introduction and Commentary (New York: Doubleday, 1981), 87–89. C. K. Barrett goes farther than most in suggesting that John had read Luke; see C. K. Barrett, *The Gospel according to St. John: An Introduction with Commentary and Notes on the Greek Text*, 2nd ed. (London: SPCK, 1978), 46; yet some connection between the third and fourth Gospels seems hard to deny.

her care for Jesus. That such an interpretation is incorrect is shown by the parable Jesus tells to illustrate the woman's situation: "'A certain creditor had two debtors; one owed five hundred denarii, and the other fifty. When they could not pay, he canceled the debts for both of them. Now which of them will love him more?' Simon answered, 'I suppose the one for whom he canceled the greater debt.' And Jesus said to him, 'You have judged rightly'" (Luke 7:41–43). Jesus makes it clear that creditor's act of forgiveness is motivated by nothing whatsoever in the situation of the debtors other than their dire need (viz., the fact that neither could pay). Correspondingly, the debtors' love is a response to, not a cause of, their debts being forgiven. If the woman's case is to be interpreted in these terms, then the love she shows Jesus in anointing his feet (vv. 38, 44–46) must be related to her being forgiven as consequence rather than cause. To be sure, the fact that Jesus' declaration, "Your sins are forgiven" (v. 48), comes only at this point in the story might seem to imply that Jesus is only now forgiving the woman's sins; but the overall logic of the passage suggests that Jesus is, again, merely declaring what is in fact already the case (after all, he has already told Simon that the woman's sins are forgiven before making any declaration to the woman herself).[42] And any lingering suspicion that the woman has somehow earned forgiveness by her love is refuted by the chapter's concluding verse, where Jesus says to her, "Your *faith* has saved you; go in peace" (v. 50). These words make it clear that it is not anything the *woman* has done, but it is her conviction regarding what *Jesus* has done that has secured her the blessing of forgiveness.

⋙⋘⋙⋘⋙⋘

These three episodes certainly do not provide anything like a fulsome summary of Jesus' prophetic office, let alone other dimensions of his earthly ministry. They do, however, illustrate something of the texture of his prophetic ministry, which, like that of the prophets of the Old Testament, takes shape in and through particular interactions. It is a ministry of "suffering" in the broad sense of exhibiting Jesus not as imposing his will on the world around him,

---

42. Careful attention to the syntax of Luke 7:47 is important here. Putting the key terms in Greek, the verse reads, "*Hou charin* I tell you, her many sins are forgiven, *hoti* she has shown much love." *Hou charin* means "for this reason" or "therefore"; but it should be linked not with "her sins are forgiven" (i.e., as giving the reason why she has been forgiven), but rather with the immediately following "I tell you" (i.e., as giving the logic behind Jesus' reporting that her sins are forgiven, viz., on the basis of the same logic described in the story of the creditor and his debtors). So too, while *hoti* is rightly rendered "for," or "because," it too serves to identify the reason why Jesus concludes that the woman has been forgiven, not the cause of her forgiveness. Combining these two points, I propose that v. 47 is best (if somewhat expansively) rendered, "In light of all that I have just said, I tell you that her many sins are forgiven: because [i.e., on the evidence of the fact that] she has shown much love."

but as responding to the contingencies of time and place. To be sure, in and through these contingencies he shows himself to be sovereign: to know the situations of those he encounters, and to speak words of truth, healing, and forgiveness that materially alter the lives of his interlocutors. He thus shows himself to be Lord and Savior—but as one who rules and saves by emptying himself of pretension, exercising authority in response to those in need, rather than the one who demands submission and service by others. In this way, his ministry exemplifies power exercised *with* and *for* others rather than *over* them.[43] Exercising power in this way does not entail any diminishment of Jesus' sovereignty—it is precisely as one who teaches with authority that Jesus proclaims, "I am among you as one who serves" (Luke 22:27)—but it does clarify the character of this power: once again, Jesus proves to be Lord precisely insofar as he is revealed as Savior.

DEAD AND BURIED

Jesus exercises his saving ministry by acts of giving. More specifically, he gives blessing, whether by means of instruction, health, forgiveness, or fellowship. And the practices of giving that mark Jesus' earthly ministry are analogous with the generous giving that defines the divine life both eternally and in relation to creation. As argued in the first part of this book, God's own triune life takes the form of eternal giving, and in creation this giving extends beyond the Godhead to constitute and include beings that are other than God. Jesus' ministry is a further extension of that giving: "I came that they may have life, and have it abundantly" (John 10:10). But while God's infinite nature means that divine giving is inexhaustible (so that no amount of giving diminishes God's ability to give still more), the earthly Jesus' giving is inherently limited because Jesus' human nature is finite. This is, again, why talk of kenosis is perfectly appropriate when speaking of the ministry of the Word of God incarnate: in giving himself for others, Jesus necessarily "empties himself" according to his human nature in a way that just does not apply to his divine nature.

As the hymn from Philippians teaches, this self-emptying extends "to the point of death—even death on a cross" (Phil. 2:8). Importantly, the point is not that Jesus' commitment to serving others takes the form of progressively wearing himself out, a self-emptying in which he finally drops dead of exhaustion. The death that comes to Jesus is inflicted on him by powers hostile to his mission of salvation and thus not in any sense a physiologically necessary or

---

43. I owe this distinction to Anna Mercedes, *Power For: Feminism and Christ's Self-Giving* (London: T&T Clark International, 2011).

natural outcome of his commitment to serving others. Neither, however, is his death simply adventitious. Although it is inflicted on him by the powers of this world, it does not come upon him unawares: "For this reason the Father loves me, because I lay down my life. . . . No one takes it from me, but I lay it down of my own accord" (John 10:17–18). For this very reason, however, Jesus' death stands as a defining feature of his ministry, as indicated by the Apostles' Creed, which, in declaiming that Jesus was "crucified, died, and was buried; he descended to the dead," uses four different verbs, describing four distinct and more or less sequential events, to communicate a single factual claim: that there was a time when Jesus was truly dead.[44] Why is this so important?

At one level, of course, death is simply a feature of human nature (see Gen. 6:3; Job 14:10–12; Ps. 90:10), so to say that Jesus died is just another way of declaring that he was fully human; but the fourfold description of his death (lacking in the equally human characteristics of birth and suffering) suggests that more is at stake than simply affirming Jesus' humanity. Alternatively, one might be tempted to argue that since only one who is truly dead can be raised from the dead, the proclamation of Jesus' death is a precondition for proclaiming his resurrection. But this explanation is inadequate, given the biblical emphasis on Jesus' death as significant in its own right. Paul certainly has no interest in marginalizing the importance of Jesus' resurrection (see, e.g., 1 Cor. 15:12–23), yet he proclaims "Christ crucified," or "the message about the cross," as "the power of God" apart from any immediate reference to the resurrection (see 1 Cor. 1:18–23; cf. Gal. 6:14; Phil. 3:18). This perspective seems consistent with the evangelists' portrayal of Jesus' own anticipation of his arrest and execution not simply as a precursor to his resurrection, but also as integral to his messianic status in its own right. For if Jesus is widely recognized as a prophet during the whole course of his ministry, it is only on the cross that he is publicly designated as "King of the Jews" (Matt. 27:37 and pars.).

---

44. The interpretation of "he descended to the dead" (*descendit ad inferos* [alt. *infernos*]) is contested. I read the clause (which has no parallel in the Nicene Creed) as emphasizing the reality of Jesus' death: "Here, we are told, we must . . . let the realization sink slowly in that Christ's life is finished and done." Alan E. Lewis, *Between Cross and Resurrection: A Theology of Holy Saturday* (Grand Rapids: Wm. B. Eerdmans Publishing Co., 2001), 38. But it has more commonly been understood as referring to Jesus' breaking the power of hell and thus as describing the first stages of his triumph over death; for extensive discussion, see Alyssa Lyra Pitstick, *Light in Darkness: Hans Urs von Balthasar and the Catholic Doctrine of Christ's Descent into Hell* (Grand Rapids: Wm. B. Eerdmans Publishing Co., 2007), chaps. 2–4. The chief difficulty with the latter interpretation is that the dramatic force of the reversal described by the creedal "On the third day he rose again" is vitiated if Jesus' descent is interpreted in triumphal terms. In this context, assimilating the harrowing of hell to the resurrection rather than the *descensus* is arguably more consistent with the biblical text most associated with the doctrine, 1 Pet. 3:18–20, which couples Jesus' "proclamation to the spirits in prison" (cf. 4:6) not with his having been "put to death in the flesh" (3:18d), but rather with his having been "made alive in the spirit" (3:18e).

To be sure, the evangelists are quite clear that from the perspective of the Roman authorities who attached this title to the cross, it is simply a summary statement of the charge against Jesus rather than an act of confession (though cf. John 19:21–22). Nevertheless, the broader biblical witness provides good reason to suppose that it is precisely in death, on the cross, that Jesus is revealed as king. This is certainly not to say that it is only on Golgotha that the idea is introduced. The Synoptic Gospels make much of the moment at Caesarea Philippi when Peter confesses Jesus as Israel's expected king by identifying him as the Messiah (Mark 8:27–29 and pars.; cf. John 11:27), and all four evangelists depict Jesus as being hailed by the crowds in messianic terms at his final entry into Jerusalem (Matt. 21:9; Mark 11:9–10; Luke 19:38; John 12:13). Yet at the same time, as the Gospels also suggest, "Messiah" is not a title that Jesus is especially eager to claim. The Synoptic writers record that Jesus, upon hearing Peter's confession at Caesarea Philippi, "sternly ordered the disciples not to tell anyone that he was the Messiah" (Matt. 16:20 and pars.), while John reports that Jesus' reactions to popular expressions of messianic enthusiasm ranged from incredulity (1:49–51; cf. 6:68–70; 16:29–32) to flight (6:15). This lack of clarity over Jesus' messianic pretensions was evidently a source of frustration to some during the course of his ministry (see 10:24–26), and it seems to have continued through his trial, where Jesus avoids a direct answer to the question of whether he is the Messiah, whether questioned by the high priest (Matt. 26:62–64; Luke 22:67–69; but cf. Mark 14:61–62) or Pilate (Matt. 27:11–14 and pars.; John 18:33–37).

It is not really credible to suppose that Jesus is simply being prudent in all this, recognizing that making an explicit claim to be the Messiah would result in his execution as a rebel against Rome (see John 11:47–50). Such carefulness is hardly consistent with Jesus' triumphal entry into Jerusalem, which was evidently both intended and perceived as fulfillment of messianic prophecy (Matt. 21:4–5; John 12:14–15).[45] The point seems rather to be that Jesus' status as Messiah is inseparable from (and thus not properly confessed apart from knowledge of) his death. Here too, Peter's confession at Caesarea Philippi represents a crucial juncture in the narrative: "From that time on, Jesus began to show his disciples that he must go to Jerusalem and undergo great suffering at the hands of the elders and chief priests and scribes, and be killed" (Matt. 16:21 and pars.). It is apparently in line with this memory that

---

45. John 12:16 reports, "His disciples did not understand these things at first; but when Jesus was glorified, then they remembered that these things had been written of him and had been done to him." Given that John records the crowd as shouting perhaps the most explicit messianic affirmations of all the evangelists (v. 13: "Hosanna! Blessed is the one who comes in the name of the Lord—the King of Israel!"), the claim that the disciples did not understand strains credulity a bit.

Christians from the beginning understood Jesus' death to have been foretold by the prophets (Acts 3:18; 17:2–3; 26:22–23; 1 Cor. 15:3; cf. Luke 24:25–26, 46). That it is precisely in his death that he is revealed as Messiah is a feature especially of the Johannine narrative (John 8:28; 12:32–33) and is reflected in the early Christian fondness for an alternative version of Ps. 96:10 that reads, "The Lord reigns from the tree."[46]

Granted that Scripture and the early church both associate Jesus' status as king with his death on the cross, what can such an association possibly mean? Here again, earthly notions of power are radically challenged. A king is a person who has power over others (see again Luke 22:25 and par.) and, as such, is supremely active; yet in death Jesus is supremely passive: increasingly subject to physical control by others in his trial and crucifixion, until in death he is finally unable to act at all.[47] Yet it is just at this point that he exercises a crucial feature of the messianic king: righteous judgment (Isa. 11:4; 16:5). For the worldly powers' execution of this one who, as sinless, was innocent (Luke 23:47; cf. Matt. 27:4, 19) amounts to judgment upon those powers: "This is the judgment, that the light has come into the world, and people loved darkness rather than light because their deeds were evil" (John 3:19). In rejecting Jesus, God's Son, the world—Jew and Gentile—rejects Israel's God, who is also Israel's rightful king. Human pretensions to know what is genuinely good and righteous are thereby exposed as a sham. It is in this way that Paul views the cross of Christ as a manifestation of power (1 Cor. 1:17–18)—not, of course, the power of the (Roman) state to humiliate and destroy its opponents, but God's power to "destroy the wisdom of the wise" (1:19) and thereby "through the foolishness of our proclamation, to save those who believe" (1:21).

This last point is crucial in reminding us that judgment is not an end in itself. Quite the contrary, Jesus insists that "I came not to judge the world, but to save the world" (John 12:47; cf. 3:17). As far as human beings are concerned, the judgment that Jesus exercises on the cross is a means to salvation, because it is designed to lead to repentance, to spur us to reject those powers and principalities—"the spiritual forces of evil" (Eph. 6:12)—that are the

46. See Justin Martyr, *Dialogue with Trypho* 73, "The Lord has reigned from the wood"; Tertullian, *Against Marcion* 3.19; Augustine, *Expositions on the Psalms* 95; cf. Epistle of Barnabas 5.13. The emendation seems to have been part of the Old Latin version of the Psalter probably originating as a Christian gloss on the original "The Lord reigns" (Ps. 96:10 MT; 95:10 LXX). Justin seems to provide a witness for a Greek version of the same expanded reading, but since no surviving text of the Septuagint includes the addition, it seems likely that whatever Greek text Justin consulted had itself been influenced by the Old Latin.

47. For a classic account of the shift from activity to passivity in the Synoptic (though not Johannine) accounts of Jesus, see Hans W. Frei, *The Identity of Jesus Christ: The Hermeneutical Bases of Dogmatic Theology* (Eugene, OR: Wipf & Stock, 1997 [1975]), esp. 150–55.

object of divine condemnation (see Col. 2:15).[48] The comprehensiveness of this divine will for salvation is suggested by the biblical affirmation that "the gospel was proclaimed even to the dead, so that, though they had been judged in the flesh as everyone is judged, they might live in the spirit as God does" (1 Pet. 4:6). In this way, for all human beings to confront the cross is to face judgment, to recognize that all our attempts to know God—the wisdom and discernment by which we seek to understand and control the terms of our existence—are bootless. For while it is true that God, as Creator, is present everywhere, upholding the creature in existence, this presence is invisible (Rom. 1:20) and so not a possible object of human discernment. By contrast, insofar as God has chosen to be visibly present in Jesus, it is in the course of his ministry (which includes both what Jesus does and what is done to him) that God is known. This was Luther's point in defining a theologian of the cross: "That person does not deserve to be called a theologian who looks upon the invisible things of God as though they were clearly perceptible in those things which have actually happened. He deserves to be called a theologian, however, who comprehends the visible and manifest things of God seen through suffering and the cross."[49] What it means for Jesus—and thus for the God of Israel—to be God, and so Lord and Savior, is revealed on the cross not exclusively (as though the other facts of his earthly ministry, his "suffering" in an expanded sense, were irrelevant) but climactically, as the culmination of his life of service (Matt. 20:28 and par.), the final and full act of giving by the one who, "having loved his own who were in the world, . . . loved them to the end" (John 13:1). So it is that the Lord reigns from the tree.

Historically speaking, of course, this reign is short-lived. The cross is not a permanent monument. Yes, at the crucifixion of the Lord of glory, the sun was darkened (Matt. 27:45 and pars.) and the veil of the temple was torn in two (27:51 and pars.); indeed, according to one evangelist the earth shook and some of the dead were raised (27:51–52). But these events were all short-lived, and (pace Pascal) Jesus does not remain on the cross "in agony until the end of the world."[50] Because he died, his agony is over, and his dead body is taken down,

48. Of course, when "the ruler of this world is judged" (John 16:11 RSV), the effect is not that he repents, but that he is "driven out" (John 12:31; cf. Luke 10:18; Rev. 12:7–9; 20:14); but this point should be taken as evidence that the devil is not the sort of being who is able to repent. See the discussion in Eugene F. Rogers, *Sexuality and the Christian Body: Their Way into the Triune God* (Oxford: Blackwell, 1999), 229–30, in dependence on the angelology outlined in Aquinas, *ST* 1.50.

49. Martin Luther, *Heidelberg Disputation*, §§19–20, in *Career of the Reformer I*, *LW* 31:40; cf. §§22, 24: "The wisdom which sees the invisible things of God in works as perceived by man is completely puffed up, blinded, and hardened. . . . Yet that wisdom is not of itself evil, . . . but without the theology of the cross[,] man misuses it in the worst manner."

50. "Jésus sera en agonie jusque'à la fin du monde; il ne faut pas dormir pendant ce temps là." Blaise Pascal, *Pensées*, ed. Léon Brunschvicg (Paris: Hachette, n.d. [1869]), 575, n. 553. The MS indicates that Pascal originally wrote *est*, which he then struck out and replaced with *sera*.

wrapped in a sheet, and laid in the tomb (Matt. 27:59–60 and pars.; cf. John 19:38–41). The story of his earthly life is ended; he is truly dead—and buried.

Although Jesus' burial is from both a narrative and creedal perspective simply confirmation of his death, the period punctuating the end of his life, that very emphasis is itself theologically suggestive. For if God elects to take flesh, and thus to be present and known not simply through a created form (as in the Old Testament theophanies), but as a creature and, more specifically, as a human creature whose life is defined by the extremes of birth and death, then it is only once that life has come to an end, once it is finally and irrevocably true that "it is finished" (John 19:30), that the work of divine self-revelation is complete. To be sure, because Jesus is the Word made flesh, at every moment of his life from the manger onward it is true that he is God; the progress of his life from infancy through childhood and adolescence and adulthood does not entail any increase in divinity, as though only at his life's end would it be true that he is divine. Here too, Jesus' humanity is perfectly ordinary. I am Ian at every point of my existence, but the question of who Ian is will only be able to be answered fully when my story is over and there is nothing more to be said about me—nothing more I might do, fail to do, or have done to me that could materially change what is true about me. So it is with Jesus. Although he is God at every moment of his life, because the content of that divine identity is disclosed in that life, it is only when that life is complete that we come to know fully who he is *as* God. To be perfect in humanity is thus for him to be dead and buried—and just as such the human life of God.[51]

And yet although Jesus' death is for all these reasons rightly regarded as the end of his story, it is not the end of Jesus. How this can be is the subject of the next chapter.

---

51. For the idea of death as the culminating moment of human self-realization, see Karl Rahner, "Ideas for a Theology of Death," in *Theology, Anthropology, Christology*, vol. 13 of *Theological Investigations*, trans. David Bourke (London: Darton, Longman & Todd, 1975), 169–86.

PART 3

The Crossing

But each of us was given grace
    according to the measure of Christ's gift.
Therefore it is said, "When he ascended on high
    he made captivity itself a captive;
    he gave gifts to his people."
(When it says, "He ascended,"
    what does it mean but that he had also descended
    into the lower parts of the earth?
He who descended is the same one
    who ascended far above all the heavens,
    so that he might fill all things.)
                      —*Ephesians 4:7–10*

6

Christus Victor

There may seem something artificial about dividing the treatment of Jesus' death and resurrection between different chapters, let alone different parts, of this book; as Rudolf Bultmann argued long ago (citing Rom. 4:25), "the cross and the resurrection form a single, indivisible cosmic event."[1] The division may seem even more questionable given that the christological topics treated in this chapter—the resurrection, ascension, and parousia—are no less features of Jesus' humanity than are his birth, suffering, and death. After all, since the divine nature cannot die, it cannot be raised from the dead; and because the divinity is omnipresent, it is only according to his human nature that Jesus can be said either to ascend to heaven from earth or return to earth from heaven. But although the events behind Good Friday and Easter both refer to the same incarnate subject, there is good reason for their separate treatment. For while it is intrinsic to human nature to be born, suffer, and die, none of the actions subsequently predicated of Jesus in the second article of the Apostles' Creed are natural to humanity. It is true that in his resurrection, ascension, and second coming, Jesus triumphs in his humanity, but the capacities by which he does so are not human ones; so as we explicate these doctrines, we necessarily speak of Jesus' humanity in a different key.

In itself, this point is not especially controversial, since Christian theologians have long distinguished between the "state of humiliation" (*status exinanitionis*) and the "state of exaltation" (*status exaltationis*) as two stages in the life of the incarnate Word, distinguished precisely by the caesura that divides his death on Good Friday afternoon from his risen life on Easter morning. Yet

1. Rudolf Bultmann, "New Testament and Mythology," in *Kerygma and Myth: A Theological Debate*, ed. Hans Werner Bartsch, trans. Reginald H. Fuller (London: SPCK, 1953), 38.

in what follows I challenge this way of construing the matter, at least insofar as the two "states" have tended to be understood as two successive narrative sequences, the first encompassing Jesus' earthly-historical life, and the second his post-resurrection existence. My own view is that the new key that must be deployed when speaking of the risen humanity of Jesus is not properly conceived in narrative terms; that is, as a sequence of distinct events, one following another, more or less analogous to those (e.g., his triumphal entry, arrest, and trial) that mark Jesus' earthly career. Instead, Jesus' resurrection, ascension, and parousia are rightly viewed as three distinct dimensions of God's eternal vindication of Jesus' finite, human life as lived from birth to death.

This position follows from my commitment to Luther's dictum that "whoever wishes to deliberate or speculate soundly about God should disregard absolutely everything except the humanity of Christ," on the grounds that "the humanity of Christ" is fully defined by the time span between Jesus' birth and death. As Gregory of Nyssa once put it, "He who had once decided to share our humanity had to experience all that belongs to our nature. Now human life is encompassed within two limits, and if he had passed through one and not touched the other, he would only have half fulfilled his purpose, having failed to reach the other limit proper to our nature."[2] Only when the full compass of a human life had been completed could Jesus, who was from the beginning of his life the Word according to *hypostasis*, be said to have taken on "all that belongs" to human *nature*. In assuming a human life, God neither could nor did take on every possibility of the many variable features of humanity; indeed, even if such a life were logically conceivable, it would hardly qualify as human, since part of what it means to be human is just to realize one particular set of features among a wide range of possible options.[3] Nevertheless, for God to be known in and as a human being, God had to assume a human life in its entirety. And this means that the revelation of God in the human being Jesus of Nazareth was complete, "perfect" in the etymological sense of the term, once Jesus' life was over, and he was dead and buried.

2. Gregory of Nyssa, "An Address on Religious Instruction," in *Christology of the Later Fathers*, ed. Edward R. Hardy (Philadelphia: Westminster Press, 1954), 309–10. Cf. Kathryn Tanner, *Jesus, Humanity and the Trinity: A Brief Systematic Theology* (Edinburgh: T&T Clark, 2001), 26–27.

3. In this context, Irenaeus of Lyon's argument that Jesus must have lived to an old age in order to have assumed a fully human life is not finally compelling because old age is more a variable feature of human existence than constitutive of it. One might well claim that the incarnation would have failed as an assumption of a fully human life if Jesus had not lived into adulthood, since adulthood (i.e., sexual maturity) is integral to the continuation of the human species: because humans are able to maintain the human species through the production of children, sexual maturity is the natural end of infancy and childhood. Old age is not the natural *end* (as opposed to the natural *outcome*) of adulthood in the same way. See Irenaeus of Lyon, *Against Heresies* 2.22.4, in *ANF* 1.

And yet for Christians it also remains decisive that the death and burial defining the end of Jesus' human life does not mark the end of what can and must be said about him. At one level this is hardly surprising, since the claim that God was born, lived, and died would not in itself amount to especially good news. Granted that Jesus benefited many of those he encountered during his earthly life through his ministries of teaching and healing, so did the merely human prophets of old, as well as his own disciples after him. Limited as they were to a very small space of time in first-century Palestine, Jesus' acts of power and his authoritative teaching can hardly in themselves be assigned the sort of cosmic significance that would establish him as Lord and Savior, even if they inspired others after him to follow his example. In light of his death on Good Friday, the messianic promise heralded by his words and deeds seems to have failed, for "the Messiah remains forever" (John 12:34), but Jesus had died. The words of the disciples on the Emmaus road express the problem perfectly: "*We had hoped* that he was the one to redeem Israel" (Luke 24:21), but events had, evidently, shown otherwise.

To be sure (and as argued in the previous chapter), the Gospels witness to a certain kind of triumph even in Jesus' death. John in particular insists that in being "lifted up" (12:32) on the cross, Jesus was enthroned as Messiah, the one in whom the judgment of the world was revealed (see 12:31). And that the Synoptic Gospels, too, view Jesus' death as a moment of revelation is reflected in the apocalyptic signs associated with the crucifixion. But however portentous these signs may have seemed to observers at the time (see Matt. 27:54 and pars.), the world did not end on Good Friday. And the fact that it did not, and that the powers of this world went on with their customary scheming, evidently unaffected by the events on Calvary, brings us back to the point that Jesus' death, however great its significance as a mark of divine solidarity with suffering humanity and divine judgment of worldly power, is not good news. And because this is so, the gloom of Cleopas and his companion on the Emmaus road was fully justified. For although God's coming among us and living a human life is in itself undoubtedly a sign of divine love and of God's commitment to be present to rather than merely in the world, still, because human lives are bound by death, this very commitment to flesh-and-blood existence seems self-defeating. Only by taking on creaturely existence can God be with creatures; but precisely in doing so, that will for communion seems foreordained to be defeated, limited by the very transience of the created nature assumed. Yes, "the Word became flesh" (John 1:14), but, as the prophet taught, "All flesh is grass" (Isa. 40:6 RSV), so that although God's Word may stand forever (Isa. 40:8), it seemingly can do so just to the extent that it is *not* flesh. If more is to be said about Jesus, it must be because his death and burial are not all that may truly be said about him.

RISEN

And, of course, that is just what the gospel proclaims: the humanity of Jesus' life does not stand as a limit to God's will to remain in communion with creatures, because the same Jesus who has died has also risen from the dead.[4] At first glance this identification of the gospel with the resurrection may seem precipitous. After all, long before the first Easter, Jesus (evidently taking up the message of John the Baptist) had preached "the good news of the kingdom" (Matt. 4:23; cf. 24:14), specifically, "The time is fulfilled, and the kingdom of God has come near" (Mark 1:15; cf. Luke 11:20; 17:20–21). These texts suggest that the content of the gospel is the earthly realization of divine rule: a polity defined by righteousness and peace (see Isa. 9:6–7; 11:1–10). Because it was the Messiah's role to establish this kingdom, it was precisely Jesus' failure to do so that made the disciples on the road to Emmaus so despondent (cf. Luke 19:11; Acts 1:6). And since on Easter morning no less than Good Friday afternoon, the gears of worldly power continued to turn as before, the news that Jesus had risen from the dead would not seem to qualify as "the good news of the kingdom." To claim that it did would seem to involve a fatal confusion of the messenger with his message.

And yet it is just such an equation of the resurrection with the good news that is implied by the early Christian identification of "the gospel of *God*" (Rom. 1:1; 2 Cor. 11:7; 1 Thess. 2:2) with "the gospel of [God's] *Son*" (Rom. 1:3, 9), or "the gospel of *Christ*" (1 Cor. 9:12; 2 Cor. 9:13; 10:14; Gal. 1:7; Phil. 1:27; 1 Thess. 3:2; cf. 2 Cor. 4:4; 2 Thess. 1:8). Luke's account of the first recorded Christian sermon makes this plain:

> You that are Israelites, listen to what I have to say: Jesus of Nazareth, a man attested to you by God with deeds of power, wonders, and signs that God did through him among you, as you yourselves know—this man, handed over to you according to the definite plan and foreknowledge of God, you crucified and killed by the hands of those outside the law. But God raised him up, having freed him from death, because it was impossible for him to be held in its power. (Acts 2:22–24)

---

4. "The fundamental Christian confession is that God raised Jesus from the dead." Ingolf U. Dalferth, *Crucified and Resurrected: Restructuring the Grammar of Christology*, trans. Jo Bennett (Grand Rapids: Baker Academic, 2015 [1994]), 39. This claim that the resurrection stands at the heart of the Christian kerygma is common to much recent theology. See, e.g., Wolfhart Pannenberg, *Systematic Theology*, 3 vols., trans. Geoffrey W. Bromiley (Grand Rapids: Wm. B. Eerdmans Publishing Co., 1988–93), 2:343–46; Robert W. Jenson, *Systematic Theology*, 2 vols. (New York: Oxford University Press, 1997–99), 1:4, 134, 195; Wolfgang Schenk, *Evangelium—Evangelien—Evangeliologie: Ein "hermeneutisches" Manifest* (Munich: Christian Kaiser, 1983), 22.

The heart of the message is clear: "This Jesus God raised up, and of that all of us are witnesses" (Acts 2:32). So it is that Paul identifies himself as an apostle "through Jesus Christ and God the Father, who raised him from the dead" (Gal. 1:1). Admittedly, the identification of the gospel with the resurrection of Jesus does not in any sense eclipse the hope for the coming of God's kingdom (1 Cor. 4:20; 6:9–10; 15:50; Gal. 5:21; cf. 2 Thess. 1:5), which Paul understands in very traditional terms as a matter of "righteousness and peace" (Rom. 14:17). The point is that Jesus' resurrection signals that this future hope has in some sense already been fulfilled.

This is so because the kingdom of God means life in the presence of God, since only where God, the source and measure of life, is present can the life of creatures be lived to the full, free from every threat to the order of righteousness and peace that God wills for creation. For this reason, the promise of God's dwelling among the people is foundational to God's covenant with Israel (Exod. 29:45–46), but the distinction between Creator and creature seems to render the promise incapable of fulfillment (1 Kgs. 8:27; 2 Chr. 6:18). As noted above, even the incarnation seems incapable of resolving this problem, since God's leading a genuinely human life entails that divine communion with humankind will be cut off by the human reality of death. Because Jesus' resurrection from the dead shows that this seemingly impassable limit is not a barrier to the divine will to dwell with creatures, the Easter message about Jesus is rightly identified with the gospel of the kingdom. The promise of Emmanuel, or God with us (Isa. 7:14; Matt. 1:23), is fulfilled permanently and irrevocably in that the crucified Jesus lives (Matt. 28:20).[5] In short, "the gospel of Christ" does not displace "the good news of the kingdom," because Jesus is (in the words of Origen of Alexandria) the *autobasileia*, himself the realization of the kingdom.[6]

But if the resurrection *signifies* the definitive triumph of God's power to live with creatures as a creature, what does it *describe?* That is, what does it mean to confess with the creeds that Jesus "rose again" on the third day? None of the canonical evangelists presumes to narrate the resurrection: when the women arrive at the tomb on Easter morning, they are told that it has already happened (Matt. 28:1–6 and pars.; cf. John 20:1–13). It is common

---

5. So, insofar as this overcoming of the barrier between God and the world is the basis for the blessing of all people through the blessing poured out on the Jews (see Eph. 3:6), Paul could speak of God having "declared the gospel beforehand to Abraham, saying, 'All the Gentiles shall be blessed in you'" (Gal. 3:8) without in any way compromising its christocentric character (3:14).

6. Origen of Alexandria, *Commentary on Matthew* 14.7; in Origen, *Spirit and Fire: A Thematic Anthology of His Writings*, ed. Hans Urs von Balthasar, trans. Robert J. Daly, SJ (Washington, DC: Catholic University of America Press, 1984 [1938]), 362.

enough to recognize that Jesus' resurrection is not simply a resuscitation, a mere return to earthly life of the sort experienced by the son of the widow of Nain (Luke 7:11–15) or Lazarus (John 11:38–44). They were raised only to die again, but "Christ, being raised from the dead, will never die again; death no longer has dominion over him" (Rom. 6:9).[7] Rather, as Paul goes on to write, "the life he lives, he lives to God" (Rom. 6:10); but what kind of a life is that? As the Gospels portray it, Jesus' risen state is characterized by a mixture of continuity and discontinuity with his prior earthly existence. On the one hand, he continues to have a body of "flesh and bones" (Luke 24:39; though cf. 1 Cor. 15:42–44) that bears the wounds of his crucifixion (John 20:20, 25–27), and which is capable of eating (Luke 24:42–43; cf. John 21:12–15). On the other hand, this body can pass through closed doors (John 20:19, 26) as well as simply vanish from sight (Luke 24:31); moreover, it is not always immediately recognizable as Jesus' body (Luke 24:15–16; John 20:14; 21:4).[8]

This mixture of continuity and discontinuity is of a piece with the rather scattered and unsystematic accounts of the resurrection appearances in the Gospels. While all four evangelists share a remarkably clear and ordered (if not entirely uniform) account of the events leading from Jesus' Last Supper through his arrest, trial, crucifixion, and burial, the stories of the resurrection appearances are notoriously varied. Mark originally seems to have lacked any accounts of the risen Jesus at all.[9] According to Matthew, he appeared to his disciples all together on a mountain in Galilee (Matt. 28:16–18). Luke, by contrast, has the risen Jesus appearing in and around Jerusalem, first to Peter and the two disciples on the Emmaus road (Luke 24:34–35), and then to all the disciples together (24:36). Finally, John speaks of an initial appearance to Mary Magdalene (20:14–17) at the tomb, followed by two appearances on successive Sundays in Jerusalem to all the disciples in a locked room (20:19, 26), and then at some later date at the lakeside in Galilee (21:1). In sharp contrast to the passion narratives, there are virtually no parallels between the resurrection accounts across the Gospels: the four versions of Jesus' various postmortem appearances are radically dissimilar.[10]

7. See, e.g., Thomas Aquinas, *ST* 3.55.2.3.

8. The accounts of the risen Jesus' "appearing" (*ōphthē*) to various individuals and groups, as recounted by Paul in 1 Cor. 15:5–7, might be taken to suggest that Jesus popped into view as suddenly as he vanished at Emmaus, but the grammar is inconclusive; moreover, the accounts of resurrection appearances narrated in the Gospels speak of Jesus coming among people (even if through closed doors!) rather than simply materializing out of thin air (though the case in Matt. 28:16–18 is admittedly ambiguous).

9. That the Second Gospel originally ended at Mark 16:8, with the women's flight from the tomb, is pretty much a matter of scholarly consensus.

10. The one clear parallel among the canonical resurrection narratives is found in Luke and John, which both tell of Jesus' appearing to all the disciples gathered together and greeting them with the words "Peace be with you" (Luke 24:36; John 20:19). The longer ending of Mark

While this contrast between the high level of agreement across the four canonical passion narratives and the idiosyncratic character of the evangelists' varied resurrection accounts might be taken as evidence against the reliability of the latter, it is better understood as reflecting the kind of "event" the resurrection is: namely, one that—unlike his death and burial—*cannot* be narrated.[11] To see why this is the case, it is important to stress once again that human life is bounded by birth and death. Resurrection does not change this. On the contrary, to distinguish resurrection from resuscitation is precisely to deny that the resurrection is a further episode in Jesus' life (i.e., something that happened after his death and burial, in the same way that his arrest happened after his triumphal entry to Jerusalem). With his death and burial, Jesus' life is over. And to deny that the resurrection is a further episode in this life is to affirm that it is precisely in the earthly life of Jesus, bounded by birth in Bethlehem at its beginning and death in Jerusalem at end, that God's life is revealed. The resurrection is not more of this life, but precisely the vindication of this life in its completeness. That is what it means to say with Paul that the life Jesus lives now, he lives to God: that he lives now exclusively by God's power and not (as was the case with the risen Lazarus, for example) through the revived or continuing power of his human nature (2 Cor. 13:4).[12]

It follows that the question of whether the resurrection is a historical event must be answered in the negative, if by "historical event" one means a happening within the spatiotemporal matrix of created cause and effect.[13] This

---

includes accounts of Jesus' appearing that correspond to the Johannine story of the appearance to Mary Magdalene (Mark 16:9), Luke's Emmaus road narrative (Mark 16:12), and the Jerusalem appearances to all the disciples gathered together (Mark 16:14); but these verses are widely agreed to be a later addition to the Gospel text (see the preceding footnote). Nor does Paul's list of resurrection appearances in 1 Cor. 15 help matters: other than the initial appearance "to Cephas [Peter], then to the twelve" (1 Cor. 15:5; cf. Luke 24:34, 36), none of the episodes listed by Paul corresponds to anything found in the Gospels.

11. "It seems that almost any selection of resurrection stories, determined by what a line of tradition made available or by theological attractiveness, could serve their purpose, since the assertion 'He was raised' *itself* could not in any case be narratively expanded." Jenson, *Systematic Theology*, 1:195.

12. Although the power by which Lazarus was raised from the dead was not human, the power by which he continued to live after having been raised was. That is, once resuscitated he continued to live by virtue of normal human processes of breathing, eating, sleeping, and so forth.

13. Here I differ from Barth, who insists on the resurrection as a "second history" that is "in the sphere of history and time no less than in the case of the words and acts and even the death of Jesus." Karl Barth, *CD* III/2:441–42. At the same time, to the extent that in using this language the essential point Barth seeks to make is that "in this time the *man* Jesus was manifested among them in the mode of *God*" (Barth, *CD* III/2:448), and that the "Easter time is simply the time of the revelation of the mystery of the preceding time of the life and death of the man Jesus" (Barth, *CD* III/2:455), the substance of my position may not be that different from his—though for me it is the very fact of this divine form of manifestation that renders reference to time problematic. Thus, although the risen Jesus interacts with his disciples, insofar as he does so as one who is risen and not simply resuscitated, he does not do so as one item in the world alongside others.

does not mean that the resurrection is a myth (i.e., a relic of prescientific cosmology), or a metaphor for the purely subjective experience of the disciples.[14] Whatever else may be said of the biblical accounts of the appearances of the risen Jesus, they are clearly intended to establish that the resurrection was real, not the product of the disciples either lying (see Matt. 27:62–66; 28:12–15) or hallucinating (Luke 24:39; John 20:27).[15] At the same time, the fact that these accounts do not fall in a consistent sequence or share a common setting indicates that the reality to which they bear witness is not of the same sort as Jesus' birth, suffering, or death.[16] Jesus is alive, but not alive as he was before. Before death he lived as a creature through created means, through the same physical and biochemical processes that sustain all human life in time and space. Now he lives still as a creature, but now sustained by God alone, independently of all created processes.

From this perspective, Bultmann was certainly right to argue that "the cross and the resurrection form a single, indivisible cosmic event," in that the resurrection is just the divine vindication of the crucified Jesus. The link between crucifixion and resurrection dates to the earliest days of Christian preaching, such that when Paul wants to summarize his message, he refers to what was already established tradition: "For I handed on to you as of first importance what I in turn had received: *that Christ died for our sins in accordance with the scriptures, and that he was buried, and that he was raised on the third day in accordance with the scriptures,* and that he appeared to Cephas, then to

14. Although the language of myth in contemporary theology is most closely associated with Rudolf Bultmann, he himself was rather careful in applying this concept to the resurrection, saying at one point that "the resurrection is not a mythological event adduced in order to prove the saving efficacy of the cross, but an article of faith just as much as the meaning of the cross itself." Bultmann, "New Testament and Mythology," 41. The fact that on p. 42 he writes, "If the event of Easter Day is in any sense an historical event additional to the event of the cross, it is nothing else than the rise of faith in the risen Lord," suggests that his view of the resurrection is best described as metaphor.

15. The idea that the resurrection appearances serve to affirm the truth of the claim that the crucified Jesus lives is not to say that they, along with reports of the empty tomb found in all four Gospels, are merely "later embellishments," added for apologetic purposes. Bultmann, "New Testament and Mythology," 39. As Bauckham notes (citing especially the work of E. P. Sanders), there is now little support for the idea that narratives naturally grow more fulsome with time (a claim flatly inconsistent with Matthew and Luke's shared tendency to abbreviate the lengthier Markan versions of stories about Jesus), or that there is any natural "direction" for the development of traditions. See Richard Bauckham, *Jesus and the Eyewitnesses: The Gospels as Eyewitness Testimony*, 2nd ed. (Grand Rapids: Wm. B. Eerdmans Publishing Co., 2017), 247, 259–60; cf. E. P. Sanders, "Historiographical Characteristics of the Gospel of John," *New Testament Studies* 53, no. 1 (2007): 17–36.

16. While Jesus' various appearances to the disciples could in principle be given spatiotemporal coordinates, it does not seem possible to identify in the same way where he was between appearances during the forty days between Easter and the ascension—or even to say that he was "in the heaven of the apocalypses" (*pace* Jenson, *Systematic Theology*, 1:197). Place and time simply cease to be appropriate categories when speaking of resurrected existence.

the twelve" (1 Cor. 15:3–5). The balance of the summary—death on the one hand and resurrection on the other—is clear. Jesus' death in itself is not good news; the resurrection is good news, but only by way of specifying *which* life has been vindicated in this way. The content of the life is the story of the man who was born of Mary and died under Pilate, and it is *that* life, which is God's life. As such, the proclamation of the resurrection does not mean the addition of further details to Jesus' life, as something that happened after his death and burial that continues his story; rather, the news of the resurrection is simply the declaration of God's verdict on the life that ended on Good Friday. It is a feature of our language (one already met in connection with our discussion of Jesus' preexistence, and which continues with the confession of his ascension, heavenly session, and return in glory) that we have no way of connecting the resurrection to Jesus' life other than by language of narrative (and thus, implicitly, temporal) succession. Yet insofar as the incarnation affirms that God has assumed a genuinely human life, bound by birth and death, the resurrection should not be understood as a quantitative extension of Jesus' life but rather as its qualitative transformation: the declaration that he lives, but in a new mode, as God lives—eternally and not in temporal sequence.

And insofar as it is the crucified who is risen, Jesus lives as king, such that the power exercised by him, power active in giving life rather than in taking it away (John 10:10; cf. Luke 22:24–27), is vindicated as *God's* power. As argued in the preceding chapter, because it is only on the cross that the character of this power, which holds nothing back in the pursuit of the righteousness and peace of God's kingdom, is fully made known (since only once all has been given is it clear that nothing has been held back), it is only as crucified that Jesus is definitively revealed as king. The proclamation that Jesus lives is thus equivalent to the claim that the crucified reigns—not merely "from the tree" (from which he has long since been taken down) but as God, which is to say, eternally. And from this perspective the fact that the one point in their otherwise quite varied post-crucifixion narratives upon which all the evangelists agree—that on Easter morning the tomb in which Jesus was buried was found empty—is significant.[17] For precisely because Jesus' death and burial are the terminus of his human life, it cannot be the case that his body stays in the

---

17. A further objection to the idea that the empty-tomb narratives were "later embellishments" invented as a bit of early Christian apologetic is that the mere fact of an empty tomb would hardly serve as compelling evidence that Jesus rose from the dead (see Matt. 27:64; 28:13). For this reason, the fact that Paul makes no mention of the empty tomb in 1 Cor. 15:3–7 shows nothing one way or the other about whether he knew of it, but only reflects the fact that it is useless for Paul's purposes in that passage, viz., to establish that a number of people had actually seen the risen Jesus. So too Luke, who clearly knew and respected the empty-tomb tradition, does not report the apostles referring to it when preaching Jesus' resurrection (see Acts 3:15; 10:41; 13:30–31).

tomb after his resurrection. If it did, then one could continue to tell stories about it (e.g., its decomposition, or its miraculous preservation, or its transportation from point A to point B); but the meaning of Jesus' resurrection is precisely that there is no more to be said about him in terms of events in time and space. The absence of his body underlines this point: Jesus' earthly story is over, to the extent that there is no more material, not even a corpse, that could provide the basis for adding to his story.[18] He reigns as the crucified and, as such, continues to bear the wounds of his crucifixion (Luke 24:39; John 20:25–27); but the body that bears these wounds is no longer situated in the realm of space and time. Once again, the resurrection adds nothing in terms of content to Jesus' story, for he reigns precisely as the one whose story ended on the cross.[19]

ASCENDED

In comparison to the resurrection, the doctrine of Christ's ascension has a relatively low profile. While commemoration of the resurrection has long shaped both the weekly and annual rhythms of Christian worship, celebration of the ascension, fixed on the penultimate Thursday of the fifty-day season of Easter, has more the flavor of a liturgical footnote.[20] Moreover, this marginal status in the tradition arguably reflects the biblical witness. Among the

---

18. Cf. Jenson, *Systematic Theology*, 1:206.
19. Karl Barth writes:

> His being as such . . . was and is the end of the old and the beginning of the new form of this world even without His resurrection and ascension. He did not and does not lack anything in Himself. What was lacking was only the men to see and hear it as the world and Word of God. . . . What was lacking was only their service of witness and proclamation. . . . It is here that His resurrection and ascension came in, and still come in. For when the New Testament speaks of these events, . . . it speaks of the perfect being of Jesus Christ, and His accomplished reconciliation of the world with God, in its character as revelation. . . . Thus the resurrection and ascension of Jesus Christ add to what He was and is and to what took place in Him, . . . only the new fact that in this event He was to be seen and was actually seen as the One He was and is. He did not become different in this event. (Karl Barth, *CD* IV/2:133)

20. Rev. 1:10 suggests that Sunday had acquired a special place in Christian consciousness as "the Lord's Day" by the end of the first century (the extent to which Paul's instruction for a collection "on the first day of every week" in 1 Cor. 16:2 reflects any widespread liturgical pattern is less clear). Early in the second century, Pliny the Younger reported to Emperor Trajan that Christians confessed to meeting regularly "on an appointed day" (*stato die*), but it is Justin Martyr in the middle of that century who gives the first clear testimony to a regular pattern of Sunday worship. Justin Martyr, *First Apology* 67, in *Apostolic Fathers with Justin Martyr and Irenaeus*.

evangelists, Matthew makes no mention of the ascension, and John refers to it only indirectly (20:17; cf. 6:62; 16:10). Mark's brief report (16:19) forms part of the Gospel's "longer ending," which is generally recognized to be a later addition to the text. Luke clearly teaches the doctrine, but he does so by way of two very different accounts: according to the first narration, Jesus ascended on Easter day itself (Luke 24:50–51), while the second dates the ascension to forty days after his resurrection (Acts 1:3, 6–10).[21] And the rest of the New Testament (apart from Hebrews, which will be discussed at greater length below) contains only a scattering of references to it (Acts 2:32–35; Rom. 8:34; Eph. 4:8–10; 1 Tim. 3:16; cf. Acts 7:56; Rom. 10:6).[22]

In addition to being a comparatively marginal topic in Scripture and tradition, the doctrine of Jesus' ascension and heavenly session raises conceptual problems: it speaks of the risen Jesus by using language of temporal succession and spatial movement that seems inconsistent with the claim that his life ended on Good Friday. Indeed, in this respect it arguably presents even more difficulties than the resurrection, which, by itself, might be taken as a simple affirmation that the crucified lives with God (cf. Matt. 22:31–32 and pars.), apart from any commitment to the idea that his risen life is such as to be capable of narration. When the proclamation of the resurrection is joined with the confession of Jesus' ascension and session, however, it all begins to look much more like an extended narrative sequence that begins with Jesus' escape from the underworld back to earth, continues in his being taken up from earth to heaven, and concludes with his entrance into the heavenly throne room, where he takes a seat at the right hand of the Father. Not only does this sequence evoke a long-antiquated three-story cosmology (viz., the underworld below, the surface of the earth, and heaven above), but it also implies that the resurrection inaugurates a further stage of Jesus' life, replete with new experiences, such that God's self-revelation in Jesus would not be defined by the completed time span extending from Christmas to Good Friday. But if Jesus' story were open-ended in that way, then it could not unequivocally be proclaimed as good news, since it would be impossible to rule out further developments that might reveal God's will toward us as perhaps not altogether gracious.

In light of these concerns, it is not surprising that the doctrine of the ascension has been subject to various forms of "demythologization" long before

21. For a thoughtful attempt to make sense of the two accounts within the context of Luke's overall literary project, see Mikael C. Parsons, *The Departure of Jesus in Luke-Acts: The Ascension Narratives in Context* (Sheffield: Sheffield Academic Press, 1987).

22. One might also view the New Testament identification of Jesus with Daniel's heavenly "Son of Man" (Matt. 24:30 and pars.; 25:31; 26:64 and pars.; Rev. 1:13; 14:14) as implying the ascension, since Jesus could only come *from* heaven if he had previously ascended *to* it.

the modern period. Thomas Aquinas, for example, was careful to state that "Christ's ascension to heaven implied no essential increase in the glory either of his body or of his soul," and in this respect it adds nothing to the resurrection.[23] Still more pointedly, the sixteenth-century Lutheran Johannes Brenz straightforwardly denied that the heaven to which Christ ascended should be interpreted in spatiotemporal terms.[24] In a similar vein, the wider Lutheran tradition (following the lead of Luther himself) has insisted that "the right hand of God" refers to God's effective power as Creator and Lord of the universe, so that the claim that Jesus ascended to God's right hand (Mark 16:19; cf. Acts 2:34) is simply a means of affirming that the crucified participates fully in God's governance of the world.[25]

From this perspective, reference to heaven as the "place" where the ascended Jesus resides is to be understood as strictly metaphorical: it is fitting for Christ to be "located" there because "heaven" is "the throne of God" (Matt. 5:34; 23:22): that is, the seat of God's power which, insofar as Jesus is God, is also "the throne . . . of the Lamb" (Rev. 22:1, 3).[26] While such language certainly does imply Jesus' absence from any place in the world, it need not be taken to entail the conclusion that heaven is yet another place, as though the incarnate Word's ascent to heaven were any more a matter of physical movement than was his "descent" to earth in the incarnation (cf. John 6:62). In order to further defend this way of interpreting Jesus' presence in heaven, however, it is important to assess more fully the dogmatic significance of Jesus' ascension and session there. A particularly powerful summary of the latter is offered by Maximus the Confessor:

23. Aquinas, *ST* 3.57.1.2. Thomas does, however, affirm that ascension entails motion, which he views as appropriate to the created nature assumed by the Word (see 3.57.1.1; cf. 3.57.2; 3.57.3.3).

24. To those who thought otherwise, Brenz mockingly inquires, "Does Jesus take little walks up there?" Johannes Brenz, *Von der Majestät unsers lieben Herrn und einigen Heilands Jesu Christi* (Tübingen: Morhart, 1567), 100–102; cited in Jenson, *Systematic Theology*, 1:203. Cf. Martin Luther, *That These Words of Christ, "This Is My Body," etc., Still Stand Firm against the Fanatics*, in vol. 37 of *LW*, ed. Robert H. Fischer (1961), 55–56.

25. "The Scriptures teach us . . . that the right hand of God is not a specific place in which a body must or may be . . . but is the almighty power of God, which at one and the same time can be nowhere [since it is not circumscribed in any one place] and yet must be everywhere [since it is by this power that God sustains creatures in being]." Luther, *That These Words of Christ*, 57. Cf. Formula of Concord, Solid Declaration 8.28, in *The Book of Concord: The Confessions of the Evangelical Lutheran Church*, ed. Robert Kolb and Timothy J. Wengert (Minneapolis: Fortress Press, 2000). For the later Lutheran Scholastics, see Heinrich Schmid, *The Doctrinal Theology of the Evangelical Lutheran Church*, 3rd ed., trans. Charles A. Hay and Henry E. Jacobs (Minneapolis: Augsburg, 1961), 403–7.

26. It is consistent with this idea that although Aquinas denies that the ascension adds anything to Jesus' post-resurrection glory, he nevertheless affirms that the doctrine is appropriate as it relates to "fittingness of place" (*aliquid quantum ad loci decentiam*). Aquinas, *ST* 3.57.1.2.

By his ascension into heaven, it is obvious that he united heaven and earth, for he entered heaven with his earthly body, which is of the same nature and consubstantial with ours, and showed that . . . all sensible nature is one, thus obscuring in himself the property of the division that cuts it in two. Then, in addition to these things, having passed with his soul and body (that is, with the whole of our nature) through all the divine and intelligible orders of heaven, he united the sensible with the intelligible and showed in himself that the convergence of the whole creation toward unity is utterly without division or disturbance. . . . And finally, after all of these things, he, considered according to the idea of his humanity, comes to God himself, having clearly "appeared," as it is written, "in the presence of God," the Father, "on our behalf" [Heb. 9:24], as a human being.[27]

If the point of the incarnation is bridging the divide between Creator and creature, then according to Maximus it is in the ascension that this goal is fully realized, because it is in ascending that Jesus crosses—and thereby bridges—all the divisions internal to the created order (e.g., earth and heaven, the sensible and the intelligible), such that they all appear together before God, joined in and united to his own person through the human nature he assumed. Importantly, this bridging does not mean the destruction of the distinctions between various types of created being, but precisely the revelation of their ontological "convergence" (*synneusis*) in the will of the one God who made them all.[28] Still less does the ascension obliterate the difference between Creator and creature. Instead, since it is precisely as creature ("with his soul and body") that Jesus comes to heaven, the ascension establishes the possibility of the mutual presence of Creator and creature *to* one another in their enduring distinction *from* one another.[29] For if the creature's presence *to God* is analytical in the doctrine of creation (since it is only by God's holding the creature in being that it can exist at all), the ascension secures the presence of God *to the creature* in and through the person of Jesus. In short, because the risen Jesus

27. Maximus the Confessor, *Ambigua* 41 (PG 91:1309B–D), in *On Difficulties in the Church Fathers: The Ambigua*, 2 vols., ed. and trans. Nicholas Constas (Cambridge, MA: Harvard University Press, 2014), 2:113, trans. alt.

28. Christ "recapitulated in himself, in a manner appropriate to God, all things, showing that the whole creation is one, . . . completed by the mutual coming together [*synodōi*] of all its members." Maximus, *Ambigua* 41.2.115 (PG 91:1312A).

29. Maximus explicitly makes this point in the same text, writing that in glory "the whole man wholly pervading the whole God, and becoming everything that God is, without, however, identity in essence [*chōris tēs kat' ousian tautotētos*]" (*Ambigua* 41.2.107 [PG 91:1308B]). Although in the earlier *Ambigua* 7, Maximus had written that by virtue of having "placed himself completely in God alone," the deified person "both is and is called God" (PG 91:1084C), the context makes it clear that there is no question of his affirming ontological identity between Creator and creature.

is seated at the Father's right hand, God's being and rule are to be identified with and thereby known in this creature, rather than treated as an inherently unknowable—and thus ultimately terrifying—power behind creation.[30]

So even though (following Thomas) the ascension adds nothing to Jesus' glory over and above the resurrection, it illuminates another dimension of his vindication by confirming that this glory is everlasting. Because Jesus is seated at the right hand, God's presence to us in Jesus is not simply the temporary divine use of created substance (as in the theophanies of the Old Testament), but the uniting of God's life with a creature, so that if it had always been the case that there can be no creature apart from God, Jesus' ascension means that henceforth there is no God apart from this creature (because this creature is no less than God). And since, as Maximus notes, this creature, in his human materiality, brings the whole of the rest of creation in his train, it follows that God has in Jesus bound the divine life to the whole of creation. In Jesus, then, we learn that there is no God apart from the world—not because God needs the world in order to be God, but because God has determined to ground the world's being not simply in God's will (as was the case in God's initial work of creation), but in God's very life (which is from the moment of the incarnation inseparable from Jesus' life).[31]

In this context, it is no accident that Maximus cites the Letter to the Hebrews as part of his account of the dogmatic significance of the ascension. Although Luke is the only New Testament author to provide a narrative of the ascension, the writer of Hebrews makes Jesus' ascension and session the central reference point for interpreting the overall significance of his ministry (1:3, 13; 7:26; 8:1; 9:24; 10:12; 12:2).[32] Specifically, the letter's author

30. In other words, the specter of the *Deus absconditus* is definitively overcome by the ascension of the *Deus revelatus*. This does not mean that the divine nature ceases to be invisible and incomprehensible, for God is never other than transcendent, and thus "a God who hides himself" (Isa. 45:15); but in assuming a human life, God hides the divine nature (which cannot be perceived) precisely in order to reveal the person of the Word and thus the identity of God. In this way the *Deus absconditus*, the mysterious and unknowable Lord of the universe, *is* just the *Deus revelatus*: the one who has appeared *sub contrario* in the human flesh of Jesus. Therefore, to continue to look for or speculate about a God above or behind the one who appears in Jesus is to have failed to take with full seriousness the claim that Jesus is God.

31. This transformation of the condition of our existence is what it means for us to be made *children* of God: as has been the case eternally for the Son, so now for us our being is not reducible to the action of the divine will, but is rooted in God's own being. We do not cease thereby to be creatures, but we cease to be subject to the vulnerability of creatures, for our lives are now lived not simply by virtue of God's favor, but actually by virtue of God's own being (Col. 3:3).

32. Indeed, it is a noted peculiarity of Hebrews in the NT canon that Jesus' exaltation to God's right hand seems to eclipse reflection on the resurrection altogether. While some critics (e.g., F. F. Bruce, William Lane) argue that the author simply subsumes the resurrection under the ascension, others maintain that the category of resurrection is conflated with (e.g., Hans Windisch, Erich Graesser) or even replaced by that of a (spiritual) ascension (e.g., Ernst

identifies the crossing of the divide between earth and heaven as the point where Jesus fulfills his messianic offices as priest (3:1; 4:14; 5:1, 5–6, 10; 6:20; 7:21–28; 8:1–4; 9:11–14; 10:11–14, 21). Indeed, it is to this end that the writer specifically emphasizes the importance of Jesus' human nature: he "had to become like his brothers and sisters in every respect" precisely "so that he might be a merciful and faithful high priest" (Heb. 2:17; cf. 4:15) and thereby make it possible for us to "approach God" (7:19).

To be sure, it would be wrong to limit Jesus' priestly work to his ascension and session, just as it would be to limit his exercise of the office of king to the cross. It is the role of the priest to mediate between God and human beings, and already during his earthly ministry Jesus exercised this mediatorial role by interceding for others in prayer (see, e.g., Luke 22:31–32; John 17:1–24); but with his ascension this intercession becomes perpetual (Rom. 8:34; Heb. 7:23–25; cf. 1 John 2:1–2).[33] That Jesus' priesthood should be associated with the *ascension* may seem counterintuitive, since it is normally by his *death* that he is understood to fulfill the role of priest by offering an atoning sacrifice to God.[34] As David Moffitt has persuasively argued, however, the association of sacrifice with death is based on a misreading both of Hebrews and of the practices of the Levitical cult on which Hebrews draws.[35] Within this latter context "sacrifice" is an extended ritual performance with many component parts. Although the death of the victim was certainly one of these components, the fact that the slaughtering was not performed at the altar suggests

---

Käsemann, Harold Attridge). See the discussion in David M. Moffitt, *Atonement and the Logic of Resurrection in the Epistle to the Hebrews* (Leiden: Brill, 2011), 3–41; I concur with Moffitt's judgment that the account of atonement in the epistle depends on (and therefore presupposes) belief in Jesus' bodily resurrection.

33. Cf. Origen of Alexandria, *Origen: Homilies on Leviticus 1–16*, trans. Gary Wayne Barkley (Washington, DC: Catholic University of America Press, 1990), 134: Jesus "now stands before the face of God interceding for us. He stands before the altar to offer a propitiation to God for us." In this context, the writer to Hebrews maintains that because Jesus was a member of the tribe of Judah rather than Levi, he could not serve as priest on earth, but only by virtue of his ascension to heaven (see Heb. 8:1–5).

34. See, e.g., John Calvin, *Institutes of the Christian Religion*, ed. John T. McNeill, trans. Ford Lewis Battles, 2 vols. (Philadelphia: Westminster Press, 1960), 502 (2.15.6): "The priestly office belongs to Christ alone because by the sacrifice of his death he blotted out our own guilt and made satisfaction for our sins. . . . Thus we see that we must begin from the death of Christ in order that the efficacy and benefit of his priesthood may reach us." Christ's death is also central to his priestly office in later Reformed and Lutheran theologies (see Heinrich Heppe, *Reformed Dogmatics*, ed. Ernst Bizer, trans. G. T. Thomson [London: George Allen & Unwin, 1950], 457–69; and Schmid, *Doctrinal Theology*, 342–70). Although Schleiermacher is harshly critical of many aspects of traditional accounts of Christ's work, Christ's "atoning death" still stands at the heart of his summary of Christ's priestly office. See Friedrich Schleiermacher, *The Christian Faith*, ed. H. R. Mackintosh and J. S. Stewart (Edinburgh: T&T Clark, 1928), §104. More recently, see Dalferth, *Crucified and Resurrected*, chap. 5.

35. See Moffitt, *Atonement and the Logic of Resurrection*, esp. chap. 4.

that it was not the focus of the rite.[36] That status is more plausibly assigned to the work reserved exclusively to the priesthood, which was not the killing of the animal, but the act of bringing the slaughtered victim's body and blood to the altar (see, e.g., Lev. 1:1–9) or, on the Day of Atonement, to the mercy seat itself in the inner sanctuary (16:12–16).[37]

Given this background, it should come as no surprise that that the author of Hebrews identifies Jesus' presentation of himself to the Father as "the centre of . . . Jesus' atoning sacrifice," so that the entrance into the heavenly sanctuary is the fulfillment of his priestly office (Heb. 6:19–20; 9:11–12, 24–25).[38] Although Jesus is also the victim whose body and blood are the means of atonement, it is not his death that defines him as priest.[39] He is priest rather as the one who lives and is therefore able to come before God in the heavenly sanctuary. And although he brings his own crucified body as an offering, the fact that he is risen—that "the life he lives, he lives to God" (Rom. 6:10), and is correspondingly "indestructible" (Heb. 7:16)—means that he is "a priest forever" (Heb. 5:6; 6:20; 7:17, 20; cf. Ps. 110:4).[40] On earth the priestly activity of bringing blood to the altar requires constant repetition, for the commission of new sins requires renewed sacrifice, but with Christ it is not so:

> When Christ came as a high priest of the good things that have come, then through the greater and perfect tent (not made with hands, that is, not of this creation), he entered once for all [*ephapax*] into the Holy Place, not with the blood of goats and calves, but with his own blood, thus obtaining eternal redemption. For if the blood of goats and bulls, with the sprinkling of the ashes of a heifer, sanctifies those who have been defiled so that their flesh is purified, how much more will the

36. See Christian Eberhart's judgment that within the overall structure of Levitical sacrifice, "die Tötung von Opfertieren zu den unwichtigeren Handlungen gehört." Christian Eberhart, *Studien zur Bedeutung der Opfer im Alten Testament: Die Signifikanz von Blut- und Verbrennungsriten im kultischen Rahmen*, Wissenschaftliche Monographien zum Alten und Neuen Testament 94 (Neukirchen-Vlyn: Neukirchener Verlag, 2002), 399; cited in Moffitt, *Atonement and the Logic of Resurrection*, 259.

37. "The most central elements of atoning sacrifices—that is, the elements most directly connected with obtaining the atoning benefit of these sacrifices—are the acts of blood manipulation and burning. These activities, by way of contrast to the act of slaughter, are exclusively the prerogatives of the priests and occur at and upon the various altars." David M. Moffitt, "Jesus' Heavenly Sacrifice in Early Christian Reception of Hebrews: A Survey," *Journal of Theological Studies*, NS, 68, part 1 (April 2017): 47, note 2; cf. Moffitt, *Atonement and the Logic of Resurrection*, 271.

38. Moffitt, "Jesus' Heavenly Sacrifice," 47.

39. Thus, the fact that Jesus was not the agent of his own death is not a point of disanalogy between his priesthood and the practice of Levitical priests (as assumed, by, e.g., Thomas Aquinas, *ST* 3.22.2.1); quite the contrary, it is fully consistent with Old Testament sacrificial practice, in which the priest receives the corpse of the victim, which has been slaughtered by another.

40. Hebrews speaks of Jesus offering his body (10:10), his blood (9:12), and himself (7:27). As Moffitt argues, blood is central because it is understood as the bearer of life (Lev. 17:11; cf. Gen. 9:4), thereby canceling the power of death let loose by the people's impurity and sin. See Moffitt, *Atonement and the Logic of Resurrection*, 256–81.

blood of Christ, who through the eternal Spirit offered himself without blemish to God, purify our conscience from dead works to worship the living God! (Heb. 9:11–14; cf. 7:27–28)

Human beings indeed continue to sin, yet because the life of the victim brought to the heavenly altar is indestructible, its effects are not finite in a way that would call for further acts of sacrifice. On the contrary, because Jesus lives, the power of his life never loses efficacy and so need be offered only once: "Nor was it to offer himself again and again, as the high priest enters the Holy Place year after year with blood that is not his own; for then he would have had to suffer again and again since the foundation of the world. But as it is, he has appeared once for all [*hapax*] at the end of the age to remove sin by the sacrifice of himself" (Heb. 9:25–26; cf. 10:10; Rom. 6:10). To invoke an image from another New Testament text, Jesus is the "Lamb standing as if it had been slaughtered" (Rev. 5:6): the one truly crucified, and continuing to bear the wounds of his crucifixion (Luke 24:39; John 20:20, 27), and yet who lives. And for Jesus to be slaughtered and yet alive (which is simply the confession that he is "crucified and risen" put into the language of the Levitical cult) is for him to be the offering that is sufficient for all time. Far from being a victim who, always dying, is (to cite again the words of Pascal) "in agony until the end of the world," he is the one who always and indefeasibly *lives* (cf. Heb. 7:8) and thereby is able to stand as surety for the life of all creatures.[41] In short, because this creature now lives God's own life before God, no creature's life can finally be separated from God's (Rom. 8:38–39).[42]

Since the doctrine of Jesus' ascension and session is in this way fundamentally a claim about the abiding power of Jesus' human life, as defined by the temporal sequence extending from Christmas to Good Friday, it should not be interpreted as describing a sequence of postmortem activities undertaken by Jesus. Indeed, when the doctrine is not viewed as part of a narrative time line, the discrepancies in Luke's dating of the ascension becomes less troubling, since the alternatives make complementary points: to say that Jesus ascended on Easter day is to characterize his risen life as from the very beginning a life in the presence of God, in distinction from a mere resuscitation; while the dating of the ascension after forty days of resurrection appearances serves to

41. "The conceptual center [of the sacrificial imagery in Hebrews] is not Jesus' earthly death outside the gates of Jerusalem, but his *living, human presence* in heaven." Moffitt, *Atonement and the Logic of Resurrection*, 284.

42. Moffitt notes that the Yom Kippur sacrifices "enabled Israel to dwell near the presence of God in relative safety, and enabled God's presence/glory to dwell among the people for another year." Moffitt, *Atonement and the Logic of Resurrection*, 272. Following this line of logic, Jesus' "indestructible life" presently at God's right hand allows for this mutual presence of God's people to God and God to God's people to be secured in perpetuity.

emphasize the human—and thus embodied—reality of Jesus' risen life (see Acts 1:3), over against the temptation to a purely spiritualized understanding of his life with God. In both cases the point is that the human being Jesus lives, but in a manner quite different from the mode of subsistence in space and time that defined his life between his birth and death. In the resurrection the terms of his human life have changed irrevocably: because "the life he lives, he lives to God" (Rom. 6:10), "even though we once knew Christ from a human point of view, we know him no longer in that way" (2 Cor. 5:16).

And yet the question remains: What can it mean to lead a truly human (viz., embodied) existence outside of space and time? For surely it is the characteristic of a body to occupy a particular space, relative to (and correspondingly dependent on) other such bodies. How then can Jesus' life at the right hand of the Father be a truly human and thus creaturely life, if God's transcendence means that this divine right hand is beyond space and time? As argued in chapter 3, that God can also be human without ceasing to be God is possible precisely by virtue of the divine transcendence, but the very asymmetry of the Creator-creature relation that makes it possible for God to become human seems to preclude any corresponding possibility of the human creature sharing the properties of divinity by living outside of space and time as God does. As Reformed theologians in particular argue, a body that cannot be assigned a definite place cannot meaningfully be designated as human. It thus seems to follow that the ascension requires some prevarication regarding either the risen Jesus' humanity (as in the Lutheran affirmation of the omnipresence of Christ's glorified humanity), or the transcendent character of heaven (as in the Reformed treatment of heaven as a "place" where a body subsists).

There is, however, a third possibility, modeled on Thomas Aquinas's account of the beatific vision. According to Thomas, the beatific vision—that is, the doctrine that human beings are able to perceive the divine essence in heaven—confronts some of the same issues of conceptual compatibility that accompany the confession of Jesus' bodily presence in heaven; for since the divine essence is transcendent, it seems to be the case *either* that whatever a creature sees is other (and thus less) than the divine essence, *or* that the creature is able to see the divine essence only by virtue of having been made divine. In short, if the seeing is truly creaturely (i.e., the creature who does the seeing remains a creature in the act of seeing), then the object seen cannot be the divine essence; and if the divine essence is indeed seen, then the observer is no longer a creature. The conundrum seems absolute, and yet, argues Thomas, Christians cannot give up the conviction that human beings in heaven, all the while remaining creatures, truly see the divine essence; for if the ultimate end of human life were anything else, it would follow that something other than God were the ultimate object of human happiness—and that conclusion would be contrary to the faith (at least according to Thomas's reading of passages like 1 Cor. 13:12; 1 John 3:2; and John 14:21).[43]

Thomas resolves this problem by appeal to a special act of God. Using the categories of Aristotelian epistemology that were current in his day, Thomas argues that we know something by apprehending its form (viz., that which defines something as the kind of thing it is—e.g., humanity), which we isolate either by abstraction from a particular material entity, or by receiving an impression on our intellect by the thing known. He maintains that neither alternative is possible in the case of the creature's knowledge of God: on the one hand, God cannot be apprehended by abstraction (since God is simple, and abstraction is possible only when an object is composite, such that its form can be distinguished from its various accompanying accidents); on the other hand, God cannot leave an impression on the created intellect (since there is no commonality between God and the intellect that would allow such an impression to be received). In short, any form that the human mind is able to generate or receive in the intellect is necessarily finite (and so other than God); this fact makes creaturely vision of God by normal processes impossible. Faced with this impasse, Aquinas suggests that in the beatific vision the divine essence is itself united to the human intellect, as both the form that is known and the form by which it is known. This is not to say that the divine essence becomes the form of the intellect (as in the process of impression described above), since that would breach the absolute distinction between Creator and creature. Instead, "the divine essence will be to the intellect as form to matter" (i.e., giving form to the intellect as other forms shape matter into particular types of things), thereby allowing us to see the divine essence by means of that essence itself.[44] In other words, while the divine essence neither is nor can be the form of any created intellect, it will by a special grace of God nevertheless relate to the intellect as a form, so that a creature's vision of the divine essence will still be a creaturely knowing (since it takes place by way of an external form) and yet have God as its object (since the form in question is that of the divine essence).[45]

43. For this and what follows, see Thomas Aquinas, *Summa Theologica*, Supplement [hereafter *ST, Suppl.*] 92.1 (New York: Benziger Bros., 1947).

44. Aquinas, *ST, Suppl.*, 92.1.

45. As Thomas puts it, because the power of our intellects is finite, "we shall see the same thing that God sees, namely His essence, but not so effectively." *ST, Suppl.*, 92.1.2; cf. 92.3: "Since then the extent of the Divine power is measured according to what it can do, if an intellect were to see in the Divine essence all that God can do, its perfection in understanding would equal in extent the Divine power in producing its effects, and thus it would comprehend the Divine power, which is impossible for any created intellect to do." In light of the Orthodox tradition's denial that the divine essence can be seen by creatures, even in glory, the fact that Thomas in this way qualifies the human capacity to see God is significant for the possibility of ecumenical rapprochement. For an extensive discussion of this question, see A. N. Williams, *The Ground of Union: Deification in Aquinas and Palamas* (Oxford: Oxford University Press, 1999).

How should this proposal be assessed? On the one hand, it certainly provides a resolution to the problem of human knowledge of the divine essence, in that God bestows on the intellect a special form that preserves the integrity of creaturely knowledge and allows that the object of such knowledge be none other than the infinite God. On the other hand, the form Thomas posits, precisely because it is the divine essence itself in distinction from our intellect, is utterly sui generis and thus without any analogue in our worldly experience of knowing. In short, Thomas simply affirms that God is able, through grace, to ensure that human beings will be able genuinely to see and know God as creatures by virtue of an unimaginable modification of their cognitive capacities. If such a resolution seems to be an instance of special pleading, Thomas would presumably reply that in the final analysis nothing other than some such sort of special pleading is possible when it is a matter of trying to speak of any sort of commensurability between the Creator and the created.

A similar strategy might be used to talk about Jesus' session at God's right hand: even as with respect to the beatific vision God provides an intellectual form corresponding to but not identical with the divine essence, so God is able to provide a "place" for the incarnate Word that is God's place (since Jesus is not other than God) without the human body becoming divine.[46] This approach avoids accounts of the ascension in which language of bodily transformation or transposition suggest that Jesus' postmortem existence is to be conceived in terms of further episodes in his life story. Resurrection and ascension are not rightly described in terms of changes either to the location or the attributes of Jesus' body, but exclusively by reference to the work of God in sustaining the humanity that was crucified.[47] This in no sense excludes Christian use of the biblical language of the "spiritual body" (1 Cor. 15:44), or of the perishable putting on the imperishable and the mortal putting on immortality (15:53–54), but it does mean that such terminology should not be understood as describing any particular properties of Jesus' glorified body. Quite the contrary, the point of the doctrines of the resurrection and ascension is to affirm that Jesus no longer lives by virtue of *any* properties of his

---

46. One might define "heaven" in similar terms: a "place" that, in contrast to the phenomenal realm of the visible universe, is God's place and yet distinct from God. The difference is that the right hand of God is such that the created body who occupies it (viz., Jesus) *is* God, so that to be present at God's right hand is quite simply *to be* God's presence. In short, heaven is the "place" where God is experienced as immediately present, and the right hand is that "place" where that experience of God's presence is God's own experience.

47. Even as the incarnation is not to be described as the preexistent *Logos* putting on flesh, as a man might a coat, neither are the resurrection and ascension to be described in terms of postmortem changes in that flesh. Both proposals misconstrue the incarnation by viewing the earthly-historical existence of Jesus as a segment of a narrative timeline that extends infinitely far in both directions, thereby conflating the eternal and the temporal.

human nature, however modified or augmented, but by God's power only. Jesus' session at the right hand is thus not another stage in his career beyond death, but just the eternal and irrevocable vindication of his crucified humanity. There are no categories available to explain this mode of existence, for it is one in which Jesus' life (that is, the sequence of events extending from birth to death, which define him as the human being he is) has ended (John 19:30)— and yet he lives. It is frankly a paradox: the paradox of the "Lamb standing as if it had been slaughtered" (Rev. 5:6).

COMING

Yet appeal to paradox may be insufficient to offset the worry that this account of the risen Jesus' life makes it appear rather inert. After all, the insistence that resurrection is not resuscitation, so that there are no further episodes in Jesus' life, and thus, strictly speaking, no further story to tell about him after Good Friday, makes it difficult to talk about his living in terms (viz., action through time, movement in space, processes of give-and-take in relation to other entities) that connote genuine liveliness. To counter this perception, it is important to recognize that a life "lived to God," like God's own life, is indeed radically different from life lived in time and space: it does not involve metabolic processes geared toward growth, maintenance, or reproduction, but is rather perfected, neither requiring nor capable of any completion. If Jesus of Nazareth, the one born of Mary and crucified by Pilate, *is* the revelation of God's Word in its fullness, then there just cannot be anything more to add to his story after Good Friday. Again, if there were, it would follow that his life was not the revelation of the Word, and that he was not the one in whom the whole fullness of deity dwelled bodily (Col. 2:9). Narrative reveals character, and because the Christian claim is just that the character of God has been definitively revealed in the life story that ends on Calvary, the confession of Jesus' resurrection, ascension, and session at God's right hand should not be understood as further episodes in that story, but simply as the vindication of that story in its completeness as God's own. And just because that life is God's life, its completeness does not mean its end. Although Jesus' life, like every human life, is bounded by death, by the power of the resurrection it is also true that this life, without ceasing to be defined by the time span extending from birth to death, has overcome death. As such, Jesus' risen life is neither a return to nor an extension of earthly life (and thus not characterized by further development that would render that earthly life incomplete), but a life that, because it is God's own, is lived as God lives: not in doing *particular* things (eating here, healing there, teaching somewhere else), but doing *all* things (i.e., upholding the whole of creation). In short, as risen, Jesus is supremely alive: the one who grounds, sustains, and empowers everything that is, and just so is "the Savior of all people, especially of those who believe" (1 Tim. 4:10).

This essential—and indeed, unsurpassable—liveliness of the risen Jesus is reflected in the last of the creedal affirmations concerning his postmortem fate: the confession that he "will come again in glory to judge the living and the dead." Once again, at first glance it seems that these words (especially when read in light of passages like 1 Thess. 4:16–17 and Rev. 1:7) must be taken as describing a further event in Jesus' story, just the sort of particular activity, marked by movement in space and time, characteristic of his earthly life in first-century Palestine. Here too, however, drawing this conclusion would vitiate the completeness of Jesus' earthly life as the revelation of the Word. And if Jesus' earthly life were incomplete in this way, then his coming in judgment would necessarily be a matter of dread, for how could one know whether the triumphant return of one whose story is incomplete were truly good news? Yet Jesus sees no basis for such fear; on the contrary, his instructions to his followers on what to do when they see "'the Son of Man coming in a cloud' with power and great glory" are these: "Stand up and raise your heads, because your redemption is drawing near" (Luke 21:28).

If the prospect of Jesus' coming again is to give rise to sure and certain hope rather than painful uncertainty, then talk of his return—the parousia—must be interpreted alongside the resurrection and ascension as a further dimension of Jesus' vindication rather than another episode in his career. And the principle that it is Christ's humanity, as defined by his finite life span, that reveals the fullness of God's will for the world provides the necessary theological grounds for rethinking the import of the biblical (and creedal) language of the parousia.[48] Once more, Jesus' coming from heaven to earth should not be understood as an event like his coming from Galilee to Jerusalem (that is, as a temporally structured movement from one location to another). Nor (the venerable tradition of referring to the parousia as the "second coming" notwithstanding) should his return be viewed as analogous to his incarnation (that is, as a transition from eternal to temporal existence). Precisely as the advent of the crucified and risen Lord, who now sits at God's right hand,

---

48. Here the rationale for demythologization, in contrast to the sort advocated by Bultmann and his followers, is strictly theological rather than apologetic; that is, it is grounded in the internal logic of the Christian confession of Jesus as Lord rather than in concern about the credibility of Christian claims in the context of modern Western culture. The problem is not that the claim of Christ's coming from heaven on a cloud is incredible in the face of current scientific cosmology, but that the interpretation of Christ's coming as an event in his life story to be located on the same narrative sequence as his baptism or his walking on water fails to take seriously that the revelation of God is defined by his earthly-historical existence.

the parousia is neither a matter of progression within time (viz., another episode in Jesus' story), nor a "movement" from eternity into time (as though Jesus were thereby initiating a second spatiotemporal life subsequent to his thirty-odd years in first-century Palestine). Rather than an event *in* time, his coming is better interpreted as the end of time. Here "end" carries the sense of both termination and fulfillment, since it means that Jesus' status as risen and ascended Lord, previously perceived only by way of extraordinary revelation (see Acts 7:56; cf. 9:3–7; Rev. 1:12–16), becomes visible to all. Indeed, because heaven is not a place in the spatiotemporal sense and yet is the seat of Jesus' glorified humanity, only as Jesus is revealed from heaven can he be visible to all, since only so is he *both* fully human (and thus visible) *and* not limited by time and space in a way that would prevent his being present to all simultaneously.

In this context, the description of Jesus as ascended to the throne of God is apt, for it points to a human analogy for his presence at the parousia that is not reducible to physical proximity. For Christ's return—precisely as the return of the human and thus embodied Christ—cannot be understood either as kind of uniform permeation of creation (as though his presence were like an infinitely extended mist or a gravitational field), or as a matter of bodily proximity to every point in creation (as though Jesus were simultaneously standing beside every creature). Neither model is consistent with Jesus' status as a concrete, particular human being. Yet to think of Jesus as seated at the heavenly throne does suggest how we might conceive of his future presence, for a monarch seated on a throne is present to everyone in the room, such that when the monarch enters, all in the room are said to be in the presence of the sovereign, wherever they may be located in relation to the throne. In a similar way, to speak of Christ's coming from heaven is to affirm a mode of divine presence that, unlike that by which God sustains creation, is, by virtue of the humanity of the incarnate Word, fully visible. The promise of the parousia (which, of course, means precisely "presence") is thus the promise of a new creation, where God no longer rules mysteriously and invisibly, "behind" the veil of created causes, but as visibly present in and to the world.

Insofar as Jesus was revealed on the cross as king, the fact that he remains the crucified, the "Lamb standing as if it had been slaughtered," means that he comes again as king. But whereas on Calvary his judgment of the world as king was evident only to those who had eyes to see (Luke 23:47), with no immediate or evident effect on the ways of power and dominion within the world, with the parousia the scope of Jesus' reign and his judgment become at once universally manifest and irresistible. Then he will come "in glory to judge the living and the dead, and his kingdom will have no end." That is, all will be subject to him, and this subjection will define the state of the world and its inhabitants into eternity. That even the dead are included in the judgment speaks to the character of God: because he is Creator, in his presence "all are alive" (Luke 20:38; cf. 1 Pet. 4:6).[49] As living, they will stand in his presence—a prospect that raises again the question of how far the incarnation and its promise of God's presence to creation is good news, for "who can endure the day of his coming, and who can stand when he appears?" (Mal. 3:2). As noted above, however, here again the principle that the parousia is not a further episode in the story of Jesus is important. If it were, then Malachi's question could only be rhetorical, since the fact that before God none is righteous (Rom. 3:10–12; cf. Ps. 14:2–3) means that no one could endure his coming. Yet because "we have seen his glory" (John 1:14), which includes "the whole fullness of deity" (Col. 2:9) that his coming is, the parousia may be anticipated with confidence rather than fear and uncertainty, in line with his instructions to the apostles. To make this point is not to claim that anyone will escape judgment, but only to recognize that the judge is the one who, having refused to be God apart from those same human beings who have no righteousness in themselves, "justifies the ungodly" (Rom. 4:5). It is for this reason, in confidence that the return of Jesus is good news, that the doctrine of the parousia forms part of the Apostles' and Nicene Creeds. Christians do not hope for Jesus' coming because they believe that they will be able to stand before him by their own power (quite the contrary, the Last Judgment is the definitive revelation of the fact that all find themselves incapable of doing so), but because they believe that he can and will cause them to stand. They will stand in him, because in him God has chosen to stand with them.

This point—that, in Jesus, God has bound God's own destiny to ours—points to a further matter attaching to the promise of Christ's return. A crucial theme of the second section of this chapter is that Jesus crosses the great divide between Creator and creature by ascending from earth to heaven, bringing his human life into God's eternal presence. But if the second article of the creed were to end with this confession, it might seem to follow that this crossing, and the redemption it signifies, is finally a matter of humanity's extraction from the world, and thus a separation of human destiny from that of other creatures. Such a picture of salvation has exercised a powerful grip on popular piety over the centuries, not only among those (like the so-called gnostics) whose views have been condemned by the church, but also

---

49. The NRSV renders Luke 20:38, "to him all *of them* are alive," but the Greek reads simply *pantes gar autō zōsin.*

among figures well within the Christian mainstream (e.g., the vision of the saints' postmortem existence in Dante's *Comedy*). Yet the idea that the destiny of human beings is fulfilled in their evacuation from earth to heaven, after which "everything [else] that belongs to this world will be burnt up by fire and reduced to nothing," is inconsistent with the biblical affirmation that the whole creation, having been "subjected to futility," now "waits with eager longing for the revealing of the children of God," in the confidence that it "will be set free from its bondage to decay and will obtain the freedom of the glory of the children of God" (Rom. 8:19–21).[50]

It is necessary to be careful here, for the interpretation of Christ's return as the fulfillment—and thus the end—of time disallows straightforwardly millenarian eschatologies: if Jesus' parousia cannot be understood as a further episode in his own history, neither can it be interpreted as the inauguration of a new earthly-historical epoch. If Jesus' earthly life ends on Good Friday and the life he lives ever after is lived to God, then the thousand-year reign mentioned in Revelation 20:6–7 cannot be taken as a literal description of a future period in space and time, and thus of a second, triumphal period of Jesus' earthly ministry supplementing the first.[51] Nevertheless, the millenarian impulse that has been found among Christians from the beginning contains a *particula veri*: the refusal to conceive the content of the Christian hope as an otherworldly, spiritualized existence abstracted from the rest of creation, and

50. The quotation in the first part of the sentence is from Schmid, *Doctrinal Theology*, 655. This idea of universal annihilation draws support from the biblical claim that on the day of the Lord "the elements will be dissolved with fire"; but crucial to interpreting this statement is the recognition that its point is by no means the denial of ultimate significance to the material world in which humanity presently lives, but rather to allow that "the earth and everything that is done on it will be disclosed" in preparation for "new heavens and a new earth, where righteousness is at home" (2 Pet. 3:10, 13). In other words, even here the point is not a definitive separation of humanity from the rest of creation, but precisely the glorification of the whole of creation as the fitting context for humanity's glorified existence. In light of the promise of a new creation, there is no justification for the claim that "not a transformation of the world, but an absolute annihilation of its substance is to be expected" (Schmid, *Doctrinal Theology*, 656).

51. Given the text's references to the coming back to life of the martyrs to share in Christ's earthly reign, such a literalistic interpretation may be held to fail by virtue of the fact that it effectively reduces resurrection to resuscitation. The traditional "Augustinian" interpretation of this passage as referring to the era of the church (viz., the historical period between Pentecost and parousia) is at least consistent with the evident location of the "millennium" on the earthly-historical plane (i.e., within space and time), as well as to its historically unremarkable character. For it is important to note that the writer of Revelation does not describe anything happening during this thousand years. They are not characterized by any specific content at all (e.g., as an era of uninterrupted plenty, or of universal peace and justice). The reader is given to understand that during this time the power of the devil is restrained prior to a final spasmodic outburst that culminates in God's definitive victory over the forces of sin and death (Rev. 20:1–3, 7–8; cf. Luke 10:18–20; 2 Thess. 2:7–10), but there is no indication that the period corresponds to any sort of universal public triumph of the church or Christianity.

the corresponding insistence that it is a fully embodied life, in which God is present to us just as one who can be seen as Jesus.[52] Such a hope is defined not by an escape from earthly existence, but rather by the transfiguration of that existence so that it is and may be sustained in God's presence. As "the first fruits of those who have died" (1 Cor. 15:20), Jesus initiates that transfigured mode of life, which the redeemed will share at his coming (15:23). To be sure, in one respect, the terms of Jesus' resurrection are unique: he is the only one who, having risen from the dead, ascends to the right hand of the Father, for he alone among human beings is Lord and God, and thus he shares in the divine rule of the universe; but the point of his ascension is not that we should follow him "up" to heaven, but that in and by the power of his enfleshment, God should come "down" to earth:

> I saw the holy city, the new Jerusalem, coming down out of heaven from God, prepared as a bride adorned for her husband. And I heard a loud voice from the throne saying,

> "See, the home of God is among mortals.
> He will dwell with them;
> they will be his peoples,
> and God himself will be with them."

> (Rev. 21:2–3)

Incarnation is the promise of Emmanuel, "God with us" (Matt. 1:23; cf. Isa. 7:14). In Bethlehem this promise was realized, as God takes flesh as Mary's son. Yet this very divine commitment to live in time seemingly renders the good news of God's coming among us fatally limited: available only to those people temporally subsequent and spatially connected to the historical life span of Jesus.[53] Only in his appearing from heaven, in that moment when he is universally revealed as Lord, is the promise that all creation may enjoy the glory of God's presence realized. So it is that the content of Christian hope as defined by Christ's return is not the evacuation of the earth, but its vindication as the home of the God who, in willing to be flesh, wills not to dwell apart from flesh.

---

52. In this context, it is probably no accident that the early apologists' rejection of the variegated movement known as Gnosticism, which was marked by a deep pessimism about materiality, was generally accompanied by a vibrant millenarian hope. See, e.g., Papias, *Fragments* 6; Justin Martyr, *Dialogue with Trypho* 80–81; Irenaeus, *Against Heresies* 5.32–36; and Tertullian, *Against Marcion* 3.25.

53. Christians have, of course, always held that the benefits of Jesus' ministry accrue to the Israelite patriarchs and matriarchs who believed in the promise of the Messiah, but this concession does not make much of a dent in the numbers of those who are apparently excluded from knowing either Christ or his benefits.

That is Christianity's hope. But what of now, when Jesus remains invisible in his place and at God's right hand, while we toil on below in a world where the realities of violence, sorrow, anger, pain, sickness, and death appear unaffected by the history of Christ's coming or the promise of his return? If the benefits of Christ's incarnation are finally a matter of future hope only, can they be free from the suspicion of false consciousness, an ideologically driven deferral of justice now in the hope of some ever-receding promise of utopia? That is the subject of the final chapter.

7

Jesus' Presence Now

It is a commonplace to say that Christian faith is suspended between past and future, between the "already" of Jesus' past earthly life and the "not yet" of his future return. The difficulty is that as the years continue to roll on, and the first century recedes into the ever more distant past, the "not yet" easily seems to overwhelm the "already," such that redemption appears to be a matter of endless deferral far removed from current experience. This gap between the content of the promised future and the present reality underwrites much modern criticism of Christianity and the church, and while this challenge is by no means new (see 2 Pet. 3:3–4), its force is enhanced by the at-best uneven character of the church's witness over the centuries, during which appeal to the promise of Jesus' coming has all too often been used to deflect attention from the needs of God's children in the here and now. For if from God's side there may be much to be said for the claim that "the Lord is not slow about his promise, . . . but is patient with you, not wanting any to perish, but all to come to repentance" (2 Pet. 3:9), the church's patience with the ways of the world often seems far more self-interested.

Be that as it may, the gap between the "already" of Jesus' earthly ministry and "not yet" of his coming again is especially pressing for the present argument, for which the humanity of Jesus is the touchstone for Christian talk about God. For in the period between ascension and parousia, Jesus' humanity is not directly perceptible to us, either as it was to his earthly companions (who could write of "what we have seen with our eyes, what we have looked at and touched with our hands, concerning the word of life," 1 John 1:1), or as it will be at his return (when "we will see him as he is," 1 John 3:2). During this time, we seemingly can access his humanity only through the Gospels: a collection of partial and not altogether consistent narratives based on the perceptions of those who did see him in bodily form. By contemporary standards the amount of material thus preserved constitutes a rather sparse biography, written down only some years after Jesus' death by evangelists who, even if drawing on eyewitness testimony, did not themselves necessarily know Jesus during his earthly life.[1] While these points need not be taken as reason for doubting the general reliability of the Gospel accounts, they do quite sharply raise the question of how we experience the humanity of Jesus Christ in the present. If the upshot of the gospel is that God, who is inherently inaccessible to us by virtue of the divine transcendence, has become present to us by living among us, then the question becomes unavoidable of how the good news that "God is with us" (Matt. 1:23) can continue to be proclaimed once Jesus has ascended to heaven.

A very traditional answer to this question is that between ascension and parousia Jesus is present (and therefore present in his humanity insofar as the presence of *Jesus*, as the incarnate Word, is necessarily a *human* presence) through the Holy Spirit. Because (as Paul puts it) "the Lord *is* the Spirit," through the Spirit we are enabled to see "the glory of the [incarnate] Lord," with the result that we "are being transformed into the same image from one degree of glory to another" (2 Cor. 3:17–18; cf. 1 Cor. 6:17; 15:45). In this way (and contrary to the impression one might get from passages like John 14:16–17; 15:26; 16:7), the Holy Spirit is not a replacement for Jesus, but that which mediates Jesus' own presence.[2] This point is crucial, for if the Spirit is the means by which the human being Jesus continues to be present in and to the world, it cannot be a substitute for his humanity, but rather its vehicle.

---

1. Although Matthew and John are traditionally identified with the eponymous apostles, whether any of the canonical evangelists knew Jesus during his life is doubted by many modern scholars, and Luke, at least, makes it clear that he did not (see Luke 1:1–3). The earliest assessment of Mark's Gospel that we possess not only denies that Mark himself knew Jesus, but explicitly dismisses the chronology of his narrative, noting that "Mark, having become the interpreter of Peter, wrote down accurately whatsoever [Peter] remembered. It was not, however, in exact order that [Mark] related the sayings or deeds of Christ. For he neither heard the Lord nor accompanied Him. But afterwards . . . he accompanied Peter, who accommodated his instructions to the necessities [of his hearers], but with no intention of giving a regular narrative of the Lord's sayings." Papias, *Fragments* 6, in *ANF* 1, trans. slightly alt. For a compelling defense of the claim that John was written by an eyewitness (though not the son of Zebedee), see Richard Bauckham, *Jesus and the Eyewitnesses: The Gospels as Eyewitness Testimony*, 2nd ed. (Grand Rapids: Wm. B. Eerdmans Publishing Co., 2017).

2. This claim that the Spirit mediates Jesus' presence should no more be taken as a slight against the distinctiveness of the Spirit than Jesus' remarks to the effect that he mediates the Father's presence (e.g., John 14:9) should be taken as impugning the integrity of the Son. Even as Jesus mediates the presence of the Father precisely in distinguishing himself from the Father as the one from whom he comes and to whom he goes (16:28), so the Spirit mediates Jesus' (human) presence by bearing witness to the Son (15:26; cf. 1 John 4:2). Insofar as the three persons are equally God and inherently present to one another, such claims should be understood as corollaries of the doctrine of the Trinity.

But how is this mediation of Christ's humanity to be understood, since the confession that Jesus is now seated at God's right hand (and thus outside the phenomenal realm of space and time) means that as a matter of faith as well as of experience, he is not now present to us in recognizably human form?

WORD AND SACRAMENT

One way this question has been answered has been to affirm Word and sacrament as a means by which the Spirit effects Jesus' presence in the world in a manner that allows him to be heard and touched, if not seen, in his humanity. Through these means, the Spirit gives Jesus' humanity an earthly-historical form in the time between his ascension and parousia, such that created realities—speech, bread, and wine—that do not stand in any direct bodily continuity with his flesh-and-blood existence in first-century Palestine are nevertheless named as his words, his body, and his blood.

Already during his earthly ministry Jesus commandeered other creatures to mediate his presence in this way when he sent forth his disciples to preach in his name (Matt. 10:5–7 and pars.; Luke 10:1–11), with the assurance that they represented him in the most fulsome possible sense: "Whoever welcomes you welcomes me, and whoever welcomes me welcomes the one who sent me" (Matt. 10:40 and pars.; cf. Luke 10:16). And after the resurrection, Jesus makes it clear that this commission continues, as he both commands his followers to "make disciples of all nations, . . . teaching them to obey everything that I have commanded you," and assures them, "I am with you always, to the end of the age" (Matt. 28:19–20; cf. John 16:12–15). But, given that the "end of the age" is precisely when Jesus comes again (Matt. 24:29–31; 25:31–32), it is not immediately clear from Jesus' words what sort of "presence" is envisaged in the meantime, when Jesus is seated at the Father's right hand in a way that is not generally visible even to the disciples, let alone to the world at large.[3]

Insofar as the language of the right hand is understood to refer to Jesus' sharing God's power as the risen Lord, his ascension entails no physical distance from the disciples or, for that matter, any other particle of the created order. In this respect (as noted in the preceding chapter), his coming again means just the public revelation of the lordship that he now exercises hiddenly. But if in this way all are present to the ascended Jesus until the parousia, Jesus is not in the same way present to the creation as a whole, or even

---

3. The New Testament does witness to at least two instances of the ascended Jesus appearing to individual disciples, in the visions granted to Stephen (Acts 7:55) and to Paul (9:3–5), but they are evidently extraordinary events (cf. 1 Cor. 15:8).

to the church in particular. Given his strong personal identification with the disciples' mission while he was still physically present on earth ("Whoever listens to you listens to me, and whoever rejects you rejects me," Luke 10:16), it is tempting to identify his continuing presence on earth directly with that of particular human individuals who continue to represent him (cf. Matt. 25:40, 45). But this will not do. It may well continue to be the case that to receive or reject a disciple is the equivalent of receiving or rejecting Jesus (cf. Gal. 4:14), but even if Paul can go so far as to say, "It is no longer I who live, but it is Christ who lives in me" (Gal. 2:20), he remains Paul and not Jesus (see 1 Cor. 1:13; cf. Acts 10:25–26; 14:13–15).

And yet insofar as Paul can talk of Christ as not only living, but also as speaking in him (2 Cor. 13:3), there is more to be said here. For although it is true that Christians are to do everything in Jesus' name (Col. 3:17), there seem to be particular circumstances in which what they say is to be regarded as though coming from the mouth of Jesus himself—so that such speech is to be regarded not merely as words, but as the Word. What speech falls in this category? At one level, it seems reasonable to include all words that are part of the public proclamation of the gospel, insofar as the point of listening to a sermon is precisely to attend to the words proclaimed, in the confidence that God can and will communicate the Word through faithful proclamation.[4] Yet although it is integral to God's intentions for the church that the word that is preached should become the Word of God, the fact that words preached are always words chosen and arranged by a particular human being means that such words do not have that status intrinsically.[5]

For this reason it would be unthinkable for the church to identify the words of even the most compelling of sermons directly with the Word of God.[6] At the same time, it may be that at least some of the words proclaimed in the church may be identified with God's Word as no sermon can be.[7]

4. The most well-known account of this principle is that of Karl Barth, who includes the Word preached along with the Word revealed (Jesus) and the Word written (Scripture) as one dimension of the threefold form of the Word of God. See Karl Barth, *CD* I/1:88–99.

5. As the devil's citation of Scripture in the temptation story indicates (see Matt. 4:5–6 and par.), even direct biblical quotation provides no guarantee that words proclaimed will communicate the Word of God.

6. To make this point is not to deny that the words proclaimed in the sermon may have communicated God's own Word, but simply to acknowledge that whether and how they may have been such is a matter of divine freedom and not human control. The church can certainly declare that a sermon is orthodox in content; but to affirm that a discourse is free from error *in fide et moribus* is worlds apart from the judgment *Deus dixit*.

7. The theology of baptism sketched out in the final, fragmentary part-volume of his *Church Dogmatics* (IV/4: §75) shows that the later Barth would not accept this possibility. His earlier views are less clear-cut. Already in *CD* I/1 he can say that the consecrated bread and wine of the Lord's Supper are "not simply and visibly there . . . as that which they want to be and should be . . . as realities of revelation and faith. They have ever and again to come into being as this." Yet

We can begin to isolate just which words these might be by noting that insofar as Jesus commands his followers to pray for (Matt. 6:10 and par.) and proclaim (10:7 and pars.) the coming of God's kingdom, the kingdom is arguably the proper content of all Christian proclamation. And insofar as Jesus, as the Emmanuel, or "God . . . with us" (Matt. 1:23; cf. Rev. 21:3), is the one in whom the kingdom is realized (Origen's *autobasileia*), to proclaim the kingdom come is just to proclaim Jesus as Lord (Rom. 10:9; cf. Phil. 2:11), even as to pray for the coming of God's kingdom is to pray for Jesus' return (1 Cor. 16:22; Rev. 22:20). At the same time, the circumstances of Jesus' coming among us, culminating in his execution by his enemies and his abandonment by his friends, reveals not simply our ignorance of God's ways, but also our sinful resistance to them. From this perspective, if the advent of the kingdom is the proper content of all Christian proclamation, that which makes this proclamation to be gospel—good news—is the declaration that the forgiveness of sins accompanies God's advent; for only as the sin by which we in various ways resist God's rule is forgiven can the fact of God's presence with us be a source of comfort rather than dread. It is thus crucial to the Christian gospel that in Jesus' ministry these two dimensions are inseparably linked: to hear that "the kingdom of God has come near" is just to be told, "Repent, and believe in the good news" (Mark 1:15); that is, to receive the gospel is to recognize both the fact of one's sin and the fact that, in Jesus, God has forgiven that sin.[8]

The central place of forgiveness for the life of faith is reflected in the fact that baptism, the rite through which a person becomes a member of the

---

while even at this point Barth clearly wants to avoid any implication that divine presence and action stand under the control of the church, he shows confidence that God, not mechanically but faithfully, fulfills God's promise to be present following upon such speech, as reflected in his approving citation of Bullinger: *Verbo Dei fiunt, quae antea non fuerant, sacramenta. Consecrantur enim verbo et sanctificata esse ostendunteur ab eo, qui instituit* (Barth, *CD* I/1:88).

8. It has been argued, perhaps most trenchantly by Andrew Sung Park, *The Wounded Heart of God: The Asian Concept of Han and the Christian Doctrine of Sin* (Nashville: Abingdon Press, 1993), that making the forgiveness of sin the heart of the gospel perversely privileges the perpetrators of evil over its victims as the beneficiaries of the good news. Against this it is worth noting that those instances where the evangelists depict Jesus as forgiving sin relate precisely to figures from society's "underside" (Matt. 9:10 and pars.; Luke 7:48; cf. John 8:1–11). This narrative observation may be taken as a sign that the concept of sin in biblical perspective covers a range of ways in which human beings are enmeshed in destructive relationships with God and one another that cannot be reduced to willful acts by the powerful against the powerless. Thus, while Park and others are right to warn against any facile theological deployment of the truth that "all are sinners," leading to a practical disregard of the ways in which different people relate to and suffer from sin, the antidote is not to dispute the foundational role of forgiveness for Christian faith, but rather to understand it always as a word spoken into a particular life by the crucified Lord rather than as a general principle by which evil is excused. For further discussion, see Ian A. McFarland, *In Adam's Fall: A Meditation on the Christian Doctrine of Original Sin* (Malden, MA: Wiley-Blackwell, 2010), esp. chaps. 7–8.

church, is precisely a baptism of repentance for the forgiveness of sins (Acts 2:38). If the declaration of forgiveness in the washing of baptism (Titus 3:5; cf. Eph. 5:26) is to be received as worthy of faith, there cannot be any doubt as to the source and guarantor of the words through which it is declared.[9] It follows that however much the church rightly demurs from identifying the words of a sermon given by even its most faithful preachers with God's, it must with equal rigor insist that when even the least faithful minister declares that a person's sins are forgiven, these words are to be received without doubt or hesitations as God's own.[10] To regard the message that the crucified Jesus is the risen Lord as good news therefore entails knowing oneself as reconciled to God in him (2 Cor. 5:19), and thus trusting that the declaration of forgiveness that effects that reconciliation counts as Jesus'— and thus God's—very own speech.

And yet although Christians, both in the rite of baptism and the declarations of absolution that follow in the life of the baptized, proclaim the forgiveness of sins in Jesus' name, so that the words declaring this forgiveness are to be heard as Jesus' own, it is not Jesus himself whose body stands at the font, forming the words. To be sure, Christians claim that the Spirit of Jesus—who is the Holy Spirit—*is* present in these events, both inspiring the words and effecting the reality of forgiveness; that is just why the word of forgiveness at the heart of Christian faith may be equated with Jesus' own words. Since the Holy Spirit is Jesus' Spirit (see Acts 16:7; Phil. 1:19), the Spirit's presence in the context of preaching and baptism may credibly be described as modes of Jesus' presence during the period between ascension and parousia. But this presence evidently does not take bodily, tangible, and perceptible form: the sound waves certainly strike our eardrums, and the water washes over us, but in neither case are we encountering Jesus in bodily form as did those who met him once in Palestine—or as we will when he comes again at the end of days. Although the Holy Spirit is certainly the Spirit of God, and thus the Spirit of Jesus, too, the very Trinitarian terms in which this identity (according to

9. "To be baptized in God's name is not to be baptized by human beings but by God himself. Although it is performed by human hands, it is nevertheless truly God's own act." Martin Luther, Large Catechism 4.10, in *The Book of Concord: The Confessions of the Evangelical Lutheran Church*, ed. Robert Kolb and Timothy J. Wengert (Minneapolis: Fortress Press, 2000), 457.

10. "Accordingly, when I say to you: 'Your sins have been forgiven,' then regard it as just as certain as if God had said it to you Himself." Martin Luther, "Gospel for the Nineteenth Sunday after Trinity: Matthew 9:1–8," in *Church Postil V*, vol. 79 of *LW*, ed. Benjamin T. G. Mayes and James L. Langebartels (St. Louis: Concordia, 2016), 79:203. The connection of absolution with baptism is a central feature of Lutheran thought: "Repentance . . . is nothing else than a return and approach to baptism, to resume and practice what has earlier been begun but abandoned. . . . As we have once obtained forgiveness of sins in baptism, so forgiveness remains day by day as long as we live" (Large Catechism 4.79, 86).

substance) must be affirmed also requires that the corresponding distinction (according to hypostasis) be made: the Spirit is not Jesus.[11]

At this point, however, the sacrament of the Eucharist, or Lord's Supper, provides a further occasion for reflection on Jesus' presence in the world between ascension and parousia. Although here, too, it is by the Spirit that words of the rite are spoken, and by which the consecration of the bread and wine is effected (as reflected in the invocation of the Spirit in the epiclesis of the eucharistic prayer), in this case the Spirit's activity is understood not only as divine *communication* of God's favor, but also as bringing about genuine *communion* with God though a bodily mediation of Jesus' presence in the consecrated elements (as implied by the common designation of the rite as "Holy Communion").[12] The declaration made to communicants as they receive the elements, "This is the body/blood of Christ," bears witness to the conviction that in this act of eating and drinking, one encounters the person of Jesus in the most direct and intimate way. And if Eucharist, unlike baptism and absolution, does not center on the forgiveness of sins,[13] its evangelical character as a proclamation of divine acceptance is clear in the declaration that Jesus' body and blood, as communicated in the bread and wine, are *"given for you"*; that is, their being shared as food and drink functions as tangible proof that Jesus comes so that sinful human beings "may have life, and have it abundantly"

---

11. Bonhoeffer distinguishes between the Holy Spirit and "the spirit of Christ" in a specifically ecclesiological context, arguing that while the former "brings individuals to Christ," the latter "deals with the historical becoming of the life of the church as a whole" and thus is more or less to be understood as the "spirit" of the community. I see no basis for such a distinction: as a human organization, any concrete Christian congregation may certainly be said to have a "spirit," which should most certainly not be identified with the Holy Spirit (here Barth's concerns about identifying any ecclesial reality straightforwardly with the divine are entirely appropriate); but neither should it be identified with Christ. To the extent that "the historical becoming of the life of the church as a whole" is faithful to its calling, it should be seen as the work of the Holy Spirit—who is just "the spirit of Christ." Dietrich Bonhoeffer, *Sanctorum Communio: A Theological Study of the Sociology of the Church*, ed. Clifford J. Green, trans. Reinhard Kraus and Nancy Lukens, Dietrich Bonhoeffer Works 1 (Minneapolis: Fortress Press, 1998), 139.

12. Admittedly, not every Christian communion confesses the presence of Jesus in the Lord's Supper, and even among those who do, the metaphysical frameworks used to describe it can differ quite profoundly from one another. Nevertheless, the confession that Christ is present in the consecrated elements is a point of significant agreement between a number of Protestant communions and the Catholic and Orthodox traditions. The recent summary statement of Catholics and Lutherans is typical of ecumenical convergence on this question: "Lutherans and Catholics agree that in the sacrament of the Lord's Supper, Jesus Christ himself is present: He is present truly, substantially, as a person, and he is present in his entirety, as Son of God and a human being." *Declaration on the Way: Church, Ministry and Eucharist* (Bishops' Committee for Ecumenical and Interreligious Affairs, United States Conference of Catholic Bishops and Evangelical Lutheran Church in America, 2015), 20.

13. Instead, the declaration of forgiveness functions as a prerequisite to sharing in the Eucharist, since only the baptized are admitted to communion, and there is an expectation that they should prepare themselves for reception by a prior act of confession.

(John 10:10). If Jesus is not present in the bodily form that he had in the first century or in which he will appear again at the end of the ages, he is, according to the majority report of the Christian tradition, nevertheless truly present and active now, materially shaping the lives of Christians under the textures and tastes of bread and wine.

THE CHURCH

And yet as important as the bodily presence of Jesus in the Eucharist may be for the piety of the individual believer and the life of the church community as a whole, Jesus' body is not visible in the consecrated elements as such. Even the Catholic doctrine of transubstantiation, which teaches that the entire substance of bread and wine is changed into the body and blood of Jesus, nevertheless holds that the accidents of bread and wine remain. And since it is the accidents that are the objects of sensory perception (i.e., appearance, texture, taste, even chemical analysis), even in the Eucharist the humanity of Jesus is not present so as to be perceived in bodily form.[14] A seemingly more somatic account of Jesus' presence is provided when the "body of Christ" is understood to name not only the eucharistic bread, but also those human bodies who, in consuming it, constitute the church.[15]

At one level, this seems like a perfectly natural extension of the logic of the eucharistic rite itself. After all, if the church is nourished by the act of feeding on Jesus' body in the Eucharist, then it makes sense that it should come to be identified as Jesus' body in the world in the time between ascension and parousia. Paul himself makes just this point when he writes, "Because there is one bread, we who are many are one body, for we all partake of the one bread" (1 Cor. 10:17).[16] And yet he also goes on to develop the imagery of the body so as to give attention to the diversity as well as the unity of the church: "For as in one body we have many members, and not all the members have the same function, so we, who are many, are one body in Christ, and individually

---

14. "What you can see . . . is the bread and cup; that's all that your eyes tell you." Augustine, "Sermon 272," in *Sermons III/7 (230–272B) on the Liturgical Seasons*, ed. John E. Rotelle, OSA, trans. Edmund Hill, OP (New Rochelle, NY: New City Press, 1993), 300, trans. alt.

15. The connection between these two referents of "body of Christ" is further suggested by the ambiguity of the creedal phrase *communio sanctorum*, which in its original significance probably referred to the Eucharist (i.e., "sharing in the holy things"), but came to be understood as defining the nature of the church as "the communion of saints."

16. Cf. Augustine, who hears Jesus saying of the Eucharist: "I am the food of grown men. Grow, and you shall feed upon me. You will not change me into yourself, as you change food into your flesh, but you will be changed into me." Augustine, *Confessions* 7.10.16, trans. Henry Chadwick (New York: Oxford University Press, 1991).

we are members one of another" (Rom. 12:4–5). The one bread gives rise to one ecclesial body, but the latter does not share the visible homogeneity of the former: for although the many members of the church are united, they remain distinct.

This sort of comparison of a community to a human body was a commonplace of ancient political rhetoric, but Paul's usage is distinctive—arguably just because he views the ecclesial body as a reality constituted by the activity of God in Christ rather than as a metaphor for purely immanent social arrangements.[17] In this context, it is important to note that Paul does not describe the church as "a" body in a way that might be extended to any more or less coherent community of human beings, but rather as *the* body of *Christ* in particular.[18] This language reinforces the point that the church's identity as a body is not something determined "from below," as a result of the various negotiations by which individuals might organize themselves into a social unit, but rather "from above," by God calling people into this body through baptism and sustaining them in it through the Eucharist. Moreover, the point of this divine activity is not that all serve the whole according to a model in which the significance of any one member is understood in terms of its benefit to the collective, but rather that all serve each other (1 Cor. 12:25)—and in such a way that the honor of the "weaker" or "less respectable" member is highlighted (12:22–24).

All of this is not to deny that the concrete forms taken by the church in history are always also a product of practical negotiations among believers, let alone that the results of such negotiations all too often bear little resemblance to the vision of mutual care described by Paul. The point remains, however, that it is not these negotiations, however faithfully or unfaithfully conducted, that define the church as the body of Christ. Rather, the church is Christ's body because God constitutes it as such, even in its imperfections—which, as the content of Paul's correspondence makes clear, were no less evident in first-century Corinth or Galatia than in subsequent times and other places. And while it is impossible to know the precise source from which Paul derived his account of the church as Christ's body, it is striking that in Luke's account of Paul's conversion, the risen Jesus himself suggests that he is to be identified with the community of believers: Paul hears a "voice saying to him, 'Saul,

17. See, e.g., E. P. Sanders, who defends "the realism of Paul's view" in his *Paul and Palestinian Judaism: A Comparison of Patterns of Religion* (London: SCM, 1977), 522–23.

18. This point counts against Wayne Meeks's contention that Paul's use of body language "is not materially different from the use by Cicero or Seneca or Plutarch." Wayne A. Meeks, *The Origins of Christian Morality: The First Two Centuries* (New Haven, CT: Yale University Press, 1993), 134. For an analysis of how Paul's use of body imagery in 1 Corinthians subverts the conservative force this image normally carries in classical rhetoric, see Dale B. Martin, *The Corinthian Body* (New Haven, CT: Yale University Press, 1995), 94–96.

Saul, why do you persecute me?'" Paul asks, "Who are you, Lord?" The reply comes, "I am Jesus, whom you are persecuting" (Acts 9:4–5; cf. Eph. 5:29–30).

And yet however much it is true for the Christian that "it is no longer I who live, but it is Christ who lives in me" (Gal. 2:20), it does not follow that whenever a Christian is struck, Jesus says "Ouch!" There is a parallel between the way in which the flesh-and-blood body of Jesus, born of Mary, is God's body because the eternal Son identifies it as his own, and that by which the body of believers is Jesus' body because the risen Jesus identifies his life with theirs. Yet the parallel is strictly limited, for the designations "God the Son" and "Jesus" are fully convertible (such that Jesus simply is the Son, and vice versa), but the terms "Jesus" and "church" are not. And this means that while the Son's identity is inseparable from Jesus (such that there is no way to identify the Son except by reference to Jesus), Jesus' identity is not inseparable from the church: whatever Jesus does, the Son does; but (as noted above) whatever the church or its members do may not in the same way be ascribed to Jesus.[19] Indeed, it may well be that it is in order to stress this point that the later texts of the Pauline corpus distinguish the church as the *body* of Christ from Jesus as its *head*, "from whom the whole body, nourished and held together by its ligaments and sinews, grows with a growth that is from God" (Col. 2:19; cf. 1:18; Eph. 5:23). On the one hand this language may seem to reduce Jesus to just one member of the body alongside the rest, yet on the other hand the fact that the member with which Jesus is identified is the head indicates that he is the source and seat of the body's identity: the one in whom the other members stand in a strictly unilateral relationship of dependence.[20]

The confession of Jesus as the ground of the church's life in this way—as the head, on whom the whole body depends and by whose power it grows (Eph. 4:16)—implies a real distinction between Jesus and the church that blocks the interpretation of the church as a simple continuation of the incarnation. As the head of the body, Jesus is a particular member of the body, distinct both

19. All this is simply to say that whatever meaning may be ascribed to the church's status as the body of Christ, it does not mean that the Word is incarnate in (and therefore hypostatically identical with) the church: only the flesh of Jesus, the one born of Mary, may without qualification be identified as the Word's.

20. One way of developing this understanding of the relationship between Jesus and the church is to note that while Jesus of Nazareth is a single person (viz., the son of Mary), the church is the body of Christ in that its members constitute a "collective person" that takes the particular form of "Christ existing as church-community" (Bonhoeffer, *Sanctorum Communio*, 121). Importantly, this does not mean that Christ absorbs the selfhood of the individual believer; indeed, at this point, insisting on a permanent distinction between Jesus and the church is crucial to preserving the integrity of its members. To be a Christian is not to lose one's identity as a specific individual who is other than Jesus, but it is to understand one's identity as grounded outside of oneself, so that "the life I now live in the flesh I live by faith in the Son of God" (Gal. 2:20; cf. Col. 3:3). In short, the individual who has responded to Jesus' call to follow him now understands him as the ground and source of her own life, as well as of the lives of neighbors.

from all the body's other members and from the body as a whole.[21] Indeed, this distinction between Jesus and the church is implicit in the conviction that it is precisely by the consumption of his *individual* body in the Eucharist that other human beings live as members of his *ecclesial* body. And yet insofar as the Spirit makes the Eucharist available for consumption though the words and deeds of these other human beings, encountering Jesus' presence in the world is bound up with encountering the body's other members. After all, when Paul insists that "all who eat and drink without discerning the body, eat and drink judgment against themselves" (1 Cor. 11:29), the discernment he appears to have in mind does not seem to relate directly to the eucharistic elements, but rather to the other members of the community. Paul reprimands the Corinthians for failing to *live* as Christ's body in the very act of celebrating the eucharistic meal that *makes* them Christ's body: "When the time comes to eat," he remarks, "each of you goes ahead with your own supper, and one goes hungry and another becomes drunk" (11:21; cf. vv. 18–19). He then gives a straightforward recommendation to address the situation that has resulted from this behavior (as a result of which "many . . . are weak and ill, and some have died," 1 Cor. 11:30): "When you come together to eat, wait for one another" (11:33).

In short, although the church cannot be identified with the person of Jesus, it nevertheless may truly be called his body in that through the Spirit it is the locus of Jesus' ongoing activity of teaching, healing, and forgiving.[22] It was by taking a human body in Mary's womb that the Word became perceptible to human beings and thus able to be known by them. In the time between his ascension and return, the humanity Jesus took from Mary cannot be perceived, but it continues to be available to human beings in Word and sacrament; and insofar as these means of grace are communicated through the lives of the church's members, the mediation of Jesus' humanity takes visibly human form. This form has both objective and subjective dimensions. Objectively, the church is the body of Christ as the set of people who have been claimed by Jesus through baptism as the body of which he is the head

21. Thus, although Karl Barth could describe the church as "the earthly-historical form of the existence of Jesus Christ himself," he was adamant that this did not justify any direct identification of the visible community with Jesus, who remains sovereign over and thus distinct from every historical, human community. Barth, *CD* IV/1:661 (and *passim* throughout this chapter, as well as in §§67 and 72); cf. IV/3.2:729, 859.

22. "Community with God exists only through Christ, but Christ is present [between ascension and parousia] only in his church-community, and therefore community with God exists only in the church." Bonhoeffer, *Sanctorum Communio*, 158; cf. 15, "Editor's Introduction," where Clifford Green points out that it was just the application of this principle that led Bonhoeffer later in his career to argue that those who separated themselves from the Confessing Church cut themselves off from salvation.

(1 Cor. 12:13; Eph. 4:4–5).[23] Subjectively, the church is Christ's body in that those who have been so claimed understand themselves as part of that body and thereby charged to see themselves as members whose various callings can only be known and fulfilled in relation to the body's other members. In this way, although the church is *constituted* as Christ's body objectively, as Jesus' presence is mediated to human beings through Word and sacrament, it is *known* as Christ's body only as the members discern the work of Jesus subjectively in one another.[24]

Jesus thus identifies with the church in such a way as to command those whom he has claimed as members of his body to look to one another in order to come to an ever-fuller understanding of who he is as Lord and Savior. And yet the way in which this happens, how Jesus is discerned in the church, is not straightforward. It certainly is not the case that discerning Christ's body in the church is a matter of perceiving how the church's members look like Jesus. On the contrary, insofar as each member of the body has its own particular place distinct from the head's position, they will all be significantly *un*like Jesus, just as they will be unlike one another.[25] For this reason, discerning Christ's body in the church does not involve coming to know Jesus' humanity in the way that it did for those who encountered him during the period of his earthly ministry. For them encountering his own individual human body, born of Mary, was the means of their coming to know who he is. Considered from this perspective, his identity has been defined by his earthly life in

---

23. Of course, in the present the number of those whom Jesus claims for his own is not limited to people who are currently, visibly members of a church (cf. John 10:16). In this context, Thomas Aquinas posited a range of degrees of human incorporation into the body of Christ. Strictly speaking, Thomas argued, only those who live with Christ in glory (viz., the saints in heaven) have been fully incorporated into his body. The lives of all other people remain at some remove from "what we will be" (1 John 3:2)—though they are all still to be counted, in various degrees, as part of the body. Some are incorporated more strongly through a faith active in love, others less so in a faith not active in love; still others are members only potentially, but with a faith that will eventually be actualized; indeed, for Thomas even those who are to be damned are, while they live, potentially members of the body of Christ, albeit in their case with a potential that will never be actualized. Thus, although believers are incorporated into Christ's body more deeply than those outside the church, it remains the case that the contours of Christ's body extend beyond the confessional boundaries of the church at any given point in time. See Aquinas, *ST* 3.8.3.

24. "So if it's you that are the body of Christ and its members, it's the mystery meaning you that has been placed on the Lord's table; what you receive is the mystery that means you. It is to what you are that you reply *Amen*, and so by replying you express your assent. What you hear, you see, is *the body of Christ*, and you answer *Amen*. So be a member of the Body of Christ, in order to make that *Amen* true." Augustine, "Sermon 272," 300.

25. Importantly, this unlikeness is fully consistent with the claim that Jesus is like us in every respect (cf. Heb. 2:17); for to be a human being is just to be one of many, each different from the rest. Indeed, for a Christian what defines a being as human is finally not any intrinsic, shared trait (e.g., reason, free will, or the like) that can be found across all members of the species; humanity is, rather, rightly defined extrinsically, by virtue of each member forming a distinctly and unsubstitutably different part of the body of which Jesus is the head.

first-century Palestine in a way that leaves nothing more to be discerned. But although Jesus' identity as Savior is determined entirely by the life he led in the first century as vindicated in its completeness by his resurrection from the dead, what it means for him to be Savior is something that cannot be known in abstraction from encounter with those whom he has in fact saved.[26] In other words, if Jesus' identity is settled (so that the only appropriate data for answering the question "Who is Jesus?" come from his earthly existence in the past), his activity is ongoing. To be sure (and as argued in the preceding chapter), Jesus' activity is *not* ongoing in the sense that he continues to perform successive bodily actions (speaking, walking, eating, etc.) in space and time; it continues rather in the Spirit: thus his whole human life, vindicated as God's own, becomes continually present in time, in the ministry of the church, as the cause of the single, complex, and temporally extended effect that is the construction of the ecclesial body.

So if we learn nothing more about *who Jesus is* by our work of discerning the body in the church, we nevertheless continue to be confronted by endlessly surprising and novel examples of *what his identity means* as we encounter the richly variegated character of the humanity he saves.[27] To discern Jesus in the church is just this: to see him active in saving by continually bringing into his body those, from Mary Magdalene and Peter on down, who by their own merits appear to have no rightful place in it.[28] In sum, we encounter Jesus in

---

26. Note, in this context, that 1 John 3:2 teaches not that what *Jesus* will be has not yet been revealed, but that "what *we* will be has not yet been revealed." To be sure, Christians await Jesus' eschatological revelation, but what is evidently to be disclosed thereby is not who Jesus is, but who we are. In line with the ancient principle that God was made human so that we might be made God (see p. 10 above): we have already seen what it means for God to become human, for that is just the content of Jesus' life, vindicated and exalted in his resurrection from the dead; what remains yet to be disclosed is what it means for us to become God.

27. It might be objected here that insofar as our understanding of any person, including Jesus, is derived from our experience of what that individual does (as illustrated in this book by the summary of the signal features of Jesus' earthly ministry in chap. 5 and, for that matter, of YHWH's history with Israel in chap. 4), any talk of Jesus' ongoing activity invariably changes our understanding of his identity. Against this line of argument, I insist on the point that the activity of Jesus that is seen in the ongoing life of the church is not any sort of series of successive deeds performed by Jesus (e.g., the saving of Peter, the saving of Mary, the saving of Paul, on down through time till the end of the age). Instead, Jesus has already acted "once for all" (Heb. 7:27; 9:12) to save, and what appears in the human lives of his followers down through the centuries is the temporally extended effect of this one long, finished act. In what appears over time, there is no variation in the content of Jesus' activity (which is entirely and only to save; cf. John 12:47), only in its various manifestations.

28. It follows that while Melanchthon's famous claim that "to know Christ is to know his benefits" in the first instance certainly means to know Christ as one's own Savior, its force cannot be limited to the individual. For insofar as my salvation is inseparable from that of the body's other members (1 Cor. 12:26; cf. Heb. 11:39–40), to know Christ's benefits is also to know him as the Savior of all those others members of the body. Philipp Melanchthon, *Loci communes*, in *Melanchthon and Bucer*, ed. Wilhelm Pauck (Philadelphia: Westminster Press, 1969), 21–22.

the church when we see the church as the manifestation of Jesus' work as Lord and Savior. For although the church is Jesus' body in a way that is dependent on (and thus distinct from) Jesus himself, it is where Jesus' work may be seen.

"ALWAYS AND EVERYWHERE"

Yet even when interpreted in a broader ecclesial context, it may seem that the sense in which Jesus may be discerned in the present falls short of what is required if his incarnate humanity is confessed as the basis for our life with God. To be sure, however poorly Christians may discern Jesus in their fellow believers, the process of discernment remains constitutive of the church's life, since being a member of the church involves celebrating the mystery of Jesus' saving presence in those, both oneself and others, who in receiving his body become his body. But even so there remains a distinction between seeing the processes whereby Jesus, in the power of the Spirit, is active in effecting salvation and seeing Jesus himself. No more than in the Eucharist, then, does the confession of the church as Christ's body lead to the kind of encounter with Jesus' humanity that would satisfy the request "Sir, we wish to see Jesus" (John 12:21).

The heart of the difficulty is the relation between Jesus' humanity and his body. For if Christians confess that in the Spirit the risen and ascended Jesus can be heard and even tasted, the fact that his earthly-historical body is utterly absent—not even present as remains in a tomb—means that he cannot be seen in such a way as to be recognized as Jesus.[29] If it is indeed the case that "he is not here" (Mark 16:6 and pars.) in a way that cannot be addressed by looking "there" instead (since the reason for the absence is that "he has been raised" and so no longer subsists anywhere in time and space), then even if he is confessed to be humanly present in Word and sacrament, he remains unavailable to us as an identifiable human being. This is the problem at the heart of the so-called scandal of particularity: the inherent finitude of Jesus' humanity, bounded by the spatiotemporal coordinates of his birth and death, seemingly poses an insuperable obstacle to his capacity (at least prior to the eschaton) to mediate God's presence to all people, let alone to the whole creation in a

---

29. In this context, the fact that even during the forty days of Easter the risen Jesus is at least on some occasions not immediately recognizable to those to whom he appears may be regarded as of some theological significance, if only as a reminder that at no point between Good Friday and the parousia is Jesus' humanity straightforwardly available for inspection. Even prior to the ascension (as well as in the extraordinary visions granted to Stephen and Paul afterward), his humanity can be seen only as he actively gives it to be seen.

way that would fulfill the promise of universal communion with God. For this reason many contemporary theologians have argued that Christians should reject the Chalcedonian position (in which the incarnation is understood as an unforeseeable and not-to-be-repeated modification of God's way of relating to creatures) in favor of a model according to which incarnation describes God's normal way of being in the world.[30] For if incarnation is viewed as a repeatable or even continuous mode of God's relating to creation, the absence of Jesus' human body from the world constitutes no barrier to God's universal presence to creatures. If God's presence in Jesus is not unique in the sense of being qualitatively different from the way in which God is present elsewhere in creation, then creaturely knowledge of God is no longer bound to this figure and his humanity.

As argued in the introduction, however, the promise of such proposals is deceptive. For absent the claim that God is uniquely present in and as the life of a particular creature (so that it is possible to say definitively that *this* one is God, and thus that God is *here* in a way that God is not present elsewhere), the good news is evacuated of meaningful content. For in that case, it is necessary to choose between one of two possibilities. On the one hand, God might be equally perceptible everywhere; but then God is insufficiently different from the world to be able to effect its salvation, since if the locus of God's becoming "flesh" is the world as a whole and every entity in it, then God's being is no longer clearly separable from that of the creatures that need saving. On the other hand, it might be that God is not directly perceptible anywhere, but then God is insufficiently present in the world to effect salvation, since on this understanding God acts *through* creatures but never *as* a creature.[31] While these considerations certainly do not resolve the theological challenges posed by the scandal of particularity, they do provide some motivation for exploring whether there might be further resources for talking about the discernment of Christ's humanity between ascension and parousia in Chalcedonian terms. That there might be is suggested by Maximus the

30. See, e.g., Catherine Keller, *On the Mystery: Discerning Divinity in Process* (Minneapolis: Fortress Press, 2008), Paul F. Knitter, *No Other Name? A Critical Survey of Christian Attitudes toward the World Religions* (Maryknoll, NY: Orbis Books, 1985); Sallie McFague, *The Body of God: An Ecological Theology* (Minneapolis: Fortress Press, 1993).

31. Might not there be a third possibility, that God is incarnate in a finite number of creatures? No less an authority than Aquinas concedes that there is no conceptual barrier to the idea of multiple incarnations of the Word (see *ST* 3.3.7); but I do not see how that possibility solves the soteriological problem of the scandal of particularity (nor does Aquinas consider it in that context). For any finite number of incarnations (China in the third century BC, Tasmania in 1400, etc.) would each have their own limited sphere of spatiotemporal "reach." Given the contingencies of human life, the only way to guarantee universal contact with God would be for God to be incarnate everywhere—which brings us back to the problem of the first option.

Confessor, one of the Chalcedonian tradition's staunchest defenders, who wrote: "For the Word of God, who is God, wishes always and everywhere to effect the mystery of his embodiment."[32]

This statement is found in the context of Maximus's attempt to explain a passage from Gregory of Nazianzus in which the Cappadocian refers to human beings as a "portion of God."[33] Maximus's primary aim in his analysis of this text is to block any interpretation that might suggest a blurring of the distinction between God and creatures: for Maximus, there is no ontological continuity between Creator and creature, and thus no possibility that the "embodiment" of which he speaks could be understood to describe God's intrinsic relation to the world as its Creator. At the same time, Maximus is equally keen to affirm that, notwithstanding the enduring ontological distinction between Creator and creature, the Christian hope of life with God includes genuine participation in the divine nature. The claim that the divine Word "wishes always and everywhere to effect the mystery of his embodiment" emerges out of his desire to defend both these convictions as fundamental to Christian faith: the divine Word is ever distinct from created substance, but this same Word also seeks continually to join the creature's life to God's own.

Crucial to Maximus's efforts to bring God and the world into the closest possible communion without collapsing them together is his insistence that the distinction between Creator and creature is defined by an inherent orientation of the latter to the former: "For it belongs to God alone to be the end, and the completion, and the impassible. . . . It belongs to creatures, on the other hand, to be moved toward that end which has no beginning, and to cease from their activity in that perfect end which is devoid of all quantity, and to experience—but not to be or to become according to essence—the

---

32. "Bouletai gar aei kai en pasin ho tou Theou Logos kai Theos tēs autou ensōmatōses energeisthai to mystērion." Maximus the Confessor, *Ambigua* 7 (PG 91:1084C–D). Maximus uses similar language elsewhere: e.g., in *Quaestiones ad Thalassium* he speaks of God's desire to be "contemplated . . . proportionately in each individual creature." Maximus, *Quaestiones ad Thalassium* 2 (PG 90:272B–C); trans. from Maximus the Confessor, *On the Cosmic Mystery of Jesus Christ: Selected Writings from St. Maximus the Confessor*, trans. Paul M. Blowers and Robert Wilken (Crestwood, NY: St. Vladimir's Seminary Press, 2003), 101.

33. Here is the complete text of the passage, taken from Gregory's *Oration* 14 ("On Love of the Poor," in PG 35:865C): "What is this wisdom that concerns me: And what is this great mystery? Or is it God's will that we, who are a portion of God [*moira tou theou*] that has flowed down from above, not become exalted and lifted up on account of this dignity, and so despise our Creator? Or is it not rather that, in our struggle and battle with the body, we should always look to Him, so that this very weakness that has been yoked to us might be an education concerning our dignity." Cited in Maximus the Confessor, *Ambigua* 7.1.87, in *On Difficulties in the Church Fathers: The Ambigua*, 2 vols., ed. and trans. Nicholas Constas (Cambridge, MA: Harvard University Press, 2014) (PG 91:1068D–1069A).

Unqualified [viz., God]."³⁴ As noted in chapter 2, Maximus uses the Greek word *logos* to explain this orientation of creature to Creator.³⁵ Drawing on John 1, he identifies the Creator with the divine Logos and then goes on to argue that each of the various beings brought into existence by the Logos has its own distinctive created *logos*, or inner principle, that defines it as the particular kind of creature it is.³⁶ It is in this context, Maximus argues, that Gregory's description of creatures as "portions of God" should be understood: because the created *logoi* are reflections (or, perhaps better, refractions) of the one divine Logos in space and time, they can rightly be described as "portions" of the uncreated God.³⁷ And by virtue of its grounding in the divine Logos, each created *logos* participates in God in accordance with its own particular way of being.³⁸

In this way, the relationship between the one divine Logos and the many created *logoi* means that the convergence of the lives of creature and Creator is rooted in the ontology of creation itself.³⁹ As "portions" of the Logos,

---

34. Maximus, *Ambigua* 7.1.87 (PG 91:1073B), trans. alt. Cf. *Ambigua* 7.1.101 (PG 91:1081A–B):

> For God is eternally an active creator, but creatures exist first in potential and only later in actuality, since it is not possible for the infinite and the finite to exist simultaneously on the same level of being. Indeed, no argument will ever be constructed to show that being and what transcends being are able to coincide, or that the measureless can be coordinated with what is subject to measure, or that the absolute can be ranked with the relative, or that something of which no specific category can positively be predicated can be placed in the same class as what is constituted by all the categories.

35. See especially pp. 65–67 above.

36. "For in their substance and formation all created things are positively defined by their own *logoi*, and by the *logoi* that exist around them and which constitute their defining limits." Maximus, *Ambigua* 7.1.101 (PG 91:1081B); cf. *Ambigua* 22.1.449 (PG 91:1256D): "If created things are many, then they must certainly be different, precisely because they are many. . . . And if the many are different, it must be understood that their *logoi*, according to which they essentially exist, are also different, since it is in these, or rather because of these *logoi*, that different things differ."

37. "We are . . . and are called 'portions of God' because of the *logoi* of our being that exist eternally in God." Maximus, *Ambigua* 7.1.103 (PG 91:1081C).

38. "For by virtue of the fact that all things have their being from God, they participate in God in a manner appropriate and proportionate to each, whether by intellect, by reason, by sensation, by vital motion, or by some essential faculty or habitual fitness." Maximus, *Ambigua* 7.1.97 (PG 91:1080B).

39. Also see Maximus the Confessor, *The Church's Mystagogy*, chap. 1, in *Maximus the Confessor: Selected Writings*, ed. G. C. Berthold (New York: Paulist Press, 1985), 186 (from PG 91:664D–665A), trans. alt.; and 187 (from PG 91:668A–B):

> Maintaining about himself as cause, beginning, and end of all beings which are by nature distinct [*diestēkota*] from one another, [God] makes them convergent in each other by the one power of their relationship to him as their beginning, . . . all things combine with all others in an unmixed [*aphytrōs*] way by the one indissoluble

all creatures naturally conform to it.[40] And yet it is also a crucial feature of Maximus's thought that the conformity of creatures to the divine Logos is not simply given.[41] The *logoi* of creatures have their ground in God in such a way that they condition the possibility of the being of the creatures whose differentiated particularities they define. But the creatures themselves come into being in an imperfect state: no creature is perfect at the moment it comes into being, because perfection is a natural attribute of divinity only. Since creatures' createdness means that they stand at an ontological distance from the uncreated Logos, who is their source and goal, their perfection can only come about through a process of movement toward the goal that follows their being created.[42] Although a creature's proper end is thus necessarily distinct from its initial state, however, and because it is part of God's intention for that creature—and thus part of its *logos*—that it should achieve that end,

---

relation to and protection of the sole beginning and cause, which nullifies and covers over all their particular relations considered according to each one's nature, *but not by dissolving or destroying them or making them not to exist*; but rather by overcoming [*nikan*] them and making them supremely manifest [*hyperphainesthai*], as the whole reveals its parts or as the whole is revealed in its cause, by which the same whole and its parts came into being and appearance. . . . As the center of straight lines that radiate from him, [Christ] does not allow by his unique, simple, and single power that the principles of beings become disjoined at the periphery but rather he circumscribes their extension in a circle and brings back to himself the distinctive elements of beings which he himself brought into existence.

40. See Maximus, *Ambigua* 7.1.95 (PG 91:1077C): "The many *logoi* are one Logos, seeing that all things are related to Him without being confused with Him."

41. At this point I differ from Jordan Daniel Wood, who has recently argued that Maximus should be interpreted as proposing just this sort of identification between creation and incarnation. See Jordan Daniel Wood, "Creation Is Incarnation: The Metaphysical Peculiarity of the *Logoi* in Maximus Confessor," *Modern Theology* 34, no. 1 (January 2018): 82–102. While there is a great deal to learn from and admire in Wood's argument, in my view he errs in collapsing the parallel Maximus draws between the incarnation on the one hand, and the Word's presence in the *logoi* of creatures on the other, into an identity. In *Ambigua* 33, for example, Maximus certainly feels free to interpret Gregory of Nazianzus's reference to the "thickening" of the eternal Logos as possibly referring either to the Word's taking flesh in Jesus, or to his concealment in the logoi of all created beings, or to his condescending to be expressed in the words of the Bible (PG 91:1285B–1288A); but it does not follow that he views all three as ontologically equivalent—especially given that Maximus explicitly contrasts the Word's "enfleshed presence [in Jesus] that is from us, because of us, and like us" with his having "hidden himself ineffably in the *logoi* [of other creatures] so as to be revealed indirectly." Thus, although in this text Maximus emphasizes that Christ is no less fully present in creatures than in Jesus, this speaks to the divine omnipresence, without reference to the fact that (*pace* Wood) in Jesus alone is the Logos hypostatically identified with a creature, such that this creature alone can be identified as the Word incarnate. After all, the claim that the Word *wishes* to effect the mystery of his embodiment in every creature implies that this goal has not yet been effected and so cannot be coeval with creation.

42. "Nothing created is its own proper end, insofar as it is not self-caused, for if it were, it would be uncreated [i.e., God], without beginning, and without motion, having now a way of being moved toward something else." Maximus, *Ambigua* 7.1.83 (PG 91:1072B–C), trans. alt.

movement toward that end is not an accidental but rather an intrinsic feature of every creature's being.[43] Thus, for a creature to achieve perfection (viz., the fulfillment of its existence as the particular kind of creature it is) is for it to conform as fully as possible to its distinctive *logos*, and thereby to the one Logos that is its source. It follows that to know a creature fully (i.e., in accord with the divine will for it that is its *logos*) is to know it in this eschatological state of being contained by God.[44]

Inasmuch as each creature has its own end, which corresponds to its *logos* (viz., its specific form of participation in the divine), so it has its own distinctive form of movement toward that end.[45] Because human beings are rational creatures, their natural movement is one of willing, so that in contrast to inanimate objects that simply respond to the push and pull of physical forces and to organisms that act by instinct, human beings are agents whose activities are marked by freedom rather than necessity.[46] This means that a human being achieves perfection when her will has "surrendered voluntarily and wholly to God, and perfectly subjected itself to His rule, by eliminating any wish that might contravene His will."[47] Again, this understanding of perfection follows from the ontology of creation: to deviate from God's will is to fail to accord in one's being with the *logos* that defines that being, and thus to undermine the very conditions of one's existence as a creature.

The distinctive form of participation in the divine nature that is the destiny of human beings is described by Maximus as deification (*theōsis*). Yet while this work of conforming to the divine is consistent with the character of humanity's *logos*, the ontological discontinuity between creature and Creator means that human beings cannot achieve such conformity by their own efforts. Indeed, although all creatures find their fulfillment as they live into the form of their particular *logoi*, which are, in turn grounded in the divine Logos, the relation of the *logoi* to the Logos remains hidden apart from the concrete appearance of the latter in time and space. It is only as the Word

43. Citing Dionysius the Areopagite, Maximus thus calls the *logoi* "divine wills" (*theia thelēmata*) and thus explains the possibility that God should say to a creature, "I do not know you" (Matt. 25:12) as referring to its not conforming to its *logos*—that is, to God's will for its being. See Maximus, *Ambigua* 7.1.109 (PG 91:1085A–C).

44. Thus, a human being is a "portion" of God in one sense simply by the sheer fact of existing, but in another, higher sense in achieving the eschatological goal of living in God. See Maximus, *Ambigua* 7.1.105 (PG 91:1084B–C).

45. "For matter is that which is moved toward coming into being [*genesin*]; and what moves it is the unmoved Logos present in the whole, which is the divine means of creating [*technē*], which we have termed nature [*physin*], and which is a form [*eidos*], and not a compound of form and matter." Maximus, *Scholia on the Divine Names* 4.26 (PG 4:296C).

46. This status is not necessarily limited to human beings. Maximus himself would have included angels in that category, and there is nothing in his ontology that would preclude other living beings, whether extraterrestrial or terrestrial, having agential characteristics.

47. Maximus, *Ambigua* 7.1.83 (PG 91:1076B).

is embodied hypostatically in Jesus, who unites in his humanity the various dimensions of created reality, that it is possible to discern the convergence of the many *logoi* in the one Logos.[48] This happens on an individual level as the human being

> places himself wholly in God alone, . . . so that he by grace is and is called God, just as God by his condescension [in taking flesh] is and is called a human being on humanity's account, so that thereby the power of this reciprocal arrangement might be displayed, which draws the human being to God through love of God by deification, and God to the human being through love of humanity by incarnation; and which, through this beautiful exchange, makes a human being God through the deification of the human being, and God a human being through the incarnation of God.[49]

It is in describing this process that Maximus speaks of the Word seeking "always and everywhere to effect the mystery of his embodiment": the mystery has its ground in the Word's bringing the divine life into communion with the created realm through the incarnation and then is completed as the created being thereby assumed is drawn by the Word to participation in the divine.

Of particular significance in the present context is that when Maximus refers to the embodiment (*ensōmatōsis*) that the Word seeks to effect "always and everywhere," he seems to have in mind both parts of this "reciprocal arrangement": the Word's taking flesh in Jesus *and* the deification of other human beings (who, unlike Jesus, are not hypostatically identical with the Word). In other words, the mystery of the Word's embodiment is not defined exclusively by the hypostatic union that constitutes the human life of Jesus, but also includes its purpose and result: that all human beings should subsist directly by the power of God just as the risen and ascended Jesus does. It is seemingly for this reason that he summarizes the arrangement as an "exchange," thereby emphasizing that the subsistence of the divine Logos in a created *logos* in the incarnation is good news because enables created *logoi*, in turn, to subsist directly in the divine Logos. Like Martin Luther's description of the relationship between Jesus and the believer as a "happy exchange" (*fröhliche Wechsel*), Maximus's "beautiful exchange" (*kalē antistrophē*) does not refer to a transfer of goods from one party to the other, but rather a sharing of goods between them. Luther, after all, conceived the language of exchange in nuptial terms, such that "what I bring and what Christ brings each becomes shared—or even reciprocally constitutive, without either party ceasing to be what it earlier

---

48. See the account of Maximus's understanding of the ascension on pp. 170–71 above.
49. Maximus, *Ambigua* 7.1.106–7 (PG 91:1084C), trans. alt.

was."[50] So too, for Maximus, the Word does not cease to be divine in becoming human, and humans do not cease to be creatures in being deified; rather, the Word adopts and human beings acquire a new mode of existence: the divine Word lives humanly *in* Jesus, thereby enabling other human beings to live divinely *through* Jesus. Although the Word's becoming human makes possible humanity's deification, both incarnation and deification can be described as the Word's embodiment: first, the Word's taking a body in Jesus, and then, on that basis, our bodies living in and by the incarnate Word.[51]

In light of this expanded understanding of the Word's embodiment, the implications of the absence of Jesus' human body from the world seem less critical for the claim that Jesus' humanity is the touchstone for our knowledge of God. It is, after all, part and parcel of the Word's assumption of human nature that Jesus be subject to death, so that his life in time and space comes to an end. And though the good news is that this one who has died now lives, having been raised from the dead, the canonical accounts of Easter morning (for all their not insignificant differences in detail) agree that a sign of this triumph is that Jesus' tomb is empty, the implication being that it is thus in both body and soul that, as the risen Lord, "the life he lives, he lives to God" (Rom. 6:10), at the right hand of the Father, and thus not in time and space. Indeed (and as noted in the previous chapter), even the promise of his coming again does not change this basic point, for insofar as his return in glory also marks the advent of a new creation, only with the end of—and thus apart from—time and space will the promise of his universal bodily presence be fulfilled. To acknowledge his humanity in the meantime requires precisely honoring the completeness of his human life as defined by the period from Christmas to Good Friday. To look for more is precisely to have failed to take *that* humanity seriously. And so it is that when, on the day of the ascension, Jesus' followers continue to look into the sky after he has been taken out of their sight, they are subject to firm, if gentle, angelic rebuke (Acts 1:11). To take Jesus' humanity seriously in the present is thus precisely to confess that it is present only in the power of the Spirit, and thus invisibly.

Therefore, in the time between ascension and parousia, Jesus' humanity is present in the bread and the wine—but it cannot be perceived there. Likewise,

---

50. Jason A. Mahn, *Becoming a Christian in Christendom: Radical Discipleship and the Way of the Cross in America's "Christian" Culture* (Minneapolis: Fortress Press, 2016), 184. For the nuptial character of the exchange in Luther, see Martin Luther, *The Freedom of a Christian*, in *Career of the Reformer I, LW* 31:351–54.

51. Human bodies, like all created substances, are already sustained by the Word in creation—but indirectly, through the mediation of created causes (e.g., air, water, food, the physical laws that ensure the integrity of our cellular structure and the coordination of cellular activity, etc.). In deification, however, our embodied lives are sustained directly by the power of the Word, independently of creaturely mediation (cf. Gal. 2:20; Col. 3:3).

although Christians confess that the church is Christ's body, of which all the baptized are members, they do not claim that seeing those members, individually or collectively, is the same as seeing Jesus. But if Maximus is right, that is just the point, since the aim of the incarnation is not that we should somehow "see" Jesus in everyone or everything, and still less that everyone and everything should *be* Jesus, but rather that everyone who is not Jesus should be just who they are by the grace and power of Jesus' Spirit:

> You are not in the flesh; you are in the Spirit, since the Spirit of God dwells in you. Anyone who does not have the Spirit of Christ does not belong to him. But if Christ is in you, though the body is dead because of sin, the Spirit is life because of righteousness. If the Spirit of him who raised Jesus from the dead dwells in you, he who raised Christ from the dead will give life to your mortal bodies also through his Spirit that dwells in you. (Rom. 8:9–11; cf. 1 Pet. 4:6)

That this fulfillment of human life is accomplished by the power of the Spirit is fully consistent with Jesus' own human life, since it was just by the grace and power of the Spirit that Jesus lived the human life he did. But precisely because the Spirit of God by which Jesus did all this is the Spirit of *Jesus* (inasmuch as Jesus is God), it is not a force or power that operates apart from or independently of Jesus. Consequently, it is not separable from him so long as he dwells in time and space (John 7:39), and so can only be poured out in the world once Jesus himself is absent in body from the world (16:7).[52] Only when seated at the right hand and thus (as described in the preceding chapter) outside of time and space, is he able in his glorified humanity to participate fully (albeit, prior to the parousia, hiddenly) in God's governance of the world; and only then is Jesus' Spirit no longer restricted to the spatio-temporal place where his body is, because his body no longer occupies that sort of place.

Thus the Spirit is in all cases the agent of the Word's embodiment, but in the present period, the Spirit effects this mystery not by making the Word live in us (as though each of us were to become individually an incarnation of the Logos in a way that displaced our own distinctive human identities), but by enabling us to live in him. In the wake of the ascension of Jesus in and with his humanity to God's right hand, we are not simply *with* God but, through the power of Jesus' Spirit, *in* God, such that we begin to share now with him life in the Spirit:

---

52. To be sure, just as the Word upholds creation at all times, so too is the Spirit always present in creation (Ps. 104:30); but, as with the Word, the operation of the Spirit is hidden apart from the incarnation: as God is only revealed *in* Jesus, so the Holy Spirit is only known *through* Jesus (see 1 John 4:1–2).

The life that God will give does not consist in the breathing of air, or in the flow of blood from the liver, but in the fact that God in God's entirety will be participated in by human beings in their entirety, so that God will be in relation to the soul as the soul is to the body, and through the soul will likewise be present in the body. . . . In this way the whole human being will be deified, being made God by the grace of the God who became human, so that the individual will remain entirely human in soul and body on account of his nature, and entirely God in soul and body owing to the grace and the splendor of the blessed glory of God.[53]

Unlike Jesus we are not and will never be the Word, whether now or in glory; but in glory our lives will be so bound to the Word, living as children of God exclusively in and by the Word, that we will in our own fashion reveal the Word's glory—which is just the glory of God. As John puts it, "What we will be has not yet been revealed. What we do know is this: when he is revealed, we will be like him, for we will see him as he is" (1 John 3:2).

This transformation is utterly dependent on Jesus' humanity—the fact that at one time "the Word became flesh and lived among us"—for evidently we can see the Word "as he is" only because he has taken (and continues in glory to retain) visible form, giving us the power to be children of God with him (John 1:12) by giving us in our humanity the same Spirit by which he was constituted as God's Son in his (Rom. 8:14–15; Gal. 4:6; cf. Luke 3:22; Rom. 1:4; 1 Pet. 1:3).[54] In short, we, as human beings, can share in the life of God only in and through the same Spirit by which God has lived the life of a human being. For although the Spirit is active in creation quite apart from the incarnation, without the incarnation this activity takes the form of sustaining us *under* God as creatures and servants, but not *with* God as friends, for because we are merely creatures, we can receive God's life only as it is given to us in creaturely form. God could not simply make us divine by fiat without obliterating the goodness of our being as creatures, and thus finally giving up on the world as good in its createdness;[55] but God can and does take on a human life so that human beings may in their humanity live with God,

---

53. Maximus, *Ambigua* 7.1.113 (PG 91:1088C), trans. alt.

54. Congar thus argues that in his humanity Jesus no less than the rest of us receives the fullness of divine sonship only in glory: "Following his resurrection, he was constituted according to the Holy Spirit as the Son of God with power. . . . Jesus' humanity, united from the very beginning to the person of the Word, has been brought to the condition of a Son of God humanity." Yves Congar, *The Word and the Spirit*, trans. David Smith (London: Geoffrey Chapman, 1986), 91.

55. In this respect, the incarnation takes nothing away from God's declaration to Moses: "No one shall see me and live" (Exod. 33:20). This statement speaks to the utter incommensurability of God in God's self and creaturely perception. But human beings can see God and live insofar as God takes on a human life; indeed, only so—as God binds God's own life to that of the creature—can they truly live (1 John 4:9).

having received the same Spirit by which he lives, and thus sharing now and in eternity a life that, while remaining fully human, is also God's. So it is that if to know God, we must finally disregard everything except the humanity of Jesus, it is because God has willed to be known just as *that* human being, and thus in *Jesus'* humanity. In the present this humanity is not visible to us, but it is mediated to us through Jesus' Spirit, which is both the Spirit of God (since Jesus is God), and also the Spirit of his humanity (since it is the Spirit by which the Word both once lived and, by the power of the resurrection, still lives a human life). For this reason, it is the Spirit of our humanity, too: the Spirit by which we, in our humanness, are able to live before God as Jesus did and does (Rom. 8:11).

And if Jesus' humanity is now present to us only in this way, in the work of the Spirit that can be recognized as Jesus' work only by faith, it is important to note that this state of affairs was not inevitable. It might have been, instead, that Easter and parousia coincided, that the triumph of Jesus' resurrection from the dead should also have been the end of time, the precise point at which his temporally and spatially limited bodily presence in Palestine should have become his universal bodily presence as triumphant Lord. Indeed, his disciples seem to have expected some such scenario (Acts 1:6), and not without reason: there was no necessity for history to have carried on after Easter morning, for the victory had been won, God's lordship vindicated, and death defeated. Objectively speaking, there was therefore nothing more to be done, nothing further to be accomplished, no reason for history to continue.

And yet, as Karl Barth rightly noted, there would have been something profoundly unsatisfactory about God's ending the world on Easter morning. God certainly could have done so, could have brought it all crashing down, stilling the powers of darkness and establishing an unconquerable empire of light. But that God did not do so may be taken as a sign that God had no desire to establish the kingdom over our heads, in spite of us, by an act of sheer power that simply crushes our feeble resistance beneath it. For such a kingdom, however glorious, would finally not have been the kingdom of Jesus, who desires us not to be servants ("because the servant does not know what the master is doing"), but friends.[56] To revert to Maximus's imagery, in such a scenario, there would have been no "beautiful exchange"—not in that there would have been no salvation, but that the shape of salvation would no longer have been one of our own appropriation of the life of God through Jesus' Spirit in faith. Instead of being free, salvation would have become automatic,

---

56. According to Barth, if God had brought the world to an end on Easter, "He might well have shown Himself to be wonderful, majestic and sovereign, but He would certainly not have been gracious." Barth, *CD* IV/3.1:333.

such that while the exchange would remain (since in such a scenario we still would have shared in the life of God), it would cease to be beautiful (because it would take the form of a divine overruling of our freedom rather than its fulfillment). That things did not happen in this way is a sign that as much as the final and definitive triumph of the kingdom is God's doing rather than ours, it is not something God wills to do without us.[57] For the point of God's victory, of Jesus' resurrection, and of our adoption as children of God is not to reduce us to nothing, to make us feel small, insignificant, or irrelevant before the overwhelming power of God. Whatever other pleasures such a kingdom might afford, it would not constitute salvation in a properly human sense, for if it is part of the *logos* of human beings that they are free, salvation—the fulfillment of such a life—must engage that freedom.[58]

It follows that for the Word to be incarnate "always and everywhere" does not mean a repetition of the one enfleshment of the Word in Jesus, still less that God's embodiment in Jesus is fundamentally the same as God's presence in the world as a whole. In this respect, the idea that the Word "wishes always and everywhere to effect the mystery of his embodiment" does nothing to lessen the scandal of particularity, or to mitigate the fact that in the period between ascension and parousia, Jesus' body cannot be discerned directly, as it was by his first disciples. For us, Jesus is available only in "what we have heard" (1 John 1:1; cf. Rom. 10:17), even if the "hearing" may be mediated through the "visible words" of the sacraments as well as the audible words of preaching.[59] Although we may well see the effects of Jesus' saving activity in the lives of those who in the strength of these words take their place in Christ's body, the church, we do not see Jesus. As the angels said to the women at the tomb, "He is not here."

And yet Jesus' absence is integral to the good news, and this in two respects. First, it confirms that the Word's relationship to the flesh and blood of Jesus was not illusory, accidental, or temporary: the Word did not float above this human existence; rather, this human being was the Word, and as such, his

---

57. "For nothing that is involuntary is durable; like streams or trees which are kept back by force. But that which is voluntary is more durable and safe. . . . Wherefore God did not think it behoved him to benefit the unwilling, but to do good to the willing. And therefore, like a tutor or physician, he partly removes and partly condones ancestral habits, . . . just as medical men do with their patients, that the medicine may be taken, being artfully blended with what is nice." Gregory of Nazianzus, *Oration* 31.25, in *Christology of the Later Fathers*, 209.

58. "The good will of Jesus Christ in the matter which here concerns us is that the world, His people and ourselves should not be merely the objects of His action but that we should be with Him as independently active and free subjects." Barth, *CD* IV/3.1:332.

59. The language of sacraments as "visible words" (*verba visibilia*) comes from Augustine, *Against Faustus the Manichaean* 19.16. For perhaps the most extensive contemporary theological elaboration of this idea, see Robert W. Jenson, *Visible Words: The Interpretation and Practice of Christian Sacraments* (Philadelphia: Fortress Press, 1978).

bodily presence in the world is bounded by the events of birth and death that define his life as truly human. So it is that in this human life no one less than God is seen, touched, and heard, and thus God's will to be with us is fully and unsurpassably revealed. But second, the uniqueness of God's incarnation in this one life, "for us and for our salvation," signals that the mystery of the Word's embodiment is not limited to God inhabiting creation, as though created existence only gained value as inhabited by the divine. Quite the contrary, the good news of the embodiment of God in Jesus is not that it should be repeated, but that it should be *inverted*; not that God should live in other human beings as God did in Jesus only, but that human beings should live in God. That is what makes it a beautiful *exchange*—that God's sharing our life in Jesus might enable us to share God's life in Jesus. It is in this sense that Jesus is truly the mediator: the one in whom the life of God and human beings, Creator and creature, subsist in communion.

It is in this way that the Word seeks to effect the mystery of his embodiment always and everywhere: not by personally appropriating all other human bodies for himself, but rather by enabling all other human bodies to appropriate *his* body by calling them to communion with himself. This appropriation, realized passively in the reception of Jesus' words (most concretely in the consumption of his own body and blood in the Eucharist), is lived out actively in community with all those others who have been called—a number that, of course, includes not only those who presently identify as members of Christ's body, but also all who more or less consciously stand outside of it. And we do this as those who do not see Jesus now; indeed, because we are able to receive Jesus' words only through the power of Jesus' Spirit, living as members of Christ's body becomes possible for us only after Jesus has ascended to the right hand of the Father and so ceased to be visible to us in time and space. Precisely because Jesus is not now seen, the believer's life now is ineluctably one of hope (Rom. 8:24–25), but if Maximus is right it is not for that reason simply one of endlessly deferred gratification (and thus of false consciousness); for because Jesus continues to live as one of us, even now we can and do live in him (Col. 3:2). Indeed, insofar as it is his Spirit that we experience as active in and among us now, bringing us to new life, we cannot help but acknowledge him, invisible though he may be: "Although you have not seen him, you love him; and even though you do not see him now, you believe in him and rejoice with an indescribable and glorious joy, for you are receiving the outcome of your faith, the salvation of your souls" (1 Pet. 1:8–9).

Conclusion

"As Is the Word, so Is God"[1]

I began this argument with a quotation from Luther to the effect that the humanity of Jesus is the key to our knowledge of God.[2] With this chapter's subtitle, I conclude with another Luther quotation that carries much the same sentiment: if the Word is God, and the Word became flesh and lived among us in Jesus, then Jesus' flesh—his earthly, temporal existence—is the measure of all our claims about who the Word is, and thus about who God is. The intervening pages have been an attempt to defend this principle, largely by way of an exposition of Chalcedonian Christology. In response to various alternatives that have been proposed in the modern period, I have defended a "Chalcedonianism without reserve," by which I mean an insistence that because Jesus of Nazareth is the Word made flesh, God is fully present and truly known in Jesus' humanity. This is good news because although we are always present *to God* by virtue of God's role as Creator, who sustains us in our being at every moment of our being, only by taking flesh does God become present *to us* by coming to be with us, making it possible for human life to be lived with (rather than merely under) God. Moreover, since the communion thereby achieved overcomes all that would separate us from God (Rom. 8:31–39), these considerations lead me to conclude that one virtue of an unreserved Chalcedonianism is its ability to give full expression to the

---

1. "Tantum est verbum, quantus est deus." Martin Luther, *Scholia in librum Genesios*, WA 9:329.31; cited in Oswald Bayer, *Martin Luther's Theology: A Contemporary Interpretation*, trans. Thomas H. Trapp (from the 3rd German ed., 2007; Grand Rapids: Wm. B. Eerdmans Publishing Co., 2008]), 351.
2. See p. 6 above.

biblical conviction that "in Christ God was reconciling the world to himself" (2 Cor. 5:19).

And yet this latter claim may seem to be undersupported, given that the foregoing chapters do not contain any formal account of how this reconciliation is achieved. Traditionally, Christology is divided between accounts of Jesus' person and his work. The former refers to the kinds of questions to which the Chalcedonian definition provides at least the basis for an answer: who Jesus is (i.e., his *identity* as the hypostasis of the second person of the Trinity), as well as the relationship between his divinity and humanity (i.e., his *ontology* as one who is both truly God and truly a human being). By contrast, the topic of Jesus' work refers to what he accomplished by virtue of his being the particular person he was. That question has typically been answered by way of a doctrine of atonement—an account of how Jesus effects the reconciliation to which Paul refers by overcoming the situation of estrangement from God caused by human sin.

Viewed from this perspective, the divide separating humanity from God is not simply ontological but also moral, a matter not merely of human beings' distance from but also of their active resistance to God. Attention to the topic of Christ's work emerges from the conviction that in light of this resistance—the human refusal to be the creatures who live by God's grace but who instead strive to be "like God" (Gen. 3:5)—it is not enough simply for Jesus to be who he is, even if who he is, is Emmanuel, or "God with us"; it is also necessary for Jesus to *do* something to counter the effects of sin. For because sin is just the rejection of God, absent such activity on Jesus' part, the revelation of God's presence could give rise only to the terror of judgment, since genuinely to be confronted by God entails precisely the recognition that rejecting God, the sole source of creaturely existence, can lead only to death. Attention to Christ's work, in short, is demanded by the recognition that humans need the assurance of God's forgiveness in addition to the knowledge of God's presence, and that such forgiveness can be received (at least according to a dominant strand of thinking in the Christian tradition) only once the demands of God's justice are satisfied. And the satisfaction of divine justice, in turn, requires the destruction of "every proud obstacle raised up against the knowledge of God" (2 Cor. 10:5).

Now it might be objected that there is something fundamentally flawed about this line of reasoning, for it seems to suggest that mercy is only possible after the requirements of justice have been fulfilled, and that forgiveness is only possible in the wake of punishment; but in common usage, to show mercy is simply to *forgo* the demands of strict justice, and to forgive, *not* to exact punishment. Moreover, the Gospels are replete with stories of Jesus declaring people's sins forgiven (including the unnamed sinner of Luke 7 discussed in chap.

5) without the evangelists offering any account of Jesus satisfying any moral, legal, or cultic requirements as a condition of his making such a declaration. Rather, they seem to view such accounts in light of a principle that is evidently accepted even by Jesus' opponents: that God has an absolutely unqualified capacity to forgive sins (Mark 2:7; Luke 5:21). From this perspective, one may perfectly well acknowledge the need for sins to be forgiven in order for human beings to live in God's presence while denying that Jesus needs to do any-thing in order to make such forgiveness possible, since the whole point of the Word's taking flesh is for God's presence to be revealed as grace, favor, and (thereby) forgiveness. Following Luther once again, it is only apart from the incarnation that God's presence will be conceived as terrifying—and apart from the incarnation God cannot be rightly conceived at all.[3] And this is just why reflection on the topic of Christ's work is so often problematic: because it depends on an understanding of God, humanity, and the moral or legal condi-tions of their communion considered apart from the fact of the incarnation, or (in the words of perhaps the most influential theologian of the atonement) *remoto Christo*.[4] But such reflection can have no theological purchase if it is true that "whoever wishes to deliberate or speculate soundly about God should disregard absolutely everything except the humanity of Christ."

And yet this very same principle also dictates that it is impossible to solve the problem of the relationship between Christ's person and work by simply dissolving the latter into the former, as though the work of salvation could be reduced to the mere fact of incarnation. A theology that takes the hypostatic union in itself as the solution to the problem of human sin can hardly be said to have taken Christ's humanity any more seriously than the most abstractly formulated model of penal substitution, for in both cases the narrated details of character and circumstance that define the particular humanity of *Christ* (in distinction from that of Mary, Peter, or no one in particular) fall to the

---

3. Admittedly, Luther did tend to think it was in some sense meaningful to speak of God apart from the incarnation, if only in a highly restricted sense:

> We have to argue in one way about God . . . as preached, revealed, offered, and worshiped, and in another way about God as he is not preached, not revealed, not offered, not worshiped. To the extent, therefore, that God hides himself and wills to be unknown to us, it is no business of ours. . . . God must therefore be left to himself in his own majesty, for in this regard we have nothing to do with him, nor has he willed that we should have anything to do with him.

So far, so good. But then Luther goes on to draw a distinction between "the word of God and God himself" that flies in the face of his own best instincts elsewhere (as expressed, e.g., in this chapter's subtitle). See Martin Luther, *On the Bondage of the Will*, in *Luther and Erasmus: Free Will and Salvation*, ed. E. Gordon Rupp and Philip S. Watson (Philadelphia: Westminster Press, 1969), 200–201.

4. Anselm of Canterbury, *Why God Became Man*, in *A Scholastic Miscellany: Anselm to Ockham*, ed. Eugene R. Fairweather (Philadelphia: Westminster Press, 1956).

wayside: all that matters is the juxtaposition of divinity and humanity, whether in conception or on the cross. Indeed, even if Christ's work is interpreted in more temporally extended fashion as a matter of perfect dependence on or obedience to God, the details of his life have no constitutive significance for our knowledge of God. Instead (in yet another form of the problem identified with the Christology of Leo's *Tome* at the beginning of this book), God is not so much known *in* Jesus as *through* him, with the Word standing behind (and thence "shining forth" from) his humanity rather than being fully identified with this human being.

Over against that sort of Christology, my aim in this book, in line with the two quotations from Luther that I have used to frame the argument, has been to develop an account of Jesus that avoids the conceptual bifurcation of his person and work by a process of christological exposition that strives for ever tighter focus on Jesus' concrete particularity as the first-century Palestinian Jew born of Mary: moving from general considerations of the ontologies of Creator and creature, through discussion of the hypostatic union, to the biblical story of the God whose Word became flesh. Even if the point of the first two chapters is to accentuate the conceptual difficulties seemingly posed by the doctrine of the incarnation by stressing the radical incommensurability of Creator and creature, the upshot of the subsequent analysis has been that in light of the reality of Jesus, the "great divide" turns out to be no divide at all, but rather the occasion for the most intimate possible communion between Creator and creature. For in the incarnation God is revealed *as* a creature and thus shown *not to be God apart from creatures*. Thus, in one crucial respect the point of the argument has been to deconstruct the very distinction employed to get it started. Although talk about God's "incarnation" cannot avoid the deployment of the concepts "divinity" and "humanity," because the incarnate one is *Jesus*, in practice all talk of "divinity" and "humanity" (as of "Creator" and "creature") must be reconstructed on the basis of his concrete form of existence.

And this brings us back to the question of Jesus' work. For if the strategy pursued in the preceding chapters is correct, then it is through attention to Jesus' work—that is, the totality of his life as lived out between Christmas and Good Friday—that one comes to know his person and thereby the natures this person hypostatizes.[5] Crucially, however, this dependence of our knowledge of Jesus' person on his work is not one of inference, as though Jesus'

---

5. Schleiermacher rightly recognized this point when he wrote that "Christ's sufferings can be thought of in connection with his redemptive activity only when regarded as a whole and a unity; to separate out any particular element and ascribe it a particular reconciling value . . . is . . . seldom free from a defiling admixture of superstition." Friedrich Schleiermacher, *The Christian Faith*, ed. H. R. Mackintosh and J. S. Stewart (Edinburgh: T&T Clark, 1989 [1929]), 437 (§101.4). I am grateful to Joshua Ralston for pointing me to this passage.

performance of certain activities (e.g., miraculous healing, stilling storms, or the spontaneous production of food and drink) or his manifesting certain qualities (e.g., faith, mercy, or justice) required him to be confessed as God by virtue of his satisfying some criterion of divinity. To interpret the relation between Jesus' person and work in those terms would, again, presuppose some knowledge of divinity apart from him, to which he could be shown to measure up. But as much as it is appropriate for Christians to argue that Jesus' career shows him to be divine (not least because Jesus himself makes just that sort of claim in John 10:38; cf. 8:17–18), the process by which his identity comes to be known is not that of Jesus' meeting the qualifications of a pre-existing job description.[6] His status is instead established by God's vindicating his life both during the course of his ministry (Matt. 3:17; 17:5 and pars.; John 12:28; cf. Matt. 12:28 and par.) and, definitively, in his resurrection from the dead (Rom. 1:4; cf. Acts 2:24; 1 Tim. 3:16) in spite of the fact that the quotidian characteristics of his life might otherwise seem to have little of the savor of divinity about them (see, e.g., Matt. 27:40–43 and par.; cf. 1 Cor. 1:23).

It is within this context only that it becomes possible to speak of Jesus' "work," in the sense of an account of what he did to effect the reconciliation of the world to God. And when framed in these terms, his work cannot be identified with a particular event (e.g., the crucifixion), or even with a pattern of behavior abstracted from his life as a whole (e.g., his obedience). Rather than being identified with something he does, his work should be understood as encompassing *everything* that he does, so that any more limited account of his work (and, of course, nothing more than a limited account can ever be presented, as explicitly noted in John 21:25) can be offered only as a kind of summary characterization of his earthly career, which is *in its entirety* the act by which God, by confronting and defeating the power of sin, reconciles the world to himself.

Earlier I stated that for the creature to encounter God absent Jesus' work of reconciliation could give rise only to the terror of judgment, since sin is just the creature's rejection of the Creator, and to encounter the Creator is for the creature to be confronted with the fact of its own creaturehood, and thus with the truth that apart from God it has no possibility of life. At first blush, this claim might seem to be yet another instance of presuming to be able to talk about divinity and humanity apart from Jesus, and thus in disregard of the principle that both are rightly known only in Jesus; yet it is justified by the fact that

---

6. To be sure, the evangelists make much of Jesus' fulfilling the words of the prophets, but these words relate to Jesus' status as Messiah, not to the claim that he is divine; in any case, even in these cases of fulfillment, it seems that the correspondence was recognized only in retrospect, not as a matter of cumulative demonstration during Jesus' lifetime (see Matt. 26:56; Luke 24:25–27; John 2:22; 12:16).

the terror of judgment is experienced when God is encountered in Jesus, too, and thus in the act of reconciliation itself no less than in any encounter with God that might take place on other terms. For Jesus is "[the] salvation, which [God has] prepared in the presence of all peoples" (Luke 2:30–31), only as the one who is also "destined for the falling and the rising of many in Israel, and to be a sign that will be opposed" (2:34). Nor should this "falling and rising" be interpreted as the description of alternative destinies for distinct groups of people; it is rather the description of the very process of salvation itself, so that it is only by falling that one comes to rise; even of those most devoted to Jesus, it may be said that "a sword will pierce your own soul too" (2:35).

None of this takes away from the fact that Jesus is the one who preaches the good news of the coming kingdom, but it does point to the incompatibility between that kingdom and sin. So it is that when Peter receives a tangible sign of the abundance of the kingdom in a miraculous catch of fish, he can only respond, "Go away from me, Lord, for I am a sinful man!" (Luke 5:8). So too, in the case of the woman with the hemorrhage (Mark 5:33 and par.), the crowd of people at Nain who witness the raising of the widow's son (Luke 7:16), the nameless woman in Simon's house (Luke 7:37–38), and with special force in the revelation of Jesus' glory on the Mount of the Transfiguration (Matt. 17:6 and pars.). Even for the outcasts and marginalized who are the most immediate beneficiaries of Jesus' ministry, the kingdom entails a new mode of life incompatible with older habits: "Stand up, take your mat and walk" (John 5:8–9; cf. Matt. 9:6 and pars.) is inseparable from "See, you have been made well! Do not sin any more, so that nothing worse happens to you" (John 5:14; cf. 8:11).

And yet it continues to be the case that Jesus' works of healing and forgiveness are unconditional: the new life that follows—by virtue of the very fact that it *follows*—is in no sense an enabling condition of Jesus' actions. Even the faith that Jesus at various points seems to imply is the means of a person's restoration (Matt. 9:22 and pars.; Mark 10:52; Luke 17:19) appears on further consideration to be no less Jesus' gift than the restoration itself (Mark 9:23–24). But this should come as no surprise, because however much it may be the experience of Jesus' contemporaries (and it was, of course, the experience only of a very few of them, even measured against the highly selective accounts found in the Gospels) that his presence portends judgment, the whole point of his ministry of reconciliation is that this judgment *not* fall on those he has come to save, however much or little they may be sensible of its justly doing so. Instead, the one on whom the unmitigated terror of judgment does fall is Jesus himself.

This has nothing to do with a need for propitiation, as though the divine honor or wrath or even justice required some sort of compensatory payment. Again, that sort of reasoning (i.e., reflections on the conditions of the

possibility of human-divine reconciliation) invariably depends on considerations derived *remoto Christo*, in which the incarnation is less the reality of
Emmanuel than a means to that end, in which only some particular features
of Jesus' human life rather than its fullness are soteriologically significant. On
such a reading, God finally stands behind rather than in Jesus' life, so that
however otherwise orthodox one's confession may be, it cannot be quite the
case that to see Jesus is to see the Father (John 12:44; 14:9). And yet if in Jesus
"the whole fullness of deity dwells bodily" (Col. 2:9), and if in this embodied
life he (in the words of the Apostles' Creed) "suffered under Pontius Pilate,
was crucified, died, and was buried," then it is certainly necessary to interpret
these events as integral to Jesus' work.

In order to avoid the implication that the ultimate truth and reality of God
stands above or behind Jesus, it is best to avoid treating his story as fundamentally a transaction between the Father and the Son (or alternatively, between
God and Satan), in which his humanity is a kind of token signifying the exchange
of moral or metaphysical currency. It seems more consistent with the logic of
the incarnation to view the story as an interaction between God and humanity
in which Jesus is precisely the one in whom the basic character or reality of both
is disclosed. Humanity is revealed at once as a creature (i.e., one utterly dependent on God) yet as having failed to live as a creature (i.e., refusing to live in this
dependence, presuming rather that human life can be earned and sustained by
one's own efforts, and thereby succumbing either to presumption or despair).
It is in this way that sin is revealed. For sin is just lawlessness (1 John 3:4), the
failure to attend to God, who is the source of the good, and thus the ground of
the created order that the law both describes and defends. And because Jesus
is God, in the rejection of Jesus, God is rejected. And whether this rejection
comes at the hands of the townsfolk of Nazareth, the leaders of Israel, the
Roman authorities, or even the ones he has called and claimed as friends; and
whether it is prompted by envy, indignation, confusion, fear, or indifference—
the witness of Scripture is that the rejection was universal, so that in the end "all
forsook him, and fled" (Mark 14:50 RSV). And in that rejection it becomes clear
that apart from God there is no future for the creature, that the only possibility is death—although because that very fact is also disclosed in the particular
circumstances of Jesus' death, it also becomes clear that even death is no barrier
to God's power to sustain the life of the creature.

And so it is that Jesus reveals what divinity is. For in that Jesus is God the
Word made flesh, the whole of his life from birth through death and resurrection reveals that God, the Creator of all things visible and invisible, eternal
and transcendent, who alone "has immortality and dwells in unapproachable
light" (1 Tim. 6:16), refuses to be God apart from human beings—indeed,
refuses to be God except *as* a human being. Although human beings in their

sin would seek to live apart from God, thereby securing for themselves only the utter and irrevocable certainty of death (Rom. 6:23), God renders this impossible by the Word (who is God) taking on "the likeness of sinful flesh" (8:3), thereby demonstrating that God *is* God in just this way and no other. So it is that the entirety of Jesus' life is his "work," for it is in all that he does, and indeed, just as he does all that he does (that is, in and through the concrete activities of hungering, thirsting, tiring, tasting, smelling, eating, drinking, sleeping, standing, walking, sweating, speaking, hearing, rejoicing, fearing, suffering, and dying), that he is Jesus and, as Jesus, God as well.

Of course, it remains possible to reject Jesus and thereby to reject God. To do so is simply to refuse to recognize oneself as someone who has been called by God in Jesus to view God's life (and thus God's story) in Jesus as one's own; that is, a refusal to take up the "power to become children of God" (John 1:12) that has been given to us in Jesus. Once again, sin is the act of rejecting God, of viewing one's life (and thus one's own story) as *only* one's own, fundamentally lived apart from and independently of God.[7] Yet in light of the incarnation, this possibility has now become untenable, because insofar as God has become flesh, our stories just are not lived apart from God. Of course, insofar as God is confessed as Creator, this is true even apart from the incarnation; but because God is transcendent and thus not to be identified with any worldly reality— even those worldly realities through which God spoke to Israel, let alone God's "eternal power and divine nature" (Rom. 1:20)—prior to the Word's taking flesh, none of those realities (including even the theophanies of the Old Testament) could be identified directly with God.[8] But because the Word has become flesh in Jesus, so that it is now true that this earthly-historical life straightforwardly *is* God's, this is no longer possible after the incarnation. To

---

7. While this phrasing may seem to suggest that the fundamental human sin is pride (that is, the presumption that one can secure one's destiny by one's own power), it is no less accurate an account of despair. To count oneself as worthless, without significance and therefore without hope, is as much to imagine one's story as solely one's own, as the Promethean presumption of self-sufficiency. In either case the essence of sin is a failure to recognize that one's life is not defined by one's own actions, but by the power and love of God, before whom no personal significance or insignificance is finally decisive.

8. Importantly, this is not to say that no event prior to the incarnation could be described as God's act. On the contrary, because God as Creator is the primary cause of everything that happens, there is no event, from the most quotidian occurrence to the parting of the Red Sea, that could *not* be so described. But insofar as (in line with Paul's remarks in Rom. 1) God's activity as primary cause is invisible (so that even the classification of an event as miraculous is a matter of faith, since even the most exacting scientific observation will be able to do no more than note the absence of any identifiable secondary cause), prior to the incarnation no such description could be judged necessary: "Everywhere there has been forgiveness of sins, the miraculous outpouring upon men of the wealth of the divine mercy, signs of the forebearance and long-suffering of God. Everywhere men are being healed of the divine wounds. But it is through Jesus that we have been enabled to see that this is so." Karl Barth, *The Epistle to the Romans*, trans. Edwin C. Hoskyns (Oxford: Oxford University Press, 1968), 106.

tell the world's—and one's own—story fully requires telling the story of Jesus, so that even if God is rejected, God can no longer be avoided. And it is the job of the church to ensure that God is not avoided by keeping the story of Jesus in circulation in such a way as to bear witness that God was here, in this utterly human life, and thus to live out the conviction that the God became flesh in Jesus just because God "desires everyone to be saved and to come to the knowledge of the truth" (1 Tim. 2:3–4).

The upshot of a "Chalcedonianism without reserve" is thus simply the firm insistence that Jesus is, in every observable feature and aspect of his existence, fully and thoroughly human; but this human being also happens to be God the Word, the eternal Son, the second person of the Trinity. As Creator, God is always sustaining every human's existence (along with that of every other creature) in every aspect of its existence; but in this one case, God identifies *this* existence, *this* life, as God's own. That is what it means for the Word to become flesh. According to this framework nothing happens to the divine nature in this becoming (i.e., there is no descent from heaven to earth). Nor is any special property or capacity given to human nature to raise it up to the divine (the fact that Christ is sinless, the biblically identified point of difference between him and the rest of us, entails no dilution of his human nature). Chalcedon rather echoes the biblical witness: that a human being is born, and this human being is God's Son—a confession that does not entail the claim that this human being has any special qualities or capacities. To be sure, because this human being is the eternal Word, the second person of the Trinity, he also has a divine nature (for how could a hypostasis possibly be confessed as divine without being God by nature, too?), but this divine nature becomes no less transcendent by virtue of the person of the Word taking flesh. After Christmas no less than before, the nature of God is invisible and ineffable, beyond all creaturely perception or description. God does not become less or other than God in the incarnation; rather, by taking created, human flesh, God lives in a form that we can see, hear, touch, and thus know—not as an object of speculative contemplation, but as Lord and Savior, as Jesus, the eternal Son, who calls us through the Spirit to be children with him of the one Father, and who thereby simultaneously reveals to us and draws us into the eternal love that is the Trinity.

And so, too, it is not the case that in taking flesh God comes under our control, reduced to the phenomenal in a way that compromises the divine transcendence. That the church should fail to honor this fact is, of course, a constant temptation, albeit one that Jesus himself warned against (Matt. 7:21). It was just the assumption that Jesus could be controlled and contained that led to the crucifixion; but the resurrection demonstrated that such efforts utterly fail to reckon with the power of God. And for this reason, all those who would know God must disregard everything except the humanity of Jesus: for it is just the humanity of Jesus that shows us that "Jesus is God's 'revelation' in a decisive sense not because he renders a dimly apprehended God clear to us, but because he challenges and queries an unusually clear sense of God."[9] Christians want to claim that in Jesus, God is *known*, and that this is *truth*. But if they are faithful to the truth of the God who is known in Jesus, they recognize that this knowledge takes proper social form not as a claim of power on their own behalf, but rather as a confession that power belongs to God, who is not subject to us, but who nevertheless enables us to bear witness to God's power which, because it "is made perfect in weakness" (2 Cor. 12:9), is properly understood as a gift that must constantly be received anew rather than held as a firmly grasped possession. Christians are called to affirm knowledge of God, but not in such a way that they are able by their own efforts to secure its fullness. To explicate this point, the Christian will refer to Jesus, not because he has provided final clarity, but because he has disclosed the radical freedom of a God who rules in and through the flux, suffering, and openness of history rather than by standing over it.

And even as in doing this for us God does not become other than God, but simply shows us who God is (and thus what it means for God to be God), so too, in calling us to be God's children, Jesus does not make us other than human. Rather, he tells us what it means to be human, which is to be children of God, and thus called by God for life with God. And so it is supremely fitting that this calling, which cannot come from anyone less than God, should be spoken by one who is, in every feature of his earthly life, no more than human, for just so may we be convinced beyond any possibility of doubt or contradiction that God's presence is no threat to our life, but, both now and into eternity, its very ground.

Christians claim that they see and know this truth in Jesus: that in his perceptible, finite humanity, they encounter no less than the infinite and invisible God. How it is that they should see and know this (and thus why it is that some do not come to such knowledge), they cannot say. For although any account of the incarnation inevitably requires talk of divinity and humanity, the confession that incarnation has taken place in the particular person Jesus of Nazareth demands that these categories be subject to a thorough rethinking and reconstruction in light of his concrete reality. This means that there is no point in trying to prove Jesus' divinity, because, if Christians are right, the content of divinity is known only by reference to Jesus. And for this reason, there remains an arresting truth in Albert Schweitzer's justly famous words:

---

9. Rowan Williams, "Trinity and Revelation," in *On Christian Theology* (Oxford: Blackwell, 2000), 138.

> He comes to us as One unknown, without a name, as of old, by the lakeside, He came to those who knew Him not. He speaks to us the same word: "Follow thou me!" and sets us to the tasks which He has to fulfill for our time. He commands. And to those who obey Him, whether they be wise or simple, He will reveal himself in the toils, the conflicts, the sufferings which they shall pass through in His fellowship, and, as an ineffable mystery, they shall learn in their own experience Who He is.[10]

And yet for all the beauty and profundity of this passage, Schweitzer doesn't get it quite right. It may indeed be said that he comes to us as One unknown, for he conforms to none of our expectations and can never be fully grasped by our knowing, remaining rather always the teacher from and about whom more both may and must be learned. But he is not without a name. On the contrary, he is "Jesus son of Joseph from Nazareth" (John 1:45), "the name given by the angel before he was conceived in the womb" (Luke 2:21), a name given because he was the one who would "save his people from their sins" (Matt. 1:21), so that the story the evangelists tell is not of an anonymous power, but very specifically "the good news of Jesus Christ, the Son of God" (Mark 1:1).

This is not a minor point. For the message of the gospel is not that of an unknown God, a *Deus absconditus* who in his transcendence is one with whom we finally can have nothing to do, whatever combination of awe, terror, respect, or fascination the thought of him may inspire. The gospel is rather that the Word, who from all eternity is God, became flesh in and as the human being named Jesus. That this one has a name, which by virtue of the incarnation is also and evermore God's name, is crucial, for it serves as a continual check on our tendency to conceive of God in other terms, by reference to whatever ideas of causation, necessity, perfection, order, goodness, truth, or beauty may press upon us in our desire to orient ourselves in the face of the experiences of contingency, vulnerability, suffering, and death that so naturally give rise to talk about God—but of a God who, without a name because beyond any possibility of naming, cannot help but be both unknown and unknowable.

Now, it may well be that statements are made about this God—the God of the philosophers, or of so-called limit experiences—that are also true of the God of Israel. Why should it not be so? But however many such statements there may be, this God is not the God of Israel, because the God of Israel has a name. The God of Israel is "the LORD," and thus not the one beyond all

---

10. Albert Schweitzer, *The Quest of the Historical Jesus: A Critical Study of Its Progress from Reimarus to Wrede*, trans. W. Montgomery (London: Adam and Charles Black, 1911), 401, trans. slightly alt.

naming, but rather the one with "the name that is above every name" (Phil. 2:9), and who, as such, takes on a creature's life and a creature's name. That is the mystery, yet (contrary to the etymology of that word) it is not a mystery before which we can only be silent, but one we are given to know (Mark 4:11) and to speak. It is the mystery that is Jesus, and thus the mystery that the "great divide" between creature and Creator is no barrier to God's becoming intimate with us, that the God who is infinite can, without in the least compromising or qualifying or abandoning that infinity, also be finite. That the One who is above can, without ceasing for a moment to be above, also be with. That the One who is eternally begotten can also be born in time. That the One who is omniscient and omnipotent can also be ignorant and weak. That the One who fills all space and time can also be located quite specifically in a stable, a carpenter's shed, or a tomb. That the One who is impassible and immortal can also suffer and die. The mystery is not that this One is divine, for that is his eternal nature: it has always been the case. The mystery is that now, at the end of all the ages, the One who is and has always been divine has become also fully human, so that we can be children of God—and thus fully human, too.

Bibliography

Anselm. *Monologion*. In *Complete Philosophical and Theological Treatises of Anselm of Canterbury*. Translated by Jasper Hopkins and Herbert Richardson. Minneapolis: Arthur J. Banning Press, 2000.

―――. *Why God Became Man*. In *A Scholastic Miscellany: Anselm to Ockham*, edited by Eugene R. Fairweather, 100–183. Philadelphia: Westminster Press, 1956.

Athanasius of Alexandria. *Against the Heathen*. In *Nicene and Post-Nicene Fathers*, 2nd series, edited by Philip Schaff and Henry Wace, vol. 4, *Athanasius: Select Works and Letters*. Boston: Hendrickson, 1995 [1892].

―――. *On the Incarnation of the Word*. In *Christology of the Later Fathers*, edited by Edward R. Hardy. Philadelphia: Westminster Press, 1954.

Augustine. *The City of God against the Pagans*. Edited and translated by R. W. Dyson. Cambridge: Cambridge University Press, 1998.

―――. *Confessions*. Translated by Henry Chadwick. Oxford: Oxford University Press, 1991.

―――. *Sermons III (51–94) on the New Testament*. Edited by John E. Rotelle, OSA. Translated by Edmund Hill, OP. Brooklyn, NY: New City Press, 1991.

―――. *Sermons III/7 (230–272B) on the Liturgical Seasons*. Edited by John E. Rotelle, OSA. Translated by Edmund Hill, OP. New Rochelle, NY: New City Press, 1993.

―――. *The Trinity*. Edited by John E. Rotelle, OSA. Translated by Edmund Hill, OP. Hyde Park, NY: New City Press, 1991.

Balthasar, Hans Urs von. *Seeing the Form*. Vol. 1 of *The Glory of the Lord: A Theological Aesthetics*. Translated by Ermo Leiva-Merikakis. San Francisco: Ignatius, 1989 [1967].

―――. *Truth of God*. Vol. 2 of *Theo-Logic*. Translated by Adrian J. Walker. San Francisco: Ignatius Press, 2004 [1985].

Bantum, Brian. *Redeeming Mulatto: A Theology of Race and Christian Hybridity*. Waco, TX: Baylor University Press, 2010.

Barrett, C. K. *The Gospel according to St. John: An Introduction with Commentary and Notes on the Greek Text*. 2nd ed. London: SPCK, 1978.

Barth, Karl. *Church Dogmatics*. 13 vols. Edited by G. W. Bromiley and T. F. Torrance. Edinburgh: T&T Clark, 1956–74.

―――. *The Epistle to the Romans*. Translated by Edwin C. Hoskyns. Oxford: Oxford University Press, 1968.

―――. *Learning Jesus Christ through the Heidelberg Catechism*. Translated by Shirley C. Guthrie. Grand Rapids: Wm. B. Eerdmans Publishing Co., 1981 [1961].

Basil of Caesarea. *Basil: Letters and Select Works*. In *Nicene and Post-Nicene Fathers*, 2nd series, edited by Philip Schaff and Henry Wace, translated by Blomfield Jackson, vol. 8. Peabody, MA: Hendrickson Publishers, 1995 [1895].

Bathrellos, Dmitri. *The Byzantine Christ: Person, Nature, and Will in the Christology of Saint Maximus the Confessor*. Oxford: Oxford University Press, 2005.

Batut, Jean-Pierre. *Pantocrator: "Dieu le Père tout-puissant" dans la théologie prénicéenne*. Paris: Institut d'Études Augustiniennes, 2009.

Bauckham, Richard. "Historiographical Characteristics of the Gospel of John." *New Testament Studies* 53, no. 1 (2007): 17–36.

———. *Jesus and the Eyewitnesses: The Gospels as Eyewitness Testimony*. 2nd ed. Grand Rapids: Wm. B. Eerdmans Publishing Co., 2017.

Bayer, Oswald. *Martin Luther's Theology: A Contemporary Interpretation*. Translated by Thomas H. Trapp. Grand Rapids: Wm. B. Eerdmans Publishing Co., 2008 [3rd German ed., 2007].

Boehmer, Julius. *Die neutestamentliche Gottesschen und die ersten drei Bitten des Vaterunsers*. Halle: Richard Mühlmann Verlagsbuchhandlung, 1917.

Boethius. *De Trinitate*. In *The Theological Tractates and the Consolation of Philosophy*. Loeb Classical Library 74. Cambridge, MA: Harvard University Press, 1973.

Bonhoeffer, Dietrich. *Sanctorum Communio: A Theological Study of the Sociology of the Church*. Edited by Clifford J. Green. Translated by Reinhard Kraus and Nancy Lukens. Dietrich Bonhoeffer Works 1. Minneapolis: Fortress Press, 1998.

The Book of Concord: The Confessions of the Evangelical Lutheran Church. Edited by Robert Kolb and Timothy J. Wengert. Minneapolis: Fortress Press, 2000.

Brenz, Johannes. *Von der Majestät unsers lieben Herrn und einigen Heilands Jesu Christi*. Tübingen: Morhart, 1567.

Brown, David. *Divine Humanity: Kenosis and the Construction of a Christian Theology*. Waco, TX: Baylor University Press, 2011.

Brown, Raymond. *The Birth of the Messiah: A Commentary on the Infancy Narratives in the Gospels of Matthew and Luke*. 2nd ed. New York: Doubleday, 1993.

Bultmann, Rudolf. "New Testament and Mythology." In *Kerygma and Myth: A Theological Debate*, edited by Hans Werner Bartsch, translated by Reginald H. Fuller, 1–44. London: SPCK, 1953.

Burrell, David B., CSC. *Aquinas: God and Action*. Chicago: University of Chicago Press, 2008 (1979).

Calvin, John. *Institutes of the Christian Religion*. Edited by John T. McNeill. Translated by Ford Lewis Battles. Philadelphia: Westminster Press, 1960.

Capes, David B. "YHWH Texts and Monotheism in Paul's Christology." In *Early Jewish and Christian Monotheism*. Edited by Loren T. Stuckenbruck and Wendy E. S. North. London: T&T Clark International, 2004.

Chemnitz, Martin. *The Two Natures of Christ*. Translated by J. A. O. Preus. St. Louis: Concordia Publishing House, 1971 [1578].

Coakley, Sarah. *Powers and Submissions: Spirituality, Philosophy, and Gender*. Malden, MA: Blackwell Publishers, 2002.

Cohen, Shaye D. "The Origins of the Matrilineal Principle in Rabbinic Law." *Association for Jewish Studies Review* 10, no. 1 (Spring 1985): 19–53.

Compendium of Creeds, Definitions, and Declarations on Matters of Faith and Morals. Edited by Heinrich Denzinger, Peter Hünermann, et al. 43rd ed. San Francisco: Ignatius Press, 2012.

Congar, Yves. *The Word and the Spirit*. Translated by David Smith. London: Geoffrey Chapman, 1986.

Copeland, Rebecca. "Remembering the Word: A Decentered Approach to Two-Natures Christology." PhD diss., Emory University, 2018.

Dalferth, Ingolf U. *Crucified and Resurrected: Restructuring the Grammar of Christology.* Translated by Jo Bennett. Grand Rapids: Baker Academic, 2015 [1994].

Darwin, Charles. *Natural Selection: Being the Second Part of His Big Species Book Written from 1856 to 1858.* Edited by R. C. Stauffer. Cambridge: Cambridge University Press, 1975.

———. *On the Origin of Species.* London: Murray, 1859.

Declaration on the Way: Church, Ministry, and Eucharist. Bishops' Committee for Ecumenical and Interreligious Affairs, United States Conference of Catholic Bishops and Evangelical Lutheran Church in America, 2015. https://download.elca.org/ELCA%20Resource%20Repository/Declaration_on_the_Way.pdf.

Derrida, Jacques. *Given Time.* Vol. 1, *Counterfeit Money.* Chicago: University of Chicago Press, 1992.

Dionysius the Areopagite. *Divine Names.* In *Pseudo-Dionysius: The Complete Works.* Translated by Colm Luibheid. New York: Paulist Press, 1987.

Early Christian Fathers. Translated and edited by Cyril C. Richardson. Library of Christian Classics 1. New York: Macmillan, 1970.

Eberhart, Christian. *Studien zur Bedeutung der Opfer im Alten Testament: Die Signifikanz von Blut- und Verbrennungsriten im kultischen Rahmen.* Wissenschaftliche Monographien zum Alten und Neuen Testament 94. Neukirchen-Vluyn: Neukirchener Verlag, 2002.

Farrer, Austin. *Finite and Infinite: A Philosophical Essay.* New York: Seabury Press, 1979 [1943].

———. *Love Almighty and Ills Unlimited: An Essay on Providence and Evil.* London: Collins, 1962.

———. *A Science of God?* London: Geoffrey Bles, 1966.

Fitzmyer, Joseph A. *The Gospel according to Luke I–IX: A New Translation with Introduction and Commentary.* New York: Doubleday, 1981.

Frank, F. H. R. *Zur Theologie A. Ritschl's.* 3rd ed. Erlangen: Andreas Deichert'sche Verlagsbuchhandlung, 1891.

Frei, Hans W. *The Identity of Jesus Christ: The Hermeneutical Bases of Dogmatic Theology.* Eugene, OR: Wipf & Stock, 1997 [1975].

Gage, Frances D. "Reminiscences by Frances D. Gage: Sojourner Truth." In *History of Woman Suffrage,* edited by Elizabeth Cady Stanton, Susan B. Anthony, and Matilda Joslyn Gage, part 1 of 3. Rochester: Charles Mann, 1887.

Gaine, Simon Francis. *Did the Saviour See the Father? Christ, Salvation and the Vision of God.* London: Bloomsbury T&T Clark, 2015.

Gathercole, Simon. *The Composition of the Gospel of Thomas: Original Language and Influences.* Society for New Testament Studies Monograph Series 151. Cambridge: Cambridge University Press, 2012.

Gerardi, Ioanni. *Loci theologici.* Edited by E. Preuss. 9 vols. Berlin: Gust. Schlawitz, 1863–75 [1610–22].

Gregory of Nazianzus. *To Cledonius against Apollinaris.* In *Christology of the Later Fathers.* Edited by Edward R. Hardy. Philadelphia: Westminster Press, 1954.

———. *The Theological Orations.* In *Christology of the Later Fathers.* Edited by Edward R. Hardy. Philadelphia: Westminster Press, 1954.

Gregory of Nyssa. "An Address on Religious Instruction." In *Christology of the Later Fathers,* edited by Edward R. Hardy, Philadelphia: Westminster Press, 1954.

Grillmeier, Aloys, SJ. *Christ in Christian Tradition*. Translated by John Bowden. Vol. 1. Louisville, KY: Westminster John Knox Press, 1995.

Hampson, Daphne. *Theology and Feminism*. Oxford: Basil Blackwell, 1990.

Heppe, Heinrich. *Reformed Dogmatics*. Edited by Ernst Bizer. Translated by G. T. Thomson. London: George Allen & Unwin, 1950 [1861].

Holldoble, Bert, and E. O. Wilson. *The Superorganism: The Beauty, Elegance, and Strangeness of Insect Societies*. New York: W. W. Norton, 2009.

Horan, Daniel C., OFM. "How Original Was Scotus on the Incarnation? Reconsidering the History of the Absolute Predestination of Christ in Light of Robert Grosseteste." *Heythrop Journal* 52 (2011): 374–91.

Irenaeus of Lyon. *Against Heresies*. In *Ante-Nicene Fathers*, edited by Alexander Roberts and James Donaldson, vol. 1, *The Apostolic Fathers with Justin Martyr and Irenaeus*. American Edition. Grand Rapids: Wm. B. Eerdmans Publishing Co., 1975 [1867].

———. *The Demonstration of the Apostolic Preaching*. Translated by Armitage Robinson. London: SPCK, 1920.

Jenson, Robert W. *Systematic Theology*. 2 vols. New York: Oxford University Press, 1997–99.

———. *Visible Words: The Interpretation and Practice of Christian Sacraments*. Philadelphia: Fortress Press, 1978.

John of Damascus. *On the Orthodox Faith*. In *Nicene and Post-Nicene Fathers*, 2nd series, translated by E. W. Watson and L. Pullan, edited by Philip Schaff and Henry Wace, vol. 9, *Hilary of Poitiers, John of Damascus*. Peabody, MA: Hendrickson Publishers, 1995 [1899].

Johnson, Luke Timothy. *The Real Jesus: The Misguided Quest for the Historical Jesus and the Truth of the Traditional Gospels*. San Francisco: HarperSanFrancisco, 1996.

Justin Martyr. *Dialogue with Trypho*. In *Ante-Nicene Fathers*, edited by Alexander Roberts and James Donaldson, vol. 1, *The Apostolic Fathers with Justin Martyr and Irenaeus*. American Edition. Grand Rapids: Wm. B. Eerdmans Publishing Co., 1975 [1867].

———. *First Apology*. In *Ante-Nicene Fathers*, edited by Alexander Roberts and James Donaldson, vol. 1, *The Apostolic Fathers with Justin Martyr and Irenaeus*. American Edition. Grand Rapids: Wm. B. Eerdmans Publishing Co., 1975 [1867].

Keller, Catherine. *On the Mystery: Discerning Divinity in Process*. Minneapolis: Fortress Press, 2008.

Knitter, Paul F. *No Other Name? A Critical Survey of Christian Attitudes toward the World Religions*. Maryknoll, NY: Orbis Books, 1985.

Larsen, Kasper Bro. "Narrative Docetism: Christology and Storytelling in the Gospel of John." In *The Gospel of John and Christian Theology*, edited by Richard Bauckham and Carl Mosser. Grand Rapids: Wm. B. Eerdmans Publishing Co., 2008.

Lash, Nicholas. "Up and Down in Christology." In *New Studies in Theology 1*, edited by Stephen Sykes and Derek Holmes. London: Duckworth, 1980.

Leontius of Byzantium. *Contra Nestorianos et Eutychianos*. In Patrologiae Cursus Completus: Series Graeca, edited by J.-P. Migne, vol. 86.1:1273A–1316B. Paris, 1865.

Lewis, Alan E. *Between Cross and Resurrection: A Theology of Holy Saturday*. Grand Rapids: Wm. B. Eerdmans Publishing Co., 2001.

Lewis, C. S. *Mere Christianity*. New York: HarperCollins, 2000 [1952].

Lossky, Vladimir. *Dogmatic Theology: Creation, God's Image in Man, and the Redeeming Work of the Trinity*. Edited by Olivier Clément and Michel Stavrou. Translated by Anthony P. Gythiel. Yonkers, NY: St. Vladimir's Seminary Press, 2017.

———. *In the Image and Likeness of God.* Edited by John H. Erickson and Thomas E. Bird. Crestwood, NY: St. Vladimir's Seminary Press, 1985.

———. *The Mystical Theology of the Eastern Church.* Cambridge: James Clarke & Co., 1957.

Louth, Andrew. *Maximus the Confessor.* London: Routledge, 1996.

Lovelock, James. *Gaia: A New Look at Life on Earth.* Oxford: Oxford University Press, 2000.

Luther, Martin. *Luther's Works.* Edited by Harold J. Grimm. American Edition. 55 vols. Philadelphia: Fortress Press/St. Louis: Concordia Publishing House, 1957–86.

———. D. Martin Luthers Werke: Kritische Gesammtausgabe. Weimar, 1883–2009.

———. *On the Bondage of the Will.* In *Luther and Erasmus: Free Will and Salvation,* edited by E. Gordon Rupp and Philip S. Watson. Philadelphia: Westminster Press, 1969.

Mahn, Jason A. *Becoming a Christian in Christendom: Radical Discipleship and the Way of the Cross in America's "Christian" Culture.* Minneapolis: Fortress Press, 2016.

Marshall, Bruce. "Do Christians Worship the God of Israel?" In *Knowing the Triune God: The Work of the Spirit in the Practices of the Church,* edited by James J. Buckley and David S. Yeago, 231–64. Grand Rapids: Wm. B. Eerdmans Publishing Co., 2001.

Martin, Dale B. *The Corinthian Body.* New Haven, CT: Yale University Press, 1995.

Mathewes, Charles T. *Evil and the Augustinian Tradition.* Cambridge: Cambridge University Press, 2001.

Maximus [Maximos] the Confessor. *Ambigua.* In Patrologiae Cursus Completus: Series Graeca, edited by J.-P. Migne, vol. 91, *Sancti Maximi Confessoris Opera omnia,* cols. 1031–1418. Paris, 1865.

———. *Disputatio cum Pyrrho.* In Patrologiae Cursus Completus: Series Graeca, edited by J.-P. Migne, vol. 91, *Sancti Maximi Confessoris Opera omnia,* cols. 287–354. Paris, 1865.

———. *On Difficulties in the Church Fathers: The Ambigua.* 2 vols. Edited and translated by Nicholas Constas. Cambridge, MA: Harvard University Press, 2014.

———. *On the Cosmic Mystery of Jesus Christ: Selected Writings from St. Maximus the Confessor.* Translated by Paul M. Blowers and Robert Wilken. Crestwood, NY: St. Vladimir's Seminary Press, 2003.

———. *Opuscula theologica et polemica.* In Patrologiae Cursus Completus: Series Graeca, edited by J.-P. Migne, vol. 91, *Sancti Maximi Confessoris Opera omnia* [vol. 2], cols. 9–286. Paris, 1865.

———. *Quaestiones ad Thalassium.* In Patrologiae Cursus Completus: Series Graeca, edited by J.-P. Migne, vol. 90, *Sancti Maximi Confessoris Opera omnia* [vol. 1], cols. 244–785. Paris, 1865.

———. *Selected Writings.* Translated by G. C. Berthold. New York: Paulist Press, 1985.

McCabe, Herbert, OP. "Aquinas on the Trinity." In *Silence and the Word: Negative Theology and Incarnation,* edited by Oliver Davies and Denys Turner, 76–93. Cambridge: Cambridge University Press, 2004.

———. *God Matters.* New York: Continuum, 2010 [1987].

McCormack, Bruce. *Orthodox and Modern: Studies in the Theology of Karl Barth.* Grand Rapids: Baker Academic, 2008.

McFague, Sallie. *The Body of God: An Ecological Theology.* Minneapolis: Fortress Press, 1993.

McFarland, Ian A. *Difference and Identity: A Theological Anthropology.* Cleveland: Pilgrim, 2001.

————. *From Nothing: A Theology of Creation*. Louisville, KY: Westminster John Knox, 2014.

————. *In Adam's Fall: A Meditation on the Christian Doctrine of Original Sin*. Malden, MA: Wiley-Blackwell, 2010.

Meeks, Wayne A. *The Origins of Christian Morality: The First Two Centuries*. New Haven, CT: Yale University Press, 1993.

Melanchthon, Philipp. *Loci communes*. In *Melanchthon and Bucer*, edited by Wilhelm Pauck. Philadelphia: Westminster Press, 1969.

Mercedes, Anna. *Power For: Feminism and Christ's Self-Giving*. London: T&T Clark International, 2011.

Moberly, R. W. L. "'Yahweh Is One': The Translation of the Shema." In *Studies in the Pentateuch*, edited by J. A. Emerton. Leiden: Brill, 1990.

Moffitt, David M. *Atonement and the Logic of Resurrection in the Epistle to the Hebrews*. Leiden: Brill, 2011.

————. "Jesus' Heavenly Sacrifice in Early Christian Reception of Hebrews: A Survey." *Journal of Theological Studies*, NS, 68, pt. 1 (April 2017): 46–71.

Moltmann, Jürgen. *God in Creation: A New Theology of Creation and the Spirit of God*. New York: Harper & Row, 1985.

Nicholas of Cusa. *Nicholas of Cusa on God as Not-Other: A Translation and Appraisal of "De li non aliud."* Translated by Jasper Hopkins. 2nd ed. Minneapolis: Arthur J. Banning Press, 1983.

O'Donovan, Oliver. *Resurrection and the Moral Order: An Outline for Evangelical Ethics*. Grand Rapids: Wm. B. Eerdmans Publishing Co., 1986.

Origen of Alexandria. *Origen: Homilies on Leviticus 1–16*. Translated by Gary Wayne Barkley. Washington, DC: Catholic University of America Press, 1990.

————. *Spirit and Fire: A Thematic Anthology of His Writings*. Edited by Hans Urs von Balthasar. Translated by Robert J. Daly, SJ. Washington, DC: Catholic University of America Press, 1984 [1938].

Otto, Rudolf. *The Idea of the Holy*. 2nd ed. Translated by John W. Harvey. New York: Oxford University Press, 1958.

Owen, John. *The Holy Spirit [Pneumatologia]*. Vol. 3 of *The Works of John Owen*, edited by William H. Goold. Carlisle, PA: Banner of Truth Trust, 1972.

Page, Ruth. *God and the Web of Creation*. London: SCM Press, 1996.

Pannenberg, Wolfhart. *Systematic Theology*. 3 vols. Translated by Geoffrey W. Bromiley. Grand Rapids: Wm. B. Eerdmans Publishing Co., 1988–93.

Papanikolaou, Aristotle. *Being with God: Trinity, Apophaticism, and Divine-Human Communion*. Notre Dame, IN: University of Notre Dame Press, 2006.

Papias. *Fragments*. In *Ante-Nicene Fathers*, edited by Alexander Roberts and James Donaldson, vol. 1, *The Apostolic Fathers with Justin Martyr and Irenaeus*. American Edition. Grand Rapids: Wm. B. Eerdmans Publishing Co., 1975 [1867].

Park, Andrew Sung. *The Wounded Heart of God: The Asian Concept of Han and the Christian Doctrine of Sin*. Nashville: Abingdon Press, 1993.

Parsons, Mikael C. *The Departure of Jesus in Luke-Acts: The Ascension Narratives in Context*. Library of New Testament Studies 21. Sheffield: Sheffield Academic Press, 1987.

Pascal, Blaise. *Pensées*. Edited by Léon Brunschvicg. Paris: Hachette, n.d. [1869].

Pawl, Timothy. *In Defense of Conciliar Christology: A Philosophical Essay*. Oxford: Oxford University Press, 2016.

Pitstick, Alyssa Lyra. *Light in Darkness: Hans Urs von Balthasar and the Catholic Doctrine of Christ's Descent into Hell*. Grand Rapids: Wm. B. Eerdmans Publishing Co., 2007.

Placher, William C. *Narratives of a Vulnerable God*. Louisville, KY: Westminster John Knox, 1994.

Rahner, Karl. *Theology, Anthropology, Christology*. Vol. 13 of *Theological Investigations*. Translated by David Bourke. London: Darton, Longman & Todd, 1975.

Ratzinger, Joseph. *Introduction to Christianity*. Translated by J. R. Foster. London: Burns & Oates, 1969.

Rogers, Eugene F. *Sexuality and the Christian Body: Their Way into the Triune God*. Oxford: Blackwell, 1999.

Ruether, Rosemary Radford. *Sexism and God-Talk: Toward Feminist Theology*. Boston: Beacon Press, 1983.

Sanders, E. P. "Historiographical Characteristics of the Gospel of John." *New Testament Studies* 53, no. 1 (2007): 17–36.

———. *Paul and Palestinian Judaism: A Comparison of Patterns of Religion*. London: SCM, 1977.

Sayers, Dorothy L. *The Mind of the Maker*. London: Methuen, 1941.

Schäfer, Peter. *Jesus in the Talmud*. Princeton, NJ: Princeton University Press, 2007.

Schenk, Wolfgang. *Evangelium—Evangelien—Evangeliologie: Ein "hermeneutisches" Manifest*. Munich: Christian Kaiser, 1983.

Schleiermacher, Friedrich. *The Christian Faith*. 2nd ed. Edited by H. R. Mackintosh and J. S. Stewart. Edinburgh: T&T Clark, 1928 [1830].

Schmid, Heinrich. *The Doctrinal Theology of the Evangelical Lutheran Church*. 3rd ed. Translated by Charles A. Hay and Henry E. Jacobs. Minneapolis: Augsburg, 1961.

Schweitzer, Albert. *The Quest of the Historical Jesus: A Critical Study of Its Progress from Reimarus to Wrede*. Translated by W. Montgomery. London: Adam and Charles Black, 1911.

Sokolowski, Robert. *Presence and Absence: A Philosophical Investigation of Language and Being*. Bloomington: Indiana University Press, 1978.

Sonderegger, Katherine. *The Doctrine of God*. Vol. 1 of *Systematic Theology*. Minneapolis: Fortress Press, 2015.

Soulen, R. Kendall. *Distinguishing the Voices*. Vol. 1 of *The Divine Name(s) and the Holy Trinity*. Louisville, KY: Westminster John Knox, 2011.

Staniloae, Dumitru. *The Person of Jesus Christ as God and Savior*. Vol. 3 of *The Experience of God: Orthodox Dogmatic Theology*. Edited and translated by Ioan Ionita. Brookline, MA: Holy Cross Orthodox Press, 2011.

Strotmann, Angelika. *"Mein Vater bist du!" (Sir. 51:10): Zur Bedeutung der Vaterschaft Gottes in kanonischen und nichtkanonischen frühjüdischen Schriften*. Frankfurt: Josef Knecht, 1991.

Studer, Basil. *Trinity and Incarnation: The Faith of the Early Church*. Edited by Andrew Louth. Translated by Matthias Westerhof. London: T&T Clark, 1993.

Sumner, Darren O. "The Twofold Life of the Word: Karl Barth's Critical Reception of the *Extra Calvinisticum*." *International Journal of Systematic Theology* 15, no. 1 (January 2013): 42–57.

Sylwanowicz, Michael. *Contingent Causality and the Foundations of Duns Scotus' "Metaphysics."* Leiden: Brill, 1996.

Synopsis purioris theologiae. Edited by Dolf te Velde. Leiden: Brill, 2015 [1625].

Tanner, Kathryn. *Christ the Key*. Cambridge: Cambridge University Press, 2010.

———. "David Brown's *Divine Humanity*." *Scottish Journal of Theology* 68, no. 1 (2015): 106–13.

———. *God and Creation in Christian Theology: Tyranny or Empowerment?* Malden, MA: Blackwell, 1988.

————. *Jesus, Humanity and the Trinity*. Edinburgh: T&T Clark, 2001.

Tanner, Norman P. *Decrees of the Ecumenical Councils*. 2 vols. Washington, DC: Georgetown University Press, 1990.

Tertullian. *Against Marcion*. In *Ante-Nicene Fathers*, edited by Alan Menzies, vol. 3, *Latin Christianity: Its Founder, Tertullian*. Grand Rapids: Wm. B. Eerdmans Publishing Co., n.d. [1885].

Thomas Aquinas. *Summa Theologiae*. Blackfriars Edition. 60 vols. London: Eyre & Spottiswood, 1964–81.

————. *Summa Theologica, Supplement*. New York: Benziger Brothers, 1947.

Thomasius, Gottfried. *Christi Person und Werk: Darstellung der evangelisch-lutherischen Dogmatik vom Mittelpunkte der Christologie aus*. 5 vols. Erlangen, 1852–1861.

Thompson, Marianne Meye. *The Incarnate Word: Perspectives on Jesus in the Fourth Gospel*. Peabody, MA: Hendrickson, 1988.

Vermes, Géza. *Jesus the Jew: A Historian's Reading of the Gospels*. Philadelphia: Fortress Press, 1981 [1973].

Watson, Francis. *Gospel Writing: A Canonical Perspective*. Grand Rapids: Wm. B. Eerdmans Publishing Co., 2013.

————. *Text and Truth: Redefining Biblical Theology*. Edinburgh: T&T Clark, 1997.

Webster, John. "The Holiness and Love of God." *Scottish Journal of Theology* 57, no. 3 (2004): 249–68.

————. *"Non ex Aequo*: God's Relation to Creatures." In *God and the Works of God*. Vol. 1 of *God without Measure: Working Papers in Christian Theology*. London: Bloomsbury T&T Clark, 2016.

White, Thomas Joseph, OP. *The Incarnate Lord: A Thomistic Study in Christology*. Washington, DC: Catholic University of America Press, 2015.

Wildman, Wesley. "Basic Christological Distinctions." *Theology Today* 64 (2007): 285–304.

Williams, A. N. *The Ground of Union: Deification in Aquinas and Palamas*. Oxford: Oxford University Press, 1999.

Williams, Dolores. *Sisters in the Wilderness: The Challenge of Womanist God-Talk*. Maryknoll, NY: Orbis Books, 1995.

Williams, Rowan. *The Edge of Words: God and the Habits of Language*. London: Bloomsbury, 2014.

————. *On Christian Theology*. Oxford: Blackwell, 2000.

Wittgenstein, Ludwig. *Tractatus Logico-Philosophicus*. Translated by D. F. Pears and B. F. McGuinness. London: Routledge, 1974 [1921].

Wood, Jordan Daniel. "Creation Is Incarnation: The Metaphysical Peculiarity of the *Logoi* in Maximus Confessor." *Modern Theology* 34, no. 1 (January 2018): 82–102.

Wyschogrod, Michael. *Abraham's Promise: Judaism and Jewish-Christian Relations*. Edited by R. Kendall Soulen. Grand Rapids: Wm. B. Eerdmans Publishing Co., 2004.

Yanofsky, Noson S. *The Outer Limits of Reason: What Science, Mathematics, and Logic Cannot Tell Us*. Boston: MIT Press, 2013.

Scripture Index

Subject Index

Lightning Source UK Ltd.
Milton Keynes UK
UKHW020234171019
351716UK00007B/1898/P